THE COMMON READER

by Virginia Woolf

Fiction

MONDAY OR TUESDAY
THE VOYAGE OUT
NIGHT AND DAY
JACOB'S ROOM
MRS. DALLOWAY
TO THE LIGHTHOUSE
ORLANDO
THE WAVES
THE YEARS
BETWEEN THE ACTS
A HAUNTED HOUSE

Biography

FLUSH: A BIOGRAPHY
ROGER FRY

Criticism, etc.

THE COMMON READER
THE SECOND COMMON READER
A ROOM OF ONE'S OWN
THREE GUINEAS
THE DEATH OF THE MOTH
THE MOMENT AND OTHER ESSAYS

VIRGINIA WOOLF

The
COMMON READER

First and Second Series
COMBINED IN ONE VOLUME

I rejoice to concur with the common reader;
for by the common sense of readers, uncorrupted
by literary prejudices, after all the refinements
of subtilty and the dogmatism of learning, must
be generally decided all claim to poetical
honours. DR. JOHNSON, *Life of Gray*

HARCOURT, BRACE AND COMPANY

NEW YORK

THE COMMON READER

COPYRIGHT, 1925, BY

HARCOURT, BRACE AND COMPANY, INC.

THE SECOND COMMON READER

COPYRIGHT, 1932, BY

HARCOURT, BRACE AND COMPANY, INC.

COMBINED EDITION IN ONE VOLUME

PUBLISHED 1948

PRINTED IN THE UNITED STATES OF AMERICA

Contents

SERIES ONE

CONTENTS

CONTENTS

TO

LYTTON STRACHEY

Some of these papers appeared originally in the *Times Literary Supplement* and the *Dial*. I have to thank the Editors for allowing me to reprint them here; some are based upon articles written for various newspapers, while others appear now for the first time.

THE COMMON READER

The Common Reader

There is a sentence in Dr. Johnson's Life of Gray which might well be written up in all those rooms, too humble to be called libraries, yet full of books, where the pursuit of reading is carried on by private people. ". . . I rejoice to concur with the common reader; for by the common sense of readers, uncorrupted by literary prejudices, after all the refinements of subtilty and the dogmatism of learning, must be finally decided all claim to poetical honours." It defines their qualities; it dignifies their aims; it bestows upon a pursuit which devours a great deal of time, and is yet apt to leave behind it nothing very substantial, the sanction of the great man's approval.

The common reader, as Dr. Johnson implies, differs from the critic and the scholar. He is worse educated, and nature has not gifted him so generously. He reads for his own pleasure rather than to impart knowledge or correct the opinions of others. Above all, he is guided by an instinct to create for himself, out of whatever odds and ends he can come by, some kind of whole—a portrait of a man, a sketch of an age, a theory of the art of writing. He never ceases, as he reads, to run up some rickety and ramshackle fabric which shall give him the temporary satisfaction of looking sufficiently like the real object to allow of affection, laughter, and argument. Hasty, inaccurate, and superficial, snatching now this poem, now that scrap of old furniture without caring where he finds it or of what nature it may be so long as it serves his purpose and rounds his structure, his deficiencies as a critic are too obvious to be pointed out; but if he has, as Dr. Johnson maintained, some say in the final distribution of poetical honours, then, perhaps, it may be worth while to write down a few of the ideas and opinions which, insignificant in themselves, yet contribute to so mighty a result.

The Pastons and Chaucer [1]

The tower of Caister Castle still rises ninety feet
into the air, and the arch still stands from which Sir
John Fastolf's barges sailed out to fetch stone for the
building of the great castle.   But now jackdaws nest
on the tower, and of the castle, which once covered six
acres of ground, only ruined walls remain, pierced by
loop-holes and surmounted by battlements, though
there are neither archers within nor cannon without.
As for the "seven religious men" and the "seven poor
folk" who should, at this very moment, be praying
for the souls of Sir John and his parents, there is no
sign of them nor sound of their prayers.   The place is
a ruin.   Antiquaries speculate and differ.

Not so very far off lie more ruins—the ruins of
Bromholm Priory, where John Paston was buried, naturally enough, since his house was only a mile or so
away, lying on low ground by the sea, twenty miles
north of Norwich.   The coast is dangerous, and the
land, even in our time, inaccessible.   Nevertheless the
little bit of wood at Bromholm, the fragment of the
true Cross, brought pilgrims incessantly to the Priory,
and sent them away with eyes opened and limbs
straightened.   But some of them with their newly-
opened eyes saw a sight which shocked them—the
grave of John Paston in Bromholm Priory without a

[1] *The Paston Letters,* edited by Dr. James Gairdner (1904), 4 vols.

tombstone. The news spread over the country-side. The Pastons had fallen; they that had been so power-ful could no longer afford a stone to put above John Paston's head. Margaret, his widow, could not pay her debts; the eldest son, Sir John, wasted his prop-erty upon women and tournaments, while the younger, John also, though a man of greater parts, thought more of his hawks than of his harvests.

The pilgrims of course were liars, as people whose eyes have just been opened by a piece of the true Cross have every right to be; but their news, none the less, was welcome. The Pastons had risen in the world. People said even that they had been bondmen not so very long ago. At any rate, men still living could re-member John's grandfather Clement tilling his own land, a hard-working peasant; and William, Clement's son, becoming a judge and buying land; and John, William's son, marrying well and buying more land and quite lately inheriting the vast new castle at Cais-ter, and all Sir John's lands in Norfolk and Suffolk. People said that he had forged the old knight's will. What wonder, then, that he lacked a tombstone? But, if we consider the character of Sir John Paston, John's eldest son, and his upbringing and his surroundings, and the relations between himself and his father as the family letters reveal them, we shall see how difficult it was, and how likely to be neglected—this business of making his father's tombstone.

For let us imagine, in the most desolate part of Eng-land known to us at the present moment, a raw, new-built house, without telephone, bathroom, or drains, arm-chairs or newspapers, and one shelf perhaps of books, unwieldy to hold, expensive to come by. The windows look out upon a few cultivated fields and a dozen hovels, and beyond them there is the sea on one side, on the other a vast fen. A single road crosses the fen, but there is a hole in it, which, one of the farm hands reports, is big enough to swallow a carriage. And, the man adds, Tom Topcroft, the mad bricklayer, has broken loose again and ranges the country half-naked, threatening to kill any one who approaches him. That is what they talk about at dinner in the desolate house, while the chimney smokes horribly, and the draught lifts the carpets on the floor. Orders are given to lock all gates at sunset, and, when the long dismal evening has worn itself away, simply and solemnly, girt about with dangers as they are, these isolated men and women fall upon their knees in prayer.

In the fifteenth century, however, the wild landscape was broken suddenly and very strangely by vast piles of brand-new masonry. There rose out of the sand-hills and heaths of the Norfolk coast a huge bulk of stone, like a modern hotel in a watering-place; but there was no parade, no lodging houses, and no pier at Yarmouth then, and this gigantic building on the out-skirts of the town was built to house one solitary old gentleman without any children—Sir John Fastolf, who had fought at Agincourt and acquired great wealth. He had fought at Agincourt and got but lit-tle reward. No one took his advice. Men spoke ill

[15]

of him behind his back. He was well aware of it; his temper was none the sweeter for it. He was a hot-tempered old man, powerful, embittered by a sense of grievance. But whether on the battlefield or at court he thought perpetually of Caister, and how, when his duties allowed, he would settle down on his father's land and live in a great house of his own building.

The gigantic structure of Caister Castle was in progress not so many miles away when the little Pastons were children. John Paston, the father, had charge of some part of the business, and the children listened, as soon as they could listen at all, to talk of stone and building, of barges gone to London and not yet returned, of the twenty-six private chambers, of the hall and chapel; of foundations, measurements, and rascally work-people. Later, in 1454, when the work was finished and Sir John had come to spend his last years at Caister, they may have seen for themselves the mass of treasure that was stored there; the tables laden with gold and silver plate; the wardrobes stuffed with gowns of velvet and satin and cloth of gold, with hoods and tippets and beaver hats and leather jackets and velvet doublets; and how the very pillow-cases on the beds were of green and purple silk. There were tapestries everywhere. The beds were laid and the bedrooms hung with tapestries representing sieges, hunting and hawking, men fishing, archers shooting, ladies playing on their harps, dallying with ducks, or a giant "bearing the leg of a bear in his hand". Such were the fruits of a well-spent life. To buy land, to build great houses, to stuff these houses full of gold and silver plate (though the privy might well be in the bedroom), was the proper aim of mankind. Mr. and Mrs. Paston spent the greater part of their energies in the same exhausting occupation. For since the passion to acquire was universal, one could never rest secure in one's possessions for long. The outlying parts of one's property were in perpetual jeopardy. The Duke of Norfolk might covet this manor, the Duke of Suffolk that. Some trumped-up excuse, as for instance that the Pastons were bondmen, gave them the right to seize the house and batter down the lodges in the owner's absence. And how could the owner of Paston and Mauteby and Drayton and Gresham be in five or six places at once, especially now that Caister Castle was his, and he must be in London trying to get his rights recognised by the King? The King was mad too, they said; did not know his own child, they said; or the King was in flight; or there was civil war in the land. Norfolk was always the most distressed of counties and its country gentlemen the most quarrelsome of mankind. Indeed, had Mrs. Paston chosen, she could have told her children how when she was a young woman a thousand men with bows and arrows and pans of burning fire had marched upon Gresham and broken the gates and mined the walls of the room where she sat alone. But much worse things than that had happened to women. She neither bewailed her lot nor thought herself a heroine. The long, long letters which she wrote so laboriously in her clear cramped hand to her husband, who was (as usual) away, make no mention of herself. The sheep had wasted the hay. Heyden's and Tuddenham's men were out. A dyke had been broken and a bullock stolen. They needed treacle badly, and really she must have stuff for a dress.

But Mrs. Paston did not talk about herself.

Thus the little Pastons would see their mother writing or dictating page after page, hour after hour, long, long letters, but to interrupt a parent who writes so laboriously of such important matters would have been a sin. The prattle of children, the lore of the nursery or schoolroom, did not find its way into these elaborate communications. For the most part her letters are the letters of an honest bailiff to his master, explaining, asking advice, giving news, rendering accounts. There was robbery and manslaughter; it was difficult to get in the rents; Richard Calle had gathered but little money; and what with one thing and another Margaret had not had time to make out, as she should have done, the inventory of the goods which her husband desired. Well might old Agnes, surveying her son's affairs rather grimly from a distance, counsel him to contrive it so that "ye may have less to do in the world; your father said, In little business lieth much rest. This world is but a thoroughfare, and full of woe; and when we depart therefrom, right nought bear with us but our good deeds and ill."

The thought of death would thus come upon them in a clap. Old Fastolf, cumbered with wealth and property, had his vision at the end of Hell fire, and shrieked aloud to his executors to distribute alms, and see that prayers were said "in perpetuum", so that his soul might escape the agonies of purgatory. William Paston, the judge, was urgent too that the monks of Norwich should be retained to pray for his soul "for ever". The soul was no wisp of air, but a solid body capable of eternal suffering, and the fire that destroyed it was as fierce as any that burnt on mortal grates. For ever there would be monks and the town of Norwich, and for ever the Chapel of Our Lady in the town of Norwich. There was something matter-of-fact, positive, and enduring in their conception both of life and of death.

With the plan of existence so vigorously marked out, children of course were well beaten, and boys and girls taught to know their places. They must acquire land; but they must obey their parents. A mother would clout her daughter's head three times a week and break the skin if she did not conform to the laws of behaviour. Agnes Paston, a lady of birth and breeding, beat her daughter Elizabeth. Margaret Paston, a softer-hearted woman, turned her daughter out of the house for loving the honest bailiff Richard Calle. Brothers would not suffer their sisters to marry beneath them, and "sell candle and mustard in Framlingham". The fathers quarrelled with the sons, and the mothers, fonder of their boys than of their girls, yet bound by all law and custom to obey their husbands, were torn asunder in their efforts to keep the peace.

[19]

With all her pains, Margaret failed to prevent rash acts on the part of her eldest son John, or the bitter words with which his father denounced him. He was a "drone among bees", the father burst out, "which labour for gathering honey in the fields, and the drone doth naught but taketh his part of it". He treated his parents with insolence, and yet was fit for no charge of responsibility abroad.

But the quarrel was ended, very shortly, by the death (22nd May 1466) of John Paston, the father, in London. The body was brought down to Bromholm to be buried. Twelve poor men trudged all the way bearing torches beside it. Alms were distributed; masses and dirges were said. Bells were rung. Great quantities of fowls, sheep, pigs, eggs, bread, and cream were devoured, ale and wine drunk, and candles burnt. Two panes were taken from the church windows to let out the reek of the torches. Black cloth was distributed, and a light set burning on the grave. But John Paston, the heir, delayed to make his father's tombstone.

He was a young man, something over twenty-four years of age. The discipline and the drudgery of a country life bored him. When he ran away from home, it was, apparently, to attempt to enter the King's household. Whatever doubts, indeed, might be cast by their enemies on the blood of the Pastons, Sir John was unmistakably a gentleman. He had inherited his lands; the honey was his that the bees had gathered with so much labour. He had the instincts of enjoy-

ment rather than of acquisition, and with his mother's
parsimony was strangely mixed something of his father's ambition. Yet his own indolent and luxurious
temperament took the edge from both. He was attractive to women, liked society and tournaments, and
court life and making bets, and sometimes, even, reading books. And so life, now that John Paston was
buried, started afresh upon rather a different foundation. There could be little outward change indeed.
Margaret still ruled the house. She still ordered the
lives of the younger children as she had ordered the
lives of the elder. The boys still needed to be beaten
into book-learning by their tutors, the girls still loved
the wrong men and must be married to the right.
Rents had to be collected; the interminable lawsuit for
the Fastolf property dragged on. Battles were fought;
the roses of York and Lancaster alternately faded and
flourished. Norfolk was full of poor people seeking
redress for their grievances, and Margaret worked for
her son as she had worked for her husband, with this
significant change only, that now, instead of confiding
in her husband, she took the advice of her priest.

But inwardly there was a change. It seems at last
as if the hard outer shell had served its purpose and
something sensitive, appreciative, and pleasure-loving
had formed within. At any rate Sir John, writing to
his brother John at home, strayed sometimes from the
business on hand to crack a joke, to send a piece of
gossip, or to instruct him, knowingly and even subtly,
upon the conduct of a love affair. Be "as lowly to the

mother as ye list, but to the maid not too lowly, nor
that ye be too glad to speed, nor too sorry to fail. And
I shall always be your herald both here, if she come
hither, and at home, when I come home, which I hope
hastily within XI. days at the furthest." And then a
hawk was to be bought, a hat, or new silk laces sent
down to John in Norfolk, prosecuting his suit flying
his hawks, and attending with considerable energy and
not too nice a sense of honesty to the affairs of the Paston estates.

The lights had long since burnt out on John Paston's
grave. But still Sir John delayed; no tomb replaced
them. He had his excuses; what with the business of
the lawsuit, and his duties at Court, and the disturbance of the civil wars, his time was occupied and his
money spent. But perhaps something strange had happened to Sir John himself, and not only to Sir John
dallying in London, but to his sister Margery falling
in love with the bailiff, and to Walter making Latin
verses at Eton, and to John flying his hawks at Paston.
Life was a little more various in its pleasures. They
were not quite so sure as the elder generation had been
of the rights of man and of the dues of God, of the
horrors of death, and of the importance of tombstones.
Poor Margaret Paston scented the change and sought
uneasily, with the pen which had marched so stiffly
through so many pages, to lay bare the root of her
troubles. It was not that the lawsuit saddened her;
she was ready to defend Caister with her own hands if
need be, "though I cannot well guide nor rule soldiers",

but there was something wrong with the family since
the death of her husband and master. Perhaps her son
had failed in his service to God; he had been too proud
or too lavish in his expenditure; or perhaps he had
shown too little mercy to the poor. Whatever the fault
might be, she only knew that Sir John spent twice as
much money as his father for less result; that they
could scarcely pay their debts without selling land,
wood, or household stuff ("It is a death to me to think
if it"); while every day people spoke ill of them in
the country because they left John Paston to lie without a tombstone. The money that might have bought
it, or more land, and more goblets and more tapestry,
was spent by Sir John on clocks and trinkets, and upon
paying a clerk to copy out Treatises upon Knighthood
and other such stuff. There they stood at Paston—
eleven volumes, with the poems of Lydgate and Chaucer among them, diffusing a strange air into the gaunt,
comfortless house, inviting men to indolence and vanity, distracting their thoughts from business, and leading them not only to neglect their own profit but to
think lightly of the sacred dues of the dead.

For sometimes, instead of riding off on his horse to
inspect his crops or bargain with his tenants, Sir John
would sit, in broad daylight, reading. There, on the
hard chair in the comfortless room with the wind lifting the carpet and the smoke stinging his eyes, he would
sit reading Chaucer, wasting his time, dreaming—or
what strange intoxication was it that he drew from
books? Life was rough, cheerless, and disappointing.

A whole year of days would pass fruitlessly in dreary business, like dashes of rain on the window pane. There was no reason in it as there had been for his father; no imperative need to establish a family and acquire an important position for children who were not born, or if born, had no right to bear their father's name. But Lydgate's poems or Chaucer's, like a mirror in which figures move brightly, silently, and compactly, showed him the very skies, fields, and people whom he knew, but rounded and complete. Instead of waiting listlessly for news from London or piecing out from his mother's gossip some country tragedy of love and jealousy, here, in a few pages, the whole story was laid before him. And then as he rode or sat at table he would remember some description or saying which bore upon the present moment and fixed it, or some string of words would charm him, and putting aside the pressure of the moment, he would hasten home to sit in his chair and learn the end of the story.

To learn the end of the story—Chaucer can still make us wish to do that. He has pre-eminently that story-teller's gift, which is almost the rarest gift among writers at the present day. Nothing happens to us as it did to our ancestors; events are seldom important; if we recount them, we do not really believe in them; we have perhaps things of greater interest to say, and for these reasons natural story-tellers like Mr. Garnett, whom we must distinguish from self-conscious story-tellers like Mr. Masefield, have become rare. For the story-teller, besides his indescribable zest for facts, must tell his story craftily, without undue stress or excitement, or we shall swallow it whole and jumble the parts together; he must let us stop, give us time to think and look about us, yet always be persuading us to move on. Chaucer was helped to this to some extent by the time of his birth; and in addition he had another advantage over the moderns which will never come the way of English poets again. England was an unspoilt country. His eyes rested on a virgin land, all unbroken grass and wood except for the small towns and an occasional castle in the building. No villa roofs peered through Kentish tree-tops; no factory chimney smoked on the hillside. The state of the country, considering how poets go to Nature, how they use her for their images and their contrasts even when they do not describe her directly, is a matter of some importance. Her cultivation or her savagery influences the poet far more profoundly than the prose writer. To the modern poet, with Birmingham, Manchester, and London the size they are, the country is the sanctuary of moral excellence in contrast with the town which is the sink of vice. It is a retreat, the haunt of modesty and virtue, where men go to hide and moralise. There is something morbid, as if shrinking from human contact, in the nature worship of Wordsworth, still more in the microscopic devotion which Tennyson lavished upon the petals of roses and the buds of lime trees. But these were great poets. In their hands, the country was no mere jeweller's shop, or museum of curious objects to be described, even more curiously, in words. Poets of smaller gift, since the view is so much spoilt, and the garden or the meadow must replace the barren heath and the precipitous mountain-side, are now confined to little landscapes, to birds' nests, to acorns with every wrinkle drawn to the life. The wider landscape is lost.

But to Chaucer the country was too large and too wild to be altogether agreeable. He turned instinctively, as if he had painful experience of their nature, from tempests and rocks to the bright May day and the jocund landscape, from the harsh and mysterious to the gay and definite. Without possessing a tithe of the virtuosity in word-painting which is the modern inheritance, he could give, in a few words, or even, when we come to look, without a single word of direct description, the sense of the open air.

And se the fresshe floures how they sprynge

—that is enough.

Nature, uncompromising, untamed, was no looking-glass for happy faces, or confessor of unhappy souls. She was herself; sometimes, therefore, disagreeable enough and plain, but always in Chaucer's pages with the hardness and the freshness of an actual presence. Soon, however, we notice something of greater importance than the gay and picturesque appearance of the mediæval world—the solidity which plumps it out, the conviction which animates the characters. There is immense variety in the *Canterbury Tales*, and yet, persisting underneath, one consistent type. Chaucer has his world; he has his young men; he has his young women. If one met them straying in Shakespeare's world one would know them to be Chaucer's, not Shakespeare's. He wants to describe a girl, and this is what she looks like:

> Ful semely hir wimpel pinched was,
> Hir nose tretys; hir eyen greye as glas;
> Hir mouth ful smal, and ther-to soft and reed;
> But sikerly she hadde a fair foreheed;
> It was almost a spanne brood, I trowe;
> For, hardily, she was nat undergrowe.

Then he goes on to develop her; she was a girl, a virgin, cold in her virginity:

> I am, thou woost, yet of thy companye,
> A mayde, and love hunting and venerye,
> And for to walken in the wodes wilde,
> And noght to been a wyf and be with childe.

Next he bethinks him how

> Discreet she was in answering alway;
> And though she had been as wise as Pallas
> No countrefeted termes hadde she
> To seme wys; but after hir degree
> She spak, and alle hir wordes more and lesse
> Souninge in vertu and in gentillesse.

Each of these quotations, in fact, comes from a different Tale, but they are parts, one feels, of the same personage, whom he had in mind, perhaps unconsciously, when he thought of a young girl, and for this reason, as she goes in and out of the *Canterbury Tales* bearing different names, she has a stability which is only to be found where the poet has made up his mind about young women, of course, but also about the world they live in, its end, its nature, and his own craft and technique, so that his mind is free to apply its force fully to its object. It does not occur to him that his Griselda might be improved or altered. There is no blur about her, no hesitation; she proves nothing; she is content to be herself. Upon her, therefore, the mind can rest with that unconscious ease which allows it, from hints and suggestions, to endow her with many more qualities than are actually referred to. Such is the power of conviction, a rare gift, a gift shared in our day by Joseph Conrad in his earlier novels, and a gift of supreme importance, for upon it the whole weight of the building depends. Once believe in Chaucer's young men and women and we have no need of preaching or protest. We know what he finds good, what evil; the less said the better. Let him get on with his story, paint knights and squires, good women and bad, cooks, shipmen, priests, and we will supply the landscape, give his society its belief, its standing towards life and death, and make of the journey to Canterbury a spiritual pilgrimage.

This simple faithfulness to his own conceptions was easier then than now in one respect at least, for Chaucer could write frankly where we must either say nothing or say it slyly. He could sound every note in the language instead of finding a great many of the best gone dumb from disuse, and thus, when struck by daring fingers, giving off a loud discordant jangle out of keeping with the rest. Much of Chaucer—a few lines perhaps in each of the Tales—is improper and gives us as we read it the strange sensation of being naked to the air after being muffled in old clothing. And, as a certain kind of humour depends upon being able to speak without self-consciousness of the parts and functions of the body, so with the advent of decency literature lost the use of one of its limbs. It lost its power to create the Wife of Bath, Juliet's nurse, and their recognisable though already colourless relation, Moll Flanders. Sterne, from fear of coarseness, is forced into indecency. He must be witty, not humorous. He must hint instead of speaking outright. Nor can we believe, with Mr. Joyce's *Ulysses* before us, that laughter of the old kind will ever be heard again.

> But, lord Christ! When that it remembreth me
> Up-on my yowthe, and on my Iolitee,
> It tikleth me aboute myn herte rote.
> Unto this day it doth myn herte bote
> That I have had my world as in my tyme.

The sound of that old woman's voice is still.

But there is another and more important reason for the surprising brightness, the still effective merriment of the *Canterbury Tales*. Chaucer was a poet; but he never flinched from the life that was being lived at the moment before his eyes. A farmyard, with its straw, its dung, its cocks and its hens is not (we have come to think) a poetic subject; poets seem either to rule out the farmyard entirely or to require that it shall be a farmyard in Thessaly and its pigs of mythological origin. But Chaucer says outright:

> Three large sowes hadde she, and namo,
> Three kyn, and eek a sheep that highte Malle;

or again,

> A yard she hadde, enclosed al aboute
> With stikkes, and a drye ditch with-oute.

He is unabashed and unafraid. He will always get close up to his object—an old man's chin—

> With thikke bristles of his berde unsofte,
> Lyk to the skin of houndfish, sharp as brere;

or an old man's neck—

> The slakke skin aboute his nekke shaketh
> Whyl that he sang;

and he will tell you what his characters wore, how they looked, what they ate and drank, as if poetry could handle the common facts of this very moment of Tuesday, the sixteenth day of April, 1387, without dirtying her hands. If he withdraws to the time of the Greeks or the Romans, it is only that his story leads him there. He has no desire to wrap himself round in antiquity, to take refuge in age, or to shirk the associations of common grocer's English.

Therefore when we say that we know the end of the journey, it is hard to quote the particular lines from which we take our knowledge. He fixed his eyes upon the road before him, not upon the world to come. He was little given to abstract contemplation. He deprecated, with peculiar archness, any competition with the scholars and divines:

> The answere of this I lete to divynis,
> But wel I woot, that in this world grey pyne is.

> What is this world? What asketh men to have?
> Now with his love, now in the colde grave
> Allone, withouten any companye,

he asks, or ponders

> O cruel goddes, that governe
> This world with binding of your worde eterne,
> And wryten in the table of athamaunt
> Your parlement, and your eterne graunt,
> What is mankinde more un-to yow holde
> Than is the sheepe, that rouketh in the folde?

Questions press upon him; he asks questions, but he is too true a poet to answer them; he leaves them unsolved, uncramped by the solution of the moment, thus fresh for the generations that come after him. In his life, too, it would be impossible to write him down a man of this party or of that, a democrat or an aristocrat. He was a staunch churchman, but he laughed at priests. He was an able public servant and a courtier, but his views upon sexual morality were extremely lax. He sympathised with poverty, but did nothing to improve the lot of the poor. It is safe to say that not a single law has been framed or one stone set upon another because of anything that Chaucer said or wrote; and yet, as we read him, we are of course absorbing morality at every pore. For among writers there are two kinds: there are the priests who take you by the hand and lead you straight up to the mystery; there are the laymen who imbed their doctrines in flesh and blood and make a complete model of the world without excluding the bad or laying stress upon the good. Wordsworth, Coleridge, and Shelley are among the priests; they give us text after text to be hung upon the wall, saying after saying to be laid upon the heart like an amulet against disaster—

Farewell, farewell, the heart that lives alone

He prayeth best that loveth best
All things both great and small

—such lines of exhortation and command spring to memory instantly. But Chaucer lets us go our ways doing the ordinary things with the ordinary people. His morality lies in the way men and women behave to each other. We see them eating, drinking, laughing, and making love, and come to feel without a word being said what their standards are and so are steeped through and through with their morality. There can be no more forcible preaching than this where all actions and passions are represented, and instead of being solemnly exhorted we are left to stray and stare and make out a meaning for ourselves. It is the morality of ordinary intercourse, the morality of the novel, which parents and librarians rightly judge to be far more persuasive than the morality of poetry.

And so, when we shut Chaucer, we feel that without a word being said the criticism is complete; what we are saying, thinking, reading, doing has been commented upon. Nor are we left merely with the sense, powerful though that is, of having been in good company and got used to the ways of good society. For as we have jogged through the real, the unadorned country-side, with first one good fellow cracking his joke or singing his song and then another, we know that though this world resembles, it is not in fact our daily world. It is the world of poetry. Everything happens here more quickly and more intensely, and with better order than in life or in prose; there is a formal elevated dullness which is part of the incantation of poetry; there are lines speaking half a second in advance what we were about to say, as if we read our thoughts before words cumbered them; and lines which we go back to read again with that heightened quality, that enchantment which keeps them glittering in the mind long afterwards. And the whole is held in its place, and its variety and divagations ordered by the power which is among the most impressive of all—the shaping power, the architect's power. It is the peculiarity of Chaucer, however, that though we feel at once this quickening, this enchantment, we cannot prove it by quotation. From most poets quotation is easy and obvious; some metaphor suddenly flowers; some passage breaks off from the rest. But Chaucer is very equal, very even-paced, very unmetaphorical. If we take six or seven lines in the hope that the quality will be contained in them it has escaped.

> My lord, ye woot that in my fadres place,
> Ye dede me strepe out of my povre wede,
> And richely me cladden, o your grace
> To yow broghte I noght elles, out of drede,
> But feyth and nakedness and maydenhede.

In its place that seemed not only memorable and moving but fit to set beside striking beauties. Cut out and taken separately it appears ordinary and quiet. Chaucer, it seems, has some art by which the most ordinary words and the simplest feelings when laid side by side make each other shine; when separated lose their lustre. Thus the pleasure he gives us is different from the pleasure that other poets give us, because it is more closely connected with what we have ourselves felt or observed. Eating, drinking and fine weather, the May, cocks and hens, millers, old peasant women, flowers—there is a special stimulus in seeing all these common things so arranged that they affect us as poetry affects us, and are yet bright, sober, precise as we see them out of doors. There is a pungency in this unfigurative language; a stately and memorable beauty in the undraped sentences which follow each other like women so slightly veiled that you see the lines of their bodies as they go—

And she set down hir water pot anon
Biside the threshold in an oxe's stall.

And then, as the procession takes its way, tranquilly,
beautifully, out from behind peeps the face of Chaucer,
grinning, malicious, in league with all foxes, donkeys,
and hens, to mock the pomp and ceremonies of life—
witty, intellectual, French, at the same time based
upon a broad bottom of English humour.

So Sir John read his Chaucer in the comfortless
room with the wind blowing and the smoke stinging,
and left his father's tombstone unmade.   But no book,
no tomb, had power to hold him long. He was one of
those ambiguous characters who haunt the boundary
line where one age merges in another and are not able
to inhabit either. At one moment he was all for buying
books cheap; next he was off to France and told his
mother, "My mind is now not most upon books".   In
his own house, where his mother Margaret was perpetually making out inventories or confiding in Gloys
the priest, he had no peace or comfort.   There was
always reason on her side; she was a brave woman, for
whose sake one must put up with the priest's insolence
and choke down one's rage when the grumbling broke
into open abuse, and "Thou proud priest" and "Thou
proud Squire" were bandied angrily about the room.
All this, with the discomforts of life and the weakness
of his own character, drove him to loiter in pleasanter
places, to put off coming, to put off writing, to put off,

[35]

year after year, the making of his father's tombstone. Yet John Paston had now lain for twelve years under the bare ground. The Prior of Bromholm sent word that the grave cloth was in tatters, and he had tried to patch it himself. Worse still, for a proud woman like Margaret Paston, the country people murmured at the Pastons' lack of piety, and other families she heard, of no greater standing than theirs, spent money in pious restoration in the very church where her husband lay unremembered. At last, turning from tournaments and Chaucer and Mistress Anne Hault, Sir John bethought him of a piece of cloth of gold which had been used to cover his father's hearse and might now be sold to defray the expenses of his tomb. Margaret had it in safe keeping; she had hoarded it and cared for it, and spent twenty marks on its repair. She grudged it; but there was no help for it. She sent it him, still distrusting his intentions or his power to put them into effect. "If you sell it to any other use," she wrote, "by my troth I shall never trust you while I live."

But this final act, like so many that Sir John had undertaken in the course of his life, was left undone. A dispute with the Duke of Suffolk in the year 1479 made it necessary for him to visit London in spite of the epidemic of sickness that was abroad; and there, in dirty lodgings, alone, busy to the end with quarrels, clamorous to the end for money, Sir John died and was buried at Whitefriars in London. He left a natural daughter; he left a considerable number of books; but his father's tomb was still unmade.

The four thick volumes of the Paston letters, however, swallow up this frustrated man as the sea absorbs a raindrop. For, like all collections of letters, they seem to hint that we need not care overmuch for the fortunes of individuals. The family will go on whether Sir John lives or dies. It is their method to heap up in mounds of insignificant and often dismal dust the innumerable trivialities of daily life, as it grinds itself out, year after year. And then suddenly they blaze up; the day shines out, complete, alive, before our eyes. It is early morning and strange men have been whispering among the women as they milk. It is evening, and there in the churchyard Warne's wife bursts out against old Agnes Paston: "All the devils of Hell draw her soul to Hell." Now it is the autumn in Norfolk and Cecily Dawne comes whining to Sir John for clothing. "Moreover, Sir, liketh it your mastership to understand that winter and cold weather draweth nigh and I have few clothes but of your gift." There is the ancient day, spread out before us, hour by hour.

But in all this there is no writing for writing's sake; no use of the pen to convey pleasure or amusement or any of the million shades of endearment and intimacy which have filled so many English letters since. Only occasionally, under stress of anger for the most part, does Margaret Paston quicken into some shrewd saw

or solemn curse. "Men cut large thongs here out of
other men's leather. . . . We beat the brushes and
other men have the birds. . . . Haste reweth . . .
which is to my heart a very spear." That is her eloquence and that her anguish. Her sons, it is true, bend
their pens more easily to their will. They jest rather
stiffly; they hint rather clumsily; they make a little
scene like a rough puppet show of the old priest's anger
and give a phrase or two directly as they were spoken
in person. But when Chaucer lived he must have heard
this very language, matter of fact, unmetaphorical,
far better fitted for narrative than for analysis, capable
of religious solemnity or of broad humour, but very
stiff material to put on the lips of men and women ac-
costing each other face to face. In short it is easy to
see, from the Paston letters, why Chaucer wrote not
Lear or *Romeo and Juliet*, but the *Canterbury Tales*.

Sir John was buried; and John the younger brother
succeeded in his turn. The Paston letters go on; life
at Paston continues much the same as before. Over it
all broods a sense of discomfort and nakedness; of un-
washed limbs thrust into splendid clothing; of tapestry
blowing on the draughty walls; of the bedroom with
its privy; of winds sweeping straight over land unmitigated by hedge or town; of Caister Castle covering
with solid stone six acres of ground, and of the plain-
faced Pastons indefatigably accumulating wealth,
treading out the roads of Norfolk, and persisting with
an obstinate courage which does them infinite credit in
furnishing the bareness of England.

[38]

On Not Knowing Greek

For it is vain and foolish to talk of Knowing Greek, since in our ignorance we should be at the bottom of any class of schoolboys, since we do not know how the words sounded, or where precisely we ought to laugh, or how the actors acted, and between this foreign people and ourselves there is not only difference of race and tongue but a tremendous breach of tradition. All the more strange, then, is it that we should wish to know Greek, try to know Greek, feel for ever drawn back to Greek, and be for ever making up some notion of the meaning of Greek, though from what incongruous odds and ends, with what slight resemblance to the real meaning of Greek, who shall say?

It is obvious in the first place that Greek literature is the impersonal literature. Those few hundred years that separate John Paston from Plato, Norwich from Athens, make a chasm which the vast tide of European chatter can never succeed in crossing. When we read Chaucer, we are floated up to him insensibly on the current of our ancestors' lives, and later, as records increase and memories lengthen, there is scarcely a figure which has not its nimbus of association, its life and letters, its wife and family, its house, its character, its happy or dismal catastrophe. But the Greeks remain in a fastness of their own. Fate has been kind there too. She has preserved them from vulgarity, Euripides was eaten by dogs; Aeschylus killed by a stone; Sappho leapt from a cliff. We know no more of them than that. We have their poetry, and that is all.

But that is not, and perhaps never can be, wholly true. Pick up any play by Sophocles, read—

Son of him who led our hosts at Troy of old, son of Agamemnon,

and at once the mind begins to fashion itself surroundings. It makes some background, even of the most provisional sort, for Sophocles; it imagines some village, in a remote part of the country, near the sea. Even nowadays such villages are to be found in the wilder parts of England, and as we enter them we can scarcely help feeling that here, in this cluster of cottages, cut off from rail or city, are all the elements of a perfect existence. Here is the Rectory; here the Manor house, the farm and the cottages; the church for worship, the club for meeting, the cricket field for play. Here life is simply sorted out into its main elements. Each man and woman has his work; each works for the health or happiness of others. And here, in this little community, characters become part of the common stock; the eccentricities of the clergyman are known; the great ladies' defects of temper; the blacksmith's feud with the milkman, and the loves and matings of the boys and girls. Here life has cut the same grooves for centuries; customs have arisen; legends have attached themselves to hilltops and solitary trees, and the village has its history, its festivals, and its rivalries.

It is the climate that is impossible. If we try to think of Sophocles here, we must annihilate the smoke and the damp and the thick wet mists. We must sharpen the lines of the hills. We must imagine a beauty of stone and earth rather than of woods and greenery. With warmth and sunshine and months of brilliant, fine weather, life of course is instantly changed; it is transacted out of doors, with the result, known to all who visit Italy, that small incidents are debated in the street, not in the sitting-room, and become dramatic; make people voluble; inspire in them that sneering, laughing, nimbleness of wit and tongue peculiar to the Southern races, which has nothing in common with the slow reserve, the low half-tones, the brooding introspective melancholy of people accustomed to live more than half the year indoors.

That is the quality that first strikes us in Greek literature, the lightning-quick, sneering, out-of-doors manner. It is apparent in the most august as well as in the most trivial places. Queens and Princesses in this very tragedy by Sophocles stand at the door bandying words like village women, with a tendency, as one might expect, to rejoice in language, to split phrases into slices, to be intent on verbal victory. The humour of the people was not good natured like that of our postmen and cabdrivers. The taunts of men lounging at the street corners had something cruel in them as well as witty. There is a cruelty in Greek tragedy which is quite unlike our English brutality. Is not Pentheus, for example, that highly respectable man, made ridiculous in the *Bacchæ* before he is destroyed? In fact, of course, these Queens and Princesses were out of doors, with the bees buzzing past them, shadows crossing them, and the wind taking their draperies. They were speaking to an enormous audience rayed round them on one of those brilliant southern days when the sun is so hot and yet the air so exciting. The poet, therefore, had to bethink him, not of some theme which could be read for hours by people in privacy, but of something emphatic, familiar, brief, that would carry, instantly and directly, to an audience of seventeen thousand people, perhaps, with ears and eyes eager and attentive, with bodies whose muscles would grow stiff if they sat too long without diversion. Music and dancing he would need, and naturally would choose one of those legends, like our Tristram and Iseult, which are known to every one in outline, so that a great fund of emotion is ready prepared, but can be stressed in a new place by each new poet.

Sophocles would take the old story of Electra, for instance, but would at once impose his stamp upon it. Of that, in spite of our weakness and distortion, what remains visible to us? That his genius was of the extreme kind in the first place; that he chose a design which, if it failed, would show its failure in gashes and ruin, not in the gentle blurring of some insignificant detail; which, if it succeeded, would cut each stroke to

[42]

the bone, would stamp each finger-print in marble. His Electra stands before us like a figure so tightly bound that she can only move an inch this way, an inch that. But each movement must tell to the utmost, or, bound as she is, denied the relief of all hints, repetitions, suggestions, she will be nothing but a dummy, tightly bound. Her words in crisis are, as a matter of fact, bare; mere cries of despair, joy, hate

οἲ ’γὼ τάλαιν’, ὄλωλα τῇδ’ ἐν ἡμέρᾳ.
παῖσον, εἰ σθένεις, διπλῆν.

But these cries give angle and outline to the play. It is thus, with a thousand differences of degree, that in English literature Jane Austen shapes a novel. There comes a moment—"I will dance with you," says Emma —which rises higher than the rest, which, though not eloquent in itself, or violent, or made striking by beauty of language, has the whole weight of the book behind it. In Jane Austen, too, we have the same sense, though the ligatures are much less tight, that her figures are bound, and restricted to a few definite movements. She, too, in her modest, everyday prose, chose the dangerous art where one slip means death.

But it is not so easy to decide what it is that gives these cries of Electra in her anguish their power to cut and wound and excite. It is partly that we know her, that we have picked up from little turns and twists of the dialogue hints of her character, of her appearance, which, characteristically, she neglected; of something suffering in her, outraged and stimulated to its utmost stretch of capacity, yet, as she herself knows ("my behaviour is unseemly and becomes me ill"), blunted and debased by the horror of her position, an unwed girl made to witness her mother's vileness and denounce it in loud, almost vulgar, clamour to the world at large. It is partly, too, that we know in the same way that Clytemnestra is no unmitigated villainess. "δεινὸν τὸ τίχτειν ἐστίν," she says—"there is a strange power in motherhood". It is no murderess, violent and un-redeemed, whom Orestes kills within the house, and Electra bids him utterly destroy—"strike again". No; the men and women standing out in the sunlight be-fore the audience on the hillside were alive enough, subtle enough, not mere figures, or plaster casts of human beings.

Yet it is not because we can analyse them into feel-ings that they impress us. In six pages of Proust we can find more complicated and varied emotions than in the whole of the *Electra*. But in the *Electra* or in the *Antigone* we are impressed by something different, by something perhaps more impressive—by heroism itself, by fidelity itself. In spite of the labour and the diffi-culty it is this that draws us back and back to the Greeks; the stable, the permanent, the original human being is to be found there. Violent emotions are needed to rouse him into action, but when thus stirred by death, by betrayal, by some other primitive calam-ity, Antigone and Ajax and Electra behave in the way in which we should behave thus struck down; the way in which everybody has always behaved; and thus we understand them more easily and more directly than we understand the characters in the *Canterbury Tales*. These are the originals, Chaucer's the varieties of the human species.

It is true, of course, that these types of the original man or woman, these heroic Kings, these faithful daughters, these tragic Queens who stalk through the ages always planting their feet in the same places, twitching their robes with the same gestures, from habit not from impulse, are among the greatest bores and the most demoralising companions in the world. The plays of Addison, Voltaire, and a host of others are there to prove it. But encounter them in Greek. Even in Sophocles, whose reputation for restraint and mastery has filtered down to us from the scholars, they are decided, ruthless, direct. A fragment of their speech broken off would, we feel, colour oceans and oceans of the respectable drama. Here we meet them before their emotions have been worn into uniformity. Here we listen to the nightingale whose song echoes through English literature singing in her own Greek tongue. For the first time Orpheus with his lute makes men and beasts follow him. Their voices ring out clear and sharp; we see the hairy tawny bodies at play in the sunlight among the olive trees, not posed gracefully on granite plinths in the pale corridors of the British Museum. And then suddenly, in the midst of all this sharpness and compression, Electra, as if she swept her veil over her face and forbade us to think of her any more, speaks of that very nightingale: "that bird dis-

[45]

traught with grief, the messenger of Zeus. Ah, queen of sorrow, Niobe, thee I deem divine—thee; who evermore weepest in thy rocky tomb".

And as she silences her own complaint, she perplexes us again with the insoluble question of poetry and its nature, and why, as she speaks thus, her words put on the assurance of immortality. For they are Greek; we cannot tell how they sounded; they ignore the obvious sources of excitement; they owe nothing of their effect to any extravagance of expression, and certainly they throw no light upon the speaker's character or the writer's. But they remain, something that has been stated and must eternally endure.

Yet in a play how dangerous this poetry, this lapse from the particular to the general must of necessity be, with the actors standing there in person, with their bodies and their faces passively waiting to be made use of! For this reason the later plays of Shakespeare, where there is more of poetry than of action, are better read than seen, better understood by leaving out the actual body than by having the body, with all its associations and movements, visible to the eye. The intolerable restrictions of the drama could be loosened, however, if a means could be found by which what was general and poetic, comment, not action, could be freed without interrupting the movement of the whole. It is this that the choruses supply; the old men or women who take no active part in the drama, the undifferentiated voices who sing like birds in the pauses of the wind; who can comment, or sum up, or allow the poet

to speak himself or supply, by contrast, another side
to his conception. Always in imaginative literature,
where characters speak for themselves and the author
has no part, the need of that voice is making itself felt.
For though Shakespeare (unless we consider that his
fools and madmen supply the part) dispensed with
the chorus, novelists are always devising some substitute—Thackeray speaking in his own person, Fielding
coming out and addressing the world before his curtain
rises. So to grasp the meaning of the play the chorus
is of the utmost importance. One must be able to
pass easily into those ecstasies, those wild and apparently irrelevant utterances, those sometimes obvious
and commonplace statements, to decide their relevance
or irrelevance, and give them their relation to the play
as a whole.

We must "be able to pass easily"; but that of course
is exactly what we cannot do. For the most part the
choruses, with all their obscurities, must be spelt out
and their symmetry mauled. But we can guess that
Sophocles used them not to express something outside
the action of the play, but to sing the praises of some
virtue, or the beauties of some place mentioned in it.
He selects what he wishes to emphasise and sings of
white Colonus and its nightingale, or of love uncon-
quered in fight. Lovely, lofty, and serene his choruses
grow naturally out of his situations, and change, not
the point of view, but the mood. In Euripides, however, the situations are not contained within themselves; they give off an atmosphere of doubt, of sug-

[47]

gestion, of questioning; but if we look to the choruses to make this plain we are often baffled rather than instructed. At once in the *Bacchæ* we are in the world of psychology and doubt; the world where the mind twists facts and changes them and makes the familiar aspects of life appear new and questionable. What is Bacchus, and who are the Gods, and what is man's duty to them, and what the rights of his subtle brain? To these questions the chorus makes no reply, or replies mockingly, or speaks darkly as if the straitness of the dramatic form had tempted Euripides to violate it in order to relieve his mind of its weight. Time is so short and I have so much to say, that unless you will allow me to place together two apparently unrelated statements and trust to you to pull them together, you must be content with a mere skeleton of the play I might have given you. Such is the argument. Euripides therefore suffers less than Sophocles and less than Aeschylus from being read privately in a room, and not seen on a hillside in the sunshine. He can be acted in the mind; he can comment upon the questions of the moment; more than the others he will vary in popularity from age to age.

If then in Sophocles the play is concentrated in the figures themselves, and in Euripides is to be retrieved from flashes of poetry and questions far flung and unanswered, Aeschylus makes these little dramas (the *Agamemnon* has 1663 lines; *Lear* about 2600), tremendous by stretching every phrase to the utmost, by sending them floating forth in metaphors, by bidding

them rise up and stalk eyeless and majestic through the
scene. To understand him it is not so necessary to understand Greek as to understand poetry. It is necessary to take that dangerous leap through the air without the support of words which Shakespeare also asks
of us. For words, when opposed to such a blast of
meaning, must give out, must be blown astray, and
only by collecting in companies convey the meaning
which each one separately is too weak to express. Con-
necting them in a rapid flight of the mind we know
instantly and instinctively what they mean, but could
not decant that meaning afresh into any other words.
There is an ambiguity which is the mark of the highest
poetry; we cannot know exactly what it means. Take
this from the *Agamemnon* for instance—

ὀμμάτων δ' ἐν ἀχηνίαις ἔρρει πᾶσ' ᾿Αφροδίτα.

The meaning is just on the far side of language. It is
the meaning which in moments of astonishing excitement and stress we perceive in our minds without
words; it is the meaning that Dostoevsky (hampered
as he was by prose and as we are by translation) leads
us to by some astonishing run up the scale of emotions
and points at but cannot indicate; the meaning that
Shakespeare succeeds in snaring.

Aeschylus thus will not give, as Sophocles gives,
the very words that people might have spoken, only so
arranged that they have in some mysterious way a
general force, a symbolic power, nor like Euripides will
he combine incongruities and thus enlarge his little

space, as a small room is enlarged by mirrors in odd corners. By the bold and running use of metaphor he will amplify and give us, not the thing itself, but the reverberation and reflection which, taken into his mind, the thing has made; close enough to the original to illustrate it, remote enough to heighten, enlarge, and make splendid.

For none of these dramatists had the license which belongs to the novelist, and, in some degree, to all writers of printed books, of modelling their meaning with an infinity of slight touches which can only be properly applied by reading quietly, carefully, and sometimes two or three times over. Every sentence had to explode on striking the ear, however slowly and beautifully the words might then descend, and however enigmatic might their final purport be. No splendour or richness of metaphor could have saved the *Agamemnon* if either images or allusions of the subtlest or most decorative had got between us and the naked cry

ὀτοτοτοῖ πόποι δᾶ. ὢ 'πολλον, ὢ 'πολλον.

Dramatic they had to be at whatever cost.

But winter fell on these villages, darkness and extreme cold descended on the hill-side. There must have been some place indoors where men could retire, both in the depths of winter and in the summer heats, where they could sit and drink, where they could lie stretched at their ease, where they could talk. It is Plato, of course, who reveals the life indoors, and de-

scribes how, when a party of friends met and had eaten
not at all luxuriously and drunk a little wine, some
handsome boy ventured a question, or quoted an opinion, and Socrates took it up, fingered it, turned it round,
looked at it this way and that, swiftly stripped it of its
inconsistencies and falsities and brought the whole company by degrees to gaze with him at the truth. It is
an exhausting process; to contract painfully upon the
exact meaning of words; to judge what each admission
involves; to follow intently, yet critically, the dwin-
dling and changing of opinion as it hardens and intensifies into truth. Are pleasure and good the same? Can
virtue be taught? Is virtue knowledge? The tired or
feeble mind may easily lapse as the remorseless questioning proceeds; but no one, however weak, can fail,
even if he does not learn more from Plato, to love
knowledge better. For as the argument mounts from
step to step, Protagoras yielding, Socrates pushing
on, what matters is not so much the end we reach
as our manner of reaching it. That all can feel—
the indomitable honesty, the courage, the love of
truth which draw Socrates and us in his wake to the
summit where, if we too may stand for a moment,
it is to enjoy the greatest felicity of which we are
capable.

Yet such an expression seems ill fitted to describe
the state of mind of a student to whom, after painful
argument, the truth has been revealed. But truth is
various; truth comes to us in different disguises; it is
not with the intellect alone that we perceive it. It is

[51]

a winter's night; the tables are spread at Agathon's house; the girl is playing the flute; Socrates has washed himself and put on sandals; he has stopped in the hall; he refuses to move when they send for him. Now Socrates has done; he is bantering Alcibiades; Alcibiades takes a fillet and binds it round "this wonderful fellow's head". He praises Socrates. "For he cares not for mere beauty, but despises more than any one can imagine all external possessions, whether it be beauty or wealth or glory, or any other thing for which the multitude felicitates the possessor. He esteems these things and us who honour them, as nothing, and lives among men, making all the objects of their admiration the playthings of his irony. But I know not if any one of you has ever seen the divine images which are within, when he has been opened and is serious. I have seen them, and they are so supremely beautiful, so golden, divine, and wonderful, that everything which Socrates commands surely ought to be obeyed even like the voice of a God." All this flows over the arguments of Plato —laughter and movement; people getting up and going out; the hour changing; tempers being lost; jokes cracked; the dawn rising. Truth, it seems, is various; Truth is to be pursued with all our faculties. Are we to rule out the amusements, the tendernesses, the frivolities of friendship because we love truth? Will truth be quicker found because we stop our ears to music and drink no wine, and sleep instead of talking through the long winter's night? It is not to the cloistered disciplinarian mortifying himself in solitude that

[52]

we are to turn, but to the well-sunned nature, the man who practises the art of living to the best advantage, so that nothing is stunted but some things are permanently more valuable than others.

So in these dialogues we are made to seek truth with every part of us. For Plato, of course, had the dramatic genius. It is by means of that, by an art which conveys in a sentence or two the setting and the atmosphere, and then with perfect adroitness insinuates itself into the coils of the argument without losing its liveliness and grace, and then contracts to bare statement, and then, mounting, expands and soars in that higher air which is generally reached only by the more extreme measures of poetry—it is this art which plays upon us in so many ways at once and brings us to an exultation of mind which can only be reached when all the powers are called upon to contribute their energy to the whole.

But we must beware. Socrates did not care for "mere beauty", by which he meant, perhaps, beauty as ornament. A people who judged as much as the Athenians did by ear, sitting out-of-doors at the play or listening to argument in the market-place, were far less apt than we are to break off sentences and appreciate them apart from the context. For them there were no Beauties of Hardy, Beauties of Meredith, Sayings from George Eliot. The writer had to think more of the whole and less of the detail. Naturally, living in the open, it was not the lip or the eye that struck them, but the carriage of the body and the proportions

[53]

of its parts. Thus when we quote and extract we do the Greeks more damage than we do the English. There is a bareness and abruptness in their literature which grates upon a taste accustomed to the intricacy and finish of printed books. We have to stretch our minds to grasp a whole devoid of the prettiness of detail or the emphasis of eloquence. Accustomed to look directly and largely rather than minutely and aslant, it was safe for them to step into the thick of emotions which blind and bewilder an age like our own. In the vast catastrophe of the European war our emotions had to be broken up for us, and put at an angle from us, before we could allow ourselves to feel them in poetry or fiction. The only poets who spoke to the purpose spoke in the sidelong, satiric manner of Wilfrid Owen and Siegfried Sassoon. It was not possible for them to be direct without being clumsy; or to speak simply of emotion without being sentimental. But the Greeks could say, as if for the first time, "Yet being dead they have not died". They could say, "If to die nobly is the chief part of excellence, to us out of all men Fortune gave this lot; for hastening to set a crown of freedom on Greece we lie possessed of praise that grows not old". They could march straight up, with their eyes open; and thus fearlessly approached, emotions stand still and suffer themselves to be looked at.

But again (the question comes back and back), Are we reading Greek as it was written when we say this? When we read these few words cut on a tombstone, a

stanza in a chorus, the end or the opening of a dialogue
of Plato's, a fragment of Sappho, when we bruise our
minds upon some tremendous metaphor in the *Agamem-*
non instead of stripping the branch of its flowers instantly as we do in reading *Lear*—are we not reading
wrongly? losing our sharp sight in the haze of associations? reading into Greek poetry not what they have
but what we lack? Does not the whole of Greece heap
itself behind every line of its literature? They admit
us to a vision of the earth unravaged, the sea unpol-
luted, the maturity, tried but unbroken, of mankind.
Every word is reinforced by a vigour which pours out
of olive-tree and temple and the bodies of the young.
The nightingale has only to be named by Sophocles
and she sings; the grove has only to be called ἄβατον,
"untrodden", and we imagine the twisted branches and
the purple violets. Back and back we are drawn to
steep ourselves in what, perhaps, is only an image of
the reality, not the reality itself, a summer's day imagined in the heart of a northern winter. Chief among
these sources of glamour and perhaps misunderstanding
is the language. We can never hope to get the whole
fling of a sentence in Greek as we do in English. We
cannot hear it, now dissonant, now harmonious, tossing sound from line to line across a page. We cannot
pick up infallibly one by one all those minute signals
by which a phrase is made to hint, to turn, to live.
Nevertheless it is the language that has us most in
bondage; the desire for that which perpetually lures us
back. First there is the compactness of the expression.

Shelley takes twenty-one words in English to translate thirteen words of Greek.

πᾶς γοῦν ποιητής γίγνεται, κἂν ἄμουσος ἦ τὸ πρίν, ὃν ἂν Ἔρως ἅψηται.

. . . For every one, even if before he were ever so undis-ciplined, becomes a poet as soon as he is touched by love.

Every ounce of fat has been pared off, leaving the flesh firm. Then, spare and bare as it is, no language can move more quickly, dancing, shaking, all alive, but controlled. Then there are the words themselves which, in so many instances, we have made expressive to us of our own emotions, *thalassa*, *thanatos*, *anthos*, *aster*—to take the first that come to hand; so clear, so hard, so intense, that to speak plainly yet fittingly without blurring the outline or clouding the depths Greek is the only expression. It is useless, then, to read Greek in translations. Translators can but offer us a vague equivalent; their language is necessarily full of echoes and associations. Professor Mackail says "wan", and the age of Burne-Jones and Morris is at once evoked. Nor can the subtler stress, the flight and the fall of the words, be kept even by the most skilful of scholars—

. . . thee, who evermore weepest in thy rocky tomb

is not

ἅτ' ἐν τάφῳ πετραίῳ,
αἰ, δακρύεις.

[56]

Further, in reckoning the doubts and difficulties there is this important problem—Where are we to laugh in reading Greek? There is a passage in the *Odyssey* where laughter begins to steal upon us, but if Homer were looking we should probably think it better to control our merriment. To laugh instantly it is almost necessary (though Aristophanes may supply us with an exception) to laugh in English. Humour, after all, is closely bound up with a sense of the body. When we laugh at the humour of Wycherley, we are laughing with the body of that burly rustic who was our common ancestor on the village green. The French, the Italians, the Americans, who derive physically from so different a stock, pause, as we pause in reading Homer, to make sure that they are laughing in the right place, and the pause is fatal. Thus humour is the first of the gifts to perish in a foreign tongue, and when we turn from Greek to Elizabethan literature it seems, after a long silence, as if our great age were ushered in by a burst of laughter.

These are all difficulties, sources of misunderstanding, of distorted and romantic, of servile and snobbish passion. Yet even for the unlearned some certainties remain. Greek is the impersonal literature; it is also the literature of masterpieces. There are no schools; no forerunners; no heirs. We cannot trace a gradual process working in many men imperfectly until it expresses itself adequately at last in one. Again, there is always about Greek literature that air of vigour which permeates an "age", whether it is the age of

Aeschylus, or Racine, or Shakespeare. One generation at least in that fortunate time is blown on to be writers to the extreme; to attain that unconsciousness which means that the consciousness is stimulated to the highest extent; to surpass the limits of small triumphs and tentative experiments. Thus we have Sappho with her constellations of adjectives, Plato daring extravagant flights of poetry in the midst of prose; Thucydides, constricted and contracted; Sophocles gliding like a shoal of trout smoothly and quietly, apparently motionless, and then with a flicker of fins off and away; while in the *Odyssey* we have what remains the triumph of narrative, the clearest and at the same time the most romantic story of the fortunes of men and women.

The *Odyssey* is merely a story of adventure, the instinctive story-telling of a sea-faring race. So we may begin it, reading quickly in the spirit of children wanting amusement to find out what happens next. But here is nothing immature; here are full-grown people, crafty, subtle, and passionate. Nor is the world itself a small one, since the sea which separates island from island has to be crossed by little hand-made boats and is measured by the flight of the sea-gulls. It is true that the islands are not thickly populated, and the people, though everything is made by hand, are not closely kept at work. They have had time to develop a very dignified, a very stately society, with an ancient tradition of manners behind it, which makes every relation at once orderly, natural, and full of reserve. Penelope crosses the room; Telemachus goes to bed;

Nausicaa washes her linen; and their actions seem laden with beauty because they do not know that they are beautiful, have been born to their possessions, are no more self-conscious than children, and yet, all those thousands of years ago, in their little islands, know all that is to be known. With the sound of the sea in their ears, vines, meadows, rivulets about them, they are even more aware than we are of a ruthless fate. There is a sadness at the back of life which they do not attempt to mitigate. Entirely aware of their own standing in the shadow, and yet alive to every tremor and gleam of existence, there they endure, and it is to the Greeks that we turn when we are sick of the vagueness, of the confusion, of the Christianity and its consolations, of our own age.

The Elizabethan Lumber Room

These magnificent volumes [1] are not often, perhaps,
read through. Part of their charm consists in the fact
that Hakluyt is not so much a book as a great bundle
of commodities loosely tied together, an emporium, a
lumber room strewn with ancient sacks, obsolete nautical instruments, huge bales of wool, and little bags of
rubies and emeralds. One is for ever untying this
packet here, sampling that heap over there, wiping the
dust off some vast map of the world, and sitting down
in semi-darkness to snuff the strange smells of silks
and leathers and ambergris, while outside tumble the
huge waves of the uncharted Elizabethan sea.

For this jumble of seeds, silks, unicorns' horns, elephants' teeth, wool, common stones, turbans, and bars
of gold, these odds and ends of priceless value and complete worthlessness, were the fruit of innumerable voyages, traffics, and discoveries to unknown lands in the
reign of Queen Elizabeth. The expeditions were
manned by "apt young men" from the West country,
and financed in part by the great Queen herself. The
ships, says Froude, were no bigger than modern
yachts. There in the river by Greenwich the fleet lay

---

[1] *Hakluyt's Collection of the Early Voyages, Travels, and Discoveries of the English Nation,* five volumes, 4to, 1810.

[61]

gathered, close to the Palace. "The Privy council looked out of the windows of the court . . . the ships thereupon discharge their ordnance . . . and the mariners they shouted in such sort that the sky rang again with the noise thereof." Then, as the ships swung down the tide, one sailor after another walked the hatches, climbed the shrouds, stood upon the mainyards to wave his friends a last farewell. Many would come back no more. For directly England and the coast of France were beneath the horizon, the ships sailed into the unfamiliar; the air had its voices, the sea its lions and serpents, its evaporations of fire and tumultuous whirlpools. But God too was very close; the clouds but sparely hid the divinity Himself; the limbs of Satan were almost visible. Familiarly the English sailors pitted their God against the God of the Turks, who "can speake never a word for dulnes, much lesse can he helpe them in such an extremitie. . . . But howsoever their God behaved himself, our God showed himself a God indeed. . . ." God was as near by sea as by land, said Sir Humphrey Gilbert, riding through the storm. Suddenly one light disappeared; Sir Humphrey Gilbert had gone beneath the waves; when morning came, they sought his ship in vain. Sir Hugh Willoughby sailed to discover the North-West Passage and made no return. The Earl of Cumberland's men, hung up by adverse winds off the coast of Cornwall for a fortnight, licked the muddy water off the deck in agony. And sometimes a ragged and worn-out man came knocking at the door of an English coun-

try house and claimed to be the boy who had left it
years ago to sail the seas. "Sir William his father, and
my lady his mother knew him not to be their son, until
they found a secret mark, which was a wart upon one
of his knees." But he had with him a black stone,
veined with gold, or an ivory tusk, or a silver ingot, and
urged on the village youth with talk of gold strewn
over the land as stones are strewn in the fields of England. One expedition might fail, but what if the passage to the fabled land of uncounted riches lay only a
little further up the coast? What if the known world
was only the prelude to some more splendid panorama?
When, after the long voyage, the ships dropped anchor
in the great river of the Plate and the men went ex-
ploring through the undulating lands, startling grazing
herds of deer, seeing the limbs of savages between the
trees, they filled their pockets with pebbles that might
be emeralds or sand that might be gold; or sometimes,
rounding a headland, they saw, far off, a string of savages slowly descending to the beach bearing on their
heads and linking their shoulders together with heavy
burdens for the Spanish King.

These are the fine stories used effectively all through
the West country to decoy "the apt young men"
lounging by the harbour-side to leave their nets and
fish for gold. But the voyagers were sober merchants
into the bargain, citizens with the good of English
trade and the welfare of English work-people at heart.
The captains are reminded how necessary it is to find
a market abroad for English wool; to discover the herb

[63]

from which blue dyes are made; above all to make inquiry as to the methods of producing oil, since all attempts to make it from radish seed have failed. They are reminded of the misery of the English poor, whose crimes, brought about by poverty, make them "daily consumed by the gallows". They are reminded how the soil of England had been enriched by the discoveries of travellers in the past; how Dr. Linaker brought seeds of the damask rose and tulipas, and how beasts and plants and herbs, "without which our life were to be said barbarous", have all come to England gradually from abroad. In search of markets and of goods, of the immortal fame success would bring them, the apt young men set sail for the North, and were left, a little company of isolated Englishmen surrounded by snow and the huts of savages, to make what bargains they could and pick up what knowledge they might before the ships returned in the summer to fetch them home again. There they endured, an isolated company, burning on the rim of the dark. One of them, carrying a charter from his company in London, went inland as far as Moscow, and there saw the Emperor "sitting in his chair of estate with his crown on his head, and a staff of goldsmiths' work in his left hand". All the ceremony that he saw is carefully written out, and the sight upon which the English merchant first set eyes has the brilliancy of a Roman vase dug up and stood for a moment in the sun, until, exposed to the air, seen by millions of eyes, it dulls and crumbles away. There, all these centuries, on the outskirts of the world, the glories of Moscow, the glories of Constantinople have flowered unseen. The Englishman was bravely dressed for the occasion, led "three fair mastiffs in coats of red cloth", and carried a letter from Elizabeth "the paper whereof did smell most fragrantly of camphor and ambergris, and the ink of perfect musk". And sometimes, since trophies from the amazing new world were eagerly awaited at home, together with unicorns' horns and lumps of ambergris and the fine stories of the engendering of whales and "debates" of elephants and dragons whose blood, mixed, congealed into vermilion, a living sample would be sent, a live savage caught somewhere off the coast of Labrador, taken to England, and shown about like a wild beast. Next year they brought him back, and took a woman savage on board to keep him company. When they saw each other they blushed; they blushed profoundly, but the sailors, though they noted it, knew not why. Later the two savages set up house together on board ship, she attending to his wants, he nursing her in sickness. But, as the sailors noted again, the savages lived together in perfect chastity.

All this, the new words, the new ideas, the waves, the savages, the adventures, found their way naturally into the plays which were being acted on the banks of the Thames. There was an audience quick to seize upon the coloured and the high-sounding; to associate those

> frigates bottom'd with rich Sethin planks,
> Topt with the lofty firs of Lebanon

with the adventures of their own sons and brothers abroad. The Verneys, for example, had a wild boy who had gone as pirate, turned Turk, and died out there, sending back to Claydon to be kept as relics of him some silk, a turban, and a pilgrim's staff. A gulf lay between the spartan domestic housecraft of the Paston women and the refined tastes of the Elizabethan Court ladies, who, grown old, says Harrison, spent their time reading histories, or "writing volumes of their own, or translating of other men's into our English and Latin tongue", while the younger ladies played the lute and the citharne and spent their leisure in the enjoyment of music. Thus, with singing and with music, springs into existence the characteristic Elizabethan extravagance; the dolphins and lavoltas of Greene; the hyperbole, more surprising in a writer so terse and muscular, of Ben Jonson. Thus we find the whole of Elizabethan literature strewn with gold and silver; with talk of Guiana's rarities, and references to that America—"O my America! my new-found-land"—which was not merely a land on the map, but symbolised the unknown territories of the soul. So, over the water, the imagination of Montaigne brooded in fascination upon savages, cannibals, society, and government.

But the mention of Montaigne suggests that though the influence of the sea and the voyages, of the lumber-room crammed with sea beasts and horns and ivory and old maps and nautical instruments, helped to inspire the greatest age of English poetry, its effects were by no means so beneficial upon English prose. Rhyme and metre helped the poets to keep the tumult of their perceptions in order. But the prose writer, without these restrictions, accumulated clauses, petered out in interminable catalogues, tripped and stumbled over the convolutions of his own rich draperies. How little Elizabethan prose was fit for its office, how exquisitely French prose was already adapted, can be seen by comparing a passage from Sidney's *Defense of Poesie* with one from Montaigne's Essays.

He beginneth not with obscure definitions, which must blur the margent with interpretations, and load the memory with doubtfulness: but he cometh to you with words set in delightful proportion, either accompanied with, or prepared for the well enchanting Skill of Music, and with a tale (forsooth) he cometh unto you, with a tale which holdeth children from play, and old men from the Chimney corner; and pretending no more, doth intend the winning of the mind from wickedness to virtue; even as the child is often brought to take most wholesome things by hiding them in such other as have a pleasant taste: which if one should begin to tell them the nature of the *Aloës* or *Rhubarbarum* they should receive, would sooner take their physic at their ears than at their mouth, so is it in men (most of which are childish in the best things, till they be cradled in their graves) glad they will be to hear the tales of Hercules. . . .

And so it runs on for seventy-six words more. Sidney's prose in an uninterrupted monologue, with sudden flashes of felicity and splendid phrases, which lends itself to lamentations and moralities, to long accumulations and catalogues, but is never quick, never collo-

[67]

quial, unable to grasp a thought closely and firmly, or to adapt itself flexibly and exactly to the chops and changes of the mind. Compared with this, Montaigne is master of an instrument which knows its own powers and limitations, and is capable of insinuating itself into crannies and crevices which poetry can never reach; of cadences different but no less beautiful; capable of subtleties and intensities which Elizabethan prose entirely ignores. He is considering the way in which certain of the ancients met death:

. . . ils l'ont faicte couler et glisser parmy la lascheté de leurs occupations accoustumées entre des garses et bons compaignons; nul propos de consolation, nulle mention de testament, nulle affectation ambitieuse de constance, nul discours de leur condition future; mais entre les jeux, les festins, facecies, entretiens communs et populaires, et la musique, et des vers amoureux.

An age seems to separate Sidney from Montaigne. The English compared with the French are as boys compared with men.

But the Elizabethan prose writers, if they have the formlessness of youth have, too, its freshness and audacity. In the same essay Sidney shapes language, masterfully and easily, to his liking; freely and naturally reaches his hand for a metaphor. To bring this prose to perfection (and Dryden's prose is very near perfection) only the discipline of the stage was necessary and the growth of self-consciousness. It is in the plays, and especially in the comic passages of the plays, that the finest Elizabethan prose is to be found. The stage was the nursery where prose learnt to find its feet. For on the stage people had to meet, to quip and crank, to suffer interruptions, to talk of ordinary things.

Cler. A box of her autumnal face, her pieced beauty! there's no man can be admitted till she be ready now-a-days, till she has painted, and perfumed, and washed, and scoured, but the boy here; and him she wipes her oiled lips upon, like a sponge. I have made a song (I pray thee hear it) on the subject. [Page sings

Still to be neat, still to be drest &c.

True. And I am clearly on the other side: I love a good dressing before any beauty o' the world. O, a woman is then like a delicate garden; nor is there one kind of it; she may vary every hour; take often counsel of her glass, and choose the best. If she have good ears, show them; good hair, lay it out; good legs, wear short clothes; a good hand, discover it often: practise any art to mend breath, cleanse teeth, repair eyebrows; paint and profess it.

So the talk runs in Ben Jonson's *Silent Woman*, knocked into shape by interruptions, sharpened by collisions, and never allowed to settle into stagnancy or swell into turbidity. But the publicity of the stage and the perpetual presence of a second person were hostile to that growing consciousness of one's self, that brooding in solitude over the mysteries of the soul, which, as the years went by, sought expression and found a champion in the sublime genius of Sir Thomas Browne. His immense egotism has paved

[69]

the way for all psychological novelists, autobiographers, confession-mongers, and dealers in the curious shades of our private life. He it was who first turned from the contacts of men with men to their lonely life within. "The world that I regard is myself; it is the microcosm of my own frame that I cast mine eye on; for the other I use it but like my globe, and turn it round sometimes for my recreation." All was mystery and darkness as the first explorer walked the catacombs swinging his lanthorn. "I feel sometimes a hell within myself; Lucifer keeps his court in my breast; Legion is revived in me." In these solitudes there were no guides and no companions. "I am in the dark to all the world, and my nearest friends behold me but in a cloud." The strangest thoughts and imaginings have play with him as he goes about his work, outwardly the most sober of mankind and esteemed the greatest physician in Norwich. He has wished for death. He has doubted all things. What if we are asleep in this world and the conceits of life are as mere dreams? The tavern music, the Ave Mary bell, the broken pot that the workman has dug out of the field—at the sight and sound of them he stops dead, as if transfixed by the astonishing vista that opens before his imagination. "We carry with us the wonders we seek without us; there is all Africa and her prodigies in us." A halo of wonder encircles everything that he sees; he turns his light gradually upon the flowers and insects and grasses at his feet so as to disturb nothing in the mysterious processes of their existence. With the same awe, mixed with a sublime complacency, he records the discovery of his own qualities and attain- ments. He was charitable and brave and averse from nothing. He was full of feeling for others and mer- ciless upon himself. "For my conversation, it is like the sun's, with all men, and with a friendly aspect to good and bad." He knows six languages, the laws, the customs and policies of several states, the names of all the constellations and most of the plants of his country, and yet, so sweeping is his imagination, so large the horizon in which he sees this little figure walking that "methinks I do not know so many as when I did but know a hundred, and had scarcely ever simpled further than Cheapside".

He is the first of the autobiographers. Swooping and soaring at the highest altitudes he stoops suddenly with loving particularity upon the details of his own body. His height was moderate, he tells us, his eyes large and luminous; his skin dark but constantly suf- fused with blushes. He dressed very plainly. He seldom laughed. He collected coins, kept maggots in boxes, dissected the lungs of frogs, braved the stench of the spermaceti whale, tolerated Jews, had a good word for the deformity of the toad, and combined a scientific and sceptical attitude towards most things with an unfortunate belief in witches. In short, as we say when we cannot help laughing at the oddities of people we admire most, he was a character, and the first to make us feel that the most sublime speculations of the human imagination are issued from a particular man, whom we can love. In the midst of the solemnities of the Urn Burial we smile when he remarks that afflictions induce callosities. The smile broadens to laughter as we mouth out the splendid pomposities, the astonishing conjectures of the *Religio Medici*. Whatever he writes is stamped with his own idiosyncrasy, and we first became conscious of impurities which hereafter stain literature with so many freakish colours that, however hard we try, make it difficult to be certain whether we are looking at a man or his writing. Now we are in the presence of sublime imagination; now rambling through one of the finest lumber rooms in the world—a chamber stuffed from floor to ceiling with ivory, old iron, broken pots, urns, unicorns' horns, and magic glasses full of emerald lights and blue mystery.

Notes on an Elizabethan Play

There are, it must be admitted, some highly formidable tracts in English literature, and chief among them that jungle, forest, and wilderness which is the Elizabethan drama. For many reasons, not here to be examined, Shakespeare stands out, Shakespeare who has had the light on him from his day to ours, Shakespeare who towers highest when looked at from the level of his own contemporaries. But the plays of the lesser Elizabethans—Greene, Dekker, Peele, Chapman, Beaumont and Fletcher,—to adventure into that wilderness is for the ordinary reader an ordeal, an upsetting experience which plies him with questions, harries him with doubts, alternately delights and vexes him with pleasures and pains. For we are apt to forget, reading, as we tend to do, only the masterpieces of a bygone age how great a power the body of a literature possesses to impose itself: how it will not suffer itself to be read passively, but takes us and reads us; flouts our preconceptions; questions principles which we had got into the habit of taking for granted, and, in fact, splits us into two parts as we read, making us, even as we enjoy, yield our ground or stick to our guns.

At the outset in reading an Elizabethan play we

are overcome by the extraordinary discrepancy between the Elizabethan view of reality and our own. The reality to which we have grown accustomed, is, speaking roughly, based upon the life and death of some knight called Smith, who succeeded his father in the family business of pitwood importers, timber merchants and coal exporters, was well known in political, temperance, and church circles, did much for the poor of Liverpool, and died last Wednesday of pneumonia while on a visit to his son at Muswell Hill. That is the world we know. That is the reality which our poets and novelists have to expound and illuminate. Then we open the first Elizabethan play that comes to hand and read how

> I once did see
> In my young travels through Armenia
> An angry unicorn in his full career
> Charge with too swift a foot a jeweller
> That watch'd him for the treasure of his brow
> And ere he could get shelter of a tree
> Nail him with his rich antlers to the earth.

Where is Smith, we ask, where is Liverpool? And the groves of Elizabethan drama echo "Where?" Exquisite is the delight, sublime the relief of being set free to wander in the land of the unicorn and the jeweller among dukes and grandees, Gonzaloes and Bellimperias, who spend their lives in murder and intrigue, dress up as men if they are women, as women if they are men, see ghosts, run mad, and die

[74]

in the greatest profusion on the slightest provocation, uttering as they fall imprecations of superb vigour or elegies of the wildest despair. But soon the low, the relentless voice, which if we wish to identify it we must suppose typical of a reader fed on modern English literature, and French and Russian, asks why, then, with all this to stimulate and enchant these old plays are for long stretches of time so intolerably dull? Is it not that literature, if it is to keep us on the alert through five acts or thirty-two chapters must somehow be based on Smith, have one toe touching Liverpool, take off into whatever heights it pleases from reality? We are not so purblind as to suppose that a man because his name is Smith and he lives at Liverpool is therefore "real". We know indeed that this reality is a chameleon. quality, the fantastic becoming as we grow used to it often the closest to the truth, the sober the furthest from it, and nothing proving a writer's greatness more than his capacity to consolidate his scene by the use of what, until he touched them, seemed wisps of cloud and threads of gossamer. Our contention merely is that there is a station, somewhere in mid-air, whence Smith and Liverpool can be seen to the best advantage; that the great artist is the man who knows where to place himself above the shifting scenery; that while he never loses sight of Liverpool he never sees it in the wrong perspective. The Elizabethans bore us, then, because their Smiths are all changed to dukes, their Liverpools to fabulous islands and palaces in Genoa.

[75]

Instead of keeping a proper poise above life they soar miles into the empyrean, where nothing is visible for long hours at a time but clouds at their revelry, and a cloud landscape is not ultimately satisfactory to human eyes. The Elizabethans bore us because they suffocate our imaginations rather than set them to work.

Still, though potent enough, the boredom of an Elizabethan play is of a different quality altogether from the boredom which a nineteenth-century play, a Tennyson or a Henry Taylor play, inflicts. The riot of images, the violent volubility of language, all that cloys and satiates in the Elizabethans yet appears to be drawn up with a roar as a feeble fire is sucked up by a newspaper. There is, even in the worst, an intermittent bawling vigour which gives us the sense in our quiet arm-chairs of ostlers and orange-girls catching up the lines, flinging them back, hissing or stamping applause. But the deliberate drama of the Victorian age is evidently written in a study. It has for audience ticking clocks and rows of classics bound in half morocco. There is no stamping, no applause. It does not, as, with all its faults, the Elizabethan audience did, leaven the mass with fire. Rhetorical and bombastic, the lines are flung and hurried into existence and reach the same impromptu felicities, have the same lip-moulded profusion and unexpected-ness, which speech sometimes achieves, but seldom in our day the deliberate, solitary pen. Indeed half the work of the dramatists one feels was done in the Elizabethan age by the public.

Against that, however, is to be set the fact that the influence of the public was in many respects detestable. To its door we must lay the greatest infliction that Elizabethan drama puts upon us—the plot; the incessant, improbable, almost unintelligible convolutions which presumably gratified the spirit of an excitable and unlettered public actually in the playhouse, but only confuse and fatigue a reader with the book before him. Undoubtedly something must happen; undoubtedly a play where nothing happens is an impossibility. But we have a right to demand (since the Greeks have proved that it is perfectly possible) that what happens shall have an end in view. It shall agitate great emotions; bring into existence memorable scenes; stir the actors to say what could not be said without this stimulus. Nobody can fail to remember the plot of the *Antigone*, because what happens is so closely bound up with the emotions of the actors that we remember the people and the plot at one and the same time. But who can tell us what happens in the *White Devil*, or the *Maid's Tragedy*, except by remembering the story apart from the emotions which it has aroused? As for the lesser Elizabethans, like Greene and Kyd, the complexities of their plots are so great, and the violence which those plots demand so terrific, that the actors themselves are obliterated and emotions which, according to our convention at least, deserve the most careful investigation, the most delicate analysis, are clean sponged off the slate. And the result is inevitable.

Outside Shakespeare and perhaps Ben Jonson, there are no characters in Elizabethan drama, only violences whom we know so little that we can scarcely care what becomes of them. Take any hero or heroine in those early plays—Bellimperia in the *Spanish Tragedy* will serve as well as another—and can we honestly say that we care a jot for the unfortunate lady who runs the whole gamut of human misery to kill herself in the end? No more than for an animated broomstick, we must reply, and in a work dealing with men and women the prevalence of broomsticks is a drawback. But the *Spanish Tragedy* is admittedly a crude forerunner, chiefly valuable because such primitive efforts lay bare the formidable framework which greater dramatists could modify, but had to use. Ford, it is claimed, is of the school of Stendhal and of Flaubert; Ford is a psychologist. Ford is an analyst. "This man", says Mr. Havelock Ellis, "writes of women not as a dramatist nor as a lover, but as one who has searched intimately and felt with instinctive sympathy the fibres of their hearts."

The play—*'Tis pity she's a Whore*—upon which this judgement is chiefly based shows us the whole nature of Annabella spun from pole to pole in a series of tremendous vicissitudes. First, her brother tells her that he loves her; next she confesses her love for him; next finds herself with child by him; next forces herself to marry Soranzo; next is discovered; next repents; finally is killed, and it is her lover and brother who kills her. To trace the trail of feelings

[78]

which such crises and calamities might be expected to breed in a woman of ordinary sensibility might have filled volumes. A dramatist of course has no volumes to fill. He is forced to contract. Even so, he can illumine; he can reveal enough for us to guess the rest. But what is it that we know without using microscopes and splitting hairs about the character of Annabella? Gropingly we make out that she is a spirited girl, with her defiance of her husband when he abuses her, her snatches of Italian song, her ready wit, her simple glad love-making. But of character as we understand the word there is no trace. We do not know how she reaches her conclusions, only that she has reached them. Nobody describes her. She is always at the height of her passion, never at its approach. Compare her with Anna Karenina. The Russian woman is flesh and blood, nerves and temperament, has heart, brain, body and mind where the English girl is flat and crude as a face painted on a playing card; she is without depth, without range, without intricacy. But as we say this we know that we have missed something. We have let the meaning of the play slip through our hands. We have ignored the emotion which has been accumulating because it has accumulated in places where we have not expected to find it. We have been comparing the play with prose, and the play, after all, is poetry.

The play is poetry we say, and the novel prose. Let us attempt to obliterate detail, and place the two before us side by side, feeling, so far as we can, the angles and edges of each, recalling each, so far as we are able, as a whole. Then, at once, the prime differences emerge; the long leisurely accumulated novel; the little contracted play; the emotion all split up, dissipated and then woven together, slowly and gradually massed into a whole, in the novel; the emotion concentrated, generalised, heightened in the play. What moments of intensity, what phrases of astonishing beauty the play shot at us!

> O, my lords,
> I but deceived your eyes with antic gesture,
> When one news straight came huddling on another
> Of death! and death! and death! still I danced forward.

or

> You have oft for these two lips
> Neglected cassia or the natural sweets
> Of the spring-violet: they are not yet much wither'd.

With all her reality, Anna Karenina could never say

> "You have oft, for these two lips
> Neglected cassia".

Some of the most profound of human emotions are therefore beyond her reach. The extremes of passion are not for the novelist; the perfect marriages of sense and sound are not for him; he must tame his swiftness to sluggardry; keep his eyes on the ground not on the sky: suggest by description, not reveal by illumination. Instead of singing

[80]

> Lay a garland on my hearse
> Of the dismal yew;
> Maidens, willow branches bear;
> Say I died true,

he must enumerate the chrysanthemums fading on the grave and the undertakers' men snuffling past in their four-wheelers. How then can we compare this lumbering and lagging art with poetry? Granted all the little dexterities by which the novelist makes us know the individual and recognise the real, the dramatist goes beyond the single and the separate, shows us not Annabella in love, but love itself; not Anna Karenina throwing herself under the train, but ruin and death and the

> . . . soul, like a ship in a black storm,
> . . . driven, I know not whither.

So with pardonable impatience we might exclaim as we shut our Elizabethan play. But what then is the exclamation with which we close *War and Peace?* Not one of disappointment; we are not left lamenting the superficiality, upbraiding the triviality of the novelist's art. Rather we are made more than ever aware of the inexhaustible richness of human sensibility. Here, in the play, we recognise the general; here, in the novel, the particular. Here we gather all our energies into a bunch and spring. Here we extend and expand and let come slowly in from all quarters deliberate impressions, accumulated messages. The mind is so saturated with sensibility, language so

inadequate to its experience, that far from ruling off
one form of literature or decreeing its inferiority to
others we complain that they are still unable to keep
pace with the wealth of material, and wait impatiently the creation of what may yet be devised to
liberate us of the enormous burden of the unexpressed.

Thus, in spite of dullness, bombast, rhetoric, and
confusion we still read the lesser Elizabethans, still
find ourselves adventuring in the land of the jeweller
and the unicorn. The familiar factories of Liverpool
fade into thin air and we scarcely recognise any likeness between the knight who imported timber and
died of pneumonia at Muswell Hill and the Armenian
Duke who fell like a Roman on his sword while the
owl shrieked in the ivy and the Duchess gave birth to
a still-born babe 'mongst women howling. To join
those territories and recognise the same man in different disguises we have to adjust and revise. But
make the necessary alterations in perspective, draw in
those filaments of sensibility which the moderns have
so marvellously developed, use instead the ear and
the eye which the moderns have so basely starved,
hear words as they are laughed and shouted, not as
they are printed in black letters on the page, see
before your eyes the changing faces and living bodies
of men and women, put yourself, in short, into a different, but not more elementary stage of your reading
development and then the true merits of Elizabethan
drama will assert themselves. The power of the
whole is undeniable. Theirs, too, is the word-coining

genius, as if thought plunged into a sea of words and
came up dripping. Theirs is that broad humour
based upon the nakedness of the body, which, however arduously the public spirited may try, is impossible, since the body is draped. Then at the back of
this, imposing not unity but some sort of stability, is
what we may briefly call a sense of the presence of
the Gods. He would be a bold critic who should
attempt to impose any creed upon the swarm and
variety of the Elizabethan dramatists, and yet it implies some timidity if we take it for granted that a
whole literature with common characteristics is a
mere evaporation of high spirits, a money-making
enterprise, a fluke of the mind which, owing to favourable circumstances, came off successfully. Even in
the jungle and the wilderness the compass still points.

> "Lord, Lord, that I were dead!"

they are for ever crying.

> O thou soft natural death that art joint-twin
> To sweetest slumber——

The pageant of the world is marvellous, but the
pageant of the world is vanity.

> glories
> Of human greatness are but pleasing dreams
> And shadows soon decaying: on the stage
> Of my mortality my youth hath acted
> Some scenes of vanity——

[83]

To die and be quit of it all is their desire; the bell
that tolls throughout the drama is death and disen-
chantment.

> All life is but a wandering to find home,
> When we're gone, we're there.

Ruin, weariness, death, perpetually death, stand
grimly to confront the other presence of Elizabethan
drama which is life: life compact of frigates, fir trees
and ivory, of dolphins and the juice of July flowers,
of the milk of unicorns and panthers' breath, of ropes
of pearl, brains of peacocks and Cretan wine. To
this, life at its most reckless and abundant, they reply

> Man is a tree that hath no top in cares,
> No root in comforts; all his power to live
> Is given to no end but t' have power to grieve.

It is this echo flung back and back from the other
side of the play which, if it has not the name, still
has the effect of the presence of the Gods.

So we ramble through the jungle, forest, and wilderness of Elizabethan drama. So we consort with
Emperors and clowns, jewellers and unicorns, and
laugh and exult and marvel at the splendour and
humour and fantasy of it all. A noble rage consumes
us when the curtain falls; we are bored too, and nauseated by the wearisome old tricks and florid bombast.
A dozen deaths of full-grown men and women move
us less than the suffering of one of Tolstoi's flies.
Wandering in the maze of the impossible and tedious

story suddenly some passionate intensity seizes us; some sublimity exalts, or some melodious snatch of song enchants. It is a world full of tedium and delight; pleasure and curiosity, of extravagant laughter, poetry, and splendour. But gradually it comes over us, what then are we being denied? What is it that we are coming to want so persistently that unless we get it instantly we must seek elsewhere? It is solitude. There is no privacy here. Always the door opens and some one comes in. All is shared, made visible, audible, dramatic. Meanwhile, as if tired with company, the mind steals off to muse in solitude; to think, not to act; to comment, not to share; to explore its own darkness, not the bright-lit-up surfaces of others. It turns to Donne, to Montaigne, to Sir Thomas Browne—the keepers of the keys of solitude.

Montaigne

Once at Bar-le-Duc Montaigne saw a portrait which René, King of Sicily, had painted of himself, and asked, "Why is it not, in like manner, lawful for every one to draw himself with a pen, as he did with a crayon?" Off-hand one might reply, Not only is it lawful, but nothing could be easier. Other people may evade us, but our own features are almost too familiar. Let us begin. And then, when we attempt the task, the pen falls from our fingers; it is a matter of profound, mysterious, and overwhelming difficulty.

After all, in the whole of literature, how many people have succeeded in drawing themselves with a pen? Only Montaigne and Pepys and Rousseau perhaps. The *Religio Medici* is a coloured glass through which darkly one sees racing stars and a strange and turbulent soul. A bright polished mirror reflects the face of Boswell peeping between other people's shoulders in the famous biography. But this talking of oneself, following one's own vagaries, giving the whole map, weight, colour, and circumference of the soul in its confusion, its variety, its imperfection— this art belonged to one man only: to Montaigne. As the centuries go by, there is always a crowd before that picture, gazing into its depths, seeing their own faces reflected in it, seeing more the longer they look, never being able to say quite what it is that they see.

New editions testify to the perennial fascination. Here is the Navarre Society in England reprinting in five fine volumes [1] Cotton's translation; while in France the firm of Louis Conard is issuing the complete works of Montaigne with the various readings in an edition to which Dr. Armaingaud has devoted a long lifetime of research.

To tell the truth about oneself, to discover oneself near at hand, is not easy.

We hear of but two or three of the ancients who have beaten this road [said Montaigne]. No one since has followed the track; 'tis a rugged road, more so than it seems, to follow a pace so rambling and uncertain, as that of the soul; to penetrate the dark profundities of its intricate internal windings; to choose and lay hold of so many little nimble motions; 'tis a new and extraordinary undertaking, and that withdraws us from the common and most recommended employments of the world.

There is, in the first place, the difficulty of expression. We all indulge in the strange, pleasant process called thinking, but when it comes to saying, even to some one opposite, what we think, then how little we are able to convey! The phantom is through the mind and out of the window before we can lay salt on its tail, or slowly sinking and returning to the profound darkness which it has lit up momentarily with a wandering light. Face, voice, and accent eke out our words and impress their feebleness with char-

---

[1] *Essays of Montaigne,* translated by Charles Cotton, 5 vols. The Navarre Society, £6:6s. net.

acter in speech. But the pen is a rigid instrument; it
can say very little; it has all kinds of habits and
ceremonies of its own. It is dictatorial too: it is
always making ordinary men into prophets, and
changing the natural stumbling trip of human speech
into the solemn and stately march of pens. It is for
this reason that Montaigne stands out from the
legions of the dead with such irrepressible vivacity.
We can never doubt for an instant that his book was
himself. He refused to teach; he refused to preach;
he kept on saying that he was just like other people.
All his effort was to write himself down, to communicate, to tell the truth, and that is a "rugged
road, more than it seems".

For beyond the difficulty of communicating oneself, there is the supreme difficulty of being oneself.
This soul, or life within us, by no means agrees with
the life outside us. If one has the courage to ask her
what she thinks, she is always saying the very opposite to what other people say. Other people, for
instance, long ago made up their minds that old
invalidish gentlemen ought to stay at home and edify
the rest of us by the spectacle of their connubial
fidelity. The soul of Montaigne said, on the contrary, that it is in old age that one ought to travel,
and marriage, which, rightly, is very seldom founded
on love, is apt to become, towards the end of life, a
formal tie better broken up. Again with politics,
statesmen are always praising the greatness of Empire, and preaching the moral duty of civilising the

[89]

savage. But look at the Spanish in Mexico, cried Montaigne in a burst of rage. "So many cities levelled with the ground, so many nations exterminated . . . and the richest and most beautiful part of the world turned upside down for the traffic of pearl and pepper! Mechanic victories!" And then when the peasants came and told him that they had found a man dying of wounds and deserted him for fear lest justice might incriminate them, Montaigne asked:

What could I have said to these people? 'Tis certain that this office of humanity would have brought them into trouble. . . . There is nothing so much, nor so grossly, nor so ordinarily faulty as the laws.

Here the soul, getting restive, is lashing out at the more palpable forms of Montaigne's great bugbears, convention and ceremony. But watch her as she broods over the fire in the inner room of that tower which, though detached from the main building, has so wide a view over the estate. Really she is the strangest creature in the world, far from heroic, variable as a weathercock, "bashful, insolent; chaste, lustful; prating, silent; laborious, delicate; ingenious, heavy; melancholic, pleasant; lying, true; knowing, ignorant; liberal, covetous, and prodigal"—in short, so complex, so indefinite, corresponding so little to the version which does duty for her in public, that a man might spend his life merely in trying to run her to earth. The pleasure of the pursuit more than rewards one for any damage that it may inflict upon one's worldly prospects. The man who is aware of himself is henceforward independent; and he is never bored, and life is only too short, and he is steeped through and through with a profound yet temperate happiness. He alone lives, while other people, slaves of ceremony, let life slip past them in a kind of dream. Once conform, once do what other people do because they do it, and a lethargy steals over all the finer nerves and faculties of the soul. She becomes all outer show and inward emptiness; dull, callous, and indifferent.

Surely then, if we ask this great master of the art of life to tell us his secret, he will advise us to withdraw to the inner room of our tower and there turn the pages of books, pursue fancy after fancy as they chase each other up the chimney, and leave the government of the world to others. Retirement and contemplation—these must be the main elements of his prescription. But no; Montaigne is by no means explicit. It is impossible to extract a plain answer from that subtle, half smiling, half melancholy man, with the heavy-lidded eyes and the dreamy, quizzical expression. The truth is that life in the country, with one's books and vegetables and flowers, is often extremely dull. He could never see that his own green peas were so much better than other people's. Paris was the place he loved best in the whole world— "jusques à ses verrues et à ses taches". As for reading, he could seldom read any book for more than an hour at a time, and his memory was so bad that he forgot what was in his mind as he walked from one room to another. Book learning is nothing to be proud of, and as for the achievements of science, what do they amount to? He had always mixed with clever men, and his father had a positive veneration for them, but he had observed that, though they have their fine moments, their rhapsodies, their visions, the cleverest tremble on the verge of folly. Observe yourself: one moment you are exalted; the next a broken glass puts your nerves on edge. All extremes are dangerous. It is best to keep in the middle of the road, in the common ruts, however muddy. In writing choose the common words; avoid rhapsody and eloquence—yet, it is true, poetry is delicious; the best prose is that which is most full of poetry.

It appears, then, that we are to aim at a democratic simplicity. We may enjoy our room in the tower, with the painted walls and the commodious bookcases, but down in the garden there is a man digging who buried his father this morning, and it is he and his like who live the real life and speak the real language. There is certainly an element of truth in that. Things are said very finely at the lower end of the table. There are perhaps more of the qualities that matter among the ignorant than among the learned. But again, what a vile thing the rabble is! "the mother of ignorance, injustice, and inconstancy. Is it reasonable that the life of a wise man should depend upon the judgment of fools?" Their minds are weak, soft and without power of resistance. They must be told what it is expedient for them to know. It is not for them to face facts as they are. The truth can only be known by the well-born soul— "l'âme bien née". Who, then, are these well-born souls, whom we would imitate, if only Montaigne would enlighten us more precisely?

But no. "Je n'enseigne poinct; je raconte." After all, how could he explain other people's souls when he could say nothing "entirely simply and solidly, without confusion or mixture, in one word", about his own, when indeed it became daily more and more in the dark to him? One quality or principle there is perhaps—that one must not lay down rules. The souls whom one would wish to resemble, like Etienne de La Boétie, for example, are always the supplest. "C'est estre, mais ce n'est pas vivre, que de se tenir attaché et obligé par necessité a un seul train." The laws are mere conventions, utterly unable to keep touch with the vast variety and turmoil of human impulses; habits and customs are a convenience devised for the support of timid natures who dare not allow their souls free play. But we, who have a private life and hold it infinitely the dearest of our possessions, suspect nothing so much as an attitude. Directly we begin to protest, to attitudinise, to lay down laws, we perish. We are living for others, not for ourselves. We must respect those who sacrifice themselves in the public service, load them with honours, and pity them for allowing, as they must, the inevitable compromise; but for ourselves let us fly fame, honour, and all offices that put us under an obligation to others. Let us simmer over our incalculable cauldron, our enthralling confusion, our hotch-potch of impulses, our perpetual miracle—for the soul throws up wonders every second. Movement and change are the essence of our being; rigidity is death; conformity is death: let us say what comes into our heads, repeat ourselves, contradict ourselves, fling out the wildest nonsense, and follow the most fantastic fancies without caring what the world does or thinks or says. For nothing matters except life; and, of course, order.

This freedom, then, which is the essence of our being, has to be controlled. But it is difficult to see what power we are to invoke to help us, since every restraint of private opinion or public law has been derided, and Montaigne never ceases to pour scorn upon the misery, the weakness, the vanity of human nature. Perhaps, then, it will be well to turn to religion to guide us? "Perhaps" is one of his favourite expressions; "perhaps" and "I think" and all those words which qualify the rash assumptions of human ignorance. Such words help one to muffle up opinions which it would be highly impolitic to speak outright. For one does not say everything; there are some things which at present it is advisable only to hint. One writes for a very few people, who understand. Certainly, seek the Divine guidance by all means, but meanwhile there is, for those who live a private life, another monitor, an invisible censor

within, "un patron au dedans", whose blame is much
more to be dreaded than any other because he knows
the truth; nor is there anything sweeter than the
chime of his approval. This is the judge to whom
we must submit; this is the censor who will help us
to achieve that order which is the grace of a well-
born soul. For "C'est une vie exquise, celle qui se
maintient en ordre jusques en son privé". But he
will act by his own light; by some internal balance
will achieve that precarious and everchanging poise
which, while it controls, in no way impedes the soul's
freedom to explore and experiment. Without other
guide, and without precedent, undoubtedly it is far
more difficult to live well the private life than the
public. It is an art which each must learn separately,
though there are, perhaps, two or three men, like
Homer, Alexander the Great, and Epaminondas
among the ancients, and Etienne de La Boétie among
the moderns, whose example may help us. But it is
an art; and the very material in which it works is
variable and complex and infinitely mysterious—human nature. To human nature we must keep close.
". . . il faut vivre entre les vivants". We must
dread any eccentricity or refinement which cuts us off
from our fellow-beings. Blessed are those who chat
easily with their neighbours about their sport or their
buildings or their quarrels, and honestly enjoy the
talk of carpenters and gardeners. To communicate
is our chief business; society and friendship our chief
delights; and reading, not to acquire knowledge, not

to earn a living, but to extend our intercourse beyond our own time and province. Such wonders there are in the world; halcyons and undiscovered lands, men with dogs' heads and eyes in their chests, and laws and customs, it may well be, far superior to our own. Possibly we are asleep in this world; possibly there is some other which is apparent to beings with a sense which we now lack.

Here then, in spite of all contradictions and of all qualifications, is something definite. These essays are an attempt to communicate a soul. On this point at least he is explicit. It is not fame that he wants; it is not that men shall quote him in years to come; he is setting up no statue in the market-place; he wishes only to communicate his soul. Communication is health; communication is truth; communication is happiness. To share is our duty; to go down boldly and bring to light those hidden thoughts which are the most diseased; to conceal nothing; to pretend nothing; if we are ignorant to say so; if we love our friends to let them know it.

". . . car, comme je scay par une trop certaine expérience, il n'est aucune si douce consolation en la perte de nos amis que celle que nous aporte la science de n'avoir rien oublié a leur dire et d'avoir eu avec eux une parfaite et entière communication.

There are people who, when they travel, wrap themselves up "se défendans de la contagion d'un air incogneu" in silence and suspicion. When they dine

they must have the same food they get at home.
Every sight and custom is bad unless it resembles
those of their own village. They travel only to return. That is entirely the wrong way to set about
it. We should start without any fixed idea where we
are going to spend the night, or when we propose to
come back; the journey is everything. Most necessary of all, but rarest good fortune, we should try to
find before we start some man of our own sort who
will go with us and to whom we can say the first
thing that comes into our heads. For pleasure has
no relish unless we share it. As for the risks—that
we may catch cold or get a headache—it is always
worth while to risk a little illness for the sake of
pleasure. "Le plaisir est des principales espèces du
profit." Besides if we do what we like, we always do
what is good for us. Doctors and wise men may object, but let us leave doctors and wise men to their
own dismal philosophy. For ourselves, who are ordinary men and women, let us return thanks to Nature
for her bounty by using every one of the senses she
has given us; vary our state as much as possible; turn
now this side, now that, to the warmth, and relish
to the full before the sun goes down the kisses of
youth and the echoes of a beautiful voice singing
Catullus. Every season is likeable, and wet days and
fine, red wine and white, company and solitude.
Even sleep, that deplorable curtailment of the joy of
life, can be full of dreams; and the most common
actions—a walk, a talk, solitude in one's own orchard

[97]

—can be enhanced and lit up by the association of the mind. Beauty is everywhere, and beauty is only two fingers' breadth from goodness. So, in the name of health and sanity, let us not dwell on the end of the journey. Let death come upon us planting our cabbages, or on horseback, or let us steal away to some cottage and there let strangers close our eyes, for a servant sobbing or the touch of a hand would break us down. Best of all, let death find us at our usual occupations, among girls and good fellows who make no protests, no lamentations; let him find us "parmy les jeux, les festins, faceties, entretiens communs et populaires, et la musique, et des vers amoureux". But enough of death; it is life that matters.

It is life that emerges more and more clearly as these essays reach not their end, but their suspension in full career. It is life that becomes more and more absorbing as death draws near, one's self, one's soul, every fact of existence: that one wears silk stockings summer and winter; puts water in one's wine; has one's hair cut after dinner; must have glass to drink from; has never worn spectacles; has a loud voice; carries a switch in one's hand; bites one's tongue; fidgets with one's feet; is apt to scratch one's ears; likes meat to be high; rubs one's teeth with a napkin (thank God, they are good!); must have curtains to one's bed; and, what is rather curious, began by liking radishes, then disliked them, and now likes them again. No fact is too little to let it slip through one's fingers and besides the interest of facts themselves, there is the strange power we have of changing facts by the force of the imagination. Observe how the soul is always casting her own lights and shadows; makes the substantial hollow and the frail substantial; fills broad daylight with dreams; is as much excited by phantoms as by reality; and in the moment of death sports with a trifle. Observe, too, her duplicity, her complexity. She hears of a friend's loss and sympathises, and yet has a bitter-sweet malicious pleasure in the sorrows of others. She believes; at the same time she does not believe. Observe her extraordinary susceptibility to impressions, especially in youth. A rich man steals because his father kept him short of money as a boy. This wall one builds not for oneself, but because one's father loved building. In short the soul is all laced about with nerves and sympathies which affect her every action, and yet, even now in 1580, no one has any clear knowledge—such cowards we are, such lovers of the smooth conventional ways—how she works or what she is except that of all things she is the most mysterious, and one's self the greatest monster and miracle in the world. ". . . plus je me hante et connois, plus ma difformitè m'estonne, moins je m'entens en moy." Observe, observe perpetually, and, so long as ink and paper exist, "sans cesse et sans travail" Montaigne will write.

But there remains one final question which, if we could make him look up from his enthralling occupation, we should like to put to this great master of the art of life. In these extraordinary volumes of short and broken, long and learned, logical and contradictory statements, we have heard the very pulse and rhythm of the soul, beating day after day, year after year through a veil which, as time goes on, fines itself almost to transparency. Here is some one who succeeded in the hazardous enterprise of living; who served his country and lived retired; was landlord, husband, father; entertained kings, loved women, and mused for hours alone over old books. By means of perpetual experiment and observation of the subtlest he achieved at last a miraculous adjustment of all these wayward parts that constitute the human soul. He laid hold of the beauty of the world with all his fingers. He achieved happiness. If he had had to live again, he said, he would have lived the same life over. But, as we watch with absorbed interest the enthralling spectacle of a soul living openly beneath our eyes, the question frames itself, Is pleasure the end of all? Whence this overwhelming interest in the nature of the soul? Why this overmastering desire to communicate with others? Is the beauty of this world enough, or is there, elsewhere, some explanation of the mystery? To this what answer can there be? There is none. There is only one more question: "Que scais-je?"

The Duchess of Newcastle[1]

". . . All I desire is fame", wrote Margaret Cavendish, Duchess of Newcastle. And while she lived her wish was granted. Garish in her dress, eccentric in her habits, chaste in her conduct, coarse in her speech, she succeeded during her lifetime in drawing upon herself the ridicule of the great and the applause of the learned. But the last echoes of that clamour have now all died away; she lives only in the few splendid phrases that Lamb scattered upon her tomb; her poems, her plays, her philosophies, her orations, her discourses —all those folios and quartos in which, she protested, her real life was shrined—moulder in the gloom of public libraries, or are decanted into tiny thimbles which hold six drops of their profusion. Even the curious student, inspired by the words of Lamb, quails before the mass of her mausoleum, peers in, looks about him, and hurries out again, shutting the door.

But that hasty glance has shown him the outlines of a memorable figure. Born (it is conjectured) in 1624, Margaret was the youngest child of a Thomas Lucas, who died when she was an infant, and her upbringing was due to her mother, a lady of remark-

[1] *The Life of William Cavendish, Duke of Newcastle, Etc.,* edited by C. H. Firth; *Poems and Fancies,* by the Duchess of Newcastle; *The World's Olio; Orations of divers Sorts Accommodated to Divers Places; Female Orations; Plays; Philosophical Letters,* etc., etc.

able character, of majestic grandeur and beauty "beyond the ruin of time". "She was very skilful in leases, and setting of lands and court keeping, ordering of stewards, and the like affairs." The wealth which thus accrued she spent, not on marriage portions, but on generous and delightful pleasures, "out of an opinion that if she bred us with needy necessity it might chance to create in us sharking qualities". Her eight sons and daughters were never beaten, but reasoned with, finely and gayly dressed, and allowed no conversation with servants, not because they are servants but because servants "are for the most part ill-bred as well as meanly born". The daughters were taught the usual accomplishments "rather for formality than for benefit", it being their mother's opinion that character, happiness, and honesty were of greater value to a woman than fiddling and singing, or "the prating of several languages".

Already Margaret was eager to take advantage of such indulgence to gratify certain tastes. Already she liked reading better than needlework, dressing and "inventing fashions" better than reading, and writing best of all. Sixteen paper books of no title, written in straggling letters, for the impetuosity of her thought always outdid the pace of her fingers, testify to the use she made of her mother's liberality. The happiness of their home life had other results as well. They were a devoted family. Long after they were married, Margaret noted, these handsome brothers and sisters, with their well-proportioned bodies, their clear complexions, brown hair, sound teeth, "tunable voices", and plain way of speaking, kept themselves "in a flock together". The presence of strangers silenced them. But when they were alone, whether they walked in Spring Gardens or Hyde Park, or had music, or supped in barges upon the water, their tongues were loosed and they made "very merry amongst themselves, . . . judging, condemning, approving, commending, as they thought good".

The happy family life had its effect upon Margaret's character. As a child, she would walk for hours alone, musing and contemplating and reasoning with herself of "everything her senses did present". She took no pleasure in activity of any kind. Toys did not amuse her, and she could neither learn foreign languages nor dress as other people did. Her great pleasure was to invent dresses for herself, which nobody else was to copy, "for", she remarks, "I always took delight in a singularity, even in accoutrements of habits".

Such a training, at once so cloistered and so free, should have bred a lettered old maid, glad of her seclusion, and the writer perhaps of some volume of letters or translations from the classics, which we should still quote as proof of the cultivation of our ancestresses. But there was a wild streak in Margaret, a love of finery and extravagance and fame, which was for ever upsetting the orderly arrangements of nature. When she heard that the Queen, since the outbreak of the Civil War, had fewer maids-of-honour than usual, she had "a great desire" to become one of them. Her mother let her go against the judgement of the rest of the family, who, knowing that she had never left home and had scarcely been beyond their sight, justly thought that she might behave at Court to her disadvantage. "Which indeed I did," Margaret confessed; "for I was so bashful when I was out of my mother's, brothers', and sisters' sight that . . . I durst neither look up with my eyes, nor speak, nor be any way sociable, insomuch as I was thought a natural fool." The courtiers laughed at her; and she retaliated in the obvious way. People were censorious; men were jealous of brains in a woman; women suspected intellect in their own sex; and what other lady, she might justly ask, pondered as she walked on the nature of matter and whether snails have teeth? But the laughter galled her, and she begged her mother to let her come home. This being refused, wisely as the event turned out, she stayed on for two years (1643-45), finally going with the Queen to Paris, and there, among the exiles who came to pay their respects to the Court, was the Marquis of Newcastle. To the general amazement, the princely nobleman, who had led the King's forces to disaster with indomitable courage but little skill, fell in love with the shy, silent, strangely dressed maid-of-honour. It was not "amorous love, but honest, honourable love", according to Margaret. She was no brilliant match; she had gained a reputation for prudery and eccentricity. What, then, could have made so great a nobleman fall at her feet? The onlookers were full of derision, disparagement, and slander. "I fear", Margaret wrote to the Marquis, "others foresee we shall be unfortunate, though we see it not ourselves, or else there would not be such pains to untie the knot of our affections." Again, "Saint Germains is a place of much slander, and thinks I send too often to you". "Pray consider", she warned him, "that I have enemies." But the match was evidently perfect. The Duke, with his love of poetry and music and play-writing, his interest in philosophy, his belief "that nobody knew or could know the cause of anything", his romantic and generous temperament, was naturally drawn to a woman who wrote poetry herself, was also a philosopher of the same way of thinking, and lavished upon him not only the admiration of a fellow-artist, but the gratitude of a sensitive creature who had been shielded and succoured by his extraordinary magnanimity. "He did approve", she wrote, "of those bashful fears which many condemned, . . . and though I did dread marriage and shunned men's company as much as I could, yet I . . . had not the power to refuse him." She kept him company during the long years of exile; she entered with sympathy, if not with understanding, into the conduct and acquirements of those horses which he trained to such perfection that the Spaniards crossed themselves and cried "Miraculo!" as they witnessed their corvets, voltoes, and pirouettes; she believed that the horses even made a "trampling

[105]

action" for joy when he came into the stables; she
pleaded his cause in England during the Protectorate;
and, when the Restoration made it possible for them
to return to England, they lived together in the
depths of the country in the greatest seclusion and
perfect contentment, scribbling plays, poems, philosophies, greeting each other's works with raptures of
delight, and confabulating doubtless upon such mar-
vels of the natural world as chance threw their way.
They were laughed at by their contemporaries;
Horace Walpole sneered at them. But there can be
no doubt that they were perfectly happy.

For now Margaret could apply herself uninter-
ruptedly to her writing. She could devise fashions
for herself and her servants. She could scribble more
and more furiously with fingers that became less and
less able to form legible letters. She could even
achieve the miracle of getting her plays acted in
London and her philosophies humbly perused by men
of learning. There they stand, in the British Museum, volume after volume, swarming with a diffused,
uneasy, contorted vitality. Order, continuity, the
logical development of her argument are all unknown
to her. No fears impede her. She has the irresponsibility of a child and the arrogance of a Duchess.
The wildest fancies come to her, and she canters
away on their backs. We seem to hear her, as the
thoughts boil and bubble, calling to John, who sat
with a pen in his hand next door, to come quick,
"John, John, I conceive!" And down it goes—what·

ever it may be; sense or nonsense; some thought on women's education—"Women live like Bats or Owls, labour like Beasts, and die like Worms, . . . the best bred women are those whose minds are civilest"; some speculation that had struck her perhaps walking that afternoon alone—why "hogs have the measles", why "dogs that rejoice swing their tails", or what the stars are made of, or what this chrysalis is that her maid has brought her, and she keeps warm in a corner of her room. On and on, from subject to subject she flies, never stopping to correct, "for there is more pleasure in making than in mending", talking aloud to herself of all those matters that filled her brain to her perpetual diversion—of wars, and boarding-schools, and cutting down trees, of grammar and morals, of monsters and the British, whether opium in small quantities is good for lunatics, why it is that musicians are mad. Looking upwards, she speculates still more ambitiously upon the nature of the moon, and if the stars are blazing jellies; looking downwards she wonders if the fishes know that the sea is salt; opines that our heads are full of fairies, "dear to God as we are"; muses whether there are not other worlds than ours, and reflects that the next ship may bring us word of a new one. In short, "we are in utter darkness". Meanwhile, what a rapture is thought!

As the vast books appeared from the stately retreat at Welbeck the usual censors made the usual objections, and had to be answered, despised, or

argued with, as her mood varied, in the preface to
every work. They said, among other things, that her
books were not her own, because she used learned
terms, and "wrote of many matters outside her ken".
She flew to her husband for help, and he answered,
characteristically, that the Duchess "had never con-
versed with any professed scholar in learning except
her brother and myself". The Duke's scholarship,
moreover, was of a peculiar nature. "I have lived in
the great world a great while, and have thought of
what has been brought to me by the senses, more than
was put into me by learned discourse; for I do not
love to be led by the nose, by authority, and old
authors; *ipse dixit* will not serve my turn." And
then she takes up the pen and proceeds, with the importunity and indiscretion of a child, to assure the
world that her ignorance is of the finest quality im-
aginable. She has only seen Des Cartes and Hobbes,
not questioned them; she did indeed ask Mr. Hobbes
to dinner, but he could not come; she often does not
listen to a word that is said to her; she does not know
any French, though she lived abroad for five years;
she has only read the old philosophers in Mr. Stanley's
account of them; of Des Cartes she has read but half
of his work on Passion; and of Hobbes only "the
little book called *De Cive*", all of which is infinitely
to the credit of her native wit, so abundant that outside succour pained it, so honest that it would not
accept help from others. It was from the plain of
complete ignorance, the untilled field of her own

consciousness, that she proposed to erect a philosophic system that was to oust all others. The results were not altogether happy. Under the pressure of such vast structures, her natural gift, the fresh and delicate fancy which had led her in her first volume to write charmingly of Queen Mab and fairyland, was crushed out of existence.

> The palace of the Queen wherein she dwells,
> Its fabric's built all of hodmandod shells;
> The hangings of a Rainbow made that's thin,
> Shew wondrous fine, when one first enters in;
> The chambers made of Amber that is clear,
> Do give a fine sweet smell, if fire be near;
> Her bed a cherry stone, is carved throughout,
> And with a butterfly's wing hung about;
> Her sheets are of the skin of Dove's eyes made
> Where on a violet bud her pillow's laid.

So she could write when she was young. But her fairies, if they survived at all, grew up into hippopotami. Too generously her prayer was granted:

> Give me the free and noble style,
> Which seems uncurb'd, though it be wild.

She became capable of involutions, and contortions and conceits of which the following is among the shortest, but not the most terrific:

> The human head may be likened to a town:
> The mouth when full, begun
> Is market day, when empty, market's done;
> The city conduct, where the water flows,
> Is with two spouts, the nostrils and the nose.

She similised, energetically, incongruously, eternally; the sea became a meadow, the sailors shepherds, the mast a maypole. The fly was the bird of summer, trees were senators, houses ships, and even the fairies, whom she loved better than any earthly thing, except the Duke, are changed into blunt atoms and sharp atoms, and take part in some of those horrible manœuvres in which she delighted to marshal the universe. Truly, "my Lady Sanspareille hath a strange spreading wit". Worse still, without an atom of dramatic power, she turned to play-writing. It was a simple process. The unwieldy thoughts which turned and tumbled within her were christened Sir Golden Riches, Moll Meanbred, Sir Puppy Dogman, and the rest, and sent revolving in tedious debate upon the parts of the soul, or whether virtue is better than riches, round a wise and learned lady who answered their questions and corrected their fallacies at considerable length in tones which we seem to have heard before.

Sometimes, however, the Duchess walked abroad. She would issue out in her own proper person, dressed in a thousand gems and furbelows, to visit the houses of the neighbouring gentry. Her pen made instant report of these excursions. She recorded how Lady C. R. "did beat her husband in a public assembly"; Sir F. O. "I am sorry to hear hath undervalued himself so much below his birth and wealth as to marry his kitchen-maid"; "Miss P. I. has become a sanctified soul, a spiritual sister, she has left curling her hair, black patches are become abominable to her, laced shoes and Galoshoes are steps to pride—she asked me what posture I thought was the best to be used in prayer". Her answer was probably unacceptable. "I shall not rashly go there again", she says of one such "gossip-making". She was not, we may hazard, a welcome guest or an altogether hospitable hostess. She had a way of "bragging of myself" which frightened visitors so that they left, nor was she sorry to see them go. Indeed, Welbeck was the best place for her, and her own company the most congenial, with the amiable Duke wandering in and out, with his plays and his speculations, always ready to answer a question or refute a slander. Perhaps it was this solitude that led her, chaste as she was in conduct, to use language which in time to come much perturbed Sir Egerton Brydges. She used, he complained, "expressions and images of extraordinary coarseness as flowing from a female of high rank brought up in courts". He forgot that this particular female had long ceased to frequent the Court; she consorted chiefly with fairies; and her friends were among the dead. Naturally, then, her language was coarse. Nevertheless, though her philosophies are futile, and her plays intolerable, and her verses mainly dull, the vask bulk of the Duchess is leavened by a vein of authentic fire. One cannot help following the lure of her erratic and lovable personality as it meanders and twinkles through page after page. There is something noble and Quixotic and high-spirited, as well as crack-brained and bird-witted, about her. Her simplicity is so open; her intelligence so active; her sympathy with fairies and animals so true and tender. She has the freakishness of an elf, the irresponsibility of some non-human creature, its heartlessness, and its charm. And although "they", those terrible critics who had sneered and jeered at her ever since, as a shy girl, she had not dared look her tormentors in the face at Court, continued to mock, few of her critics, after all, had the wit to trouble about the nature of the universe, or cared a straw for the sufferings of the hunted hare, or longed, as she did, to talk to some one "of Shakespeare's fools". Now, at any rate, the laugh is not all on their side.

But laugh they did. When the rumour spread that the crazy Duchess was coming up from Welbeck to pay her respects at Court, people crowded the streets to look at her, and the curiosity of Mr. Pepys twice brought him to wait in the Park to see her pass. But the pressure of the crowd about her coach was too great. He could only catch a glimpse of her in her silver coach with her footmen all in velvet, a velvet cap on her head, and her hair about her ears. He could only see for a moment between the white curtains the face of "a very comely woman", and on she drove through the crowd of staring Cockneys, all pressing to catch a glimpse of that romantic lady, who stands in the picture at Welbeck, with large melancholy eyes, and something fastidious and fantastic in her bearing, touching a table with the tips of long pointed fingers in the calm assurance of immortal fame.

Rambling Round Evelyn

Should you wish to make sure that your birthday will be celebrated three hundred years hence, your best course is undoubtedly to keep a diary. Only first be certain that you have the courage to lock your genius in a private book and the humour to gloat over a fame that will be yours only in the grave. For the good diarist writes either for himself alone or for a posterity so distant that it can safely hear every secret and justly weigh every motive. For such an audience there is need neither of affectation nor of restraint. Sincerity is what they ask, detail, volume; skill with the pen comes in conveniently, but brilliance is not necessary; genius is a hindrance even; and should you know your business and do it manfully, posterity will let you off mixing with great men, reporting famous affairs, or having lain with the first ladies in the land.

The diary, for whose sake we are remembering the three hundredth anniversary of the birth of John Evelyn,[1] is a case in point. It is sometimes composed like a memoir, sometimes jotted down like a calendar; but he never used its pages to reveal the secrets of his heart, and all that he wrote might have been read aloud in the evening with a calm conscience to his children. If we wonder, then, why we still trouble

[1] Written in 1920.

[113]

to read what we must consider the uninspired work
of a good man we have to confess, first that diaries
are always diaries, books, that is, that we read in
convalescence, on horseback, in the grip of death;
second, that this reading, about which so many fine
things have been said, is for the most part mere
dreaming and idling; lying in a chair with a book;
watching the butterflies on the dahlias; a profitless
occupation which no critic has taken the trouble to
investigate, and on whose behalf only the moralist
can find a good word to say. For he will allow it to
be an innocent employment; and happiness, he will
add, though derived from trivial sources, has probably done more to prevent human beings from changing their religions and killing their kings than either
philosophy or the pulpit.

It may be well, indeed, before reading much further in Evelyn's book, to decide where it is that our
modern view of happiness differs from his. Ignorance, surely, ignorance is at the bottom of it; his
ignorance, and our comparative erudition. No one
can read the story of Evelyn's foreign travels without
envying in the first place his simplicity of mind, in
the second his activity. To take a simple example
of the difference between us—that butterfly will sit
motionless on the dahlia while the gardener trundles
his barrow past it, but let him flick the wings with
the shadow of a rake, and off it flies, up it goes, instantly on the alert. So, we may reflect, a butterfly
sees but does not hear; and here no doubt we are

much on a par with Evelyn. But as for going into the house to fetch a knife and with that knife dissecting a Red Admiral's head, as Evelyn would have done, no sane person in the twentieth century would entertain such a project for a second. Individually we may know as little as Evelyn, but collectively we know so much that there is little incentive to venture on private discoveries. We seek the encyclopædia, not the scissors; and know in two minutes not only more than was known to Evelyn in his lifetime, but that the mass of knowledge is so vast that it is scarcely worth while to possess a single crumb. Ignorant, yet justly confident that with his own hands he might advance not merely his private knowledge but the knowledge of mankind, Evelyn dabbled in all the arts and sciences, ran about the Continent for ten years, gazed with unflagging gusto upon hairy women and rational dogs, and drew inferences and framed speculations which are now only to be matched by listening to the talk of old women round the village pump. The moon, they say, is so much larger than usual this autumn that no mushrooms will grow, and the carpenter's wife will be brought to bed of twins. So Evelyn, Fellow of the Royal Society, a gentleman of the highest culture and intelligence, carefully noted all comets and portents, and thought it a sinister omen when a whale came up the Thames. In 1658, too, a whale had been seen. "That year died Cromwell." Nature, it seems, was determined to stimulate the devotion of her seventeenth-century ad-

mirers by displays of violence and eccentricity from
which she now refrains. There were storms, floods,
and droughts; the Thames frozen hard; comets flaring
in the sky. If a cat so much as kittened in Evelyn's
bed the kitten was inevitably gifted with eight legs,
six ears, two bodies, and two tails.

But to return to happiness. It sometimes appears
that if there is an insoluble difference between our
ancestors and ourselves it is that we draw our happiness from different sources. We rate the same
things at different values. Something of this we may
ascribe to their ignorance and our knowledge. But
are we to suppose that ignorance alters the nerves
and the affections? Are we to believe that it would
have been an intolerable penance for us to live familiarly with the Elizabethans? Should we have
found it necessary to leave the room because of
Shakespeare's habits, and to have refused Queen
Elizabeth's invitation to dinner? Perhaps so. For
Evelyn was a sober man of unusual refinement, and
yet he pressed into a torture chamber as we crowd to
see the lions fed.

. . . they first bound his wrists with a strong rope or small
cable, and one end of it to an iron ring made fast to the wall
about four feet from the floor, and then his feet with another
cable, fastened about five feet farther than his utmost length
to another ring on the floor of the room. Thus suspended,
and yet lying but aslant, they slid a horse of wood under the
rope which bound his feet, which so exceedingly stiffened it,
as severed the fellow's joints in miserable sort, drawing him

out at length in an extraordinary manner, he having only a pair of linen drawers upon his naked body . . .

And so on. Evelyn watched this to the end, and then remarked that "the spectacle was so uncomfortable that I was not able to stay the sight of another", as we might say that the lions growl so loud and the sight of raw meat is so unpleasant that we will now visit the penguins. Allowing for his discomfort, there is enough discrepancy between his view of pain and ours to make us wonder whether we see any fact with the same eyes, marry any woman from the same motives, or judge any conduct by the same standards. To sit passive when muscles tore and bones cracked, not to flinch when the wooden horse was raised higher and the executioner fetched a horn and poured two buckets of water down the man's throat, to suffer this iniquity on a suspicion of robbery which the man denied—all this seems to put Evelyn in one of those cages where we still mentally seclude the riff-raff of Whitechapel. Only it is obvious that we have somehow got it wrong. If we could maintain that our susceptibility to suffering and love of justice were proof that all our humane instincts were as highly developed as these, then we could say that the world improves, and we with it. But let us get on with the diary.

In 1652, when it seemed that things had settled down unhappily enough, "all being entirely in the rebels' hands", Evelyn returned to England with his wife, his Tables of Veins and Arteries, his Venetian glass and the rest of his curiosities, to lead the life of a country gentleman of strong Royalist sympathies at Deptford. What with going to church and going to town, settling his accounts and planting his garden —"I planted the orchard at Sayes Court; new moon, wind west"—his time was spent much as ours is. But there was one difference which it is difficult to illustrate by a single quotation, because the evidence is scattered all about in little insignificant phrases. The general effect of them is that he used his eyes. The visible world was always close to him. The visible world has receded so far from us that to hear all this talk of buildings and gardens, statues and carving, as if the look of things assailed one out of doors as well as in, and were not confined to a few small canvases hung upon the wall, seems strange. No doubt there are a thousand excuses for us; but hitherto we have been finding excuses for him. Wherever there was a picture to be seen by Julio Romano, Polydore, Guido, Raphael, or Tintoretto, a finely-built house, a prospect, or a garden nobly designed, Evelyn stopped his coach to look at it, and opened his diary to record his opinion. On August 27 Evelyn, with Dr. Wren and others, was in St. Paul's surveying "the general decay of that ancient and venerable church"; held with Dr. Wren another judgement from the rest; and had a mind to build it with "a noble cupola, a form of church building not as yet known in England but of wonderful grace", in which Dr. Wren concurred.

Six days later the Fire of London altered their plans. It was Evelyn again who, walking by himself, chanced to look in at the window of "a poor solitary thatched house in a field in our parish", there saw a young man carving at a crucifix, was overcome with an enthusiasm which does him the utmost credit, and carried Grinling Gibbons and his carving to Court.

Indeed, it is all very well to be scrupulous about the sufferings of worms and sensitive to the dues of servant girls, but how pleasant also if, with shut eyes, one could call up street after street of beautiful houses. A flower is red; the apples rosy-gilt in the afternoon sun; a picture has charm, especially as it displays the character of a grandfather and dignifies a family descended from such a scowl; but these are scattered fragments—little relics of beauty in a world that has grown indescribably drab. To our charge of cruelty Evelyn might well reply by pointing to Bayswater and the purlieus of Clapham; and if he should assert that nothing now has character or conviction, that no farmer in England sleeps with an open coffin at his bedside to remind him of death, we could not retort effectually offhand. True, we like the country. Evelyn never looked at the sky.

But to return. After the Restoration Evelyn emerged in full possession of a variety of accomplishments which in our time of specialists seems remarkable enough. He was employed on public business; he was Secretary to the Royal Society; he wrote plays and poems; he was the first authority upon trees and gardens in England; he submitted a design for the rebuilding of London; he went into the question of smoke and its abatement—the lime trees in St. James's Park being, it is said, the result of his cogitations; he was commissioned to write a history of the Dutch war—in short, he completely outdid the Squire of "The Princess", whom in many respects he anticipated—

> A lord of fat prize oxen and of sheep,
> A raiser of huge melons and of pine,
> A patron of some thirty charities,
> A pamphleteer on guano and on grain,
> A quarter sessions chairman abler none.

All that he was, and shared with Sir Walter another characteristic which Tennyson does not mention. He was, we cannot help suspecting, something of a bore, a little censorious, a little patronising, a little too sure of his own merits, and a little obtuse to those of other people. Or what is the quality, or absence of quality, that checks our sympathies partly, perhaps, it is due to some inconsistency which it would be harsh to call by so strong a name as hypocrisy. Though he deplored the vices of his age he could never keep away from the centre of them. "The luxurious dallying and profaneness" of the Court, the sight of "Mrs. Nelly" looking over her garden wall and holding "very familiar discourse" with King Charles on the green walk below, caused him acute disgust; yet he could never decide to break with the Court and retire to "my poor but quiet villa", which was of course the apple of his eye and one of the show-places in England. Then, though he loved his daughter Mary, his grief at her death did not prevent him from counting the number of empty coaches drawn by six horses apiece that attended her funeral. His women friends combined virtue with beauty to such an extent that we can hardly credit them with wit into the bargain. Poor Mrs. Godolphin at least, whom he celebrated in a sincere and touching biography, "loved to be at funerals" and chose habitually "the dryest and leanest morsels of meat", which may be the habits of an angel but do not present her friendship with Evelyn in an alluring light. But it is Pepys who sums up our case against Evelyn; Pepys who said of him after a long morning's entertainment: "In fine a most excellent person he is and must be allowed a little for a little conceitedness; but he may well be so, being a man so much above others". The words exactly hit the mark, "A most excellent person he was"; but a little conceited.

Pepys it is who prompts us to another reflection, inevitable, unnecessary, perhaps unkind. Evelyn was no genius. His writing is opaque rather than transparent; we see no depths through it, nor any very secret movements of mind or heart. He can neither make us hate a regicide nor love Mrs. Godolphin beyond reason. But he writes a diary; and he writes it supremely well. Even as we drowse, somehow or other the bygone gentleman sets up, through three centuries, a perceptible tingle of communication, so that without laying stress on anything in particular, stopping to dream, stopping to laugh, stopping merely to look, we are yet taking notice all the time. His garden for example—how delightful is his disparagement of it, and how acid his criticism of the gardens of others! Then, we may be sure, the hens at Sayes Court laid the very best eggs in England, and when the Tsar drove a wheelbarrow through his hedge what a catastrophe it was, and we can guess how Mrs. Evelyn dusted and polished, and how Evelyn himself grumbled, and how punctilious and efficient and trustworthy he was, how prone to give advice, how ready to read his own works aloud, and how affectionate, withal, lamenting bitterly but not effusively, for the man with the long-drawn sensitive face was never that, the death of the little prodigy Richard, and recording how "after evening prayers was my child buried near the rest of his brothers—my very dear children." He was not an artist; no phrases linger in the mind; no paragraphs build themselves up in memory; but as an artistic method this of going on with the day's story circumstantially, bringing in people who will never be mentioned again, leading up to crises which never take place, introducing Sir Thomas Browne but never letting him speak, has its fascination. All through his pages good men, bad men, celebrities, nonentities are coming into the room and going out again. The greater number we scarcely notice; the door shuts upon them and they disappear.

But now and again the sight of a vanishing coat-tail suggests more than a whole figure sitting still in a full light. They have struck no attitude, arranged no mantle. Little they think that for three hundred years and more they will be looked at in the act of jumping a gate, or observing, like the old Marquis of Argyle, that the turtle doves in the aviary are owls. Our eyes wander from one to the other; our affections settle here or there—on hot-tempered Captain Wray, for instance, who was choleric, had a dog that killed a goat, was for shooting the goat's owner, was for shooting his horse when it fell down a precipice; on Mr. Saladine; on Mr. Saladine's beautiful daughter; on Captain Wray lingering at Geneva to make love to Mr. Saladine's daughter; on Evelyn himself most of all, grown old, walking in his garden at Wooton, his sorrows smoothed out, his grandson doing him credit, the Latin quotations falling pat from his lips, his trees flourishing, and the butterflies flying and flaunting on his dahlias too.

Defoe[1]

The fear which attacks the recorder of centenaries lest he should find himself measuring a diminishing spectre and forced to foretell its approaching dissolution is not only absent in the case of *Robinson Crusoe* but the mere thought of it is ridiculous. It may be true that *Robinson Crusoe* is two hundred years of age upon the twenty-fifth of April 1919, but far from raising the familiar speculations as to whether people now read it and will continue to read it, the effect of the bicentenary is to make us marvel that *Robinson Crusoe*, the perennial and immortal, should have been in existence so short a time as that. The book resembles one of the anonymous productions of the race itself rather than the effort of a single mind; and as for celebrating its centenary we should as soon think of celebrating the centenaries of Stonehenge itself. Something of this we may attribute to the fact that we have all had *Robinson Crusoe* read aloud to us as children, and were thus much in the same state of mind towards Defoe and his story that the Greeks were in towards Homer. It never occurred to us that there was such a person as Defoe, and to have been told that *Robinson Crusoe* was the work of a man with a pen in his hand would either have disturbed us unpleasantly or meant nothing at all. The impressions of childhood are those that

[1] Written in 1919.

last longest and cut deepest. It still seems that the name of Daniel Defoe has no right to appear upon the title-page of *Robinson Crusoe*, and if we celebrate the bi-centenary of the book we are making a slightly unnecessary allusion to the fact that, like Stonehenge, it is still in existence.

The great fame of the book has done its author some injustice; for while it has given him a kind of anonymous glory it has obscured the fact that he was a writer of other works which, it is safe to assert, were not read aloud to us as children. Thus when the Editor of the *Christian World* in the year 1870 appealed to "the boys and girls of England" to erect a monument upon the grave of Defoe, which a stroke of lightning had mutilated, the marble was inscribed to the memory of the author of *Robinson Crusoe*. No mention was made of *Moll Flanders*. Considering the topics which are dealt with in that book, and in *Roxana*, *Captain Singleton*, *Colonel Jack* and the rest, we need not be surprised, though we may be indignant, at the omission. We may agree with Mr. Wright, the biographer of Defoe, that these "are not works for the drawing-room table". But unless we consent to make that useful piece of furniture the final arbiter of taste, we must deplore the fact that their superficial coarseness, or the universal celebrity of *Robinson Crusoe*, has led them to be far less widely famed than they deserve. On any monument worthy of the name of monument the names of *Moll Flanders* and *Roxana*, at least, should be carved as deeply as the name of Defoe.

They stand among the few English novels which we can call indisputably great. The occasion of the bi-centenary of their more famous companion may well lead us to consider in what their greatness, which has so much in common with his, may be found to consist.

Defoe was an elderly man when he turned novelist, many years the predecessor of Richardson and Fielding, and one of the first indeed to shape the novel and launch it on its way. But it is unnecessary to labour the fact of his precedence, except that he came to his novel-writing with certain conceptions about the art which he derived partly from being himself one of the first to practise it. The novel had to justify its existence by telling a true story and preaching a sound moral. "This supplying a story by invention is certainly a most scandalous crime," he wrote. "It is a sort of lying that makes a great hole in the heart, in which by degrees a habit of lying enters in." Either in the preface or in the text of each of his works, therefore, he takes pains to insist that he has not used his invention at all but has depended upon facts, and that his purpose has been the highly moral desire to convert the vicious or to warn the innocent. Happily these were principles that tallied very well with his natural disposition and endowments. Facts had been drilled into him by sixty years of varying fortunes before he turned his experience to account in fiction. "I have some time ago summed up the Scenes of my life in this distich," he wrote:

No man has tasted differing fortunes more,
And thirteen times I have been rich and poor.

He had spent eighteen months in Newgate and talked
with thieves, pirates, highwaymen, and coiners before
he wrote the history of Moll Flanders. But to have
facts thrust upon you by dint of living and accident is
one thing; to swallow them voraciously and retain the
imprint of them indelibly, is another. It is not merely
that Defoe knew the stress of poverty and had talked
with the victims of it, but that the unsheltered life, exposed to circumstances and forced to shift for itself,
appealed to him imaginatively as the right matter for
his art. In the first pages of each of his great novels
he reduces his hero or heroine to such a state of un-
friended misery that their existence must be a continued struggle, and their survival at all the result of
luck and their own exertions. Moll Flanders was born
in Newgate of a criminal mother; Captain Singleton
was stolen as a child and sold to the gipsies; Colonel
Jack, though "born a gentleman, was put 'prentice to
a pickpocket"; Roxana starts under better auspices,
but, having married at fifteen, she sees her husband go
bankrupt and is left with five children in "a condition
the most deplorable that words can express".

Thus each of these boys and girls has the world
to begin and the battle to fight for himself. The situation thus created was entirely to Defoe's liking.
From her very birth or with half a year's respite at
most, Moll Flanders, the most notable of them, is

goaded by "that worst of devils, poverty", forced to earn her living as soon as she can sew, driven from place to place, making no demands upon her creator for the subtle domestic atmosphere which he was unable to supply, but drawing upon him for all he knew of strange people and customs. From the outset the burden of proving her right to exist is laid upon her. She has to depend entirely upon her own wits and judgement, and to deal with each emergency as it arises by a rule-of-thumb morality which she has forged in her own head. The briskness of the story is due partly to the fact that having transgressed the accepted laws at a very early age she has henceforth the freedom of the outcast. The one impossible event is that she should settle down in comfort and security. But from the first the peculiar genius of the author asserts itself, and avoids the obvious danger of the novel of adventure. He makes us understand that Moll Flanders was a woman on her own account and not only material for a succession of adventures. In proof of this she begins, as Roxana also begins, by falling passionately, if unfortunately, in love. That she must rouse herself and marry some one else and look very closely to her settlements and prospects is no slight upon her passion, but to be laid to the charge of her birth; and, like all Defoe's women, she is a person of robust understanding. Since she makes no scruple of telling lies when they serve her purpose, there is something undeniable about her truth when she speaks it. She has no time to waste upon the refinements of personal affection; one tear is dropped, one moment of despair allowed, and then "on with the story". She has a spirit that loves to breast the storm. She delights in the exercise of her own powers. When she discovers that the man she has married in Virginia is her own brother she is violently disgusted; she insists upon leaving him; but as soon as she sets foot in Bristol, "I took the diversion of going to Bath, for as I was still far from being old so my humour, which was always gay, continued so to an extreme". Heartless she is not, nor can any one charge her with levity; but life delights her, and a heroine who lives has us all in tow. Moreover, her ambition has that slight strain of imagination in it which puts it in the category of the noble passions. Shrewd and practical of necessity, she is yet haunted by a desire for romance and for the quality which to her perception makes a man a gentleman. "It was really a true gallant spirit he was of, and it was the more grievous to me. 'Tis something of relief even to be undone by a man of honour rather than by a scoundrel," she writes when she had misled a highwayman as to the extent of her fortune. It is in keeping with this temper that she should be proud of her final partner because he refuses to work when they reach the plantations but prefers hunting, and that she should take pleasure in buying him wigs and silver-hilted swords "to make him appear, as he really was, a very fine gentleman". Her very love of hot weather is in keeping, and the passion with which she kissed the ground that her son had trod on, and her noble tolerance of every kind of fault so long as it is not "complete baseness of spirit, imperious, cruel, and relentless when uppermost, abject and low-spirited when down". For the rest of the world she has nothing but good-will.

Since the list of the qualities and graces of this seasoned old sinner is by no means exhausted we can well understand how it was that Borrow's apple-woman on London Bridge called her "blessed Mary" and valued her book above all the apples on her stall; and that Borrow, taking the book deep into the booth, read till his eyes ached. But we dwell upon such signs of character only by way of proof that the creator of Moll Flanders was not, as he has been accused of being, a mere journalist and literal recorder of facts with no conception of the nature of psychology. It is true that his characters take shape and substance of their own accord, as if in despite of the author and not altogether to his liking. He never lingers or stresses any point of subtlety or pathos, but presses on imperturbably as if they came there without his knowledge. A touch of imagination, such as that when the Prince sits by his son's cradle and Roxana observes how "he loved to look at it when it was asleep", seems to mean much more to us than to him. After the curiously modern dissertation upon the need of communicating matters of importance to a second person lest, like the thief in Newgate, we should talk of it in our sleep, he apologises for his digression. He seems to have taken his characters so deeply into his mind that he lived them without exactly knowing how; and, like all unconscious artists, he leaves more gold in his work than his own generation was able to bring to the surface.

The interpretation that we put on his characters might therefore well have puzzled him. We find for ourselves meanings which he was careful to disguise even from himself. Thus it comes about that we admire Moll Flanders far more than we blame her. Nor can we believe that Defoe had made up his mind as to the precise degree of her guilt, or was unaware that in considering the lives of the abandoned he raised many deep questions and hinted, if he did not state, answers quite at variance with his professions of belief. From the evidence supplied by his essay upon the "Education of Women" we know that he had thought deeply and much in advance of his age upon the capacities of women, which he rated very high, and the injustice done to them, which he rated very harsh.

I have often thought of it as one of the most barbarous customs in the world, considering us as a civilised and a Christian country, that we deny the advantages of learning to women. We reproach the sex every day with folly and impertinence; which I am confident, had they the advantages of education equal to us, they would be guilty of less than ourselves.

The advocates of women's rights would hardly care, perhaps, to claim Moll Flanders and Roxana among their patron saints; and yet it is clear that Defoe not only intended them to speak some very modern doctrines upon the subject, but placed them in circumstances where their peculiar hardships are displayed in such a way as to elicit our sympathy. Courage, said Moll Flanders, was what women needed, and the power to "stand their ground"; and at once gave practical demonstration of the benefits that would result. Roxana, a lady of the same profession, argues more subtly against the slavery of marriage. She "had started a new thing in the world" the merchant told her; "it was a way of arguing contrary to the general practise". But Defoe is the last writer to be guilty of bald preaching. Roxana keeps our attention because she is blessedly unconscious that she is in any good sense an example to her sex and is thus at liberty to own that part of her argument is "of an elevated strain which was really not in my thoughts at first, at all". The knowledge of her own frailties and the honest questioning of her own motives, which that knowledge begets, have the happy result of keeping her fresh and human when the martyrs and pioneers of so many problem novels have shrunken and shrivelled to the pegs and props of their respective creeds.

But the claim of Defoe upon our admiration does not rest upon the fact that he can be shown to have anticipated some of the views of Meredith, or to have written scenes which (the odd suggestion occurs) might have been turned into plays by Ibsen. Whatever his ideas upon the position of women, they are an incidental result of his chief virtue, which is that he deals

with the important and lasting side of things and not
with the passing and trivial. He is often dull. He
can imitate the matter-of-fact precision of a scientific traveller until we wonder that his pen could trace
or his brain conceive what has not even the excuse of
truth to soften its dryness. He leaves out the whole
of vegetable nature, and a large part of human nature.
All this we may admit, though we have to admit defects as grave in many writers whom we call great.
But that does not impair the peculiar merit of what
remains. Having at the outset limited his scope and
confined his ambitions he achieves a truth of insight
which is far rarer and more enduring than the truth of
fact which he professed to make his aim. Moll Flanders and her friends recommended themselves to him
not because they were, as we should say, "picturesque";
nor, as he affirmed, because they were examples of evil
living by which the public might profit. It was their
natural veracity, bred in them by a life of hardship,
that excited his interest. For them there were no
excuses; no kindly shelter obscured their motives.
Poverty was their taskmaster. Defoe did not pronounce more than a judgement of the lips upon their
failings. But their courage and resource and tenacity
delighted him. He found their society full of good
talk, and pleasant stories, and faith in each other,
and morality of a home-made kind. Their fortunes
had that infinite variety which he praised and relished
and beheld with wonder in his own life. These men
and women, above all, were free to talk openly of the

passions and desires which have moved men and women since the beginning of time, and thus even now they keep their vitality undiminished. There is a dignity in everything that is looked at openly. Even the sordid subject of money, which plays so large a part in their histories, becomes not sordid but tragic when it stands not for ease and consequence but for honour, honesty and life itself. You may object that Defoe is humdrum, but never that he is engrossed with petty things.

He belongs, indeed, to the school of the great plain writers, whose work is founded upon a knowledge of what is most persistent, though not most seductive, in human nature. The view of London from Hungerford Bridge, grey, serious, massive, and full of the subdued stir of traffic and business, prosaic if it were not for the masts of the ships and the towers and domes of the city, brings him to mind. The tattered girls with violets in their hands at the street corners, and the old weather-beaten women patiently displaying their matches and bootlaces beneath the shelter of arches, seem like characters from his books. He is of the school of Crabbe, and of Gissing, and not merely a fellow pupil in the same stern place of learning, but its founder and master.

Addison [1]

In July, 1843, Lord Macaulay pronounced the opinion that Joseph Addison had enriched our literature with compositions "that will live as long as the English language". But when Lord Macaulay pronounced an opinion it was not merely an opinion. Even now, at a distance of seventy-six years, the words seem to issue from the mouth of the chosen representative of the people. There is an authority about them, a sonority, a sense of responsibility, which put us in mind of a Prime Minister making a proclamation on behalf of a great empire rather than of a journalist writing about a deceased man of letters for a magazine. The article upon Addison is, indeed, one of the most vigorous of the famous essays. Florid, and at the same time extremely solid, the phrases seem to build up a monument, at once square and lavishly festooned with ornament, which should serve Addison for shelter so long as one stone of Westminster Abbey stands upon another. Yet, though we may have read and admired this particular essay times out of number (as we say when we have read anything three times over), it has never occurred to us, strangely enough, to believe that it is true. That is apt to happen to the admiring reader of Macaulay's essays. While delighting in their richness, force, and variety, and finding every judgement, how-

[1] Written in 1919.

ever emphatic, proper in its place, it seldom occurs to us to connect these sweeping assertions and undeniable convictions with anything so minute as a human being. So it is with Addison. "If we wish", Macaulay writes, "to find anything more vivid than Addison's best portraits, we must go either to Shakespeare or to Cervantes". "We have not the least doubt that if Addison had written a novel on an extensive plan it would have been superior to any that we possess." His essays, again, "fully entitle him to the rank of a great poet"; and, to complete the edifice, we have Voltaire proclaimed "the prince of buffoons", and together with Swift forced to stoop so low that Addison takes rank above them both as a humorist.

Examined separately, such flourishes of ornament look grotesque enough, but in their place—such is the persuasive power of design—they are part of the decoration; they complete the monument. Whether Addison or another is interred within, it is a very fine tomb. But now that two centuries have passed since the real body of Addison was laid by night under the Abbey floor, we are, through no merit of our own, partially qualified to test the first of the flourishes on that fictitious tombstone to which, though it may be empty, we have done homage, in a formal kind of way, these sixty-seven years. The compositions of Addison will live as long as the English language. Since every moment brings proof that our mother tongue is more lusty and lively than sorts with complete sedateness or chastity, we need only concern ourselves with the vitality of

Addison. Neither lusty nor lively is the adjective we should apply to the present condition of the *Tatler* and the *Spectator*. To take a rough test, it is possible to discover how many people in the course of a year borrow Addison's works from the public library, and a particular instance affords us the not very encouraging information that during nine years two people yearly take out the first volume of the *Spectator*. The second volume is less in request than the first. The inquiry is not a cheerful one. From certain marginal comments and pencil marks it seems that these rare devotees seek out only the famous passages and, as their habit is, score what we are bold enough to consider the least admirable phrases. No; if Addison lives at all, it is not in the public libraries. It is in libraries that are markedly private, secluded, shaded by lilac trees and brown with folios, that he still draws his faint, regular breath. If any man or woman is going to solace himself with a page of Addison before the June sun is out of the sky to-day, it is in some such pleasant retreat as this.

Yet all over England at intervals, perhaps wide ones, we may be sure that there are people engaged in reading Addison, whatever the year or season. For Addison is very well worth reading. The temptation to read Pope on Addison, Macaulay on Addison, Thackeray on Addison, Johnson on Addison rather than Addison himself is to be resisted, for you will find, if you study the *Tatler* and the *Spectator*, glance at *Cato*, and run through the remainder of the six moderate-sized volumes, that Addison is neither Pope's Addison nor anybody else's Addison, but a separate, independent individual still capable of casting a clear-cut shape of himself upon the consciousness, turbulent and distracted as it is, of nineteen hundred and nineteen. It is true that the fate of the lesser shades is always a little precarious. They are so easily obscured or distorted. It seems so often scarcely worth while to go through the cherishing and humanising process which is necessary to get into touch with a writer of the second class who may, after all, have little to give us. The earth is crusted over them; their features are obliterated, and perhaps it is not a head of the best period that we rub clean in the end, but only the chip of an old pot. The chief difficulty with the lesser writers, however, is not only the effort. It is that our standards have changed. The things that they like are not the things that we like; and as the charm of their writing depends much more upon taste than upon conviction, a change of manners is often quite enough to put us out of touch altogether. That is one of the most troublesome barriers between ourselves and Addison. He attached great importance to certain qualities. He had a very precise notion of what we are used to call "niceness" in man or woman. He was extremely fond of saying that men ought not to be atheists, and that women ought not to wear large petticoats. This directly inspires in us not so much a sense of distaste as a sense of difference. Dutifully, if at

[140]

all, we strain our imaginations to conceive the kind of audience to whom these precepts were addressed. The *Tatler* was published in 1709; the *Spectator* a year or two later. What was the state of England at that particular moment? Why was Addison so anxious to insist upon the necessity of a decent and cheerful religious belief? Why did he so constantly, and in the main kindly, lay stress upon the foibles of women and their reform? Why was he so deeply impressed with the evils of party government? Any historian will explain; but it is always a misfortune to have to call in the services of any historian. A writer should give us direct certainty; explanations are so much water poured into the wine. As it is, we can only feel that these counsels are addressed to ladies in hoops and gentlemen in wigs—a vanished audience which has learnt its lesson and gone its way and the preacher with it. We can only smile and marvel and perhaps admire the clothes.

And that is not the way to read. To be thinking that dead people deserved these censures and admired this morality, judged the eloquence, which we find so frigid, sublime, the philosophy to us so superficial, profound, to take a collector's joy in such signs of antiquity, is to treat literature as if it were a broken jar of undeniable age but doubtful beauty, to be stood in a cabinet behind glass doors. The charm which still makes *Cato* very readable is much of this nature. When Syphax exclaims,

So, where our wide Numidian wastes extend,
Sudden, th' impetuous hurricanes descend,
Wheel through the air, in circling eddies play,
Tear up the sands, and sweep whole plains away,
The helpless traveller, with wild surprise,
Sees the dry desert all around him rise,
And smother'd in the dusty whirlwind dies,

we cannot help imagining the thrill in the crowded theatre, the feathers nodding emphatically on the ladies' heads, the gentlemen leaning forward to tap their canes, and every one exclaiming to his neighbour how vastly fine it is and crying "Bravo!" But how can *we* be excited? And so with Bishop Hurd and his notes—his "finely observed", his "wonderfully exact, both in the sentiment and expression", his serene confidence that when "the present humour of idolising Shakespeare is over", the time will come when *Cato* is "supremely admired by all candid and judicious critics". This is all very amusing and productive of pleasant fancies, both as to the faded frippery of our ancestors' minds and the bold opulence of our own. But it is not the intercourse of equals, let alone that other kind of intercourse, which as it makes us contemporary with the author, persuades us that his object is our own. Occasionally in *Cato* one may pick up a few lines that are not obsolete; but for the most part the tragedy which Dr. Johnson thought "unquestionably the noblest production of Addison's genius" has become collector's literature.

Perhaps most readers approach the essays also with

some suspicion as to the need of condescension in their minds. The question to be asked is whether Addison, attached as he was to certain standards of gentility, morality, and taste, has not become one of those people of exemplary character and charming urbanity who must never be talked to about anything more exciting than the weather. We have some slight suspicion that the *Spectator* and the *Tatler* are nothing but talk, couched in perfect English, about the number of fine days this year compared with the number of wet the year before. The difficulty of getting on to equal terms with him is shown by the little fable which he introduces into one of the early numbers of the *Tatler*, of "a young gentleman, of moderate understanding, but great vivacity, who . . . had got a little smattering of knowledge, just enough to make an atheist or a free-thinker, but not a philosopher, or a man of sense". This young gentleman visits his father in the country, and proceeds "to enlarge the narrowness of the country notions; in which he succeeded so well, that he had seduced the butler by his table-talk, and staggered his eldest sister. . . . 'Till one day, talking of his setting dog . . . said 'he did not question but Tray was as immortal as any one of the family'; and in the heat of the argument told his father, that for his own part, 'he expected to die like a dog'. Upon which, the old man, starting up in a very great passion, cried out, 'Then, sirrah, you shall live like one'; and taking his cane in his hand, cudgelled him out of his system. This had so good an effect upon him, that he took up from

that day, fell to reading good books, and is now a
bencher in the Middle-Temple." There is a good deal
of Addison in that story: his dislike of "dark and uncomfortable prospects"; his respect for "principles
which are the support, happiness, and glory of all public societies, as well as private persons"; his solicitude
for the butler; and his conviction that to read good
books and become a bencher in the Middle Temple is
the proper end for a very vivacious young gentleman.
This Mr. Addison married a countess, "gave his little
senate laws", and, sending for young Lord Warwick,
made that famous remark about seeing how a Christian can die which has fallen upon such evil days that
our sympathies are with the foolish, and perhaps fuddled, young peer rather than with the frigid gentleman, not too far gone for a last spasm of self-com-
placency, upon the bed.

Let us rub off such incrustations, so far as they are
due to the corrosion of Pope's wit or the deposit of
mid-Victorian lachrymosity, and see what, for us in
our time, remains. In the first place, there remains the
not despicable virtue, after two centuries of existence,
of being readable. Addison can fairly lay claim to
that; and then, slipped in on the tide of the smooth,
well-turned prose, are little eddies, diminutive water-
falls, agreeably diversifying the polished surface. We
begin to take note of whims, fancies, peculiarities on
the part of the essayist which light up the prim, impeccable countenance of the moralist and convince us that,
however tightly he may have pursed his lips, his eyes

are very bright and not so shallow after all. He is alert
to his finger tips. Little muffs, silver garters, fringed
gloves draw his attention; he observes with a keen,
quick glance, not unkindly, and full rather of amusement than of censure. To be sure, the age was rich in
follies. Here were coffee-houses packed with politicians talking of Kings and Emperors and letting their
own small affairs go to ruin. Crowds applauded the
Italian opera every night without understanding a
word of it. Critics discoursed of the unities. Men
gave a thousand pounds for a handful of tulip roots.
As for women—or "the fair sex", as Addison liked to
call them—their follies were past counting. He did
his best to count them, with a loving particularity
which roused the ill humour of Swift. But he did it
very charmingly, with a natural relish for the task, as
the following passage shows:

> I consider woman as a beautiful romantic animal, that may
> be adorned with furs and feathers, pearls and diamonds,
> ores and silks. The lynx shall cast its skin at her feet to
> make her a tippet; the peacock, parrot, and swan, shall pay
> contributions to her muff; the sea shall be searched for shells,
> and the rocks for gems; and every part of nature furnish out
> its share towards the embellishment of a creature that is the
> most consummate work of it. All this I shall indulge them
> in; but as for the petticoat I have been speaking of, I neither
> can nor will allow it.

In all these matters Addison was on the side of sense
and taste and civilisation. Of that little fraternity,
often so obscure and yet so indispensable, who in every

age keep themselves alive to the importance of art and letters and music, watching, discriminating, denouncing and delighting, Addison was one—distinguished and strangely contemporary with ourselves. It would have been, so one imagines, a great pleasure to take him a manuscript; a great enlightenment, as well as a great honour, to have his opinion. In spite of Pope, one fancies that his would have been criticism of the best order, open-minded and generous to novelty, and yet, in the final resort, unfaltering in its standards. The boldness which is a proof of vigour is shown by his defence of "Chevy Chase". He had so clear a notion of what he meant by the "very spirit and soul of fine writing" as to track it down in an old barbarous ballad or rediscover it in "that divine work" "Paradise Lost". Moreover, far from being a connoisseur only of the still, settled beauties of the dead, he was aware of the present; a severe critic of its "Gothic taste", vigilant in protecting the rights and honours of the language, and all in favour of simplicity and quiet. Here we have the Addison of Will's and Button's, who, sitting late into the night and drinking more than was good for him, gradually overcame his taciturnity and began to talk. Then he "chained the attention of every one to him". "Addison's conversation", said Pope, "had something in it more charming than I have found in any other man." One can well believe it, for his essays at their best preserve the very cadence of easy yet exquisitely modulated conversation—the smile checked before it has broadened into laughter, the thought lightly turned from frivolity or abstraction, the ideas springing, bright, new, various, with the utmost spontaneity. He seems to speak what comes into his head, and is never at the trouble of raising his voice. But he has described himself in the character of the lute better than any one can do it for him.

The lute is a character directly opposite to the drum, that sounds very finely by itself, or in a very small concert. Its notes are exquisitely sweet, and very low, easily drowned in a multitude of instruments, and even lost among a few, unless you give a particular attention to it. A lute is seldom heard in a company of more than five, whereas a drum will show itself to advantage in an assembly of 500. The lutanists, therefore, are men of a fine genius, uncommon reflection, great affability, and esteemed chiefly by persons of a good taste, who are the only proper judges of so delightful and soft a melody.

Addison was a lutanist. No praise, indeed, could be less appropriate than Lord Macaulay's. To call Addison on the strength of his essays a great poet, or to prophesy that if he had written a novel on an extensive plan it would have been "superior to any that we possess", is to confuse him with the drums and trumpets; it is not merely to overpraise his merits, but to overlook them. Dr. Johnson superbly, and, as his manner is, once and for all has summed up the quality of Addison's poetic genius:

His poetry is first to be considered; of which it must be confessed that it has not often those felicities of diction which

[147]

give lustre to sentiments, or that vigour of sentiment that animates diction; there is little of ardour, vehemence, or transport; there is very rarely the awfulness of grandeur, and not very often the splendour of elegance. He thinks justly; but he thinks faintly.

The Sir Roger de Coverley papers are those which have the most resemblance, on the surface, to a novel. But their merit consists in the fact that they do not adumbrate, or initiate, or anticipate anything; they exist, perfect, complete, entire in themselves. To read them as if they were a first hesitating experiment containing the seed of greatness to come is to miss the peculiar point of them. They are studies done from the outside by a quiet spectator. When read together they compose a portrait of the Squire and his circle all in characteristic positions—one with his rod, another with his hounds—but each can be detached from the rest without damage to the design or harm to himself. In a novel, where each chapter gains from the one before it or adds to the one that follows it, such separations would be intolerable. The speed, the intricacy, the design, would be mutilated. These particular qualities are perhaps lacking, but nevertheless Addison's method has great advantages. Each of these essays is very highly finished. The characters are defined by a succession of extremely neat, clean strokes. Inevitably, where the sphere is so narrow—an essay is only three or four pages in length—there is not room for great depth or intricate subtlety. Here, from the *Spectator*, is a good example of the witty and decisive

manner in which Addison strikes out a portrait to fill
the little frame:

Sombrius is one of these sons of sorrow. He thinks himself
obliged in duty to be sad and disconsolate. He looks on a
sudden fit of laughter as a breach of his baptismal vow. An
innocent jest startles him like blasphemy. Tell him of one
who is advanced to a title of honour, he lifts up his hands
and eyes; describe a public ceremony, he shakes his head; shew
him a gay equipage, he blesses himself. All the little ornaments of life are pomps and vanities. Mirth is wanton, and
wit profane. He is scandalized at youth for being lively, and
at childhood for being playful. He sits at a christening, or
at a marriage-feast, as at a funeral; sighs at the conclusion
of a merry story, and grows devout when the rest of the company grow pleasant. After all Sombrius is a religious man,
and would have behaved himself very properly, had he lived
when Christianity was under a general persecution.

The novel is not a development from that model,
for the good reason that no development along these
lines is possible. Of its kind such a portrait is perfect; and when we find, scattered up and down the
Spectator and the *Tatler*, numbers of such little masterpieces with fancies and anecdotes in the same style,
some doubt as to the narrowness of such a sphere becomes inevitable. The form of the essay admits of
its own particular perfection; and if anything is perfect the exact dimensions of its perfection become im-
material. One can scarcely settle whether, on the
whole, one prefers a raindrop to the River Thames.
When we have said all that we can say against them—
that many are dull, others superficial, the allegories

[149]

faded, the piety conventional, the morality trite—there still remains the fact that the essays of Addison are perfect essays. Always at the highest point of any art there comes a moment when everything seems in a conspiracy to help the artist, and his achievement becomes a natural felicity on his part of which he seems, to a later age, half-unconscious. So Addison, writing day after day, essay after essay, knew instinctively and exactly how to do it. Whether it was a high thing, or whether it was a low thing, whether an epic is more profound or a lyric more passionate, undoubtedly it is due to Addison that prose is now prosaic—the medium which makes it possible for people of ordinary intelligence to communicate their ideas to the world. Addison is the respectable ancestor of an innumerable progeny. Pick up the first weekly journal and the article upon the "Delights of Summer" or the "Approach of Age" will show his influence. But it will also show, unless the name of Mr. Max Beerbohm, our solitary essayist, is attached to it, that we have lost the art of writing essays. What with our views and our virtues, our passions and profundities, the shapely silver drop, that held the sky in it and so many bright little visions of human life, is now nothing but a hold-all knobbed with luggage packed in a hurry. Even so, the essayist will make an effort, perhaps without knowing it, to write like Addison.

In his temperate and reasonable way Addison more than once amused himself with speculations as to the fate of his writings. He had a just idea of their nature and value. "I have new-pointed all the batteries of ridicule", he wrote. Yet, because so many of his darts had been directed against ephemeral follies, "absurd fashions, ridiculous customs, and affected forms of speech", the time would come, in a hundred years, perhaps, when his essays, he thought, would be "like so many pieces of old plate, where the weight will be regarded, but the fashion lost". Two hundred years have passed; the plate is worn smooth; the pattern almost rubbed out; but the metal is pure silver.

The Lives of the Obscure

Five shillings, perhaps, will secure a life subscription to this faded, out-of-date, obsolete library, which with a little help from the rates, is chiefly subsidised from the shelves of clergymen's widows, and country gentlemen inheriting more books than their wives like to dust. In the middle of the wide airy room, with windows that look to the sea and let in the shouts of men crying pilchards for sale on the cobbled street below, a row of vases stands, in which specimens of the local flowers droop, each with its name inscribed beneath. The elderly, the marooned, the bored, drift from newspaper to newspaper, or sit holding their heads over back numbers of *The Illustrated London News* and the *Wesleyan Chronicle*. No one has spoken aloud here since the room was opened in 1854. The obscure sleep on the walls, slouching against each other as if they were too drowsy to stand upright. Their backs are flaking off; their titles often vanished. Why disturb their sleep? Why re-open those peaceful graves, the librarian seems to ask, peering over his spectacles, and resenting the duty, which indeed has become laborious, of retrieving from among those nameless tombstones Nos. 1763, 1080, and 606.

I

THE TAYLORS AND THE EDGEWORTHS

For one likes romantically to feel oneself a deliverer advancing with lights across the waste of years to the rescue of some stranded ghost—a Mrs. Pilkington, a Rev. Henry Elman, a Mrs. Ann Gilbert—waiting, appealing, forgotten, in the growing gloom. Possibly they hear one coming. They shuffle, they preen, they bridle. Old secrets well up to their lips. The divine relief of communication will soon again be theirs. The dust shifts and Mrs. Gilbert—but the contact with life is instantly salutary. Whatever Mrs. Gilbert may be doing, she is not thinking about us. Far from it. Colchester, about the year 1800, was for the young Taylors, as Kensington had been for their mother, "a very Elysium". There were the Strutts, the Hills, the Stapletons; there was poetry, philosophy, engraving. For the young Taylors were brought up to work hard, and if, after a long day's toil upon their father's pictures, they slipped round to dine with the Strutts they had a right to their pleasure. Already they had won prizes in Darton and Harvey's pocketbook. One of the Strutts knew James Montgomery, and there was talk, at those gay parties, with the Moorish decorations and all the cats—for old Ben Strutt was a bit of a character: did not communicate; would not let his daughters eat meat, so no wonder they died of consumption—there was talk of printing a joint volume to be called *The Associate Minstrels*, to which James, if not Robert himself, might contribute. The Stapletons were poetical, too. Moira and Bithia would wander over the old town wall at Balkerne Hill reading poetry by moonlight. Perhaps there was a little too much poetry in Colchester in 1800. Looking back in the middle of a prosperous and vigorous life, Ann had to lament many broken careers, much unfulfilled promise. The Stapletons died young, perverted, miserable; Jacob, with his "dark, scorn-speaking countenance", who had vowed that he would spend the night looking for Ann's lost bracelet in the street, disappeared, "and I last heard of him vegetating among the ruins of Rome—himself too much a ruin"; as for the Hills, their fate was worst of all. To submit to public baptism was flighty, but to marry Captain M.! Anybody could have warned pretty Fanny Hill against Captain M. Yet off she drove with him in his fine phaeton. For years nothing more was heard of her. Then one night, when the Taylors had moved to Ongar and old Mr. and Mrs. Taylor were sitting over the fire, thinking how, as it was nine o'clock, and the moon was full, they ought, according to their promise, to look at it and think of their absent children, there came a knock at the door. Mrs. Taylor went down to open it. But who was this sad, shabby-looking woman outside? "Oh, don't you remember the Strutts and the Stapletons, and how you warned me against Captain M.?" cried Fanny Hill, for it was Fanny Hill—poor Fanny Hill, all worn and sunk; poor Fanny Hill, that used

[155]

to be so sprightly. She was living in a lone house not far from the Taylors, forced to drudge for her husband's mistress, for Captain M. had wasted all her fortune, ruined all her life.

Ann married Mr. G., of course—of course. The words toll persistently through these obscure volumes. For in the vast world to which the memoir writers admit us there is a solemn sense of something unescapable, of a wave gathering beneath the frail flotilla and carrying it on. One thinks of Colchester in 1800. Scribbling verses, reading Montgomery—so they begin; the Hills, the Stapletons, the Strutts disperse and disappear as one knew they would; but here, after long years, is Ann still scribbling, and at last here is the poet Montgomery himself in her very house, and she begging him to consecrate her child to poetry by just holding him in his arms, and he refusing (for he is a bachelor), but taking her for a walk, and they hear the thunder, and she thinks it the artillery, and he says in a voice which she will never, never forget: "Yes! The artillery of Heaven!" It is one of the attractions of the unknown, their multitude, their vastness; for, instead of keeping their identity separate, as remarkable people do, they seem to merge into one another, their very boards and title-pages and frontispieces dissolving, and their innumerable pages melting into continuous years so that we can lie back and look up into the fine mist-like substance of countless lives, and pass unhindered from century to century, from life to life. Scenes detach themselves. We watch groups. Here is young Mr. Elman talking to Miss Biffen at Brighton. She has neither arms nor legs; a footman carries her in and out. She teaches miniature painting to his sister. Then he is in the stage coach on the road to Oxford with Newman. Newman says nothing. Elman nevertheless reflects that he has known all the great men of his time. And so back and so forwards, he paces eternally the fields of Sussex until, grown to an extreme old age, there he sits in his Rectory thinking of Newman, thinking of Miss Biffen, and making —it is his great consolation—string bags for missionaries. And then? Go on looking. Nothing much happens. But the dim light is exquisitely refreshing to the eyes. Let us watch little Miss Frend trotting along the Strand with her father. They meet a man with very bright eyes. "Mr. Blake," says Mr. Frend. It is Mrs. Dyer who pours out tea for them in Clifford's Inn. Mr. Charles Lamb has just left the room. Mrs. Dyer says she married George because his washerwoman cheated him so. What do you think George paid for his shirts, she asks? Gently, beautifully, like the clouds of a balmy evening, obscurity once more traverses the sky, an obscurity which is not empty but thick with the star dust of innumerable lives. And suddenly there is a rift in it, and we see a wretched little packet-boat pitching off the Irish coast in the middle of the nineteenth century. There is an unmistakable air of 1840 about the tarpaulins and the hairy monsters in sou'westers lurching and spitting over the sloping decks, yet treating the solitary young woman who stands in shawl and poke bonnet gazing, gazing, not without kindness. No, no, no! She will not leave the deck. She will stand there till it is quite dark, thank you! "Her great love of the sea . . . drew this exemplary wife and mother every now and then irresistibly away from home. No one but her husband knew where she had gone, and her children learnt only later in life that on these occasions, when suddenly she disappeared for a few days, she was taking short sea voyages . . ." a crime which she expiated by months of work among the Midland poor. Then the craving would come upon her, would be confessed in private to her husband, and off she stole again—the mother of Sir George Newnes.

One would conclude that human beings were happy, endowed with such blindness to fate, so indefatigable an interest in their own activities, were it not for those sudden and astonishing apparitions staring in at us, all taut and pale in their determination never to be forgotten, men who have just missed fame, men who have passionately desired redress—men like Haydon, and Mark Pattison, and the Rev. Blanco White. And in the whole world there is probably but one person who looks up for a moment and tries to interpret the menacing face, the furious beckoning fist, before, in the multitude of human affairs, fragments of faces, echoes of voices, flying coat-tails, and bonnet strings disappearing down the shrubbery walks, one's attention is distracted for ever. What is that enormous wheel, for example, careering downhill in Berkshire in the eighteenth century? It runs faster and faster; suddenly a youth jumps out from within; next moment it leaps over the edge of a chalk pit and is dashed to smithereens. This is Edgeworth's doing—Richard Lovell Edgeworth, we mean, the portentous bore.

For that is the way he has come down to us in his two volumes of memoirs—Byron's bore, Day's friend, Maria's father, the man who almost invented the telegraph, and did, in fact, invent machines for cutting turnips, climbing walls, contracting on narrow bridges and lifting their wheels over obstacles—a man meritorious, industrious, advanced, but still, as we investigate his memoirs, mainly a bore. Nature endowed him with irrepressible energy. The blood coursed through his veins at least twenty times faster than the normal rate. His face was red, round, vivacious. His brain raced. His tongue never stopped talking. He had married four wives and had nineteen children, including the novelist Maria. Moreover, he had known every one and done everything. His energy burst open the most secret doors and penetrated to the most private apartments. His wife's grandmother, for instance, disappeared mysteriously every day. Edgeworth blundered in upon her and found her, with her white locks flowing and her eyes streaming, in prayer before a crucifix. She was a Roman Catholic then, but why a penitent? He found out somehow that her husband had been killed in a duel, and she had married the man who killed him. "The consolations of religion are fully equal to its terrors," Dick Edgeworth

[159]

reflected as he stumbled out again. Then there was
the beautiful young woman in the castle among the
forests of Dauphiny. Half paralysed, unable to speak
above a whisper, there she lay when Edgeworth broke
in and found her reading. Tapestries flapped on the
castle walls; fifty thousand bats—"odious animals
whose stench is uncommonly noisome"—hung in clus-
ters in the caves beneath. None of the inhabitants understood a word she said. But to the Englishman she
talked for hour after hour about books and politics
and religion. He listened; no doubt he talked. He
sat dumbfounded. But what could one do for her?
Alas, one must leave her lying among the tusks, and
the old men, and the cross-bows, reading, reading, reading. For Edgeworth was employed in turning the
Rhone from its course. He must get back to his job.
One reflection he would make. "I determined on steadily persevering in the cultivation of my understanding."

He was impervious to the romance of the situations
in which he found himself. Every experience served
only to fortify his character. He reflected, he observed,
he improved himself daily. You can improve, Mr.
Edgeworth used to tell his children, every day of your
life. "He used to say that with this power of improving they might in time be anything, and without
it in time they would be nothing." Imperturbable, indefatigable, daily increasing in sturdy self-assurance,
he has the gift of the egoist. He brings out, as he
bustles and bangs on his way, the diffident, shrinking

figures who would otherwise be drowned in darkness.
The aged lady, whose private penance he disturbed, is
only one of a series of figures who start up on either
side of his progress, mute, astonished, showing us in a
way that is even now unmistakable, their amazement
at this well-meaning man who bursts in upon them at
their studies and interrupts their prayers. We see him
through their eyes; we see him as he does not dream
of being seen. What a tyrant he was to his first wife!
How intolerably she suffered! But she never utters a
word. It is Dick Edgeworth who tells her story in
complete ignorance that he is doing anything of the
kind. "It was a singular trait of character in my wife,"
he observes, "who had never shown any uneasiness at
my intimacy with Sir Francis Delaval, that she should
take a strong dislike to Mr. Day. A more dangerous
and seductive companion than the one, or a more moral
and improving companion than the other, could not be
found in England." It was, indeed, very singular.

For the first Mrs. Edgeworth was a penniless girl,
the daughter of a ruined country gentleman, who sat
over his fire picking cinders from the hearth and throwing them into the grate, while from time to time he
ejaculated "Hein! Heing!" as yet another scheme for
making his fortune came into his head. She had had no
education. An itinerant writing-master had taught her
to form a few words. When Dick Edgeworth was an
undergraduate and rode over from Oxford she fell in
love with him and married him in order to escape the
poverty and the mystery and the dirt, and to have a

husband and children like other women. But with what result? Gigantic wheels ran downhill with the bricklayer's son inside them. Sailing carriages took flight and almost wrecked four stage coaches. Machines did cut turnips, but not very efficiently. Her little boy was allowed to roam the country like a poor man's son, bare-legged, untaught. And Mr. Day, coming to breakfast and staying to dinner, argued incessantly about scientific principles and the laws of nature.

But here we encounter one of the pitfalls of this nocturnal rambling among forgotten worthies. It is so difficult to keep, as we must with highly authenticated people, strictly to the facts. It is so difficult to refrain from making scenes which, if the past could be recalled, might perhaps be found lacking in accuracy. With a character like Thomas Day, in particular, whose history surpasses the bounds of the credible, we find ourselves oozing amazement, like a sponge which has absorbed so much that it can retain no more but fairly drips. Certain scenes have the fascination which belongs rather to the abundance of fiction than to the sobriety of fact. For instance, we conjure up all the drama of poor Mrs. Edgeworth's daily life; her bewilderment, her loneliness, her despair, how she must have wondered whether any one really wanted machines to climb walls, and assured the gentlemen that turnips were better cut simply with a knife, and so blundered and floundered and been snubbed that she dreaded the almost daily arrival of the tall young man with his pompous, melancholy face, marked by the smallpox, his profusion of uncombed black hair, and his finical cleanliness of hands and person. He talked fast, fluently, incessantly, for hours at a time about philosophy and nature, and M. Rousseau. Yet it was her house; she had to see to his meals, and, though he ate as though he were half asleep, his appetite was enormous. But it was no use complaining to her husband. Edgeworth said, "She lamented about trifles." He went on to say: "The lamenting of a female with whom we live does not render home delightful." And then, with his obtuse open-mindedness, he asked her what she had to complain of? Did he ever leave her alone? In the five or six years of their married life he had slept from home not more than five or six times. Mr. Day could corroborate that. Mr. Day corroborated everything that Mr. Edgeworth said. He egged him on with his experiments. He told him to leave his son without education. He did not care a rap what the people of Henley said. In short, he was at the bottom of all the absurdities and extravagances which made Mrs. Edgeworth's life a burden to her.

Yet let us choose another scene—one of the last that poor Mrs. Edgeworth was to behold. She was returning from Lyons, and Mr. Day was her escort. A more singular figure, as he stood on the deck of the packet which took them to Dover, very tall, very upright, one finger in the breast of his coat, letting the wind blow his hair out, dressed absurdly, though in the height of fashion, wild, romantic, yet at the same time authoritative and pompous, could scarcely be imagined; and this strange creature, who loathed women, was in charge of a lady who was about to become a mother, had adopted two orphan girls, and had set himself to win the hand of Miss Elizabeth Sneyd by standing between boards for six hours daily in order to learn to dance. Now and again he pointed his toe with rigid precision; then, waking from the congenial dream into which the dark clouds, the flying waters, and the shadow of England upon the horizon had thrown him, he rapped out an order in the smart, affected tones of a man of the world. The sailors stared, but they obeyed. There was something sincere about him, something proudly indifferent to what you thought; yes, something comforting and humane, too, so that Mrs. Edgeworth for her part was determined never to laugh at him again. But men were strange; life was difficult, and with a sigh of bewilderment, perhaps of relief, poor Mrs. Edgeworth landed at Dover, was brought to bed of a daughter, and died.

Day meanwhile proceeded to Lichfield. Elizabeth Sneyd, of course, refused him—gave a great cry, people said; exclaimed that she had loved Day the blackguard, but hated Day the gentleman, and rushed from the room. And then, they said, a terrible thing happened. Mr. Day, in his rage, bethought him of the orphan, Sabrina Sydney, whom he had bred to be his wife; visited her at Sutton Coldfield; flew into a passion at the sight of her; fired a pistol at her skirts, poured melted sealing wax over her arms, and boxed her ears. "No; I could never have done that," Mr. Edgeworth used to say, when people described the scene. And whenever to the end of his life he thought of Thomas Day he fell silent. So great, so passionate, so inconsistent—his life had been a tragedy, and in thinking of his friend, the best friend he had ever had, Richard Edgeworth fell silent.

It is almost the only occasion upon which silence is recorded of him. To muse, to repent, to contemplate were foreign to his nature. His wife and friends and children are silhouetted with extreme vividness upon a broad disc of interminable chatter. Upon no other background could we realise so clearly the sharp fragment of his first wife, or the shades and depths which make up the character, at once humane and brutal, advanced and hidebound of the inconsistent philosopher, Thomas Day. But his power is not limited to people; landscapes, groups, societies seem, even as he describes them, to split off from him, to be projected away, so that we are able to run just ahead of him and anticipate his coming. They are brought out all the more vividly by the extreme incongruity which so often marks his comment and stamps his presence; they live with a peculiar beauty, fantastic, solemn, mysterious, in contrast with Edgeworth, who is none of these things. In particular, he brings before us a garden in Cheshire, the garden of a parsonage, an ancient but commodious parsonage.

One pushed through a white gate and found oneself in a grass court, small but well kept, with roses grow-

ing in the hedges and grapes hanging from the walls.
But what, in the name of wonder, were those objects in
the middle of the grass plot? Through the dusk of an
autumn evening there shone out an enormous white
globe. Round it at various distances were others of
different sizes—the planets and their satellites, it
seemed. But who could have placed them there, and
why? The house was silent; the windows shut; nobody was stirring. Then, furtively peeping from behind a curtain, appeared for a second the face of an
elderly man, handsome, dishevelled, distraught. It
vanished.

In some mysterious way, human beings inflict
their own vagaries upon nature. Moths and birds
must have flitted more silently through the little garden; over everything must have brooded the same fantastic peace. Then, red-faced, garrulous, inquisitive,
in burst Richard Lovell Edgeworth. He looked at the
globes; he satisfied himself that they were of "accurate
design and workmanlike construction". He knocked
at the door. He knocked and knocked. No one came.
At length, as his impatience was overcoming him,
slowly the latch was undone, gradually the door was
opened; a clergyman, neglected, unkempt, but still a
gentleman, stood before him. Edgeworth named himself, and they retired to a parlour littered with books
and papers and valuable furniture now fallen to decay.
At last, unable to control his curiosity any longer,
Edgeworth asked what were the globes in the garden?

Instantly the clergyman displayed extreme agitation. It was his son who had made them, he exclaimed; a boy of genius, a boy of the greatest industry, and of virtue and acquirements far beyond his age. But he had died. His wife had died. Edgeworth tried to turn the conversation, but in vain. The poor man rushed on passionately, incoherently about his son, his genius, his death. "It struck me that his grief had injured his understanding," said Edgeworth, and he was becoming more and more uncomfortable when the door opened and a girl of fourteen or fifteen, entering with a tea-tray in her hand, suddenly changed the course of his host's conversation. Indeed, she was beautiful; dressed in white; her nose a shade too prominent, perhaps—but no, her proportions were exquisitely right. "She is a scholar and an artist!" the clergyman exclaimed as she left the room. But why did she leave the room? If she was his daughter why did she not preside at the tea-table? Was she his mistress? Who was she? And why was the house in this state of litter and decay? Why was the front door locked? Why was the clergyman apparently a prisoner, and what was his secret story? Questions began to crowd into Edgeworth's head as he sat drinking his tea; but he could only shake his head and make one last reflection, "I feared that something was not right," as he shut the white wicket gate behind him, and left alone for ever in the untidy house among the planets and their satellites, the mad clergyman and the lovely girl.

II

LAETITIA PILKINGTON

Let us bother the librarian once again. Let us ask him to reach down, dust, and hand over to us that little brown book over there, the Memoirs of Mrs. Pilkington, three volumes bound in one, printed by Peter Hoey in Dublin, MDCCLXXVI. The deepest obscurity shades her retreat; the dust lies heavy on her tomb—one board is loose, that is to say, and nobody has read her since early in the last century when a reader, presumably a lady, whether disgusted by her obscenity or stricken by the hand of death, left off in the middle and marked her place with a faded list of goods and groceries. If ever a woman wanted a champion, it is obviously Laetitia Pilkington. Who then was she?

Can you imagine a very extraordinary cross between Moll Flanders and Lady Ritchie, between a rolling and rollicking woman of the town and a lady of breeding and refinement? Laetitia Pilkington (1712-1759) was something of the sort—shady, shifty, adventurous, and yet, like Thackeray's daughter, like Miss Mitford, like Madame de Sévigné and Jane Austen and Maria Edgeworth, so imbued with the old traditions of her sex that she wrote, as ladies talk, to give pleasure. Throughout her *Memoirs*, we can never forget that it is her wish to entertain, her unhappy fate to sob. Dabbing her eyes and controlling her anguish, she begs us to forgive an odious breach of manners which only the suffering of a lifetime, the intolerable persecutions of Mr. P——n, the malignant, she must say the h——h, spite of Lady C——t can excuse. For who should know better than the Earl of Killmallock's great-granddaughter that it is the part of a lady to hide her sufferings? Thus Laetitia is in the great tradition of English women of letters. It is her duty to entertain; it is her instinct to conceal. Still, though her room near the Royal Exchange is threadbare, and the table is spread with old play-bills instead of a cloth, and the butter is served in a shoe, and Mr. Worsdale has used the teapot to fetch small beer that very morning, still she presides, still she entertains. Her language is a trifle coarse, perhaps. But who taught her English? The great Doctor Swift.

In all her wanderings, which were many and in her failings, which were great, she looked back to those early Irish days when Swift had pinched her into propriety of speech. He had beaten her for fumbling at a drawer: he had daubed her cheeks with burnt cork to try her temper; he had bade her pull off her shoes and stockings and stand against the wainscot and let him measure her. At first she had refused; then she had yielded. "Why," said the Dean, "I suspected you had either broken Stockings or foul toes, and in either case should have delighted to expose you." Three feet two inches was all she measured, he declared, though, as Laetitia complained, the weight of Swift's hand on her head had made her shrink to half her size.

But she was foolish to complain. Probably she owed her intimacy to that very fact—she was only three feet two. Swift had lived a lifetime among the giants; now there was a charm in dwarfs. He took the little creature into his library. "'Well,' said he, 'I have brought you here to show you all the Money I got when I was in the Ministry, but don't steal any of it.' 'I won't, indeed, Sir,' said I; so he opened a Cabinet, and showed me a whole parcel of empty drawers. 'Bless me,' says he, 'the Money is flown.'" There was a charm in her surprise; there was a charm in her humility. He could beat her and bully her, make her shout when he was deaf, force her husband to drink the lees of the wine, pay their cab fares, stuff guineas into a piece of gingerbread, and relent surprisingly, as if there were something grimly pleasing to him in the thought of so foolish a midget setting up to have a life and a mind of her own. For with Swift she was herself; it was the effect of his genius. She had to pull off her stockings if he told her to. So, though his satire terrified her, and she found it highly unpleasant to dine at the Deanery and see him watching, in the great glass which hung before him for that purpose, the butler stealing beer at the sideboard, she knew that it was a privilege to walk with him in his garden; to hear him talk of Mr. Pope and quote Hudibras; and then be hustled back in the rain to save coach hire, and then to sit chatting in the parlour with Mrs. Brent, the housekeeper, about the Dean's oddity and charity, and how the sixpence he saved on the coach he gave to the lame old man who sold gingerbread at the corner, while the Dean dashed up the front stairs and down the back so violently that she was afraid he would fall and hurt himself.

But memories of great men are no infallible specific. They fall upon the race of life like beams from a lighthouse. They flash, they shock, they reveal, they vanish. To remember Swift was of little avail to Laetitia when the troubles of life came thick about her. Mr. Pilkington left her for Widow W—rr—n. Her father—her dear father—died. The sheriff's officers insulted her. She was deserted in an empty house with two children to provide for. The tea chest was secured, the garden gate locked, and the bills left unpaid. And still she was young and attractive and gay, with an inordinate passion for scribbling verses and an incredible hunger for reading books. It was this that was her undoing. The book was fascinating and the hour late. The gentleman would not lend it, but would stay till she had finished. They sat in her bedroom. It was highly indiscreet, she owned. Suddenly twelve watchmen broke through the kitchen window, and Mr. Pilkington appeared with a cambric handkerchief tied about his neck. Swords were drawn and heads broken. As for her excuse, how could one expect Mr. Pilkington and the twelve watchmen to believe that? Only reading! Only sitting up late to finish a new book! Mr. Pilkington and the watchmen interpreted the situation

[171]

as such men would. But lovers of learning, she is persuaded, will understand her passion and deplore its consequences.

And now what was she to do? Reading had played her false, but still she could write. Ever since she could form her letters, indeed, she had written, with incredible speed and considerable grace, odes, addresses, apostrophes to Miss Hoadley, to the Recorder of Dublin, to Dr. Delville's place in the country. "Hail, happy Delville, blissful seat!" "Is there a man whose fixed and steady gaze———"—the verses flowed without the slightest difficulty on the slightest occasion. Now, therefore, crossing to England, she set up, as her advertisement had it, to write letters upon any subject, except the law, for twelve pence ready money, and no trust given. She lodged opposite White's Chocolate House, and there, in the evening, as she watered her flowers on the leads, the noble gentlemen in the window across the road drank her health, sent her over a bottle of burgundy; and later she heard old Colonel —— crying, "Poke after me, my lord, poke after me," as he shepherded the D—— of M—lb—gh up her dark stairs. That lovely gentleman, who honoured his title by wearing it, kissed her, complimented her, opened his pocket-book, and left her with a banknote for fifty pounds upon Sir Francis Child. Such tributes stimulated her pen to astonishing outbursts of impromptu gratitude. If, on the other hand, a gentleman refused to buy or a lady hinted impropriety, this same flowery pen writhed and twisted in agonies of

hate and vituperation. "Had I said that your F——r
died Blaspheming the Almighty", one of her accusa-
tions begins, but the end is unprintable. Great ladies
were accused of every depravity, and the clergy, unless their taste in poetry was above reproach, suffered
an incessant castigation. Mr. Pilkington, she never
forgot, was a clergyman.

Slowly but surely the Earl of Killmallock's great-
granddaughter descended in the social scale. From St.
James's Street and its noble benefactors she migrated
to Green Street to lodge with Lord Stair's *valet de
chambre* and his wife, who washed for persons of distinction. She, who had dallied with dukes, was glad
for company's sake to take a hand at quadrille with
footmen and laundresses and Grub Street writers, who,
as they drank porter, sipped green tea, and smoked tobacco, told stories of the utmost scurrility about their
masters and mistresses. The spiciness of their conversation made amends for the vulgarity of their manners. From them Laetitia picked up those anecdotes
of the great which sprinkled her pages with dashes and
served her purpose when subscribers failed and landladies grew insolent. Indeed, it was a hard life—to
trudge to Chelsea in the snow wearing nothing but a
chintz gown and be put off with a beggarly half-crown
by Sir Hans Sloane; next to tramp to Ormond Street
and extract two guineas from the odious Dr. Meade,
which, in her glee, she tossed in the air and lost in a
crack of the floor; to be insulted by footmen; to sit
down to a dish of boiling water because her land-

[173]

lady must not guess that a pinch of tea was beyond her means. Twice on moonlight nights, with the lime trees in flower, she wandered in St. James's Park and contemplated suicide in Rosamond's Pond. Once, musing among the tombs in Westminster Abbey, the door was locked on her, and she had to spend the night in the pulpit wrapped in a carpet from the Communion Table to protect herself from the assaults of rats. "I long to listen to the young-ey'd cherubims!" she exclaimed. But a very different fate was in store for her. In spite of Mr. Colley Cibber, and Mr. Richardson, who supplied her first with gilt-edged notepaper and then with baby linen, those harpies, her landladies, after drinking her ale, devouring her lobsters, and failing often for years at a time to comb their hair, succeeded in driving Swift's friend, and the Earl's great-granddaughter, to be imprisoned with common debtors in the Marshalsea.

Bitterly she cursed her husband who had made her a lady of adventure instead of what nature intended, "a harmless household dove". More and more wildly she ransacked her brains for anecdotes, memories, scandals, views about the bottomless nature of the sea, the inflammable character of the earth—anything that would fill a page and earn her a guinea. She remembered that she had eaten plovers' eggs with Swift. "Here, Hussey," said he, "is a Plover's egg. King William used to give crowns apiece for them. . . ." Swift never laughed, she remembered. He used to suck in his cheeks instead of laughing. And what else could she remember? A great many gentlemen, a great many landladies; how the window was thrown up when her father died, and her sister came downstairs with the sugar-basin, laughing. All had been bitterness and struggle, except that she had loved Shakespeare, known Swift, and kept through all the shifts and shades of an adventurous career a gay spirit, something of a lady's breeding, and the gallantry which, at the end of her short life, led her to crack her joke and enjoy her duck with death at her heart and duns at her pillow.

III

MISS ORMEROD [1]

The trees stood massively in all their summer foliage spotted and grouped upon a meadow which sloped gently down from the big white house. There were unmistakable signs of the year 1835 both in the trees and in the sky, for modern trees are not nearly so voluminous as these ones, and the sky of those days had a kind of pale diffusion in its texture which was different from the more concentrated tone of the skies we know.

Mr. George Ormerod stepped from the drawing-room window of Sedbury House, Gloucestershire, wearing a tall furry hat and white trousers strapped under his instep; he was closely, though deferentially, fol-

[1] Founded upon the Life of Eleanor Ormerod, by Robert Wallace Murray. 1904.

[175]

lowed by a lady wearing a yellow-spotted dress over a crinoline, and behind her, singly and arm in arm, came nine children in nankeen jackets and long white drawers. They were going to see the water let out of a pond.

The youngest child, Eleanor, a little girl with a pale face, rather elongated features, and black hair, was left by herself in the drawing-room, a large sallow apartment with pillars, two chandeliers, for some reason enclosed in holland bags, and several octagonal tables some of inlaid wood and others of greenish malachite. At one of these little Eleanor Ormerod was seated in a high chair.

"Now, Eleanor," said her mother, as the party assembled for the expedition to the pond, "here are some pretty beetles. Don't touch the glass. Don't get down from your chair, and when we come back little George will tell you all about it."

So saying, Mrs. Ormerod placed a tumbler of water containing about half a dozen great water grubs in the middle of the malachite table, at a safe distance from the child, and followed her husband down the slope of old-fashioned turf towards a cluster of extremely old-fashioned sheep; opening, directly she stepped on to the terrace, a tiny parasol of bottle green silk with a bottle green fringe, though the sky was like nothing so much as a flock bed covered with a counterpane of white dimity.

The plump pale grubs gyrated slowly round and round in the tumbler. So simple an entertainment must surely soon have ceased to satisfy. Surely Eleanor would shake the tumbler, upset the grubs, and scramble down from her chair. Why, even a grown person can hardly watch those grubs crawling down the glass wall, then floating to the surface, without a sense of boredom not untinged with disgust. But the child sat perfectly still. Was it her custom, then, to be entertained by the gyrations of grubs? Her eyes were reflective, even critical. But they shone with increasing excitement. She beat one hand upon the edge of the table. What was the reason? One of the grubs had ceased to float: he lay at the bottom; the rest, descending, proceeded to tear him to pieces.

"And how has little Eleanor enjoyed herself?" asked Mr. Ormerod, in rather a deep voice, stepping into the room and with a slight air of heat and of fatigue upon his face.

"Papa," said Eleanor, almost interrupting her father in her eagerness to impart her observation, "I saw one of the grubs fall down and the rest came and ate him!"

"Nonsense, Eleanor," said Mr. Ormerod. "You are not telling the truth." He looked severely at the tumbler in which the beetles were still gyrating as before.

"Papa, it was true!"

"Eleanor, little girls are not allowed to contradict their fathers," said Mrs. Ormerod, coming in through the window, and closing her green parasol with a snap.

"Let this be a lesson," Mr. Ormerod began, signing to the other children to approach, when the door opened, and the servant announced,

[177]

"Captain Fenton."

Captain Fenton "was at times thought to be tedious in his recurrence to the charge of the Scots Greys in which he had served at the battle of Waterloo."

But what is this crowd gathered round the door of the George Hotel in Chepstow? A faint cheer rises from the bottom of the hill. Up comes the mail coach, horses steaming, panels mud-splashed. "Make way! Make way!" cries the ostler and the vehicle dashes into the courtyard, pulls up sharp before the door. Down jumps the coachman, the horses are led off, and a fine team of spanking greys is harnessed with incredible speed in their stead. Upon all this—coachman, horses, coach, and passengers—the crowd looked with gaping admiration every Wednesday evening all through the year. But to-day, the twelfth of March, 1852, as the coachman settled his rug, and stretched his hands for the reins, he observed that instead of being fixed upon him, the eyes of the people of Chepstow darted this way and that. Heads were jerked. Arms flung out. Here a hat swooped in a semi-circle. Off drove the coach almost unnoticed. As it turned the corner all the outside passengers craned their necks, and one gentleman rose to his feet and shouted, "There! there! there!" before he was bowled into eternity. It was an insect—a red-winged insect. Out the people of Chepstow poured into the high road; down the hill they ran; always the insect flew in front of them; at length by Chepstow Bridge a young man, throwing his bandanna over the blade of an oar, captured it alive and presented it to a highly respectable elderly gentleman who now came puffing upon the scene—Samuel Budge, doctor, of Chepstow. By Samuel Budge it was presented to Miss Ormerod; by her sent to a professor at Oxford. And he, declaring it "a fine specimen of the rose underwinged locust" added the gratifying information that it "was the first of the kind to be captured so far west."

And so, at the age of twenty-four Miss Eleanor Ormerod was thought the proper person to receive the gift of a locust.

When Eleanor Ormerod appeared at archery meetings and croquet tournaments young men pulled their whiskers and young ladies looked grave. It was so difficult to make friends with a girl who could talk of nothing but black beetles and earwigs—"Yes, that's what she likes, isn't it queer?—Why, the other day Ellen, Mama's maid, heard from Jane, who's under-kitchenmaid at Sedbury House, that Eleanor tried to boil a beetle in the kitchen saucepan and he wouldn't die, and swam round and round, and she got into a terrible state and sent the groom all the way to Gloucester to fetch chloroform—all for an insect, my dear!—and she gives the cottagers shillings to collect beetles for her—and she spends hours in her bedroom cutting them up—and she climbs trees like a boy to find wasps' nests—oh, you can't think what they don't say about her in the village—for she does look so odd, dressed anyhow, with that great big nose and those bright little eyes, so like a caterpillar herself, I always think—but of course she's wonderfully clever and very good, too, both of them. Georgiana has a lending library for the cottagers, and Eleanor never misses a service—but there she is—that short pale girl in the large bonnet. Do go and talk to her, for I'm sure I'm too stupid, but you'd find plenty to say—" But neither Fred nor Arthur, Henry nor William found anything to say—

". . . probably the lecturer would have been equally well pleased had none of her own sex put in an appearance."

This comment upon a lecture delivered in the year 1889 throws some light, perhaps, upon archery meetings in the 'fifties.

It being nine o'clock on a February night some time about 1862 all the Ormerods were in the library; Mr. Ormerod making architectural designs at a table; Mrs. Ormerod lying on a sofa making pencil drawings upon grey paper; Eleanor making a model of a snake to serve as a paper weight; Georgiana making a copy of the font in Tidenham Church; some of the others examining books with beautiful illustrations; while at intervals someone rose, unlocked the wire book case, took down a volume for instruction or entertainment, and perused it beneath the chandelier.

Mr. Ormerod required complete silence for his studies. His word was law, even to the dogs, who, in the absence of their master, instinctively obeyed the eldest male person in the room. Some whispered colloquy there might be between Mrs. Ormerod and her daughters—

"The draught under the pew was really worse than ever this morning, Mama—"

"And we could only unfasten the latch in the chancel because Eleanor happened to have her ruler with her—"

"—hm—m—m. Dr. Armstrong—Hm—m—m—"

"—Anyhow things aren't as bad with us as they are at Kinghampton. They say Mrs. Briscoe's Newfoundland dog follows her right up to the chancel rails when she takes the sacrament—"

"And the turkey is still sitting on its eggs in the pulpit."

—"The period of incubation for a turkey is between three and four weeks"—said Eleanor, thoughtfully looking up from her cast of the snake and forgetting, in the interest of her subject, to speak in a whisper.

"Am I to be allowed no peace in my own house?" Mr. Ormerod exclaimed angrily, rapping with his ruler on the table, upon which Mrs. Ormerod half shut one eye and squeezed a little blob of Chinese white on to her high light, and they remained silent until the servants came in, when everyone, with the exception of Mrs. Ormerod, fell on their knees. For she, poor lady, suffered from a chronic complaint and left the family party forever a year or two later, when the green sofa was moved into the corner, and the drawings given to her nieces in memory of her. But Mr. Ormerod went on making architectural drawings at nine p.m. every night (save on Sundays when he read a sermon) until he too lay upon the green sofa, which had not been used since Mrs. Ormerod lay there, but still looked much the same. "We deeply felt the happiness of ministering to his welfare," Miss Ormerod wrote, "for he would not hear of our leaving him for even twenty-four hours and he objected to visits from my brothers excepting occasionally for a short time. They, not being used to the gentle ways necessary for an aged invalid, worried him . . . the Thursday following, the 9th October, 1873, he passed gently away at the mature age of eighty-seven years." Oh, graves in country churchyards—respectable burials—mature old gentlemen—D.C.L., LL.D., F.R.S., F.S.A.—lots of letters come after your names, but lots of women are buried with you!

There remained the Hessian Fly and the Bot—mysterious insects! Not, one would have thought, among God's most triumphant creations, and yet—if you see them under a microscope!—the Bot, obese, globular, obscene; the Hessian, booted, spurred, whiskered, cadaverous. Next slip under the glass an innocent grain; behold it pock-marked and livid; or take this strip of hide, and note those odious pullulating lumps —well, what does the landscape look like then?

The only palatable object for the eye to rest on in acres of England is a lump of Paris Green. But English people won't use microscopes; you can't make them use Paris Green either—or if they do, they let it drip. Dr. Ritzema Bos is a great stand-by. For they won't take a woman's word. And indeed, though for the sake of the Ox Warble one must stretch a point, there are matters, questions of stock infestation, things one has to go into—things a lady doesn't even like to see, much less discuss, in print—"these, I say, I intend to leave entirely to the Veterinary surgeons. My brother —oh, he's dead now—a very good man—for whom I collected wasps' nests—lived at Brighton and wrote about wasps—he, I say, wouldn't let me learn anatomy, never liked me to do more than take sections of teeth."

Ah, but Eleanor, the Bot and the Hessian have more power over you than Mr. Edward Ormerod himself. Under the microscope you clearly perceive that these insects have organs, orifices, excrement; they do, most emphatically, copulate. Escorted on the one side by the Bos or Warble, on the other by the Hessian Fly, Miss Ormerod advanced statelily, if slowly, into the open. Never did her features show more sublime than when lit up by the candour of her avowal. "This is excrement; these, though Ritzema Bos is positive to the contrary, are the generative organs of the male. I've proved it." Upon her head the hood of Edinburgh most fitly descended; pioneer of purity even more than of Paris Green.

"If you're sure I'm not in your way," said Miss Lipscomb unstrapping her paint box and planting her tripod firmly in the path, "—I'll try to get a picture of those lovely hydrangeas against the sky—What flowers you have in Penzance!"

The market gardener crossed his hands on his hoe,

slowly twined a piece of bass round his finger, looked at the sky, said something about the sun, also about the prevalence of lady artists, and then, with a nod of his head, observed sententiously that it was to a lady that he owed everything he had.

"Ah?" said Miss Lipscomb, flattered, but already much occupied with her composition.

"A lady with a queer-sounding name," said Mr. Pascoe, "but that's the lady I've called my little girl after —I don't think there's such another in Christendom."

Of course it was Miss Ormerod, equally of course Miss Lipscomb was the sister of Miss Ormerod's family doctor; and so she did no sketching that morning, but left with a handsome bunch of grapes instead—for every flower had drooped, ruin had stared him in the face—he had written, not believing one bit what they told him—to the lady with the queer name, back there came a book "In-ju-ri-ous In-sects," with the page turned down, perhaps by her very hand, also a letter which he kept at home under the clock, but he knew every word by heart, since it was due to what she said there that he wasn't a ruined man—and the tears ran down his face and Miss Lipscomb, clearing a space on the lodging-house table, wrote the whole story to her brother.

"The prejudice against Paris Green certainly seems to be dying down," said Miss Ormerod when she read it.—"But now," she sighed rather heavily, being no longer young and much afflicted with the gout, "now it's the sparrows."

[184]

One might have thought that *they* would have left her alone—innocent dirt-grey birds, taking more than their share of the breakfast crumbs, otherwise inoffensive. But once you look through a microscope—once you see the Hessian and the Bot as they really are—there's no peace for an elderly lady pacing her terrace on a fine May morning. For example, why, when there are crumbs enough for all, do only the sparrows get them? Why not swallows or martins? Why—oh, here come the servants for prayers—

"Forgive us our trespasses as we forgive them that trespass against us. . . . For thine is the Kingdom and the power and the glory, for ever and ever. Amen—"

"The Times, ma'am—"

"Thank you, Dixon. . . . The Queen's birthday! We must drink her Majesty's health in the old white port, Dixon. Home Rule—tut—tut—tut. All that madman Gladstone. My father would have thought the world was coming to an end, and I'm not at all sure that it isn't. I must talk to Dr. Lipscomb—"

Yet all the time in the tail of her eye she saw myriads of sparrows, and retiring to the study proclaimed in a pamphlet of which 36,000 copies were gratuitously distributed that the sparrow is a pest.

"When he eats an insect," she said to her sister Georgiana, "which isn't often, it's one of the few insects that one wants to keep—one of the very few," she added with a touch of acidity natural to one whose investigations have all tended to the discredit of the insect race.

[185]

"But there'll be some very unpleasant consequences to face," she concluded—"Very unpleasant indeed."

Happily the port was now brought in, the servants assembled; and Miss Ormerod, rising to her feet, gave the toast "Her Blessed Majesty." She was extremely loyal, and moreover she liked nothing better than a glass of her father's old white port. She kept his pigtail, too, in a box.

Such being her disposition it went hard with her to analyse the sparrow's crop, for the sparrow she felt, symbolises something of the homely virtue of English domestic life, and to proclaim it stuffed with deceit was disloyal to much that she, and her fathers before her, held dear. Sure enough the clergy—the Rev. J. E. Walker—denounced her for her brutality; "God Save the Sparrow!" exclaimed the Animal's Friend; and Miss Carrington, of the Humanitarian League, replied in a leaflet described by Miss Ormerod as "spirity, discourteous, and inaccurate."

"Well," said Miss Ormerod to her sister, "it did me no harm before to be threatened to be shot at, also hanged in effigy, and other little attentions."

"Still it was very disagreeable, Eleanor—more disagreeable I believe, to me than to you," said Georgiana. Soon Georgiana died. She had however finished the beautiful series of insect diagrams at which she worked every morning in the dining-room and they were presented to Edinburgh University. But Eleanor was never the same woman after that.

Dear forest fly—flour moths—weevils—grouse and

[186]

cheese flies—beetles—foreign correspondents—eel worms—ladybirds—wheat midges—resignation from the Royal Agricultural Society—gall mites—boot beetles—Announcement of honorary degree to be conferred—feelings of appreciation and anxiety—paper on wasps—last annual report warnings of serious illness—proposed pension—gradual loss of strength—Finally Death.

That is life, so they say.

"It does no good to keep people waiting for an answer," sighed Miss Ormerod, "though I don't feel as able as I did since that unlucky accident at Waterloo. And no one realises what the strain of the work is—often I'm the only lady in the room, and the gentlemen so learned, though I've always found them most helpful, most generous in every way. But I'm growing old, Miss Hartwell, that's what it is. That's what led me to be thinking of this difficult matter of flour infestation in the middle of the road so that I didn't see the horse until he had poked his nose into my ear. . . . Then there's this nonsense about a pension. What could possess Mr. Barron to think of such a thing? I should feel inexpressibly lowered if I accepted a pension. Why, I don't altogether like writing LL.D. after my name, though Georgie would have liked it. All I ask is to be let go on in my own quiet way. Now where is Messrs. Langridge's sample? We must take that first. 'Gentlemen, I have examined your sample and find . . .' "

"If any one deserves a thorough good rest it's you, Miss Ormerod," said Dr. Lipscomb, who had grown a little white over the ears. "I should say the farmers of England ought to set up a statue to you, bring offerings of corn and wine—make you a kind of Goddess, eh—what was her name?"

"Not a very shapely figure for a Goddess," said Miss Ormerod with a little laugh. "I should enjoy the wine though. You're not going to cut me off my one glass of port surely?"

"You must remember," said Dr. Lipscomb, shaking his head, "how much your life means to others."

"Well, I don't know about that," said Miss Ormerod, pondering a little. "To be sure, I've chosen my epitaph. 'She introduced Paris Green into England,' and there might be a word or two about the Hessian fly—that, I do believe, was a good piece of work."

"No need to think about epitaphs yet," said Dr. Lipscomb.

"Our lives are in the hands of the Lord," said Miss Ormerod simply.

Dr. Lipscomb bent his head and looked out of the window. Miss Ormerod remained silent.

"English entomologists care little or nothing for objects of practical importance," she exclaimed suddenly. "Take this question of flour infestation—I can't say how many grey hairs that hasn't grown me."

"Figuratively speaking, Miss Ormerod," said Dr. Lipscomb, for her hair was still raven black.

"Well, I do believe all good work is done in concert," Miss Ormerod continued. "It is often a great comfort to me to think that."

"It's beginning to rain," said Dr. Lipscomb. "How will your enemies like that, Miss Ormerod?"

"Hot or cold, wet or dry, insects always flourish!" cried Miss Ormerod, energetically sitting up in bed.

"Old Miss Ormerod is dead," said Mr. Drummond, opening The Times on Saturday, July 20th, 1901.

"Old Miss Ormerod?" asked Mrs. Drummond.

Jane Austen

It is probable that if Miss Cassandra Austen had had her way, we should have had nothing of Jane Austen's except her novels. To her elder sister alone did she write freely; to her alone she confided her hopes and, if rumour is true, the one great disappointment of her life; but when Miss Cassandra Austen grew old, and the growth of her sister's fame made her suspect that a time might come when strangers would pry and scholars speculate, she burnt, at great cost to herself, every letter that could gratify their curiosity, and spared only what she judged too trivial to be of interest.

Hence our knowledge of Jane Austen is derived from a little gossip, a few letters, and her books. As for the gossip, gossip which has survived its day is never despicable; with a little rearrangement it suits our purpose admirably. For example, Jane "is not at all pretty and very prim, unlike a girl of twelve . . . Jane is whimsical and affected," says little Philadelphia Austen of her cousin. Then we have Mrs. Mitford, who knew the Austens as girls and thought Jane "the prettiest, silliest, most affected, husband-hunting butterfly she ever remembers". Next, there is Miss Mitford's anonymous friend "who visits her now [and] says that she has stiffened into the most perpendicular, precise, taciturn piece of 'single blessedness' that ever existed, and that, until *Pride and Prejudice* showed what a precious gem was hidden in that unbending case, she was no more regarded in society than a poker or firescreen. . . . The case is very different now," the good lady goes on; "she is still a poker—but a poker of whom everybody is afraid. . . . A wit, a delineator of character, who does not talk is terrific indeed!" On the other side, of course, there are the Austens, a race little given to panegyric of themselves, but nevertheless, they say, her brothers "were very fond and very proud of her. They were attached to her by her talents, her virtues, and her engaging manners, and each loved afterwards to fancy a resemblance in some niece or daughter of his own to the dear sister Jane, whose perfect equal they yet never expected to see." Charming but perpendicular, loved at home but feared by strangers, biting of tongue but tender of heart—these contrasts are by no means incompatible, and when we turn to the novels we shall find ourselves stumbling there too over the same complexities in the writer.

To begin with, that prim little girl whom Philadelphia found so unlike a child of twelve, whimsical and affected, was soon to be the authoress of an astonishing and unchildish story, *Love and Freindship*,[1] which, incredible though it appears, was written at the age of fifteen. It was written, apparently, to amuse the schoolroom; one of the stories in the same book is dedicated with mock solemnity to her brother; another

---

[1] *Love and Freindship,* Chatto and Windus.

is neatly illustrated with water-colour heads by her sister. There are jokes which, one feels, were family property; thrusts of satire, which went home because all little Austens made mock in common of fine ladies who "sighed and fainted on the sofa".

Brothers and sisters must have laughed when Jane read out loud her last hit at the vices which they all abhorred. "I die a martyr to my grief for the loss of Augustius. One fatal swoon has cost me my life. Beware of Swoons, Dear Laura. . . . Run mad as often as you chuse, but do not faint. . . ." And on she rushed, as fast as she could write and quicker than she could spell, to tell the incredible adventures of Laura and Sophia, of Philander and Gustavus, of the gentleman who drove a coach between Edinburgh and Stirling every other day, of the theft of the fortune that was kept in the table drawer, of the starving mothers and the sons who acted Macbeth. Undoubtedly, the story must have roused the schoolroom to uproarious laughter. And yet, nothing is more obvious than that this girl of fifteen, sitting in her private corner of the common parlour, was writing not to draw a laugh from brother and sisters, and not for home consumption. She was writing for everybody, for nobody, for our age, for her own; in other words, even at that early age Jane Austen was writing. One hears it in the rhythm and shapeliness and severity of the sentences. "She was nothing more than a mere good tempered, civil, and obliging young woman; as such we could scarcely dislike her—she was only an

object of contempt." Such a sentence is meant to outlast the Christmas holidays. Spirited, easy, full of
fun, verging with freedom upon sheer nonsense,—
Love and Freindship is all that, but what is this note
which never merges in the rest, which sounds distinctly
and penetratingly all through the volume? It is the
sound of laughter. The girl of fifteen is laughing, in
her corner, at the world.

Girls of fifteen are always laughing. They laugh
when Mr. Binney helps himself to salt instead of
sugar. They almost die of laughing when old Mrs.
Tomkins sits down upon the cat. But they are crying
the moment after. They have no fixed abode from
which they see that there is something eternally laughable in human nature, some quality in men and women
that for ever excites our satire. They do not know
that Lady Greville who snubs, and poor Maria who
is snubbed, are permanent features of every ballroom.
But Jane Austen knew it from her birth upwards.
One of those fairies who perch upon cradles must
have taken her a flight through the world directly she
was born. When she was laid in the cradle again
she knew not only what the world looked like, but had
already chosen her kingdom. She had agreed that if
she might rule over that territory, she would covet no
other. Thus at fifteen she had few illusions about
other people and none about herself. Whatever she
writes is finished and turned and set in its relation,
not to the parsonage, but to the universe. She is impersonal; she is inscrutable. When the writer, Jane

Austen, wrote down in the most remarkable sketch in the book a little of Lady Greville's conversation, there is no trace of anger at the snub which the clergyman's daughter, Jane Austen, once received. Her gaze passes straight to the mark, and we know precisely where, upon the map of human nature, that mark is. We know because Jane Austen kept to her compact; she never trespassed beyond her boundaries. Never, even at the emotional age of fifteen, did she round upon herself in shame, obliterate a sarcasm in a spasm of compassion, or blur an outline in a mist of rhapsody. Spasms and rhapsodies, she seems to have said, pointing with her stick, end *there;* and the boundary line is perfectly distinct. But she does not deny that moons and mountains and castles exist—on the other side. She has even one romance of her own. It is for the Queen of Scots. She really admired her very much. "One of the first characters in the world," she called her, "a bewitching Princess whose only friend was then the Duke of Norfolk, and whose only ones now Mr. Whitaker, Mrs. Lefroy, Mrs. Knight and myself." With these words her passion is neatly circumscribed, and rounded with a laugh. It is amusing to remember in what terms the young Brontës wrote, not very much later, in their northern parsonage, about the Duke of Wellington.

The prim little girl grew up. She became "the prettiest, silliest, most affected husband-hunting butterfly" Mrs. Mitford ever remembered, and, incidentally, the authoress of a novel called *Pride and Prejudice,* which,

written stealthily under cover of a creaking door, lay
for many years unpublished. A little later, it is
thought, she began another story, *The Watsons*, and
being for some reason dissatisfied with it, left it unfinished. Unfinished and unsuccessful, it may throw
more light upon its writer's genius than the polished
masterpiece blazing in universal fame. Her difficulties
are more apparent in it, and the method she took to
overcome them less artfully concealed. To begin with,
the stiffness and the bareness of the first chapters prove
that she was one of those writers who lay their facts out
rather baldly in the first version and then go back and
back and back and cover them with flesh and atmosphere. How it would have been done we cannot say—
by what suppressions and insertions and artful devices.
But the miracle would have been accomplished; the dull
history of fourteen years of family life would have been
converted into another of those exquisite and apparently effortless introductions; and we should never
have guessed what pages of preliminary drudgery Jane
Austen forced her pen to go through. Here we perceive that she was no conjuror after all. Like other
writers, she had to create the atmosphere in which her
own peculiar genius could bear fruit. Here she fum-
bles; here she keeps us waiting. Suddenly, she has
done it; now things can happen as she likes things to
happen. The Edwards' are going to the ball. The
Tomlinsons' carriage is passing; she can tell us that
Charles is "being provided with his gloves and told to
keep them on"; Tom Musgrove retreats to a remote

corner with a barrel of oysters and is famously snug.
Her genius is freed and active. At once our senses
quicken; we are possessed with the peculiar intensity
which she alone can impart. But of what is it all composed? Of a ball in a country town; a few couples
meeting and taking hands in an assembly room; a
little eating and drinking; and for catastrophe, a boy
being snubbed by one young lady and kindly treated
by another. There is no tragedy and no heroism. Yet
for some reason the little scene is moving out of all
proportion to its surface solemnity. We have been
made to see that if Emma acted so in the ball-room,
how considerate, how tender, inspired by what sincerity
of feeling she would have shown herself in those graver
crises of life which, as we watch her, come inevitably
before our eyes. Jane Austen is thus a mistress of
much deeper emotion than appears upon the surface.
She stimulates us to supply what is not there. What
she offers is, apparently, a trifle, yet is composed of
something that expands in the reader's mind and
endows with the most enduring form of life scenes
which are outwardly trivial. Always the stress is laid
upon character. How, we are made to wonder, will
Emma behave when Lord Osborne and Tom Musgrove
make their call at five minutes before three, just as
Mary is bringing in the tray and the knife-case? It
is an extremely awkward situation. The young men
are accustomed to much greater refinement. Emma
may prove herself ill-bred, vulgar, a nonentity. The
turns and twists of the dialogue keep us on the tenter-

hooks of suspense. Our attention is half upon the present moment, half upon the future. And when, in the end, Emma behaves in such a way as to vindicate our highest hopes of her, we are moved as if we had been made witnesses of a matter of the highest importance. Here, indeed, in this unfinished and in the main inferior story are all the elements of Jane Austen's greatness. It has the permanent quality of literature. Think away the surface animation, the likeness to life, and there remains to provide a deeper pleasure, an exquisite discrimination of human values. Dismiss this too from the mind and one can dwell with extreme satisfaction upon the more abstract art which, in the ball-room scene, so varies the emotions and proportions the parts that it is possible to enjoy it, as one enjoys poetry, for itself, and not as a link which carries the story this way and that.

But the gossip says of Jane Austen that she was perpendicular, precise, and taciturn—"a poker of whom everybody is afraid". Of this too there are traces; she could be merciless enough; she is one of the most consistent satirists in the whole of literature. Those first angular chapters of *The Watsons* prove that hers was not a prolific genius; she had not, like Emily Brontë, merely to open the door to make herself felt. Humbly and gaily she collected the twigs and straws out of which the nest was to be made and placed them neatly together. The twigs and straws were a little dry and a little dusty in themselves. There was the big house and the little house; a tea party, a dinner

[198]

party, and an occasional picnic; life was hedged in by
valuable connections and adequate incomes; by muddy
roads, wet feet, and a tendency on the part of the
ladies to get tired; a little money supported it, a little
consequence, and the education commonly enjoyed by
upper middle-class families living in the country.
Vice, adventure, passion were left outside. But of
all this prosiness, of all this littleness, she evades nothing, and nothing is slurred over. Patiently and precisely she tells us how they "made no stop anywhere
till they reached Newbury, where a comfortable meal,
uniting dinner and supper, wound up the enjoyments
and fatigues of the day". Nor does she pay to conventions merely the tribute of lip homage; she believes
in them besides accepting them. When she is describing a clergyman, like Edmund Bertram, or a sailor, in
particular, she appears debarred by the sanctity of his
office from the free use of her chief tool, the comic
genius, and is apt therefore to lapse into decorous
panegyric or matter-of-fact description. But these are
exceptions; for the most part her attitude recalls the
anonymous ladies' ejaculation—"A wit, a delineator
of character, who does not talk is terrific indeed!"
She wishes neither to reform nor to annihilate; she
is silent; and that is terrific indeed. One after another
she creates her fools, her prigs, her worldlings, her Mr.
Collins', her Sir Walter Elliotts, her Mrs. Bennetts.
She encircles them with the lash of a whip-like phrase
which, as it runs round them, cuts out their silhouettes
for ever. But there they remain; no excuse is found

for them and no mercy shown them. Nothing remains
of Julia and Maria Bertram when she has done with
them; Lady Bertram is left "sitting and calling to Pug
and trying to keep him from the flower beds" eternally.
A divine justice is meted out; Dr. Grant, who begins
by liking his goose tender, ends by bringing on "apo-
plexy and death, by three great institutionary dinners
in one week". Sometimes it seems as if her creatures
were born merely to give Jane Austen the supreme delight of slicing their heads off. She is satisfied; she is
content; she would not alter a hair on anybody's head,
or move one brick or one blade of grass in a world
which provides her with such exquisite delight.

Nor, indeed, would we. For even if the pangs of
outraged vanity, or the heat of moral wrath, urged us
to improve away a world so full of spite, pettiness,
and folly, the task is beyond our powers. People are
like that—the girl of fifteen knew it; the mature
woman proves it. At this very moment some Lady
Bertram finds it almost too trying to keep Pug from
the flower beds; she sends Chapman to help Miss
Fanny, a little late. The discrimination is so perfect,
the satire so just that, consistent though it is, it almost
escapes our notice. No touch of pettiness, no hint of
spite, rouses us from our contemplation. Delight
strangely mingles with our amusement. Beauty illumines these fools.

That elusive quality is indeed often made up of
very different parts, which it needs a peculiar genius
to bring together. The wit of Jane Austen has for

partner the perfection of her taste. Her fool is a fool,
her snob is a snob, because he departs from the model
of sanity and sense which she has in mind, and conveys to us unmistakably even while she makes us
laugh. Never did any novelist make more use of an
impeccable sense of human values. It is against the
disc of an unerring heart, an unfailing good taste, an
almost stern morality, that she shows up those deviations from kindness, truth, and sincerity which are
among the most delightful things in English literature.
She depicts a Mary Crawford in her mixture of good
and bad entirely by this means. She lets her rattle
on against the clergy, or in favour of a baronetage
and ten thousand a year with all the ease and spirit
possible; but now and again she strikes one note of her
own, very quietly, but in perfect tune, and at once
all Mary Crawford's chatter, though it continues to
amuse, rings flat. Hence the depth, the beauty, the
complexity of her scenes. From such contrasts there
comes a beauty, a solemnity even which are not only as
remarkable as her wit, but an inseparable part of it.
In *The Watsons* she gives us a foretaste of this power;
she makes us wonder why an ordinary act of kindness,
as she describes it, becomes so full of meaning. In her
masterpieces, the same gift is brought to perfection.
Here is nothing out of the way; it is midday in Northamptonshire; a dull young man is talking to rather a
weakly young woman on the stairs as they go up to
dress for dinner, with housemaids passing. But, from
triviality, from commonplace, their words become sud-

denly full of meaning, and the moment for both one of the most memorable in their lives. It fills itself; it shines; it glows; it hangs before us, deep, trembling, serene for a second; next, the housemaid passes, and this drop in which all the happiness of life has collected gently subsides again to become part of the ebb and flow of ordinary existence.

What more natural then, with this insight into their profundity, than that Jane Austen should have chosen to write of the trivialities of day to day existence, of parties, picnics, and country dances? No "suggestions to alter her style of writing" from the Prince Regent or Mr. Clarke could tempt her; no romance, no adventure, no politics or intrigue could hold a candle to life on a country-house staircase as she saw it. Indeed, the Prince Regent and his librarian had run their heads against a very formidable obstacle; they were trying to tamper with an incorruptible conscience, to disturb an infallible discretion. The child who formed her sentences so finely when she was fifteen never ceased to form them, and never wrote for the Prince Regent or his Librarian, but for the world at large. She knew exactly what her powers were, and what material they were fitted to deal with as material should be dealt with by a writer, whose standard of finality was high. There were impressions that lay outside her province; emotions that by no stretch or artifice could be properly coated and covered by her own resources. For example, she could not make a girl talk enthusiastically of banners and chapels. She could not throw herself wholeheartedly into a romantic moment. She had all sorts of devices for evading scenes of passion. Nature and its beauties she approached in a sidelong way of her own. She describes a beautiful night without once mentioning the moon. Nevertheless, as we read the few formal phrases about "the brilliancy of an unclouded night and the contrast of the deep shade of the woods" the night is at once as "solemn, and soothing, and lovely" as she tells us, quite simply, that it was.

The balance of her gifts was singularly perfect. Among her finished novels there are no failures, and among her many chapters few that sink markedly below the level of the others. But, after all, she died at the age of forty-two. She died at the height of her powers. She was still subject to those changes which often make the final period of a writer's career the most interesting of all. Vivacious, irrepressible, gifted with an invention of great vitality, there can be no doubt that she would have written more, had she lived, and it is tempting to consider whether she would not have written differently. The boundaries were marked; moons, mountains, and castles lay on the other side. But was she not sometimes tempted to trespass for a minute? Was she not beginning, in her own gay and brilliant manner, to contemplate a little voyage of discovery?

Let us take *Persuasion*, the last completed novel, and look by its light at the books she might have written had she lived. There is a peculiar beauty and a peculiar dullness in *Persuasion*. The dullness is that which so often marks the transition stage between two different periods. The writer is a little bored. She has grown too familiar with the ways of her world; she no longer notes them freshly. There is an asperity in her comedy which suggests that she has almost ceased to be amused by the vanities of a Sir Walter or the snobbery of a Miss Elliott. The satire is harsh, and the comedy crude. She is no longer so freshly aware of the amusements of daily life. Her mind is not altogether on her object. But, while we feel that Jane Austen has done this before, and done it better, we also feel that she is trying to do something which she has never yet attempted. There is a new element in *Persuasion*, the quality, perhaps, that made Dr. Whewell fire up and insist that it was "the most beautiful of her works". She is beginning to discover that the world is larger, more mysterious, and more romantic than she had supposed. We feel it to be true of herself when she says of Anne: "She had been forced into prudence in her youth, she learned romance as she grew older—the natural sequel of an unnatural beginning". She dwells frequently upon the beauty and the melancholy of nature, upon the autumn where she had been wont to dwell upon the spring. She talks of the "influence so sweet and so sad of autumnal months in the country". She marks "the tawny leaves and withered hedges". "One does not love a place the less because one has suffered in it", she observes. But it is not only in a new sensibility to nature that we detect the change. Her attitude to life itself is altered. She is seeing it, for the greater part of the book, through the eyes of a woman who, unhappy herself, has a special sympathy for the happiness and unhappiness of others, which, until the very end, she is forced to comment upon in silence. Therefore the observation is less of facts and more of feelings than is usual. There is an expressed emotion in the scene at the concert and in the famous talk about woman's constancy which proves not merely the biographical fact that Jane Austen had loved, but the æsthetic fact that she was no longer afraid to say so. Experience, when it was of a serious kind, had to sink very deep, and to be thoroughly disinfected by the passage of time, before she allowed herself to deal with it in fiction. But now, in 1817, she was ready. Outwardly, too, in her circumstances, a change was imminent. Her fame had grown very slowly. "I doubt", wrote Mr. Austen Leigh, "whether it would be possible to mention any other author of note whose personal obscurity was so complete." Had she lived a few more years only, all that would have been altered. She would have stayed in London, dined out, lunched out, met famous people, made new friends, read, travelled, and carried back to the quiet country cottage a hoard of observations to feast upon at leisure.

And what effect would all this have had upon the six novels that Jane Austen did not write? She would not have written of crime, of passion, or of adventure. She would not have been rushed by the importunity

of publishers or the flattery of friends into sloven-
liness or insincerity. But she would have known more.
Her sense of security would have been shaken. Her
comedy would have suffered. She would have trusted
less (this is already perceptible in *Persuasion*) to dialogue and more to reflection to give us a knowledge
of her characters. Those marvellous little speeches
which sum up, in a few minutes' chatter, all that we
need in order to know an Admiral Croft or a Mrs.
Musgrove for ever, that shorthand, hit-or-miss method
which contains chapters of analysis and pyschology,
would have become too crude to hold all that she now
perceived of the complexity of human nature. She
would have devised a method, clear and composed as
ever, but deeper and more suggestive, for conveying
not only what people say, but what they leave unsaid;
not only what they are, but what life is. She would
have stood farther away from her characters, and seen
them more as a group, less as individuals. Her satire,
while it played less incessantly, would have been more
stringent and severe. She would have been the forerunner of Henry James and of Proust—but enough.
Vain are these speculations: the most perfect artist
among women, the writer whose books are immortal,
died "just as she was beginning to feel confidence in
her own success".

Modern Fiction

In making any survey, even the freest and loosest, of modern fiction it is difficult not to take it for granted that the modern practice of the art is somehow an improvement upon the old. With their simple tools and primitive materials, it might be said, Fielding did well and Jane Austen even better, but compare their opportunities with ours! Their masterpieces certainly have a strange air of simplicity. And yet the analogy between literature and the process, to choose an example, of making motor cars scarcely holds good beyond the first glance. It is doubtful whether in the course of the centuries, though we have learnt much about making machines, we have learnt anything about making literature. We do not come to write better; all that we can be said to do is to keep moving, now a little in this direction, now in that, but with a circular tendency should the whole course of the track be viewed from a sufficiently lofty pinnacle. It need scarcely be said that we make no claim to stand, even momentarily, upon that vantage ground. On the flat, in the crowd, half blind with dust, we look back with envy to those happier warriors, whose battle is won and whose achievements wear so serene an air of accomplishment that we can scarcely refrain from whispering that the fight was not so fierce for them as for us. It is for the historian of literature to decide; for him to say if we are now beginning or ending or standing in the middle of a great period of prose fiction, for down in the plain little is visible. We only know that certain gratitudes and hostilities inspire us; that certain paths seem to lead to fertile land, others to the dust and the desert; and of this perhaps it may be worth while to attempt some account.

Our quarrel, then, is not with the classics, and if we speak of quarrelling with Mr. Wells, Mr. Bennett, and Mr. Galsworthy it is partly that by the mere fact of their existence in the flesh their work has a living, breathing, every-day imperfection which bids us take what liberties with it we choose. But it is also true that, while we thank them for a thousand gifts, we reserve our unconditional gratitude for Mr. Hardy, for Mr. Conrad, and in a much lesser degree for the Mr. Hudson, of *The Purple Land*, *Green Mansions*, and *Far Away and Long Ago*. Mr. Wells, Mr. Bennett, and Mr. Galsworthy have excited so many hopes and disappointed them so persistently that our gratitude largely takes the form of thanking them for having shown us what they might have done but have not done; what we certainly could not do, but as certainly, perhaps, do not wish to do. No single phrase will sum up the charge or grievance which we have to bring against a mass of work so large in its volume and embodying so many qualities, both admirable and the reverse. If we tried to formulate our meaning in one word we should say that these three writers are materialists. It is because they are concerned not with the spirit but with the body that they have disappointed us, and left us with the feeling that the sooner English fiction turns its back upon them, as politely as may be, and marches, if only into the desert, the better for its soul. Naturally, no single word reaches the centre of three separate targets. In the case of Mr. Wells it falls notably wide of the mark. And yet even with him it indicates to our thinking the fatal alloy in his genius, the great clod of clay that has got itself mixed up with the purity of his inspiration. But Mr. Bennett is perhaps the worst culprit of the three, inasmuch as he is by far the best workman. He can make a book so well constructed and solid in its craftsmanship that it is difficult for the most exacting of critics to see through what chink or crevice decay can creep in. There is not so much as a draught between the frames of the windows, or a crack in the boards. And yet—if life should refuse to live there? That is a risk which the creator of *The Old Wives' Tale*, George Cannon, Edwin Clayhanger, and hosts of other figures, may well claim to have surmounted. His characters live abundantly, even unexpectedly, but it remains to ask how do they live, and what do they live for? More and more they seem to us, deserting even the well-built villa in the Five Towns, to spend their time in some softly padded first-class railway carriage, pressing bells and buttons innumerable; and the destiny to which they travel so luxuriously becomes more and more unquestionably an eternity of bliss spent in the very best hotel in Brighton. It can scarcely be said of Mr. Wells that he is a materialist in the sense that he takes too much delight in the solidity of his fabric. His mind is too generous in its sympathies to allow him to spend much time in making things shipshape and substantial. He is a materialist from sheer goodness of heart, taking upon his shoulders the work that ought to have been discharged by Government officials, and in the plethora of his ideas and facts scarcely having leisure to realise, or forgetting to think important, the crudity and coarseness of his human beings. Yet what more damaging criticism can there be both of his earth and of his Heaven than that they are to be inhabited here and hereafter by his Joans and his Peters? Does not the inferiority of their natures tarnish whatever institutions and ideals may be provided for them by the generosity of their creator? Nor, profoundly though we respect the integrity and humanity of Mr. Galsworthy, shall we find what we seek in his pages.

If we fasten, then, one label on all these books, on which is one word materialists, we mean by it that they write of unimportant things; that they spend immense skill and immense industry making the trivial and the transitory appear the true and the enduring.

We have to admit that we are exacting, and, further, that we find it difficult to justify our discontent by explaining what it is that we exact. We frame our question differently at different times. But it reappears most persistently as we drop the finished novel on the crest of a sigh—Is it worth while? What is the point of it all? Can it be that owing to one of those little deviations which the human spirit seems to make from time to time Mr. Bennett has come down with his magnificent apparatus for catching life just an inch or two on the wrong side? Life escapes; and perhaps without life nothing else is worth while. It is a confession of vagueness to have to make use of such a figure as this, but we scarcely better the matter by speaking, as critics are prone to do, of reality. Admitting the vagueness which afflicts all criticism of novels, let us hazard the opinion that for us at this moment the form of fiction most in vogue more often misses than secures the thing we seek. Whether we call it life or spirit, truth or reality, this, the essential thing, has moved off, or on, and refuses to be contained any longer in such ill-fitting vestments as we provide. Nevertheless, we go on perseveringly, conscientiously, constructing our two and thirty chapters after a design which more and more ceases to resemble the vision in our minds. So much of the enormous labour of proving the solidity, the likeness to life, of the story is not merely labour thrown away but labour misplaced to the extent of obscuring and blotting out the light of the conception. The writer seems constrained, not by his own free will but by some powerful and unscrupulous tyrant who has him in thrall to provide a plot, to provide comedy, tragedy, love, interest, and an air of probability embalming the whole so impeccable that if all his figures were to come to life they would find themselves dressed down to the last button of their coats in the fashion of the hour. The tyrant is obeyed; the novel is done to a turn. But sometimes, more and more often as time goes by, we suspect a momentary doubt, a spasm of rebellion, as the pages fill themselves in the customary way. Is life like this? Must novels be like this?

Look within and life, it seems, is very far from being "like this". Examine for a moment an ordinary mind on an ordinary day. The mind receives a myriad impressions—trivial, fantastic, evanescent, or engraved with the sharpness of steel. From all sides they come, an incessant shower of innumerable atoms; and as they fall, as they shape themselves into the life of Monday or Tuesday, the accent falls differently from of old; the moment of importance came not here but there; so that if a writer were a free man and not a slave, if he could write what he chose, not what he must, if he could base his work upon his own feeling and not upon convention, there would be no plot, no comedy, no tragedy, no love interest or catastrophe in the accepted style, and perhaps not a single button sewn on as the Bond Street tailors would have it. Life is not a series of gig lamps symmetrically arranged; but a luminous halo, a semi-transparent envelope surrounding us from the beginning of consciousness to the end. Is it not the task of the nov-

elist to convey this varying, this unknown and uncir-
cumscribed spirit, whatever aberration or complexity
it may display, with as little mixture of the alien and
external as possible? We are not pleading merely
for courage and sincerity; we are suggesting that the
proper stuff of fiction is a little other than custom
would have us believe it.

It is, at any rate, in some such fashion as this that
we seek to define the quality which distinguishes the
work of several young writers, among whom Mr.
James Joyce is the most notable, from that of their
predecessors. They attempt to come closer to life,
and to preserve more sincerely and exactly what interests and moves them, even if to do so they must
discard most of the conventions which are commonly
observed by the novelist. Let us record the atoms as
they fall upon the mind in the order in which they
fall, let us trace the pattern, however disconnected
and incoherent in appearance, which each sight or
incident scores upon the consciousness. Let us not
take it for granted that life exists more fully in what
is commonly thought big than in what is commonly
thought small. Any one who has read *The Portrait
of the Artist as a Young Man* or, what promises to
be a far more interesting work, *Ulysses*,[1] now appearing in the *Little Review*, will have hazarded some
theory of this nature as to Mr. Joyce's intention. On
our part, with such a fragment before us, it is hazarded rather than affirmed; but whatever the intention

[1] Written April 1919.

of the whole there can be no question but that it is of the utmost sincerity and that the result, difficult or unpleasant as we may judge it, is undeniably important. In contrast with those whom we have called materialists Mr. Joyce is spiritual; he is concerned at all costs to reveal the flickerings of that innermost flame which flashes its messages through the brain, and in order to preserve it he disregards with complete courage whatever seems to him adventitious, whether it be probability, or coherence or any other of these signposts which for generations have served to support the imagination of a reader when called upon to imagine what he can neither touch nor see. The scene in the cemetery, for instance, with its brilliancy, its sordidity, its incoherence, its sudden lightning flashes of significance, does undoubtedly come so close to the quick of the mind that, on a first reading at any rate, it is difficult not to acclaim a masterpiece. If we want life itself here, surely we have it. Indeed, we find ourselves fumbling rather awkwardly if we try to say what else we wish, and for what reason a work of such originality yet fails to compare, for we must take high examples, with *Youth* or *The Mayor of Casterbridge*. It fails because of the comparative poverty of the writer's mind, we might say simply and have done with it. But it is possible to press a little further and wonder whether we may not refer our sense of being in a bright yet narrow room, confined and shut in, rather than enlarged and set free, to some limitation imposed by the method as well as

[214]

by the mind. Is it the method that inhibits the creative power? Is it due to the method that we feel neither jovial nor magnanimous, but centred in a self which, in spite of its tremor of susceptibility, never embraces or creates what is outside itself and beyond? Does the emphasis laid, perhaps didactically, upon indecency, contribute to the effect of something angular and isolated? Or is it merely that in any effort of such originality it is much easier, for contemporaries especially, to feel what it lacks than to name what it gives? In any case it is a mistake to stand outside examining "methods". Any method is right, every method is right, that expresses what we wish to express, if we are writers; that brings us closer to the novelist's intention if we are readers. This method has the merit of bringing us closer to what we were prepared to call life itself; did not the reading of *Ulysses* suggest how much of life is excluded or ignored, and did it not come with a shock to open *Tristram Shandy* or even *Pendennis* and be by them convinced that there are not only other aspects of life, but more important ones into the bargain.

However this may be, the problem before the novelist at present, as we suppose it to have been in the past, is to contrive means of being free to set down what he chooses. He has to have the courage to say that what interests him is no longer "this" but "that": out of "that" alone must he construct his work. For the moderns "that", the point of interest, lies very likely in the dark places of psychology. At

once, therefore, the accent falls a little differently;
the emphasis is upon something hitherto ignored; at
once a different outline of form becomes necessary,
difficult for us to grasp, incomprehensible to our
predecessors. No one but a modern, perhaps no one
but a Russian, would have felt the interest of the
situation which Tchekov has made into the short story
which he calls "Gusev". Some Russian soldiers lie ill
on board a ship which is taking them back to Russia.
We are given a few scraps of their talk and some of
their thoughts; then one of them dies and is carried
away; the talk goes on among the others for a time,
until Gusev himself dies, and looking "like a carrot
or a radish" is thrown overboard. The emphasis is
laid upon such unexpected places that at first it
seems as if there were no emphasis at all; and then,
as the eyes accustom themselves to twilight and discern the shapes of things in a room we see how complete the story is, how profound, and how truly in
obedience to his vision Tchekov has chosen this, that,
and the other, and placed them together to compose
something new. But it is impossible to say "this is
comic", or "that is tragic", nor are we certain, since
short stories, we have been taught, should be brief and
conclusive, whether this, which is vague and inconclusive, should be called a short story at all.

The most elementary remarks upon modern English
fiction can hardly avoid some mention of the Russian
influence, and if the Russians are mentioned one runs
the risk of feeling that to write of any fiction save

theirs is waste of time. If we want understanding of the soul and heart where else shall we find it of comparable profundity? If we are sick of our own materialism the least considerable of their novelists has by right of birth a natural reverence for the human spirit. "Learn to make yourself akin to people. . . . But let this sympathy be not with the mind—for it is easy with the mind—but with the heart, with love towards them." In every great Russian writer we seem to discern the features of a saint, if sympathy for the sufferings of others, love towards them, endeavour to reach some goal worthy of the most exacting demands of the spirit constitute saintliness. It is the saint in them which confounds us with a feeling of our own irreligious triviality, and turns so many of our famous novels to tinsel and trickery. The conclusions of the Russian mind, thus comprehensive and compassionate, are inevitably, perhaps, of the utmost sadness. More accurately indeed we might speak of the inconclusiveness of the Russian mind. It is the sense that there is no answer, that if honestly examined life presents question after question which must be left to sound on and on after the story is over in hopeless interrogation that fills us with a deep, and finally it may be with a resentful, despair. They are right perhaps; unquestionably they see further than we do and without our gross impediments of vision. But perhaps we see something that escapes them, or why should this voice of protest mix itself with our gloom? The voice of protest is the voice of another and an ancient civilisation which seems to have bred in us the instinct to enjoy and fight rather than to suffer and understand. English fiction from Sterne to Meredith bears witness to our natural delight in humour and comedy, in the beauty of earth, in the activities of the intellect, and in the splendour of the body. But any deductions that we may draw from the comparison of two fictions so immeasurably far apart are futile save indeed as they flood us with a view of the infinite possibilities of the art and remind us that there is no limit to the horizon, and that nothing—no "method", no experiment, even of the wildest—is forbidden, but only falsity and pretence. "The proper stuff of fiction" does not exist; everything is the proper stuff of fiction, every feeling, every thought; every quality of brain and spirit is drawn upon; no perception comes amiss. And if we can imagine the art of fiction come alive and standing in our midst, she would undoubtedly bid us break her and bully her, as well as honour and love her, for so her youth is renewed and her sovereignty assured.

Jane Eyre and Wuthering Heights[1]

Of the hundred years that have passed since Charlotte Brontë was born, she, the centre now of so much legend, devotion, and literature, lived but thirty-nine. It is strange to reflect how different those legends might have been had her life reached the ordinary human span. She might have become, like some of her famous contemporaries, a figure familiarly met with in London and elsewhere, the subject of pictures and anecdotes innumerable, the writer of many novels, of memoirs possibly, removed from us well within the memory of the middle-aged in all the splendour of established fame. She might have been wealthy, she might have been prosperous. But it is not so. When we think of her we have to imagine some one who had no lot in our modern world; we have to cast our minds back to the 'fifties of the last century, to a remote parsonage upon the wild Yorkshire moors. In that parsonage, and on those moors, unhappy and lonely, in her poverty and her exaltation, she remains for ever.

These circumstances, as they affected her character, may have left their traces on her work. A novelist, we reflect, is bound to build up his structure with

[1] Written in 1916.

[219]

much very perishable material which begins by lending it reality and ends by cumbering it with rubbish. As we open *Jane Eyre* once more we cannot stifle the suspicion that we shall find her world of imagination as antiquated, mid-Victorian, and out of date as the parsonage on the moor, a place only to be visited by the curious, only preserved by the pious. So we open *Jane Eyre;* and in two pages every doubt is swept clean from our minds.

Folds of scarlet drapery shut in my view to the right hand; to the left were the clear panes of glass, protecting, but not separating me from the drear November day. At intervals, while turning over the leaves of my book, I studied the aspect of that winter afternoon. Afar, it offered a pale blank of mist and cloud; near, a scene of wet lawn and storm-beat shrub, with ceaseless rain sweeping away wildly before a long and lamentable blast.

There is nothing there more perishable than the moor itself, or more subject to the sway of fashion than the "long and lamentable blast". Nor is this exhilaration short-lived. It rushes us through the entire volume, without giving us time to think, without letting us lift our eyes from the page. So intense is our absorption that if some one moves in the room the movement seems to take place not there but up in Yorkshire. The writer has us by the hand, forces us along her road, makes us see what she sees, never leaves us for a moment or allows us to forget her.[1]

[1] Charlotte and Emily Brontë had much the same sense of colour. ". . . we saw—ah! it was beautiful—a splendid place carpeted with crimson, and crimson-covered chairs and tables, and a pure white ceil-

At the end we are steeped through and through with the genius, the vehemence, the indignation of Charlotte Brontë. Remarkable faces, figures of strong outline and gnarled feature have flashed upon us in passing; but it is through her eyes that we have seen them. Once she is gone, we seek for them in vain. Think of Rochester and we have to think of Jane Eyre. Think of the moor, and again, there is Jane Eyre. Think of the drawing-room, even, those "white carpets on which seemed laid brilliant garlands of flowers", that "pale Parian mantelpiece" with its Bohemia glass of "ruby red" and the "general blending of snow and fire"—what is all that except Jane Eyre?

The drawbacks of being Jane Eyre are not far to seek. Always to be a governess and always to be in love is a serious limitation in a world which is full, after all, of people who are neither one nor the other. The characters of a Jane Austen or of a Tolstoi have a million facets compared with these. They live and are complex by means of their effect upon many different people who serve to mirror them in the round. They move hither and thither whether their creators

---

ing bordered by gold, a shower of glass drops hanging in silver chains from the centre, and shimmering with little soft tapers" (*Wuthering Heights*). Yet it was merely a very pretty drawing-room, and within it a boudoir, both spread with white carpets, on which seemed laid brilliant garlands of flowers; both ceiled with snowy mouldings of white grapes and vine leaves, beneath which glowed in rich contrast crimson couches and ottomans; while the ornaments on the pale Parian mantelpiece were of sparkling Bohemia glass, ruby red; and between the windows large mirrors repeated the general blending of snow and fire.

watch them or not, and the world in which they live seems to us an independent world which we can visit, now that they have created it, by ourselves. Thomas Hardy is more akin to Charlotte Brontë in the power of his personality and the narrowness of his vision. But the differences are vast. As we read *Jude the Obscure* we are not rushed to a finish; we brood and ponder and drift away from the text in plethoric trains of thought which build up round the characters an atmosphere of question and suggestion of which they are themselves, as often as not, unconscious. Simple peasants as they are, we are forced to confront them with destinies and questionings of the hugest import, so that often it seems as if the most important characters in a Hardy novel are those which have no names. Of this power, of this speculative curiosity, Charlotte Brontë has no trace. She does not attempt to solve the problems of human life; she is even unaware that such problems exist; all her force, and it is the more tremendous for being constricted, goes into the assertion, "I love", "I hate", "I suffer".

For the self-centred and self-limited writers have a power denied the more catholic and broad-minded. Their impressions are close packed and strongly stamped between their narrow walls. Nothing issues from their minds which has not been marked with their own impress. They learn little from other writers, and what they adopt they cannot assimilate. Both Hardy and Charlotte Brontë appear to have founded their styles upon a stiff and decorous journalism. The staple of their prose is awkward and unyielding. But both with labour and the most obstinate integrity by thinking every thought until it has subdued words to itself, have forged for themselves a prose which takes the mould of their minds entire; which has, into the bargain, a beauty, a power, a swiftness of its own. Charlotte Brontë, at least, owed nothing to the reading of many books. She never learnt the smoothness of the professional writer, or acquired his ability to stuff and sway his language as he chooses. "I could never rest in communication with strong, discreet, and refined minds, whether male or female," she writes, as any leader-writer in a provincial journal might have written; but gathering fire and speed goes on in her own authentic voice "till I had passed the outworks of conventional reserve and crossed the threshold of confidence, and won a place by their hearts' very hearthstone". It is there that she takes her seat; it is the red and fitful glow of the heart's fire which illumines her page. In other words, we read Charlotte Brontë not for exquisite observation of character—her characters are vigorous and elementary; not for comedy—hers is grim and crude; not for a philosophic view of life—hers is that of a country parson's daughter; but for her poetry. Probably that is so with all writers who have, as she has, an overpowering personality, who, as we should say in real life, have only to open the door to make themselves felt. There is in them some untamed ferocity perpetually at war with the accepted order

[223]

of things which makes them desire to create instantly rather than to observe patiently. This very ardour, rejecting half shades and other minor impediments, wings its way past the daily conduct of ordinary people and allies itself with their more inarticulate passions. It makes them poets, or, if they choose to write in prose, intolerant of its restrictions. Hence it is that both Emily and Charlotte are always invoking the help of nature. They both feel the need of some more powerful symbol of the vast and slumbering passions in human nature than words or actions can convey. It is with a description of a storm that Charlotte ends her finest novel *Villette*. "The skies hang full and dark—a wrack sails from the west; the clouds cast themselves into strange forms." So she calls in nature to describe a state of mind which could not otherwise be expressed. But neither of the sisters observed nature accurately as Dorothy Wordsworth observed it, or painted it minutely as Tennyson painted it. They seized those aspects of the earth which were most akin to what they themselves felt or imputed to their characters, and so their storms, their moors, their lovely spaces of summer weather are not ornaments applied to decorate a dull page or display the writer's powers of observation—they carry on the emotion and light up the meaning of the book.

The meaning of a book, which lies so often apart from what happens and what is said and consists rather in some connection which things in themselves different have had for the writer, is necessarily hard to grasp. Especially this is so when, like the Brontës, the writer is poetic, and his meaning inseparable from his language, and itself rather a mood than a particular observation. *Wuthering Heights* is a more difficult book to understand than *Jane Eyre*, because Emily was a greater poet than Charlotte. When Charlotte wrote she said with eloquence and splendour and passion "I love", "I hate", "I suffer". Her experience, though more intense, is on a level with our own. But there is no "I" in *Wuthering Heights*. There are no governesses. There are no employers. There is love, but it is not the love of men and women. Emily was inspired by some more general conception. The impulse which urged her to create was not her own suffering or her own injuries. She looked out upon a world cleft into gigantic disorder and felt within her the power to unite it in a book. That gigantic ambition is to be felt throughout the novel— a struggle, half thwarted but of superb conviction, to say something through the mouths of her characters which is not merely "I love" or "I hate", but "we, the whole human race" and "you, the eternal powers . . ." the sentence remains unfinished. It is not strange that it should be so; rather it is astonishing that she can make us feel what she had it in her to say at all. It surges up in the half-articulate words of Catherine Earnshaw, "If all else perished and *he* remained, I should still continue to be; and if all else remained and he were annihilated, the universe would turn to a mighty stranger; I should not seem part of it". It breaks out again in the presence of the dead. "I see a repose that neither earth nor hell can break, and I feel an assurance of the endless and shadowless hereafter—the eternity they have entered—where life is boundless in its duration, and love in its sympathy and joy in its fulness." It is this suggestion of power underlying the apparitions of human nature, and lifting them up into the presence of greatness that gives the book its huge stature among other novels. But it was not enough for Emily Brontë to write a few lyrics, to utter a cry, to express a creed. In her poems she did this once and for all, and her poems will perhaps outlast her novel. But she was novelist as well as poet. She must take upon herself a more laborious and a more ungrateful task. She must face the fact of other existences, grapple with the mechanism of external things, build up, in recognisable shape, farms and houses and report the speeches of men and women who existed independently of herself. And so we reach these summits of emotion not by rant or rhapsody but by hearing a girl sing old songs to herself as she rocks in the branches of a tree; by watching the moor sheep crop the turf; by listening to the soft wind breathing through the grass. The life at the farm with all its absurdities and its improbability is laid open to us. We are given every opportunity of comparing *Wuthering Heights* with a real farm and Heathcliff with a real man. How, we are allowed to ask, can there be truth or insight or the finer shades of emotion in men and women who so little resemble

what we have seen ourselves? But even as we ask it
we see in Heathcliff the brother that a sister of genius
might have seen; he is impossible we say, but nevertheless no boy in literature has so vivid an existence
as his. So it is with the two Catherines; never could
women feel as they do or act in their manner, we say.
All the same, they are the most lovable women in
English fiction. It is as if she could tear up all that
we know human beings by, and fill these unrecognisable transparences with such a gust of life that they
transcend reality. Hers, then, is the rarest of all
powers. She could free life from its dependence on
facts; with a few touches indicate the spirit of a face
so that it needs no body; by speaking of the moor
make the wind blow and the thunder roar.

George Eliot

To read George Eliot attentively is to become aware how little one knows about her. It is also to become aware of the credulity, not very creditable to one's insight, with which, half consciously and partly maliciously, one had accepted the late Victorian version of a deluded woman who held phantom sway over subjects even more deluded than herself. At what moment, and by what means her spell was broken it is difficult to ascertain. Some people attribute it to the publication of her *Life*. Perhaps George Meredith, with his phrase about the "mercurial little showman" and the "errant woman" on the dais, gave point and poison to the arrows of thousands incapable of aiming them so accurately, but delighted to let fly. She became one of the butts for youth to laugh at, the convenient symbol of a group of serious people who were all guilty of the same idolatry and could be dismissed with the same scorn. Lord Acton had said that she was greater than Dante; Herbert Spencer exempted her novels, as if they were not novels, when he banned all fiction from the London Library. She was the pride and paragon of her sex. Moreover, her private record was not more alluring than her public. Asked to describe an afternoon at the Priory, the story-teller always intimated that the memory of those serious Sunday afternoons had come to tickle his sense of humour. He had been so much alarmed by the grave lady in her low chair; he had been so anxious to say the intelligent thing. Certainly, the talk had been very serious, as a note in the fine clear hand of the great novelist bore witness. It was dated on the Monday morning, and she accused herself of having spoken without due forethought of Marivaux when she meant another; but no doubt, she said, her listener had already supplied the correction. Still, the memory of talking about Marivaux to George Eliot on a Sunday afternoon was not a romantic memory. It had faded with the passage of the years. It had not become picturesque.

Indeed, one cannot escape the conviction that the long, heavy face with its expression of serious and sullen and almost equine power has stamped itself depressingly upon the minds of people who remember George Eliot, so that it looks out upon them from her pages. Mr. Gosse has lately described her as he saw her driving through London in a victoria—

a large, thick-set sybil, dreamy and immobile, whose massive features, somewhat grim when seen in profile, were incongruously bordered by a hat, always in the height of Paris fashion, which in those days commonly included an immense ostrich feather.

Lady Ritchie, with equal skill, has left a more intimate indoor portrait:

She sat by the fire in a beautiful black satin gown, with a green shaded lamp on the table beside her, where I saw Ger-

man books lying and pamphlets and ivory paper-cutters. She
was very quiet and noble, with two steady little eyes and a
sweet voice. As I looked I felt her to be a friend, not exactly
a personal friend, but a good and benevolent impulse.

A scrap of her talk is preserved. "We ought to respect our influence," she said. "We know by our
own experience how very much others affect our lives,
and we must remember that we in turn must have the
same effect upon others." Jealously treasured, committed to memory, one can imagine recalling the
scene, repeating the words, thirty years later and
suddenly, for the first time, bursting into laughter.
In all these records one feels that the recorder,
even when he was in the actual presence, kept his
distance and kept his head, and never read the novels
in later years with the light of a vivid, or puzzling,
or beautiful personality dazzling in his eyes. In
fiction, where so much of personality is revealed, the
absence of charm is a great lack; and her critics, who
have been, of course, mostly of the opposite sex, have
resented, half consciously perhaps, her deficiency in
a quality which is held to be supremely desirable in
women. George Eliot was not charming; she was
not strongly feminine; she had none of those eccentricities and inequalities of temper which give to so
many artists the endearing simplicity of children.
One feels that to most people, as to Lady Ritchie, she
was "not exactly a personal friend, but a good and
benevolent impulse". But if we consider these portraits more closely we shall find that they are all the

portraits of an elderly celebrated woman, dressed in black satin, driving in her victoria, a woman who has been through her struggle and issued from it with a profound desire to be of use to others, but with no wish for intimacy, save with the little circle who had known her in the days of her youth. We know very little about the days of her youth; but we do know that the culture, the philosophy, the fame, and the influence were all built upon a very humble foundation—she was the grand-daughter of a carpenter.

The first volume of her life is a singularly depressing record. In it we see her raising herself with groans and struggles from the intolerable boredom of petty provincial society (her father had risen in the world and become more middle class, but less picturesque) to be the assistant editor of a highly intellectual London review, and the esteemed companion of Herbert Spencer. The stages are painful as she reveals them in the sad soliloquy in which Mr. Cross condemned her to tell the story of her life. Marked in early youth as one "sure to get something up very soon in the way of a clothing club", she proceeded to raise funds for restoring a church by making a chart of ecclesiastical history; and that was followed by a loss of faith which so disturbed her father that he refused to live with her. Next came the struggle with the translation of Strauss, which, dismal and "soul-stupefying" in itself, can scarcely have been made less so by the usual feminine tasks of ordering a household and nursing a dying father, and the distressing conviction, to one so dependent upon affection, that by becoming a blue-stocking she was forfeiting her brother's respect. "I used to go about like an owl," she said, "to the great disgust of my brother." "Poor thing," wrote a friend who saw her toiling through Strauss with a statue of the risen Christ in front of her, "I do pity her sometimes, with her pale sickly face and dreadful headaches, and anxiety, too, about her father." Yet, though we cannot read the story without a strong desire that the stages of her pilgrimage might have been made, if not more easy, at least more beautiful, there is a dogged determination in her advance upon the citadel of culture which raises it above our pity. Her development was very slow and very awkward, but it had the irresistible impetus behind it of a deep-seated and noble ambition. Every obstacle at length was thrust from her path. She knew every one. She read everything. Her astonishing intellectual vitality had triumphed. Youth was over, but youth had been full of suffering. Then, at the age of thirty-five, at the height of her powers, and in the fullness of her freedom, she made the decision which was of such profound moment to her and still matters even to us, and went to Weimar, alone with George Henry Lewes.

The books which followed so soon after her union testify in the fullest manner to the great liberation which had come to her with personal happiness. In themselves they provide us with a plentiful feast. Yet at the threshold of her literary career one may

find in some of the circumstances of her life influences
that turned her mind to the past, to the country village, to the quiet and beauty and simplicity of childish
memories and away from herself and the present.
We understand how it was that her first book was
Scenes of Clerical Life, and not *Middlemarch*. Her
union with Lewes had surrounded her with affection,
but in view of the circumstances and of the conventions it had also isolated her. "I wish it to be understood," she wrote in 1857, "that I should never invite any one to come and see me who did not ask
for the invitation." She had been "cut off from what
is called the world", she said later, but she did not
regret it. By becoming thus marked, first by circumstances and later, inevitably, by her fame, she lost the
power to move on equal terms unnoted among her
kind; and the loss for a novelist was serious. Still,
basking in the light and sunshine of *Scenes of Clerical
Life*, feeling the large mature mind spreading itself
with a luxurious sense of freedom in the world of
her "remotest past", to speak of loss seems inappropriate. Everything to such a mind was gain. All
experience filtered down through layer after layer of
perception and reflection, enriching and nourishing.
The utmost we can say, in qualifying her attitude
towards fiction by what little we know of her life, is
that she had taken to heart certain lessons not usually
learnt early, if learnt at all, among which, perhaps,
the most branded upon her was the melancholy virtue
of tolerance; her sympathies are with the everyday

lot, and play most happily in dwelling upon the
homespun of ordinary joys and sorrows. She has
none of that romantic intensity which is connected
with a sense of one's own individuality, unsated and
unsubdued, cutting its shape sharply upon the background of the world. What were the loves and sorrows of a snuffy old clergyman, dreaming over his
whisky, to the fiery egotism of Jane Eyre? The
beauty of those first books, *Scenes of Clerical Life*,
Adam Bede, *The Mill on the Floss*, is very great.
It is impossible to estimate the merit of the Poysers,
the Dodsons, the Gilfils, the Bartons, and the rest
with all their surroundings and dependencies, because
they have put on flesh and blood and we move among
them, now bored, now sympathetic, but always with
that unquestioning acceptance of all that they say and
do, which we accord to the great originals only. The
flood of memory and humour which she pours so
spontaneously into one figure, one scene after another,
until the whole fabric of ancient rural England is
revived, has so much in common with a natural
process that it leaves us with little consciousness that
there is anything to criticise. We accept; we feel
the delicious warmth and release of spirit which the
great creative writers alone procure for us. As one
comes back to the books after years of absence they
pour out, even against our expectation, the same store
of energy and heat, so that we want more than anything to idle in the warmth as in the sun beating
down from the red orchard wall. If there is an ele-

ment of unthinking abandonment in thus submitting
to the humours of Midland farmers and their wives,
that, too, is right in the circumstances. We scarcely
wish to analyse what we feel to be so large and deeply
human. And when we consider how distant in time
the world of Shepperton and Hayslope is, and how
remote the minds of farmer and agricultural labourers
from those of most of George Eliot's readers, we can
only attribute the ease and pleasure with which we
ramble from house to smithy, from cottage parlour
to rectory garden, to the fact that George Eliot makes
us share their lives, not in a spirit of condescension
or of curiosity, but in a spirit of sympathy. She is
no satirist. The movement of her mind was too slow
and cumbersome to lend itself to comedy. But she
gathers in her large grasp a great bunch of the main
elements of human nature and groups them loosely
together with a tolerant and wholesome understanding which, as one finds upon re-reading, has not only
kept her figures fresh and free, but has given them an
unexpected hold upon our laughter and tears. There
is the famous Mrs. Poyser. It would have been easy
to work her idiosyncrasies to death, and, as it is, perhaps, George Eliot gets her laugh in the same place
a little too often. But memory, after the book is
shut, brings out, as sometimes in real life, the details
and subtleties which some more salient characteristic
has prevented us from noticing at the time. We
recollect that her health was not good. There were
occasions upon which she said nothing at all. She

was patience itself with a sick child. She doted upon Totty. Thus one can muse and speculate about the greater number of George Eliot's characters and find, even in the least important, a roominess and margin where those qualities lurk which she has no call to bring from their obscurity.

But in the midst of all this tolerance and sympathy there are, even in the early books, moments of greater stress. Her humour has shown itself broad enough to cover a wide range of fools and failures, mothers and children, dogs and flourishing midland fields, farmers, sagacious or fuddled over their ale, horse-dealers, inn-keepers, curates, and carpenters. Over them all broods a certain romance, the only romance that George Eliot allowed herself—the romance of the past. The books are astonishingly readable and have no trace of pomposity or pretence. But to the reader who holds a large stretch of her early work in view it will become obvious that the mist of recollection gradually withdraws. It is not that her power diminishes, for, to our thinking, it is at its highest in the mature *Middlemarch*, the magnificent book which with all its imperfections is one of the few English novels written for grown-up people. But the world of fields and farms no longer contents her. In real life she had sought her fortunes elsewhere; and though to look back into the past was calming and consoling, there are, even in the early works, traces of that troubled spirit, that exacting and questioning and baffled presence who was George Eliot herself. In

[237]

Adam Bede there is a hint of her in Dinah. She shows herself far more openly and completely in Maggie in *The Mill on the Floss*. She is Janet in *Janet's Repentance*, and Romola, and Dorothea seeking wisdom and finding one scarcely knows what in marriage with Ladislaw. Those who fall foul of George Eliot do so, we incline to think, on account of her heroines; and with good reason; for there is no doubt that they bring out the worst of her, lead her into difficult places, make her self-conscious, didactic, and occasionally vulgar. Yet if you could delete the whole sisterhood you would leave a much smaller and a much inferior world, albeit a world of greater artistic perfection and far superior jollity and comfort. In accounting for her failure, in so far as it was a failure, one recollects that she never wrote a story until she was thirty-seven, and that by the time she was thirty-seven she had come to think of herself with a mixture of pain and something like resentment. For long she preferred not to think of herself at all. Then, when the first flush of creative energy was exhausted and self-confidence had come to her, she wrote more and more from the personal standpoint, but she did so without the unhesitating abandonment of the young. Her self-consciousness is always marked when her heroines say what she herself would have said. She disguised them in every possible way. She granted them beauty and wealth into the bargain; she invented, more improbably, a taste for brandy. But the disconcerting and stimulating fact remained that

she was compelled by the very power of her genius
to step forth in person upon the quiet bucolic
scene.

The noble and beautiful girl who insisted upon
being born into the Mill on the Floss is the most
obvious example of the ruin which a heroine can
strew about her. Humour controls her and keeps her
lovable so long as she is small and can be satisfied
by eloping with the gipsies or hammering nails into
her doll; but she develops; and before George Eliot
knows what has happened she has a full-grown woman
on her hands demanding what neither gipsies nor
dolls, nor St. Ogg's itself is capable of giving her.
First Philip Wakem is produced, and later Stephen
Guest. The weakness of the one and the coarseness
of the other have often been pointed out; but both,
in their weakness and coarseness, illustrate not so
much George Eliot's inability to draw the portrait of
a man, as the uncertainty, the infirmity, and the fumbling which shook her hand when she had to conceive
a fit mate for a heroine. She is in the first place
driven beyond the home world she knew and loved,
and forced to set foot in middle-class drawing-rooms
where young men sing all the summer morning and
young women sit embroidering smoking-caps for
bazaars. She feels herself out of her element, as her
clumsy satire of what she calls "good society" proves.

Good society has its claret and its velvet carpets, its dinner
engagements six weeks deep, its opera, and its faëry ball rooms
. . . gets its science done by Faraday and its religion by the

superior clergy who are to be met in the best houses; how should it have need of belief and emphasis?

There is no trace of humour or insight there, but only the vindictiveness of a grudge which we feel to be personal in its origin. But terrible as the complexity of our social system is in its demands upon the sympathy and discernment of a novelist straying across the boundaries, Maggie Tulliver did worse than drag George Eliot from her natural surroundings. She insisted upon the introduction of the great emotional scene. She must love; she must despair; she must be drowned clasping her brother in her arms. The more one examines the great emotional scenes the more nervously one anticipates the brewing and gathering and thickening of the cloud which will burst upon our heads at the moment of crisis in a shower of disillusionment and verbosity. It is partly that her hold upon dialogue, when it is not dialect, is slack; and partly that she seems to shrink with an elderly dread of fatigue from the effort of emotional concentration. She allows her heroines to talk too much. She has little verbal felicity. She lacks the unerring taste which chooses one sentence and compresses the heart of the scene within that. "Whom are you going to dance with?" asked Mr. Knightley, at the Westons' ball. "With you, if you will ask me," said Emma; and she has said enough. Mrs. Casaubon would have talked for an hour and we should have looked out of the window.

Yet, dismiss the heroines without sympathy, confine George Eliot to the agricultural world of her
"remotest past", and you not only diminish her greatness but lose her true flavour. That greatness is here
we can have no doubt. The width of the prospect,
the large strong outlines of the principal features, the
ruddy light of the early books, the searching power
and reflective richness of the later tempt us to linger
and expatiate beyond our limits. But it is upon the
heroines that we would cast a final glance. "I have
always been finding out my religion since I was a
little girl," says Dorothea Casaubon. "I used to pray
so much—now I hardly ever pray. I try not to have
desires merely for myself. . . ." She is speaking for
them all. That is their problem. They cannot live
without religion, and they start out on the search for
one when they are little girls. Each has the deep
feminine passion for goodness, which makes the place
where she stands in aspiration and agony the heart
of the book—still and cloistered like a place of worship, but that she no longer knows to whom to pray.
In learning they seek their goal; in the ordinary tasks
of womanhood; in the wider service of their kind.
They do not find what they seek, and we cannot wonder. The ancient consciousness of woman, charged
with suffering and sensibility, and for so many ages
dumb, seems in them to have brimmed and overflowed
and uttered a demand for something—they scarcely
know what—for something that is perhaps incompatible with the facts of human existence. George

Eliot had far too strong an intelligence to tamper with those facts, and too broad a humour to mitigate the truth because it was a stern one. Save for the supreme courage of their endeavour, the struggle ends, for her heroines, in tragedy, or in a compromise that is even more melancholy. But their story is the incomplete version of the story of George Eliot herself. For her, too, the burden and the complexity of womanhood were not enough; she must reach beyond the sanctuary and pluck for herself the strange bright fruits of art and knowledge. Clasping them as few women have ever clasped them, she would not renounce her own inheritance—the difference of view, the difference of standard—nor accept an inappropriate reward. Thus we behold her, a memorable figure, inordinately praised and shrinking from her fame, despondent, reserved, shuddering back into the arms of love as if there alone were satisfaction and, it might be, justification, at the same time reaching out with "a fastidious yet hungry ambition" for all that life could offer the free and inquiring mind and confronting her feminine aspirations with the real world of men. Triumphant was the issue for her, whatever it may have been for her creations, and as we recollect all that she dared and achieved, how with every obstacle against her—sex and health and convention—she sought more knowledge and more freedom till the body, weighted with its double burden, sank worn out, we must lay upon her grave whatever we have it in our power to bestow of laurel and rose.

The Russian Point of View

Doubtful as we frequently are whether either the French or the Americans, who have so much in common with us, can yet understand English literature, we must admit graver doubts whether, for all their enthusiasm, the English can understand Russian literature. Debate might protract itself indefinitely as to what we mean by "understand". Instances will occur to everybody of American writers in particular who have written with the highest discrimination of our literature and of ourselves; who have lived a lifetime among us, and finally have taken legal steps to become subjects of King George. For all that, have they understood us, have they not remained to the end of their days foreigners? Could any one believe that the novels of Henry James were written by a man who had grown up in the society which he describes, or that his criticism of English writers was written by a man who had read Shakespeare without any sense of the Atlantic Ocean and two or three hundred years on the far side of it separating his civilisation from ours? A special acuteness and detachment, a sharp angle of vision the foreigner will often achieve; but not that absence of self-consciousness, that ease and fellowship and sense of common values which make for intimacy, and sanity, and the quick give and take of familiar intercourse.

Not only have we all this to separate us from Russian literature, but a much more serious barrier—the difference of language. Of all those who feasted upon Tolstoi, Dostoevsky, and Tchekov during the past twenty years, not more than one or two perhaps have been able to read them in Russian. Our estimate of their qualities has been formed by critics who have never read a word of Russian, or seen Russia, or even heard the language spoken by natives; who have had to depend, blindly and implicitly, upon the work of translators.

What we are saying amounts to this, then, that we have judged a whole literature stripped of its style. When you have changed every word in a sentence from Russian to English, have thereby altered the sense a little, the sound, weight, and accent of the words in relation to each other completely, nothing remains except a crude and coarsened version of the sense. Thus treated, the great Russian writers are like men deprived by an earthquake or a railway accident not only of all their clothes, but also of something subtler and more important—their manners, the idiosyncrasies of their characters. What remains is, as the English have proved by the fanaticism of their admiration, something very powerful and very impressive, but it is difficult to feel sure, in view of these mutilations, how far we can trust ourselves not to impute, to distort, to read into them an emphasis which is false.

They have lost their clothes, we say, in some terrible

catastrophe, for some such figure as that describes the simplicity, the humanity, startled out of all effort to hide and disguise its instincts, which Russian literature, whether it is due to translation, or to some more profound cause, makes upon us. We find these qualties steeping it through, as obvious in the lesser writers as in the greater. "Learn to make yourselves akin to people. I would even like to add: make yourself indispensable to them. But let this sympathy be not with the mind—for it is easy with the mind—but with the heart, with love towards them." "From the Russian," one would say instantly, wherever one chanced on that quotation. The simplicity, the absence of effort, the assumption that in a world bursting with misery the chief call upon us is to understand our fellow-sufferers, "and not with the mind—for it is easy with the mind—but with the heart"—this is the cloud which broods above the whole of Russian literature, which lures us from our own parched brilliancy and scorched thoroughfares to expand in its shade—and of course with disastrous results. We become awkward and self-conscious; denying our own qualities, we write with an affectation of goodness and simplicity which is nauseating in the extreme. We cannot say "Brother" with simple conviction. There is a story by Mr. Galsworthy in which one of the characters so addresses another (they are both in the depths of misfortune). Immediately everything becomes strained and affected. The English equivalent for "Brother" is "Mate"—a very different word, with something sardonic in it, an indefinable suggestion of humour. Met though they are in the depths of misfortune the two Englishmen who thus accost each other will, we are sure, find a job, make their fortunes, spend the last years of their lives in luxury, and leave a sum of money to prevent poor devils from calling each other "Brother" on the Embankment. But it is common suffering, rather than common happiness, effort, or desire that produces the sense of brotherhood. It is the "deep sadness" which Dr. Hagberg Wright finds typical of the Russian people that creates their literature.

A generalisation of this kind will, of course, even if it has some degree of truth when applied to the body of literature, be changed profoundly when a writer of genius sets to work on it. At once other questions arise. It is seen that an "attitude" is not simple; it is highly complex. Men reft of their coats and their manners, stunned by a railway accident, say hard things, harsh things, unpleasant things, difficult things, even if they say them with the abandonment and simplicity which catastrophe has bred in them. Our first impressions of Tchekov are not of simplicity but of bewilderment. What is the point of it, and why does he make a story out of this? we ask as we read story after story. A man falls in love with a married woman, and they part and meet, and in the end are left talking about their position and by what means they can be free from "this intolerable bondage".

" 'How? How?' he asked, clutching his head. . . . And it seemed as though in a little while the solution would be found and then a new and splendid life would begin." That is the end. A postman drives a student to the station and all the way the student tries to make the postman talk, but he remains silent. Suddenly the postman says unexpectedly, "It's against the regulations to take any one with the post." And he walks up and down the platform with a look of anger on his face. "With whom was he angry? Was it with people, with poverty, with the autumn nights?" Again, that story ends.

But is it the end, we ask? We have rather the feeling that we have overrun our signals; or it is as if a tune had stopped short without the expected chords to close it. These stories are inconclusive, we say, and proceed to frame a criticism based upon the assumption that stories ought to conclude in a way that we recognise. In so doing we raise the question of our own fitness as readers. Where the tune is familiar and the end emphatic—lovers united, villains discomfited, intrigues exposed—as it is in most Victorian fiction, we can scarcely go wrong, but where the tune is unfamiliar and the end a note of interrogation or merely the information that they went on talking, as it is in Tchekov, we need a very daring and alert sense of literature to make us hear the tune, and in particular those last notes which complete the harmony. Probably we have to read a great many stories before we feel, and the feeling is essential to our satisfaction, that we hold the parts together, and that Tchekov was not merely rambling disconnectedly, but struck now this note, now that with intention, in order to complete his meaning.

We have to cast about in order to discover where the emphasis in these strange stories rightly comes. Tchekov's own words give us a lead in the right direction. ". . . such a conversation as this between us", he says, "would have been unthinkable for our parents. At night they did not talk, but slept sound; we, our generation, sleep badly, are restless, but talk a great deal, and are always trying to settle whether we are right or not." Our literature of social satire and psychological finesse both sprang from that restless sleep, that incessant talking; but after all, there is an enormous difference between Tchekov and Henry James, between Tchekov and Bernard Shaw. Obviously—but where does it arise? Tchekov, too, is aware of the evils and injustices of the social state; the condition of the peasants appals him, but the reformer's zeal is not his—that is not the signal for us to stop. The mind interests him enormously; he is a most subtle and delicate analyst of human relations. But again, no; the end is not there. Is it that he is primarily interested not in the soul's relation with other souls, but with the soul's relation to health—with the soul's relation to goodness? These stories are always showing us some affectation, pose, insincerity. Some woman has got into a false relation; some man has been perverted by the inhumanity of his circumstances. The soul is ill; the soul is cured; the soul is not cured. Those are the emphatic points in his stories.

Once the eye is used to these shades, half the "conclusions" of fiction fade into thin air; they show like transparences with a light behind them—gaudy, glaring, superficial. The general tidying up of the last chapter, the marriage, the death, the statement of values so sonorously trumpeted forth, so heavily underlined, become of the most rudimentary kind. Nothing is solved, we feel; nothing is rightly held together. On the other hand, the method which at first seemed so casual, inconclusive, and occupied with trifles, now appears the result of an exquisitely original and fastidious taste, choosing boldly, arranging infallibly, and controlled by an honesty for which we can find no match save among the Russians themselves. There may be no answer to these questions, but at the same time let us never manipulate the evidence so as to produce something fitting, decorous, agreeable to our vanity. This may not be the way to catch the ear of the public; after all, they are used to louder music, fiercer measures; but as the tune sounded, so he has written it. In consequence, as we read these little stories about nothing at all, the horizon widens; the soul gains an astonishing sense of freedom.

In reading Tchekov we find ourselves repeating the word "soul" again and again. It sprinkles his pages. Old drunkards use it freely; ". . . you are high up in the service, beyond all reach, but haven't real soul, my dear boy . . . there's no strength in it." Indeed, it is the soul that is the chief character in Russian fiction. Delicate and subtle in Tchekov, subject to an in-

[249]

finite number of humours and distempers, it is of
greater depth and volume in Dostoevsky, liable to
violent diseases and raging fevers, but still the pre-
dominant concern. Perhaps that is why it needs so
great an effort on the part of an English reader to read
The Brothers Karamazov or *The Possessed* a second
time. The "soul" is alien to him. It is even antipathetic. It has little sense of humour and no sense
of comedy. It is formless. It has slight connection
with the intellect. It is confused, diffuse, tumultuous,
incapable, it seems, of submitting to the control of logic
or the discipline of poetry. The novels of Dostoevsky
are seething whirlpools, gyrating sandstorms, water-
spouts which hiss and boil and suck us in. They are
composed purely and wholly of the stuff of the soul.
Against our wills we are drawn in, whirled round,
blinded, suffocated, and at the same time filled with a
giddy rapture. Out of Shakespeare there is no more
exciting reading. We open the door and find ourselves
in a room full of Russian generals, the tutors of Russian generals, their step-daughters and cousins and
crowds of miscellaneous people who are all talking at
the tops of their voices about their most private affairs. But where are we? Surely it is the part of a
novelist to inform us whether we are in an hotel, a
flat, or hired lodging. Nobody thinks of explaining.
We are souls, tortured, unhappy souls, whose only
business it is to talk, to reveal, to confess, to draw up
at whatever rending of flesh and nerve those crabbed
sins which crawl on the sand at the bottom of us. But,

as we listen, our confusion slowly settles. A rope is
flung to us; we catch hold of a soliloquy; holding on
by the skin of our teeth, we are rushed through the
water; feverishly, wildly, we rush on and on, now sub-
merged, now in a moment of vision understanding
more than we have ever understood before, and receiving such revelations as we are wont to get only
from the press of life at its fullest. As we fly we
pick it all up—the names of the people, their relationships, that they are staying in an hotel at Roulet-
tenburg, that Polina is involved in an intrigue with the
Marquis de Grieux—but what unimportant matters
these are compared with the soul! It is the soul that
matters, its passion, its tumult, its astonishing medley
of beauty and vileness. And if our voices suddenly rise
into shrieks of laughter, or if we are shaken by the
most violent sobbing, what more natural?—it hardly
calls for remark. The pace at which we are living is
so tremendous that sparks must rush off our wheels
as we fly. Moreover, when the speed is thus increased
and the elements of the soul are seen, not separately in
scenes of humour or scenes of passion as our slower
English minds conceive them, but streaked, involved,
inextricably confused, a new panorama of the human
mind is revealed. The old divisions melt into each
other. Men are at the same time villains and saints;
their acts are at once beautiful and despicable. We
love and we hate at the same time. There is none of
that precise division between good and bad to which
we are used. Often those for whom we feel most affec-

tion are the greatest criminals, and the most abject sinners move us to the strongest admiration as well as love.

Dashed to the crest of the waves, bumped and battered on the stones at the bottom, it is difficult for an English reader to feel at ease. The process to which he is accustomed in his own literature is reversed. If we wished to tell the story of a General's love affair (and we should find it very difficult in the first place not to laugh at a General), we should begin with his house; we should solidify his surroundings. Only when all was ready should we attempt to deal with the General himself. Moreover, it is not the samovar but the teapot that rules in England; time is limited; space crowded; the influence of other points of view, of other books, even of other ages, makes itself felt. Society is sorted out into lower, middle, and upper classes, each with its own traditions, its own manners, and, to some extent, its own language. Whether he wishes it or not, there is a constant pressure upon an English novelist to recognise these barriers, and, in consequence, order is imposed on him and some kind of form; he is inclined to satire rather than to compassion, to scrutiny of society rather than understanding of individuals themselves.

No such restraints were laid on Dostoevsky. It is all the same to him whether you are noble or simple, a tramp or a great lady. Whoever you are, you are the vessel of this perplexed liquid, this cloudy, yeasty, precious stuff, the soul. The soul is not restrained by barriers. It overflows, it floods, it mingles with the souls of others. The simple story of a bank clerk who could not pay for a bottle of wine spreads, before we know what is happening, into the lives of his father-in-law and the five mistresses whom his father-in-law treated abominably, and the postman's life, and the charwoman's, and the Princesses' who lodged in the same block of flats; for nothing is outside Dostoevsky's province; and when he is tired, he does not stop, he goes on. He cannot restrain himself. Out it tumbles upon us, hot, scalding, mixed, marvellous, terrible, oppressive—the human soul.

There remains the greatest of all novelists—for what else can we call the author of *War and Peace?* Shall we find Tolstoi, too, alien, difficult, a foreigner? Is there some oddity in his angle of vision which, at any rate until we have become disciples and so lost our bearings, keeps us at arm's length in suspicion and bewilderment? From his first words we can be sure of one thing at any rate—here is a man who sees what we see, who proceeds, too, as we are accustomed to proceed, not from the inside outwards, but from the outside inwards. Here is a world in which the postman's knock is heard at eight o'clock, and people go to bed between ten and eleven. Here is a man, too, who is no savage, no child of nature; he is educated; he has had every sort of experience. He is one of those born aristocrats who have used their privileges to the full. He is metropolitan, not suburban. His senses, his intellect, are acute, powerful, and well nourished. There is something proud and superb in the attack of such a mind and such a body upon life. Nothing seems to escape him. Nothing glances off him unrecorded. Nobody, therefore, can so convey the excitement of sport, the beauty of horses, and all the fierce desirability of the world to the senses of a strong young man. Every twig, every feather sticks to his magnet. He notices the blue or red of a child's frock; the way a horse shifts its tail; the sound of a cough; the action of a man trying to put his hands into pockets that have been sewn up. And what his infallible eye reports of a cough or a trick of the hands his infallible brain refers to something hidden in the character so that we know his people, not only by the way they love and their views on politics and the immortality of the soul, but also by the way they sneeze and choke. Even in a translation we feel that we have been set on a mountain-top and had a telescope put into our hands. Everything is astonishingly clear and absolutely sharp. Then, suddenly, just as we are exulting, breathing deep, feeling at once braced and purified, some detail—perhaps the head of a man— comes at us out of the picture in an alarming way, as if extruded by the very intensity of its life. "Suddenly a strange thing happened to me: first I ceased to see what was around me; then his face seemed to vanish till only the eyes were left, shining over against mine; next the eyes seemed to be in my own head, and then all became confused—I could see nothing and was forced to shut my eyes, in order to break loose from the feeling of pleasure and fear which his gaze was producing in me. . . ." Again and again we share Masha's feelings in *Family Happiness*. One shuts one's eyes to escape the feeling of pleasure and fear. Often it is pleasure that is uppermost. In this very story there are two descriptions, one of a girl walking in a garden at night with her lover, one of a newly married couple prancing down their drawing-room, which so convey the feeling of intense happiness that we shut the book to feel it better. But always there is an element of fear which makes us, like Masha, wish to escape from the gaze which Tolstoi fixes on us. Does it arise from the sense, which in real life might harass us, that such happiness as he describes is too intense to last, that we are on the edge of disaster? Or is it not that the very intensity of our pleasure is somehow questionable and forces us to ask, with Pozdnyshev in the Kreutzer Sonata, "But why live?" Life dominates Tolstoi as the soul dominates Dostoevsky. There is always at the centre of all the brilliant and flashing petals of the flower this scorpion, "Why live?" There is always at the centre of the book some Olenin, or Pierre, or Levin who gathers into himself all experience, turns the world round between his fingers, and never ceases to ask even as he enjoys it, what is the meaning of it, and what should be our aims. It is not the priest who shatters our desires most effectively; it is the man who has known them, and loved them himself. When he derides them, the world indeed turns to dust and ashes beneath our feet. Thus fear mingles with our pleasure, and of the three great Russian writers, it is Tolstoi who most enthralls us and most repels.

But the mind takes its bias from the place of its birth, and no doubt, when it strikes upon a literature so alien as the Russian, flies off at a tangent far from the truth.

Outlines

I

Speaking truthfully, *Mary Russell Mitford and Her
Surroundings* is not a good book. It neither enlarges
the mind nor purifies the heart. There is nothing in
it about Prime Ministers and not very much about
Miss Mitford. Yet, as one is setting out to speak the
truth, one must own that there are certain books which
can be read without the mind and without the heart,
but still with considerable enjoyment. To come to the
point, the great merit of these scrapbooks, for they
can scarcely be called biographies, is that they license
mendacity. One cannot believe what Miss Hill says
about Miss Mitford, and thus one is free to invent
Miss Mitford for oneself. Not for a second do we
accuse Miss Hill of telling lies. That infirmity is
entirely ours. For example: "Alresford was the birth-
place of one who loved nature as few have loved her,
and whose writings 'breathe the air of the hayfields and
the scent of the hawthorn boughs', and seem to waft to
us 'the sweet breezes that blow over ripened corn-
fields and daisied meadows'." It is perfectly true
that Miss Mitford was born at Alresford, and yet,
when it is put like that, we doubt whether she was ever
born at all. Indeed she was, says Miss Hill; she was

[257]

born "on the 16th December, 1787. 'A pleasant house in truth it was,' Miss Mitford writes. 'The breakfast-room . . . was a lofty and spacious apartment.' " So Miss Mitford was born in the breakfast-room about eight-thirty on a snowy morning between the Doctor's second and third cups of tea. "Pardon me," said Mrs. Mitford, turning a little pale, but not omitting to add the right quantity of cream to her husband's tea, "I feel . . ." That is the way in which Mendacity begins. There is something plausible and even ingenious in her approaches. The touch about the cream, for instance, might be called historical, for it is well known that when Mary won £20,000 in the Irish lottery, the Doctor spent it all upon Wedgwood china, the winning number being stamped upon the soup plates in the middle of an Irish harp, the whole being surmounted by the Mitford arms, and encircled by the motto of Sir John Bertram, one of William the Conqueror's knights, from whom the Mitfords claimed descent. "Observe," says Mendacity, "with what an air the Doctor drinks his tea, and how she, poor lady, contrives to curtsey as she leaves the room." Tea? I inquire, for the Doctor, though a fine figure of a man, is already purple and profuse, and foams like a crimson cock over the frill of his fine laced shirt. "Since the ladies have left the room," Mendacity begins, and goes on to make up a pack of lies with the sole object of proving that Dr. Mitford kept a mistress in the purlieus of Reading and paid her money on the pretence that he was investing it in a new method of

lighting and heating houses invented by the Marquis
de Chavannes. It came to the same thing in the end
—to the King's Bench Prison, that is to say; but
instead of allowing us to recall the literary and historical associations of the place, Mendacity wanders off
to the window and distracts us again by the plati-
tudinous remark that it is still snowing. There is
something very charming in an ancient snowstorm.
The weather has varied almost as much in the course
of generations as mankind. The snow of those days
was more formally shaped and a good deal softer
than the snow of ours, just as an eighteenth-century
cow was no more like our cows than she was like the
florid and fiery cows of Elizabethan pastures. Sufficient attention has scarcely been paid to this aspect of
literature, which, it cannot be denied, has its importance.

Our brilliant young men might do worse, when in
search of a subject, than devote a year or two to cows
in literature, snow in literature, the daisy in Chaucer
and in Coventry Patmore. At any rate, the snow falls
heavily. The Portsmouth mail-coach has already lost
its way; several ships have foundered, and Margate
pier has been totally destroyed. At Hatfield Peveral
twenty sheep have been buried, and though one supports itself by gnawing wurzels which it has found near
it, there is grave reason to fear that the French king's
coach has been blocked on the road to Colchester. It is
now the 16th of February, 1808.

Poor Mrs. Mitford! Twenty-one years ago she

left the breakfast-room, and no news has yet been received of her child. Even Mendacity is a little ashamed of itself, and, picking up *Mary Russell Mitford and Her Surroundings*, assures us that everything will come right if we possess ourselves in patience. The French king's coach was on its way to Bocking; at Bocking lived Lord and Lady Charles Murray-Aynsley; and Lord Charles was shy. Lord Charles had always been shy. Once when Mary Mitford was five years old—sixteen years, that is, before the sheep were lost and the French king went to Bocking—Mary "threw him into an agony of blushing by running up to his chair in mistake for that of my papa". He had indeed to leave the room. Miss Hill, who, somewhat strangely, finds the society of Lord and Lady Charles pleasant, does not wish to quit it without "introducing an incident in connection with them which took place in the month of February, 1808". But is Miss Mitford concerned in it? we ask, for there must be an end of trifling. To some extent, that is to say, Lady Charles was a cousin of the Mitfords, and Lord Charles was shy. Mendacity is quite ready to deal with "the incident" even on these terms; but, we repeat, we have had enough of trifling. Miss Mitford may not be a great woman; for all we know she was not even a good one; but we have certain responsibilities as a reviewer which we are not going to evade.

There is, to begin with, English literature. A sense of the beauty of nature has never been altogether absent, however much the cow may change from age to age, from English poetry. Nevertheless, the difference between Pope and Wordsworth in this respect is very considerable. *Lyrical Ballads* was published in 1798; *Our Village* in 1824. One being in verse and the other in prose, it is not necessary to labour a comparison which contains, however, not only the elements of justice, but the seeds of many volumes. Like her great predecessor, Miss Mitford much preferred the country to the town; and thus, perhaps, it may not be inopportune to dwell for a moment upon the King of Saxony, Mary Anning, and the ichthyosaurus. Let alone the fact that Mary Anning and Mary Mitford had a Christian name in common, they are further connected by what can scarcely be called a fact, but may, without hazard, be called a probability. Miss Mitford was looking for fossils at Lyme Regis only fifteen years before Mary Anning found one. The King of Saxony visited Lyme in 1844, and seeing the head of an ichthyosaurus in Mary Anning's window, asked her to drive to Pinny and explore the rocks. While they were looking for fossils, an old woman seated herself in the King's coach—was she Mary Mitford? Truth compels us to say that she was not; but there is no doubt, and we are not trifling when we say it, that Mary Mitford often expressed a wish that she had known Mary Anning, and it is singularly unfortunate to have to state that she never did. For we have reached the year 1844; Mary Mitford is fifty-seven years of age, and so far, thanks to Mendacity and its trifling ways, all we know of her is that she did not know Mary

[261]

Anning, had not found an ichthyosaurus, had not been out in a snowstorm, and had not seen the King of France.

It is time to wring the creature's neck, and begin again at the very beginning.

What considerations, then, had weight with Miss Hill when she decided to write *Mary Russell Mitford and Her Surroundings?* Three emerge from the rest, and may be held of paramount importance. In the first place, Miss Mitford was a lady; in the second, she was born in the year 1787; and in the third, the stock of female characters who lend themselves to biographic treatment by their own sex is, for one reason or another, running short. For instance, little is known of Sappho, and that little is not wholly to her credit. Lady Jane Grey has merit, but is undeniably obscure. Of George Sand, the more we know the less we approve. George Eliot was led into evil ways which not all her philosophy can excuse. The Brontës, however highly we rate their genius, lacked that indefinable something which marks the lady; Harriet Martineau was an atheist; Mrs. Browning was a married woman; Jane Austen, Fanny Burney, and Maria Edgeworth have been done already; so that, what with one thing and another, Mary Russell Mitford is the only woman left.

There is no need to labour the extreme importance of the date when we see the word "surroundings" on the back of a book. Surroundings, as they are called, are invariably eighteenth-century surroundings. When we come, as of course we do, to that phrase which relates how "as we looked upon the steps leading down from the upper room, we fancied we saw the tiny figure jumping from step to step", it would be the grossest outrage upon our sensibilities to be told that those steps were Athenian, Elizabethan, or Parisian. They were, of course, eighteenth-century steps, leading down from the old panelled room into the shady garden, where, tradition has it, William Pitt played marbles, or, if we like to be bold, where on still summer days we can almost fancy that we hear the drums of Bonaparte on the coast of France. Bonaparte is the limit of the imagination on one side, as Monmouth is on the other; it would be fatal if the imagination took to toying with Prince Albert or sporting with King John. But fancy knows her place, and there is no need to labour the point that her place is the eighteenth century. The other point is more obscure. One must be a lady. Yet what that means, and whether we like what it means, may both be doubtful. If we say that Jane Austen was a lady and that Charlotte Brontë was not one, we do as much as need be done in the way of definition, and commit ourselves to neither side.

It is undoubtedly because of their reticence that Miss Hill is on the side of the ladies. They sigh things off and they smile things off, but they never seize the silver table by the legs or dash the teacups on the floor. It is in many ways a great convenience to have a subject who can be trusted to live a long life without once raising her voice. Sixteen years is a considerable stretch of time, but of a lady it is enough to say, "Here Mary Mitford passed sixteen years of her life and here she got to know and love not only their own beautiful grounds but also every turn of the surrounding shady lanes." Her loves were vegetable, and her lanes were shady. Then, of course, she was educated at the school where Jane Austen and Mrs. Sherwood had been educated. She visited Lyme Regis, and there is mention of the Cobb. She saw London from the top of St. Paul's, and London was much smaller then than it is now. She changed from one charming house to another, and several distinguished literary gentlemen paid her compliments and came to tea. When the dining-room ceiling fell down it did not fall on her head, and when she took a ticket in a lottery she did win the prize. If in the foregoing sentences there are any words of more than two syllables, it is our fault and not Miss Hill's; and to do that writer justice, there are not many whole sentences in the book which are neither quoted from Miss Mitford nor supported by the authority of Mr. Crissy.

But how dangerous a thing is life! Can one be sure that anything not wholly made of mahogany will to the very end stand empty in the sun? Even cupboards have their secret springs, and when, inadvertently we are sure, Miss Hill touches this one, out, terrible to relate, topples a stout old gentleman. In plain English, Miss Mitford had a father. There is nothing actually improper in that. Many women have had fathers. But Miss Mitford's father was kept in a cupboard; that is to say, he was not a nice father. Miss Hill even goes so far as to conjecture that when "an imposing procession of neighbours and friends" followed him to the grave, "we cannot help thinking that this was more to show sympathy and respect for Miss Mitford than from special respect for him". Severe as the judgement is, the gluttonous, bibulous, amorous old man did something to deserve it. The less said about him the better. Only, if from your earliest childhood your father has gambled and speculated, first with your mother's fortune, then with your own, spent your earnings, driven you to earn more, and spent that too; if in old age he has lain upon a sofa and insisted that fresh air is bad for daughters, if, dying at length, he has left debts that can only be paid by selling everything you have or sponging upon the charity of friends—then even a lady sometimes raises her voice. Miss Mitford herself spoke out once. "It was grief to go; there I had toiled and striven and tasted as deeply of bitter anxiety, of fear, and of hope as often falls to the lot of woman." What language for a lady to use! for a lady, too, who owns a teapot. There is a drawing of the teapot at the bottom of the page. But it is now of no avail; Miss Mitford has smashed it to smithereens. That is the worst of writing about ladies; they have fathers as well as teapots. On the other hand, some pieces of Dr. Mitford's Wedgwood dinner service are still in existence, and a copy of Adam's Geography, which Mary won as a prize at school, is "in our temporary possession". If there is nothing improper in the suggestion, might not the next book be devoted entirely to them?

II

DR. BENTLEY

As we saunter through those famous courts where Dr. Bentley once reigned supreme we sometimes catch sight of a figure hurrying on its way to Chapel or Hall which, as it disappears, draws our thoughts enthusiastically after it. For that man, we are told, has the whole of Sophocles at his finger-ends; knows Homer by heart; reads Pindar as we read the *Times;* and spends his life, save for these short excursions to eat and pray, wholly in the company of the Greeks. It is true that the infirmities of our education prevent us from appreciating his emendations as they deserve; his life's work is a sealed book to us; none the less, we treasure up the last flicker of his black gown, and feel as if a bird of Paradise had flashed by us, so bright is his spirit's raiment, and in the murk of a November evening we had been privileged to see it winging its way to roost in fields of amaranth and beds of moly. Of all men, great scholars are the most mysterious, the most august. Since it is unlikely that we shall ever be admitted to their intimacy, or see much more of them than a black gown crossing a court at dusk, the best we can do is to read their lives—for example, the *Life of Dr. Bentley* by Bishop Monk.

There we shall find much that is odd and little that
is reassuring. The greatest of our scholars, the man
who read Greek as the most expert of us read English
not merely with an accurate sense of meaning and
grammar but with a sensibility so subtle and widespread that he perceived relations and suggestions of
language which enabled him to fetch up from oblivion
lost lines and inspire new life into the little fragments
that remained, the man who should have been steeped
in beauty (if what they say of the Classics is true) as
a honey-pot is ingrained with sweetness was, on the
contrary, the most quarrelsome of mankind.

"I presume that there are not many examples of an
individual who has been a party in six distinct suits
before the Court of King's Bench within the space of
three years", his biographer remarks; and adds that
Bentley won them all. It is difficult to deny his conclusion that though Dr. Bentley might have been a
first-rate lawyer or a great soldier "such a display
suited any character rather than that of a learned and
dignified clergyman". Not all these disputes, however, sprung from his love of literature. The charges
against which he had to defend himself were directed
against him as Master of Trinity College, Cambridge.
He was habitually absent from chapel; his expenditure upon building and upon his household was excessive; he used the college seal at meetings which did
not consist of the statutable number of sixteen, and
so on. In short, the career of the Master of Trinity
was one continuous series of acts of aggression and

defiance, in which Dr. Bentley treated the Society of
Trinity College as a grown man might treat an im-
portunate rabble of street boys. Did they dare to hint
that the staircase at the Lodge which admitted four
persons abreast was quite wide enough?—did they refuse to sanction his expenditure upon a new one?
Meeting them in the Great Court one evening after
chapel he proceeded urbanely to question them. They
refused to budge. Whereupon, with a sudden alteration of colour and voice, Bentley demanded whether
"they had forgotten his rusty sword?" Mr. Michael
Hutchinson and some others, upon whose backs the
weight of that weapon would have first descended,
brought pressure upon their seniors. The bill for
£350 was paid and their preferment secured. But
Bentley did not wait for this act of submission to finish
his staircase.

So it went on, year after year. Nor was the arrogance of his behaviour always justified by the splendour or utility of the objects he had in view—the creation of the Backs, the erection of an observatory, the
foundation of a laboratory. More trivial desires were
gratified with the same tyranny. Sometimes he
wanted coal; sometimes bread and ale; and then
Madame Bentley, sending her servant with a snuff-
box in token of authority, got from the butteries at
the expense of the college a great deal more of these
commodities than the college thought that Dr. Bentley
ought to require. Again, when he had four pupils to
lodge with him who paid him handsomely for their

board, it was drawn from the College, at the command of the snuff-box, for nothing. The principles of "delicacy and good feeling" which the Master might have been expected to observe (great scholar as he was, steeped in the wine of the classics) went for nothing. His argument that the "few College loaves" upon which the four young patricians were nourished were amply repaid by the three sash windows which he had put into their rooms at his own expense failed to convince the Fellows. And when, on Trinity Sunday 1719, the Fellows found the famous College ale not to their liking, they were scarcely satisfied when the butler told them that it had been brewed by the Master's orders, from the Master's malt, which was stored in the Master's granary, and though damaged by "an insect called the weevil" had been paid for at the very high rates which the Master demanded.

Still these battles over bread and beer are trifles and domestic trifles at that. His conduct in his profession will throw more light upon our inquiry. For, released from brick and building, bread and beer, patricians and their windows, it may be found that he expanded in the atmosphere of Homer, Horace, and Manilius, and proved in his study the benign nature of those influences which have been wafted down to us through the ages. But there the evidence is even less to the credit of the dead languages. He acquitted himself magnificently, all agree, in the great controversy about the letters of Phalaris. His temper was excellent and his learning prodigious. But that triumph was suc-

ceeded by a series of disputes which force upon us the
extraordinary spectacle of men of learning and genius,
of authority and divinity, brawling about Greek and
Latin texts, and calling each other names for all the
world like bookies on a racecourse or washerwomen in
a back street. For this vehemence of temper and viru-
lence of language were not confined to Bentley alone;
they appear unhappily characteristic of the profession
as a whole. Early in life, in the year 1691, a quarrel
was fastened upon him by his brother chaplain Hody
for writing Malelas, not as Hody preferred, Malela.
A controversy in which Bentley displayed learning and
wit, and Hody accumulated endless pages of bitter
argument against the letter *s* ensued. Hody was
worsted, and "there is too much reason to believe, that
the offence given by this trivial cause was never afterwards healed". Indeed, to mend a line was to break a
friendship. James Gronovius of Leyden—"homun-
culus eruditione mediocri, ingenio nullo", as Bentley
called him—attacked Bentley for ten years because
Bentley had succeeded in correcting a fragment of
Callimachus where he had failed.

But Gronovius was by no means the only scholar
who resented the success of a rival with a rancour that
grey hairs and forty years spent in editing the classics
failed to subdue. In all the chief towns of Europe lived
men like the notorious de Pauw of Utrecht, "a person
who has justly been considered the pest and disgrace
of letters", who, when a new theory or new edition
appeared, banded themselves together to deride and

humiliate the scholar. ". . . all his writings", Bishop
Monk remarks of de Pauw, "prove him to be devoid
of candour, good faith, good manners, and every gentlemanly feeling: and while he unites all the defects
and bad qualities that were ever found in a critic or
commentator, he adds one peculiar to himself, an incessant propensity to indecent allusions." With such
tempers and such habits it is not strange that the scholars of those days sometimes ended lives made intolerable by bitterness, poverty, and neglect by their own
hands, like Johnson, who after a lifetime spent in the
detection of minute errors of construction, went mad
and drowned himself in the meadows near Notting-
ham. On May 20, 1712, Trinity College was shocked
to find that the professor of Hebrew, Dr. Sike, had
hanged himself "some time this evening, before candle-
light, in his sash". When Kuster died, it was reported
that he, too, had killed himself. And so, in a sense, he
had. For when his body was opened "there was found
a cake of sand along the lower region of his belly.
This, I take it, was occasioned by his sitting nearly
double, and writing on a very low table, surrounded
with three or four circles of books placed on the
ground, which was the situation we usually found him
in." The minds of poor schoolmasters, like John Ker
of the dissenting Academy, who had had the high
gratification of dining with Dr. Bentley at the Lodge,
when the talk fell upon the use of the word *equidem*,
were so distorted by a lifetime of neglect and study
that they went home, collected all uses of the word

equidem which contradicted the Doctor's opinion, returned to the Lodge, anticipating in their simplicity a warm welcome, met the Doctor issuing to dine with the Archbishop of Canterbury, followed him down the street in spite of his indifference and annoyance, and, being refused even a word of farewell, went home to brood over their injuries and wait the day of revenge.

But the bickerings and animosities of the smaller fry were magnified, not obliterated, by the Doctor himself in the conduct of his own affairs. The courtesy and good temper which he had shown in his early controversies had worn away. ". . . a course of violent animosities and the indulgence of unrestrained indignation for many years had impaired both his taste and judgement in controversy", and he condescended, though the subject in dispute was the Greek Testament, to call his antagonist "maggot", "vermin", "gnawing rat", and "cabbage head", to refer to the darkness of his complexion, and to insinuate that his wits were crazed, which charge he supported by dwelling on the fact that his brother, a clergyman, wore a beard to his girdle.

Violent, pugnacious, and unscrupulous, Dr. Bentley survived these storms and agitations, and remained, though suspended from his degrees and deprived of his mastership, seated at the Lodge imperturbably. Wearing a broad-brimmed hat indoors to protect his eyes, smoking his pipe, enjoying his port, and expounding to his friends his doctrine of the digamma, Bentley lived those eighty years which, he said, were long

[272]

enough "to read everything which was worth reading", "Et tunc", he added, in his peculiar manner,

Et tunc magna mei sub terris ibit imago.

A small square stone marked his grave in Trinity College, but the Fellows refused to record upon it the fact that he had been their Master.

But the strangest sentence in this strange story has yet to be written, and Bishop Monk writes it as if it were a commonplace requiring no comment. "For a person who was neither a poet, nor possessed of poetical taste to venture upon such a task was no common presumption." The task was to detect every slip of language in *Paradise Lost*, and all instances of bad taste and incorrect imagery. The result was notoriously lamentable. Yet in what, we may ask, did it differ from those in which Bentley was held to have acquitted himself magnificently? And if Bentley was incapable of appreciating the poetry of Milton, how can we accept his verdict upon Horace and Homer? And if we cannot trust implicitly to scholars, and if the study of Greek is supposed to refine the manners and purify the soul—but enough. Our scholar has returned from Hall; his lamp is lit; his studies are resumed; and it is time that our profane speculations should have an end. Besides, all this happened many, many years ago.

III

LADY DOROTHY NEVILL

She had stayed, in a humble capacity, for a week in the ducal household. She had seen the troops of highly decorated human beings descending in couples to eat, and ascending in couples to bed. She had, surreptitiously, from a gallery, observed the Duke himself dusting the miniatures in the glass cases, while the Duchess let her crochet fall from her hands as if in utter disbelief that the world had need of crochet. From an upper window she had seen, as far as eye could reach, gravel paths swerving round isles of greenery and losing themselves in little woods designed to shed the shade without the severity of forests; she had watched the ducal carriage bowling in and out of the prospect, and returning a different way from the way it went. And what was her verdict? "A lunatic asylum."

It is true that she was a lady's-maid, and that Lady Dorothy Nevill, had she encountered her on the stairs, would have made an opportunity to point out that that is a very different thing from being a lady.

My mother never failed to point out the folly of workwomen, shop-girls, and the like calling each other "Ladies". All this sort of thing seemed to her to be mere vulgar humbug, and she did not fail to say so.

What can we point out to Lady Dorothy Nevill? that with all her advantages she had never learned to spell?

[274]

that she could not write a grammatical sentence? that she lived for eighty-seven years and did nothing but put food into her mouth and slip gold through her fingers? But delightful though it is to indulge in righteous indignation, it is misplaced if we agree with the lady's-maid that high birth is a form of congenital insanity, that the sufferer merely inherits the diseases of his ancestors, and endures them, for the most part very stoically, in one of those comfortably padded lunatic asylums which are known, euphemistically, as the stately homes of England.

Moreover, the Walpoles are not ducal. Horace Walpole's mother was a Miss Shorter; there is no mention of Lady Dorothy's mother in the present volume, but her great-grandmother was Mrs. Oldfield the actress, and, to her credit, Lady Dorothy was "exceedingly proud" of the fact. Thus she was not an extreme case of aristocracy; she was confined rather to a bird-cage than to an asylum; through the bars she saw people walking at large, and once or twice she made a surprising little flight into the open air. A gayer, brighter, more vivacious specimen of the caged tribe can seldom have existed; so that one is forced at times to ask whether what we call living in a cage is not the fate that wise people, condemned to a single sojourn upon earth, would choose. To be at large is, after all, to be shut out; to waste most of life in accumulating the money to buy and the time to enjoy what the Lady Dorothys find clustering and glowing about their cradles when their eyes first open—as hers

opened in the year 1826 at number eleven Berkeley
Square. Horace Walpole had lived there. Her father, Lord Orford, gambled it away in one night's
play the year after she was born. But Wolterton Hall,
in Norfolk, was full of carving and mantelpieces, and
there were rare trees in the garden, and a large and
famous lawn. No novelist could wish a more charming and even romantic environment in which to set the
story of two little girls, growing up, wild yet secluded,
reading Bossuet with their governess, and riding out
on their ponies at the head of the tenantry on polling
day. Nor can one deny that to have had the author
of the following letter among one's ancestors would
have been a source of inordinate pride. It is addressed
to the Norwich Bible Society, which had invited Lord
Orford to become its president:

I have long been addicted to the Gaming Table. I have
lately taken to the Turf. I fear I frequently blaspheme.
But I have never distributed religious tracts. All this was
known to you and your Society. Notwithstanding which you
think me a fit person to be your president. God forgive your
hypocrisy.

It was not Lord Orfold who was in the cage on that
occasion. But, alas! Lord Orford owned another
country house, Ilsington Hall, in Dorsetshire, and
there Lady Dorothy came in contact first with the mulberry tree, and later with Mr. Thomas Hardy; and
we get our first glimpse of the bars. We do not pretend to the ghost of an enthusiasm for Sailors' Homes

[276]

in general; no doubt mulberry trees are much nicer to look at; but when it comes to calling people "vandals" who cut them down to build houses, and to having footstools made from the wood, and to carving upon those footstools inscriptions which testify that "often and often has King George III. taken his tea" under this very footstool, then we want to protest—"Surely you must mean Shakespeare?" But as her subsequent remarks upon Mr. Hardy tend to prove, Lady Dorothy does not mean Shakespeare. She "warmly appreciated" the works of Mr. Hardy, and used to complain "that the county families were too stupid to appreciate his genius at its proper worth". George the Third drinking his tea; the county families failing to appreciate Mr. Hardy: Lady Dorothy is undoubtedly behind the bars.

Yet no story more aptly illustrates the barrier which we perceive hereafter between Lady Dorothy and the outer world than the story of Charles Darwin and the blankets. Among her recreations Lady Dorothy made a hobby of growing orchids, and thus got into touch with "the great naturalist". Mrs. Darwin, inviting her to stay with them, remarked with apparent simplicity that she had heard that people who moved much in London society were fond of being tossed in blankets. "I am afraid," her letter ended, "we should hardly be able to offer you anything of that sort." Whether in fact the necessity of tossing Lady Dorothy in a blanket had been seriously debated at Down, or whether Mrs. Darwin obscurely hinted her sense of some incongruity between her husband and the lady of the orchids, we do not know. But we have a sense of two worlds in collision; and it is not the Darwin world that emerges in fragments. More and more do we see Lady Dorothy hopping from perch to perch, picking at groundsel here, and at hempseed there, indulging in exquisite trills and roulades, and sharpening her beak against a lump of sugar in a large, airy, magnificently equipped bird-cage. The cake was full of charming diversions. Now she illuminated leaves which had been macerated to skeletons; now she interested herself in improving the breed of donkeys; next she took up the cause of silkworms, almost threatened Australia with a plague of them, and "actually succeeded in obtaining enough silk to make a dress"; again she was the first to discover that wood, gone green with decay, can be made, at some expense, into little boxes; she went into the question of funguses and established the virtues of the neglected English truffle; she imported rare fish; spent a great deal of energy in vainly trying to induce storks and Cornish choughs to breed in Sussex; painted on china; emblazoned heraldic arms, and, attaching whistles to the tails of pigeons, produced wonderful effects "as of an aerial orchestra" when they flew through the air. To the Duchess of Somerset belongs the credit of investigating the proper way of cooking guinea-pigs; but Lady Dorothy was one of the first to serve up a dish of these little creatures at luncheon in Charles Street.

[278]

But all the time the door of the cage was ajar. Raids were made into what Mr. Nevill calls "Upper Bohemia"; from which Lady Dorothy returned with "authors, journalists, actors, actresses, or other agreeable and amusing people". Lady Dorothy's judgement is proved by the fact that they seldom misbehaved, and some indeed became quite domesticated, and wrote her "very gracefully turned letters". But once or twice she made a flight beyond the cage herself. "These horrors", she said, alluding to the middle class, "are so clever and we are so stupid; but then look how well they are educated, while our children learn nothing but how to spend their parents' money!" She brooded over the fact. Something was going wrong. She was too shrewd and too honest not to lay the blame partly at least upon her own class. "I suppose she can just about read?" she said of one lady calling herself cultured; and of another, "She is indeed curious and well adapted to open bazaars." But to our thinking her most remarkable flight took place a year or two before her death, in the Victoria and Albert Museum:

I do so agree with you, she wrote—though I ought not to say so—that the upper class are very—I don't know what to say—but they seem to take no interest in anything—but golfing, etc. One day I was at the Victoria and Albert Museum, just a few sprinkles of legs, for I am sure they looked too frivolous to have bodies and souls attached to them—but what softened the sight to my eyes were 2 little Japs poring over each article with a handbook . . . our bodies, of course, giggling and looking at nothing. Still worse, not one soul of the higher class visible: in fact I never heard of any one of them knowing of the place, and for this we are spending millions—it is all too painful.

It was all too painful, and the guillotine, she felt, loomed ahead. That catastrophe she was spared, for who could wish to cut off the head of a pigeon with a whistle attached to its tail? But if the whole bird-cage had been overturned and the aerial orchestra sent screaming and fluttering through the air, we can be sure, as Mr. Joseph Chamberlain told her, that her conduct would have been "a credit to the British aristocracy".

IV

ARCHBISHOP THOMSON

The origin of Archbishop Thomson was obscure. His great-uncle "may reasonably be supposed" to have been "an ornament to the middle classes". His aunt married a gentleman who was present at the murder of Gustavus III. of Sweden; and his father met his death at the age of eighty-seven by treading on a cat in the early hours of the morning. The physical vigour which this anecdote implies was combined in the Archbishop with powers of intellect which promised success in whatever profession he adopted. At Oxford it seemed likely that he would devote himself to philosophy or science. While reading for his degree he found time to write the *Outlines of the Laws of Thought*, which "immediately became a recognised text-book for Oxford classes". But though poetry, philosophy, medicine, and the law held out their temptations he put such thoughts aside, or never entertained them, having made up his mind from the first to dedicate himself to Divine service. The measure of his success in the more exalted sphere is attested by the following facts: Ordained deacon in 1842 at the age of twenty-three, he became Dean and Bursar of Queen's College, Oxford, in 1845; Provost in 1855, Bishop of Gloucester and Bristol in 1861, and Archbishop of York in 1862. Thus at the early age of forty-three he stood next in rank to the Archbishop of Canterbury himself; and it was commonly though erroneously expected that he would in the end attain to that dignity also.

It is a matter of temperament and belief whether you read this list with respect or with boredom; whether you look upon an archbishop's hat as a crown or as an extinguisher. If, like the present reviewer, you are ready to hold the simple faith that the outer order corresponds to the inner—that a vicar is a good man, a canon a better man, and an archbishop the best man of all—you will find the study of the Archbishop's life one of extreme fascination. He has turned aside from poetry and philosophy and law, and specialised in virtue. He has dedicated himself to the service of the Divine. His spiritual proficiency has been such that he has developed from deacon to dean, from dean to bishop, and from bishop to archbishop in the short

space of twenty years. As there are only two arch-
bishops in the whole of England the inference seems to
be that he is the second best man in England; his hat
is the proof of it. Even in a material sense his hat
was one of the largest; it was larger than Mr. Gladstone's; larger than Thackeray's; larger than Dickens';
it was in fact, so his hatter told him and we are inclined to agree, an "eight full". Yet he began much
as other men begin. He struck an undergraduate in a
fit of temper and was rusticated; he wrote a text-book
of logic and rowed a very good oar. But after he was
ordained his diary shows that the specialising process
had begun. He thought a great deal about the state
of his soul; about "the monstrous tumour of Simony";
about Church reform; and about the meaning of Christianity. "Self-renunciation," he came to the conclusion, "is the foundation of Christian Religion and
Christian Morals. . . . The highest wisdom is that
which can enforce and cultivate this self-renunciation.
Hence (against Cousin) I hold that religion is higher
far than philosophy." There is one mention of chem-
ists and capillarity, but science and philosophy were,
even at this early stage, in danger of being crowded
out. Soon the diary takes a different tone. "He
seems," says his biographer, "to have had no time for
committing his thoughts to paper"; he records his engagements only, and he dines out almost every night.
Sir Henry Taylor, whom he met at one of these parties, described him as "simple, solid, good, capable, and
pleasing". Perhaps it was his solidity combined with

his "eminently scientific" turn of mind, his blandness
as well as his bulk, that impressed some of these great
people with the confidence that in him the Church had
found a very necessary champion. His "brawny logic"
and massive frame seemed to fit him to grapple with a
task that taxed the strongest—how, that is, to recon-
cile the scientific discoveries of the age with religion,
and even prove them "some of its strongest witnesses
for the truth". If any one could do this Thomson
could; his practical ability, unhampered by any mystical or dreaming tendency, had already proved itself in
the conduct of the business affairs of his College.
From Bishop he became almost instantly Archbishop;
and in becoming Archbishop he became Primate of
England, Governor of the Charterhouse and King's
College, London, patron of one hundred and twenty
livings, with the Archdeaconries of York, Cleveland,
and the East Riding in his gift, and the Canonries and
Prebends in York Minster. Bishopthorpe itself was
an enormous palace; he was immediately faced by the
"knotty question" of whether to buy all the furniture
—"much of it only poor stuff"—or to furnish the house
anew, which would cost a fortune. Moreover there
were seven cows in the park; but these, perhaps, were
counterbalanced by nine children in the nursery. Then
the Prince and Princess of Wales came to stay, and
the Archbishop took upon himself the task of furnishing the Princess's apartments. He went up to London
and bought eight Moderator lamps, two Spanish figures holding candles, and reminded himself of the

[283]

necessity of buying "soap for Princess". But meanwhile far more serious matters claimed every ounce of
his strength. Already he had been exhorted to "wield
the sure lance of your brawny logic against the sophis-
tries" of the authors of *Essays and Reviews,* and had
responded in a work called *Aids to Faith.* Near at
hand the town of Sheffield, with its large population
of imperfectly educated working men, was a breeding
ground of scepticism and discontent. The Archbishop
made it his special charge. He was fond of watching
the rolling of armour plate, and constantly addressed
meetings of working men. "Now what are these Nihil-
isms, and Socialisms, and Communisms, and Fenian-
isms, and Secret Societies—what do they all mean?" he
asked. "Selfishness," he replied, and "assertion of one
class against the rest is at the bottom of them all."
There was a law of nature, he said, by which wages
went up and wages went down. "You must accept the
declivity as well as the ascent. . . . If we could only
get people to learn that, then things would go on a
great deal better and smoother." And the working
men of Sheffield responded by giving him five hundred
pieces of cutlery mounted in sterling silver. But presumably there were a certain number of knives among
the spoons and the forks.

Bishop Colenso, however, was far more troublesome
than the working men of Sheffield; and the Ritualists
vexed him so persistently that even his vast strength
felt the strain. The questions which were referred to
him for decision were peculiarly fitted to tease and an-

noy even a man of his bulk and his blandness. Shall
a drunkard found dead in a ditch, or a burglar who
has fallen through a skylight, be given the benefit of
the Burial Service? he was asked. The question of
lighted candles was "most difficult"; the wearing of
coloured stoles and the administration of the mixed
chalice taxed him considerably; and finally there was
the Rev. John Purchas, who, dressed in cope, alb,
biretta and stole "cross-wise", lit candles and extinguished them "for no special reason"; filled a vessel
with black powder and rubbed it into the foreheads of
his congregation; and hung over the Holy Table "a
figure, image, or stuffed skin of a dove, in a flying attitude". The Archbishop's temper, usually so positive
and imperturbable, was gravely ruffled. "Will there
ever come a time when it will be thought a crime to
have striven to keep the Church of England as representing the common sense of the Nation?" he asked.
"I suppose it may, but I shall not see it. I have gone
through a good deal, but I do not repent of having
done my best." If, for a moment, the Archbishop
himself could ask such a question, we must confess to
a state of complete bewilderment. What has become
of our superlatively good man? He is harassed and
cumbered; spends his time settling questions about
stuffed pigeons and coloured petticoats; writes over
eighty letters before breakfast sometimes; scarcely has
time to run over to Paris and buy his daughter a bonnet; and in the end has to ask himself whether one of
these days his conduct will not be considered a crime.

Was it a crime? And if so, was it his fault? Did he not start out in the belief that Christianity had something to do with renunciation and was not entirely a matter of common sense? If honours and obligations, pomps and possessions, accumulated and encrusted him, how, being an Archbishop, could he refuse to accept them? Princesses must have their soap; palaces must have their furniture; children must have their cows. And, pathetic though it seems, he never completely lost his interest in science. He wore a pedometer; he was one of the first to use a camera; he believed in the future of the typewriter; and in his last years he tried to mend a broken clock. He was a delightful father too; he wrote witty, terse, sensible letters; his good stories were much to the point; and he died in harness. Certainly he was a very able man, but if we insist upon goodness—is it easy, is it possible, for a good man to be an Archbishop?

The Patron and the Crocus

Young men and women beginning to write are generally given the plausible but utterly impracticable advice to write what they have to write as shortly as possible, as clearly as possible, and without other thought in their minds except to say exactly what is in them. Nobody ever adds on these occasions the one thing needful: "And be sure you choose your patron wisely", though that is the gist of the whole matter. For a book is always written for somebody to read, and, since the patron is not merely the paymaster, but also in a very subtle and insidious way the instigator and inspirer of what is written, it is of the utmost importance that he should be a desirable man.

But who, then, is the desirable man—the patron who will cajole the best out of the writer's brain and bring to birth the most varied and vigorous progeny of which he is capable? Different ages have answered the question differently. The Elizabethans, to speak roughly, chose the aristocracy to write for and the playhouse public. The eighteenth-century patron was a combination of coffee-house wit and Grub Street bookseller. In the nineteenth century the great writers wrote for the half-crown magazines and the leisured classes. And looking back and applauding the splendid results of these different alliances, it all seems enviably simple, and plain as a pikestaff compared with

[287]

our own predicament—for whom should we write? For the present supply of patrons is of unexampled and bewildering variety. There is the daily Press, the weekly Press, the monthly Press; the English public and the American public; the best-seller public and the worst-seller public; the high-brow public and the red-blood public; all now organised self-conscious entities capable through their various mouthpieces of making their needs known and their approval or displeasure felt. Thus the writer who has been moved by the sight of the first crocus in Kensington Gardens has, before he sets pen to paper, to choose from a crowd of competitors the particular patron who suits him best. It is futile to say, "Dismiss them all; think only of your crocus", because writing is a method of communication; and the crocus is an imperfect crocus until it has been shared. The first man or the last may write for himself alone, but he is an exception and an unenviable one at that, and the gulls are welcome to his works if the gulls can read them.

Granted, then, that every writer has some public or other at the end of his pen, the high-minded will say that it should be a submissive public, accepting obediently whatever he likes to give it. Plausible as the theory sounds, great risks are attached to it. For in that case the writer remains conscious of his public, yet is superior to it—an uncomfortable and unfortunate combination, as the works of Samuel Butler, George Meredith, and Henry James may be taken to prove. Each despised the public; each desired a public; each

failed to attain a public; and each wreaked his failure
upon the public by a succession, gradually increasing
in intensity, of angularities, obscurities, and affectations which no writer whose patron was his equal and
friend would have thought it necessary to inflict.
Their crocuses in consequence are tortured plants, beautiful and bright, but with something wry-necked about
them, malformed, shrivelled on the one side, overblown
on the other. A touch of the sun would have done
them a world of good. Shall we then rush to the opposite extreme and accept (if in fancy alone) the flattering proposals which the editors of the *Times* and the
Daily News may be supposed to make us—"Twenty
pounds down for your crocus in precisely fifteen hundred words, which shall blossom upon every breakfast
table from John o' Groats to the Land's End before
nine o'clock to-morrow morning with the writer's name
attached"?

But will one crocus be enough, and must it not be
a very brilliant yellow to shine so far, to cost so much,
and to have one's name attached to it? The Press is
undoubtedly a great multiplier of crocuses. But if we
look at some of these plants, we shall find that they
are only very distantly related to the original little yellow or purple flower which pokes up through the grass
in Kensington Gardens about this time of year. The
newspaper crocus is amazing but still a very different
plant. It fills precisely the space allotted to it. It
radiates a golden glow. It is genial, affable, warm-
hearted. It is beautifully finished, too, for let nobody

[289]

think that the art of "our dramatic critic" of the *Times* or of Mr. Lynd of the *Daily News* is an easy one. It is no despicable feat to start a million brains running at nine o'clock in the morning, to give two million eyes something bright and brisk and amusing to look at. But the night comes and these flowers fade. So little bits of glass lose their lustre if you take them out of the sea; great prima donnas howl like hyenas if you shut them up in telephone boxes; and the most brilliant of articles when removed from its element is dust and sand and the husks of straw. Journalism embalmed in a book is unreadable.

The patron we want, then, is one who will help us to preserve our flowers from decay. But as his qualities change from age to age, and it needs considerable integrity and conviction not to be dazzled by the pretensions or bamboozled by the persuasions of the competing crowd, this business of patron-finding is one of the tests and trials of authorship. To know whom to write for is to know how to write. Some of the modern patron's qualities are, however, fairly plain. The writer will require at this moment, it is obvious, a patron with the book-reading habit rather than the play-going habit. Nowadays, too, he must be instructed in the literature of other times and races. But there are other qualities which our special weaknesses and tendencies demand in him. There is the question of indecency, for instance, which plagues us and puzzles us much more than it did the Elizabethans. The twentieth-century patron must be immune from shock.

He must distinguish infallibly between the little clod of manure which sticks to the crocus of necessity, and that which is plastered to it out of bravado. He must be a judge, too, of those social influences which inevitably play so large a part in modern literature, and able to say which matures and fortifies, which inhibits and makes sterile. Further, there is emotion for him to pronounce on, and in no department can he do more useful work than in bracing a writer against sentimentality on the one hand and a craven fear of expressing his feeling on the other. It is worse, he will say, and perhaps more common, to be afraid of feeling than to feel too much. He will add, perhaps, something about language, and point out how many words Shakespeare used and how much grammar Shakespeare violated, while we, though we keep our fingers so demurely to the black notes on the piano, have not appreciably improved upon *Antony and Cleopatra*. And if you can forget your sex altogether, he will say, so much the better; a writer has none. But all this is by the way—elementary and disputable. The patron's prime quality is something different, only to be expressed perhaps by the use of that convenient word which cloaks so much—atmosphere. It is necessary that the patron should shed and envelop the crocus in an atmosphere which makes it appear a plant of the very highest importance, so that to misrepresent it is the one outrage not to be forgiven this side of the grave. He must make us feel that a single crocus, if it be a real crocus, is enough for him; that he does not want to be lec-

[291]

tured, elevated, instructed, or improved; that he is sorry that he bullied Carlyle into vociferation, Tennyson into idyllics, and Ruskin into insanity; that he is now ready to efface himself or assert himself as his writers require; that he is bound to them by a more than maternal tie; that they are twins indeed, one dying if the other dies, one flourishing if the other flourishes; that the fate of literature depends upon their happy alliance—all of which proves, as we began by saying, that the choice of a patron is of the highest importance. But how to choose rightly? How to write well? Those are the questions.

The Modern Essay

As Mr. Rhys truly says, it is unnecessary to go profoundly into the history and origin of the essay—whether it derives from Socrates or Siranney the Persian—since, like all living things, its present is more important than its past. Moreover, the family is widely spread; and while some of its representatives have risen in the world and wear their coronets with the best, others pick up a precarious living in the gutter near Fleet Street. The form, too, admits variety. The essay can be short or long, serious or trifling, about God and Spinoza, or about turtles and Cheapside. But as we turn over the pages of these five little volumes,[1] containing essays written between 1870 and 1920, certain principles appear to control the chaos, and we detect in the short period under review something like the progress of history.

Of all forms of literature, however, the essay is the one which least calls for the use of long words. The principle which controls it is simply that it should give pleasure; the desire which impels us when we take it from the shelf is simply to receive pleasure. Everything in an essay must be subdued to that end. It should lay us under a spell with its first word, and we should only wake, refreshed, with its last. In the interval we may pass through the most various experi-

---

[1] *Modern English Essays,* edited by Ernest Rhys, 5 vols. (Dent).

ences of amusement, surprise, interest, indignation;
we may soar to the heights of fantasy with Lamb or
plunge to the depths of wisdom with Bacon, but we
must never be roused. The essay must lap us about
and draw its curtain across the world.

So great a feat is seldom accomplished, though the
fault may well be as much on the reader's side as on
the writer's. Habit and lethargy have dulled his palate. A novel has a story, a poem rhyme; but what art
can the essayist use in these short lengths of prose to
sting us wide awake and fix us in a trance which is not
sleep but rather an intensification of life—a basking,
with every faculty alert, in the sun of pleasure? He
must know—that is the first essential—how to write.
His learning may be as profound as Mark Pattison's,
but in an essay it must be so fused by the magic of
writing that not a fact juts out, not a dogma tears the
surface of the texture. Macaulay in one way, Froude
in another, did this superbly over and over again.
They have blown more knowledge into us in the course
of one essay than the innumerable chapters of a hundred text-books. But when Mark Pattison has to tell
us, in the space of thirty-five little pages, about Montaigne, we feel that he had not previously assimilated
M. Grün. M. Grün was a gentleman who once wrote
a bad book. M. Grün and his book should have been
embalmed for our perpetual delight in amber. But the
process is fatiguing; it requires more time and perhaps
more temper than Pattison had at his command. He

served M. Grün up raw, and he remains a crude berry among the cook meats, upon which our teeth must grate for ever. Something of the sort applies to Matthew Arnold and a certain translator of Spinoza. Literal truth-telling and finding fault with a culprit for his good are out of place in an essay, where everything should be for our good and rather for eternity than for the March number of the *Fortnightly Review*. But if the voice of the scold should never be heard in this narrow plot, there is another voice which is as a plague of locusts—the voice of a man stumbling drowsily among loose words, clutching aimlessly at vague ideas, the voice, for example, of Mr. Hutton in the following passage:

Add to this that his married life was very brief, only seven years and a half, being unexpectedly cut short, and that his passionate reverence for his wife's memory and genius—in his own words, "a religion"—was one which, as he must have been perfectly sensible, he could not make to appear otherwise than extravagant, not to say an hallucination, in the eyes of the rest of mankind, and yet that he was possessed by an irresistible yearning to attempt to embody it in all the tender and enthusiastic hyperbole of which it is so pathetic to find a man who gained his fame by his "dry-light" a master, and it is impossible not to feel that the human incidents in Mr. Mill's career are very sad.

A book could take that blow, but it sinks an essay. A biography in two volumes is indeed the proper depositary; for there, where the licence is so much wider, and hints and glimpses of outside things make part of the feast (we refer to the old type of Victorian volume), these yawns and stretches hardly matter, and have indeed some positive value of their own. But that value, which is contributed by the reader, perhaps illicitly, in his desire to get as much into the book from all possible sources as he can, must be ruled out here.

There is no room for the impurities of literature in an essay. Somehow or other, by dint of labour or bounty of nature, or both combined, the essay must be pure—pure like water or pure like wine, but pure from dullness, deadness, and deposits of extraneous matter. Of all writers in the first volume, Walter Pater best achieves this arduous task, because before setting out to write his essay ("Notes on Leonardo da Vinci") he has somehow contrived to get his material fused. He is a learned man, but it is not knowledge of Leonardo that remains with us, but a vision, such as we get in a good novel where everything contributes to bring the writer's conception as a whole before us. Only here, in the essay, where the bounds are so strict and facts have to be used in their nakedness, the true writer like Walter Pater makes these limitations yield their own quality. Truth will give it authority; from its narrow limits he will get shape and intensity; and then there is no more fitting place for some of those ornaments which the old writers loved and we, by calling them ornaments, presumably despise. Nowadays nobody would have the courage to embark on the once famous description of Leonardo's lady who has

[296]

learned the secrets of the grave; and has been a diver in deep seas and keeps their fallen day about her; and trafficked for strange webs with Eastern merchants; and, as Leda, was the mother of Helen of Troy, and, as Saint Anne, the mother of Mary . . .

The passage is too thumb-marked to slip naturally into the context. But when we come unexpectedly upon "the smiling of women and the motion of great waters", or upon "full of the refinement of the dead, in sad, earth-coloured raiment, set with pale stones", we suddenly remember that we have ears and we have eyes, and that the English language fills a long array of stout volumes with innumerable words, many of which are of more than one syllable. The only living Englishman who ever looks into these volumes is, of course, a gentleman of Polish extraction. But doubtless our abstention saves us much gush, much rhetoric, much high-stepping and cloud-prancing, and for the sake of the prevailing sobriety and hard-headedness we should be willing to barter the splendour of Sir Thomas Browne and the vigour of Swift.

Yet, if the essay admits more properly than biography or fiction of sudden boldness and metaphor, and can be polished till every atom of its surface shines, there are dangers in that too. We are soon in sight of ornament. Soon the current, which is the life-blood of literature, runs slow; and instead of sparkling and flashing or moving with a quieter impulse which has a deeper excitement, words coagulate together in frozen sprays which, like the grapes on a Christmas-tree, glitter for a single night, but are dusty and garish the day after. The temptation to decorate is great where the theme may be of the slightest. What is there to interest another in the fact that one has enjoyed a walking tour, or has amused oneself by rambling down Cheapside and looking at the turtles in Mr. Sweeting's shop window? Stevenson and Samuel Butler chose very different methods of exciting our interest in these domestic themes. Stevenson, of course, trimmed and polished and set out his matter in the traditional eighteenth-century form. It is admirably done, but we cannot help feeling anxious, as the essay proceeds, lest the material may give out under the craftsman's fingers. The ingot is so small, the manipulation so incessant. And perhaps that is why the peroration—

To sit still and contemplate—to remember the faces of women without desire, to be pleased by the great deeds of men without envy, to be everything and everywhere in sympathy and yet content to remain where and what you are—

has the sort of insubstantiality which suggests that by the time he got to the end he had left himself nothing solid to work with. Butler adopted the very opposite method. Think your own thoughts, he seems to say, and speak them as plainly as you can. These turtles in the shop window which appear to leak out of their shells through heads and feet suggest a fatal faithfulness to a fixed idea. And so, striding unconcernedly from one idea to the next, we traverse a large stretch of ground; observe that a wound in the solicitor is a very serious thing; that Mary Queen of Scots wears surgical boots and is subject to fits near the Horse Shoe in Tottenham Court Road; take it for granted that no one really cares about Æschylus; and so, with many amusing anecdotes and some profound reflections, reach the peroration, which is that, as he had been told not to see more in Cheapside than he could get into twelve pages of the *Universal Review*, he had better stop. And yet obviously Butler is at least as careful of our pleasure as Stevenson; and to write like oneself and call it not writing is a much harder exercise in style than to write like Addison and call it writing well.

But, however much they differ individually, the Victorian essayists yet had something in common. They wrote at greater length than is now usual, and they wrote for a public which had not only time to sit down to its magazine seriously, but a high, if peculiarly Victorian, standard of culture by which to judge it. It was worth while to speak out upon serious matters in an essay; and there was nothing absurd in writing as well as one possibly could when, in a month or two, the same public which had welcomed the essay in a magazine would carefully read it once more in a book. But a change came from a small audience of cultivated people to a larger audience of people who were not quite so cultivated. The change was not altogether for the worse. In volume iii. we find Mr. Birrell and Mr. Beerbohm. It might even be said that there was a reversion to the classic type, and that the essay by losing its size and something of its sonority was approaching more nearly the essay of Addison and Lamb. At any rate, there is a great gulf between Mr. Birrell on Carlyle and the essay which one may suppose that Carlyle would have written upon Mr. Birrell. There is little similarity between *A Cloud of Pinafores*, by Max Beerbohm, and *A Cynic's Apology*, by Leslie Stephen. But the essay is alive; there is no reason to despair. As the conditions change so the essayist, most sensitive of all plants to public opinion, adapts himself, and if he is good makes the best of the change, and if he is bad the worst. Mr. Birrell is certainly good; and so we find that, though he has dropped a considerable amount of weight, his attack is much more direct and his movement more supple. But what did Mr. Beerbohm give to the essay and what did he take from it? That is a much more complicated question, for here we have an essayist who has concentrated on the work and is without doubt the prince of his profession.

What Mr. Beerbohm gave was, of course, himself. This presence, which has haunted the essay fitfully from the time of Montaigne, had been in exile since the death of Charles Lamb. Matthew Arnold was never to his readers Matt, nor Walter Pater affectionately abbreviated in a thousand homes to Wat. They gave us much, but that they did not give. Thus, some time in the nineties, it must have surprised readers accustomed to exhortation, information, and denunciation to find themselves familiarly addressed by a voice which seemed to belong to a man no larger than themselves. He was affected by private joys and sorrows, and had no gospel to preach and no learning to impart. He was himself, simply and directly, and himself he has remained. Once again we have an essayist capable of using the essayist's most proper but most dangerous and delicate tool. He has brought personality into literature, not unconsciously and impurely, but so consciously and purely that we do not know whether there is any relation between Max the essayist and Mr. Beerbohm the man. We only know that the spirit of personality permeates every word that he writes. The triumph is the triumph of style. For it is only by knowing how to write that you can make use in literature of your self; that self which, while it is essential to literature, is also its most dangerous antagonist. Never to be yourself and yet always—that is the problem. Some of the essayists in Mr. Rhys' collection, to be frank, have not altogether succeeded in solving it. We are nauseated by the sight of trivial personalities decomposing in the eternity of print. As talk, no doubt, it was charming, and certainly the writer is a good fellow to meet over a bottle of beer. But literature is stern; it is no use being charming, virtuous, or even learned and brilliant into the bargain, unless, she seems to reiterate, you fulfil her first condition—to know how to write.

This art is possessed to perfection by Mr. Beerbohm. But he has not searched the dictionary for polysyllables. He has not moulded firm periods or seduced our ears with intricate cadences and strange melodies.

[301]

Some of his companions—Henley and Stevenson, for example—are momentarily more impressive. But *A Cloud of Pinafores* had in it that indescribable inequality, stir, and final expressiveness which belong to life and to life alone. You have not finished with it because you have read it, any more than friendship is ended because it is time to part. Life wells up and alters and adds. Even things in a book-case change if they are alive; we find ourselves wanting to meet them again; we find them altered. So we look back upon essay after essay by Mr. Beerbohm, knowing that, come September or May, we shall sit down with them and talk. Yet it is true that the essayist is the most sensitive of all writers to public opinion. The drawing-room is the place where a great deal of reading is done nowadays, and the essays of Mr. Beerbohm lie, with an exquisite appreciation of all that the position exacts, upon the drawing-room table. There is no gin about; no strong tobacco; no puns, drunkenness, or insanity. Ladies and gentlemen talk together, and some things, of course, are not said.

But if it would be foolish to attempt to confine Mr. Beerbohm to one room, it would be still more foolish, unhappily, to make him, the artist, the man who gives us only his best, the representative of our age. There are no essays by Mr. Beerbohm in the fourth or fifth volumes of the present collection. His age seems already a little distant, and the drawing-room table, as it recedes, begins to look rather like an altar where, once upon a time, people deposited offerings—fruit from their own orchards, gifts carved with their own hands. Now once more the conditions have changed. The public needs essays as much as ever, and perhaps even more. The demand for the light middle not exceeding fifteen hundred words, or in special cases seventeen hundred and fifty, much exceeds the supply. Where Lamb wrote one essay and Max perhaps writes two, Mr. Belloc at a rough computation produces three hundred and sixty-five. They are very short, it is true. Yet with what dexterity the practised essayist will utilise his space—beginning as close to the top of the sheet as possible, judging precisely how far to go, when to turn, and how, without sacrificing a hair's-breadth of paper, to wheel about and alight accurately upon the last word his editor allows! As a feat of skill it is well worth watching. But the personality upon which Mr. Belloc, like Mr. Beerbohm, depends suffers in the process. It comes to us not with the natural richness of the speaking voice, but strained and thin and full of mannerisms and affectations, like the voice of a man shouting through a megaphone to a crowd on a windy day. "Little friends, my readers," he says in the essay called "An Unknown Country", and he goes on to tell us how—

There was a shepherd the other day at Findon Fair who had come from the east by Lewes with sheep, and who had in his eyes that reminiscence of horizons which makes the eyes of shepherds and of mountaineers different from the eyes of other men. . . . I went with him to hear what he had to say, for shepherds talk quite differently from other men.

[303]

Happily this shepherd had little to say, even under the stimulus of the inevitable mug of beer, about the Unknown Country, for the only remark that he did make proves him either a minor poet, unfit for the care of sheep, or Mr. Belloc himself masquerading with a fountain pen. That is the penalty which the habitual essayist must now be prepared to face. He must masquerade. He cannot afford the time either to be himself or to be other people. He must skim the surface of thought and dilute the strength of personality. He must give us a worn weekly halfpenny instead of a solid sovereign once a year.

But it is not Mr. Belloc only who has suffered from the prevailing conditions. The essays which bring the collection to the year 1920 may not be the best of their authors' work, but, if we except writers like Mr. Conrad and Mr. Hudson, who have strayed into essay writing accidentally, and concentrate upon those who write essays habitually, we shall find them a good deal affected by the change in their circumstances. To write weekly, to write daily, to write shortly, to write for busy people catching trains in the morning or for tired people coming home in the evening, is a heartbreaking task for men who know good writing from bad. They do it, but instinctively draw out of harm's way anything precious that might be damaged by contact with the public, or anything sharp that might irritate its skin. And so, if one reads Mr. Lucas, Mr. Lynd, or Mr. Squire in the bulk, one feels that a common greyness silvers everything. They are as far removed from the extravagant beauty of Walter Pater as they are from the intemperate candour of Leslie Stephen. Beauty and courage are dangerous spirits to battle in a column and a half; and thought, like a brown paper parcel in a waistcoat pocket, has a way of spoiling the symmetry of an article. It is a kind, tired, apathetic world for which they write, and the marvel is that they never cease to attempt, at least, to write well.

But there is no need to pity Mr. Clutton Brock for this change in the essayist's conditions. He has clearly made the best of his circumstances and not the worst. One hesitates even to say that he has had to make any conscious effort in the matter, so naturally has he effected the transition from the private essayist to the public, from the drawing-room to the Albert Hall. Paradoxically enough, the shrinkage in size has brought about a corresponding expansion of individuality. We have no longer the "I" of Max and of Lamb, but the "we" of public bodies and other sublime personages. It is "we" who go to hear the *Magic Flute;* "we" who ought to profit by it; "we", in some mysterious way, who, in our corporate capacity, once upon a time actually wrote it. For music and literature and art must submit to the same generalisation or they will not carry to the farthest recesses of the Albert Hall. That the voice of Mr. Clutton Brock, so sincere and so disinterested, carries such a distance and reaches so many without pandering to the weakness of the mass or its passions must be a matter of legitimate satisfaction to us all. But while "we" are gratified, "I", that

[305]

unruly partner in the human fellowship, is reduced to despair. "I" must always think things for himself, and feel things for himself. To share them in a diluted form with the majority of well-educated and well-intentioned men and women is for him sheer agony; and while the rest of us listen intently and profit profoundly, "I" slips off to the woods and the fields and rejoices in a single blade of grass or a solitary potato.

In the fifth volume of modern essays, it seems, we have got some way from pleasure and the art of writing. But in justice to the essayists of 1920 we must be sure that we are not praising the famous because they have been praised already and the dead because we shall never meet them wearing spats in Piccadilly. We must know what we mean when we say that they can write and give us pleasure. We must compare them; we must bring out the quality. We must point to this and say it is good because it is exact, truthful, and imaginative:

Nay, retire men cannot when they would; neither will they, when it were Reason; but are impatient of Privateness, even in age and sickness, which require the shadow: like old Townsmen: that will still be sitting at their street door, though thereby they offer Age to Scorn . . .

and to this, and say it is bad because it is loose, plausible, and commonplace:

With courteous and precise cynicism on his lips, he thought of quiet virginal chambers, of waters singing under the moon, of terraces where taintless music sobbed into the open night,

[306]

of pure maternal mistresses with protecting arms and vigilant eyes, of fields slumbering in the sunlight, of leagues of ocean heaving under warm tremulous heavens, of hot ports, gorgeous and perfumed. . . .

It goes on, but already we are bemused with sound and neither feel nor hear. The comparison makes us suspect that the art of writing has for backbone some fierce attachment to an idea. It is on the back of an idea, something believed in with conviction or seen with precision and thus compelling words to its shape, that the diverse company which included Lamb and Bacon, and Mr. Beerbohm and Hudson, and Vernon Lee and Mr. Conrad, and Leslie Stephen and Butler and Walter Pater reaches the farther shore. Very various talents have helped or hindered the passage of the idea into words. Some scrape through painfully; others fly with every wind favouring. But Mr. Belloc and Mr. Lucas and Mr. Lynd and Mr. Squire are not fiercely attached to anything in itself. They share the contemporary dilemma—that lack of an obstinate conviction which lifts ephemeral sounds through the misty sphere of anybody's language to the land where there is a perpetual marriage, a perpetual union. Vague as all definitions are, a good essay must have this permanent quality about it; it must draw its curtain round us, but it must be a curtain that shuts us in, not out.

Joseph Conrad[1]

Suddenly, without giving us time to arrange our thoughts or prepare our phrases, our guest has left us; and his withdrawal without farewell or ceremony is in keeping with his mysterious arrival, long years ago, to take up his lodging in this country. For there was always an air of mystery about him. It was partly his Polish birth, partly his memorable appearance, partly his preference for living in the depths of the country, out of ear-shot of gossips, beyond reach of hostesses, so that for news of him one had to depend upon the evidence of simple visitors with a habit of ringing door-bells who reported of their unknown host that he had the most perfect manners, the brightest eyes, and spoke English with a strong foreign accent.

Still, though it is the habit of death to quicken and focus our memories, there clings to the genius of Conrad something essentially, and not accidentally, difficult of approach. His reputation of later years was, with one obvious exception, undoubtedly the highest in England; yet he was not popular. He was read with passionate delight by some; others he left cold and lustreless. Among his readers were people of the most opposite ages and sympathies. Schoolboys of fourteen, driving their way through Marryat, Scott, Henty, and Dickens, swallowed him down with the rest; while

[1] August, 1924.

the seasoned and the fastidious, who in process of time
have eaten their way to the heart of literature and
there turn over and over a few precious crumbs, set Conrad scrupulously upon their banqueting table. One
source of difficulty and disagreement is, of course, to be
found, where men have at all times found it, in his
beauty. One opens his pages and feels as Helen must
have felt when she looked in her glass and realised that,
do what she would, she could never in any circumstances pass for a plain woman. So Conrad had been
gifted, so he had schooled himself, and such was his
obligation to a strange language wooed characteristically for its Latin qualities rather than its Saxon that
it seemed impossible for him to make an ugly or insignificant movement of the pen. His mistress, his style,
is a little somnolent sometimes in repose. But let
somebody speak to her, and then how magnificently
she bears down upon us, with what colour, triumph,
and majesty! Yet it is arguable that Conrad would
have gained both in credit and in popularity if he had
written what he had to write without this incessant
care for appearances. They block and impede and
distract, his critics say, pointing to those famous passages which it is becoming the habit to lift from their
context and exhibit among other cut flowers of English
prose. He was self-conscious and stiff and ornate, they
complain, and the sound of his own voice was dearer
to him than the voice of humanity in its anguish. The
criticism is familiar, and as difficult to refute as the
remarks of deaf people when *Figaro* is played. They

see the orchestra; far off they hear a dismal scrape of sound; their own remarks are interrupted, and, very naturally, they conclude that the ends of life would be better served if instead of scraping Mozart those fifty fiddlers broke stones upon the road. That beauty teaches, that beauty is a disciplinarian, how are we to convince them, since her teaching is inseparable from the sound of her voice and to that they are deaf? But read Conrad, not in birthday books but in the bulk, and he must be lost indeed to the meaning of words who does not hear in that rather stiff and sombre music, with its reserve, its pride, its vast and implacable integrity, how it is better to be good than bad, how loyalty is good and honesty and courage, though ostensibly Conrad is concerned merely to show us the beauty of a night at sea. But it is ill work dragging such intimations from their element. Dried in our little saucers, without the magic and mystery of language, they lose their power to excite and goad; they lose the drastic power which is a constant quality of Conrad's prose.

For it was by virtue of something drastic in him, the qualities of a leader and captain, that Conrad kept his hold over boys and young people. Until *Nostromo* was written his characters, as the young were quick to perceive, were fundamentally simple and heroic, however subtle the mind and indirect the method of their creator. They were seafarers, used to solitude and silence. They were in conflict with Nature, but at peace with man. Nature was their an-

[311]

tagonist; she it was who drew forth honour, magnanimity, loyalty, the qualities proper to man; she who in sheltered bays reared to womanhood beautiful girls unfathomable and austere. Above all, it was Nature who turned out such gnarled and tested characters as Captain Whalley and old Singleton, obscure but glorious in their obscurity, who were to Conrad the pick of our race, the men whose praises he was never tired of celebrating:

They had been strong as those are strong who know neither doubts nor hopes. They had been impatient and enduring, turbulent and devoted, unruly and faithful. Well-meaning people had tried to represent these men as whining over every mouthful of their food, as going about their work in fear of their lives. But in truth they had been men who knew toil, privation, violence, debauchery—but knew not fear, and had no desire of spite in their hearts. Men hard to manage, but easy to inspire; voiceless men—but men enough to scorn in their hearts the sentimental voices that bewailed the hardness of their fate. It was a fate unique and their own; the capacity to bear it appeared to them the privilege of the chosen! Their generation lived inarticulate and indispensable, without knowing the sweetness of affections or the refuge of a home—and died free from the dark menace of a narrow grave. They were the everlasting children of the mysterious sea.

Such were the characters of the early books—*Lord Jim*, *Typhoon*, *The Nigger of the "Narcissus"*, *Youth;* and these books, in spite of the changes and fashions, are surely secure of their place among our classics. But they reach this height by means of qualities which the simple story of adventure, as Marryat told it, or Feni-

more Cooper, has no claim to possess. For it is clear
that to admire and celebrate such men and such deeds,
romantically, whole-heartedly and with the fervour of
a lover, one must be possessed of the double vision;
one must be at once inside and out. To praise their
silence one must possess a voice. To appreciate their
endurance one must be sensitive to fatigue. One must
be able to live on equal terms with the Whalleys and
the Singletons and yet hide from their suspicious eyes
the very qualities which enable one to understand
them. Conrad alone was able to live that double life,
for Conrad was compound of two men; together with
the sea captain dwelt that subtle, refined, and fastidious analyst whom he called Marlow. "A most discreet, understanding man", he said of Marlow.

Marlow was one of those born observers who are
happiest in retirement. Marlow liked nothing better
than to sit on deck, in some obscure creek of the
Thames, smoking and recollecting; smoking and specu-
lating; sending after his smoke beautiful rings of words
until all the summer's night became a little clouded
with tobacco smoke. Marlow, too, had a profound
respect for the men with whom he had sailed; but he
saw the humour of them. He nosed out and described
in masterly fashion those livid creatures who prey successfully upon the clumsy veterans. He had a flair
for human deformity; his humour was sardonic. Nor
did Marlow live entirely wreathed in the smoke of his
own cigars. He had a habit of opening his eyes suddenly and looking—at a rubbish heap, at a port, at a

[313]

shop counter—and then complete in its burning ring of light that thing is flashed bright upon the mysterious background. Introspective and analytical, Marlow was aware of this peculiarity. He said the power came to him suddenly. He might, for instance, overhear a French officer murmur "Mon Dieu, how the time passes!"

Nothing [he comments] could have been more commonplace than this remark; but its utterance coincided for me with a moment of vision. It's extraordinary how we go through life with eyes half shut, with dull ears, with dormant thoughts. . . . Nevertheless, there can be but few of us who had never known one of these rare moments of awakening, when we see, hear, understand, ever so much—everything —in a flash, before we fall back again into our agreeable somnolence. I raised my eyes when he spoke, and I saw him as though I had never seen him before.

Picture after picture he painted thus upon that dark background; ships first and foremost, ships at anchor, ships flying before the storm, ships in harbour; he painted sunsets and dawns; he painted the night; he painted the sea in every aspect; he painted the gaudy brilliancy of Eastern ports, and men and women, their houses and their attitudes. He was an accurate and unflinching observer, schooled to that "absolute loyalty towards his feelings and sensations", which, Conrad wrote, "an author should keep hold of in his most exalted moments of creation". And very quietly and compassionately Marlow sometimes lets fall a few words of epitaph which remind us, with all that beauty and brilliancy before our eyes, of the darkness of the background.

Thus a rough-and-ready distinction would make us say that it is Marlow who comments, Conrad who creates. It would lead us, aware that we are on dangerous ground, to account for that change which, Conrad tells us, took place when he had finished the last story in the *Typhoon* volume—"a subtle change in the nature of the inspiration"—by some alteration in the relationship of the two old friends. ". . . it seemed somehow that there was nothing more in the world to write about." It was Conrad, let us suppose, Conrad the creator, who said that, looking back with sorrowful satisfaction upon the stories he had told; feeling as he well might that he could never better the storm in *The Nigger of the "Narcissus"*, or render more faithful tribute to the qualities of British seamen than he had done already in *Youth* and *Lord Jim*. It was then that Marlow, the commentator, reminded him how, in the course of nature, one must grow old, sit smoking on deck, and give up seafaring. But, he reminded him, those strenuous years had deposited their memories; and he even went so far perhaps as to hint that, though the last word might have been said about Captain Whalley and his relation to the universe, there remained on shore a number of men and women whose relationships, though of a more personal kind, might be worth looking into. If we further suppose that there was a volume of Henry James on board and that Marlow gave his friend the

book to take to bed with him, we may seek support
in the fact that it was in 1905 that Conrad wrote a
very fine essay upon that master.

For some years, then, it was Marlow who was the
dominant partner. *Nostromo, Chance, The Arrow of
Gold* represent that stage of the alliance which some
will continue to find the richest of all. The human
heart is more intricate than the forest, they will say;
it has its storms; it has its creatures of the night; and
if as novelist you wish to test man in all his relationships, the proper antagonist is man; his ordeal is in
society, not solitude. For them there will always be
a peculiar fascination in the books where the light of
those brilliant eyes falls not only upon the waste of
waters but upon the heart in its perplexity. But it
must be admitted that, if Marlow thus advised Conrad to shift his angle of vision, the advice was bold.
For the vision of a novelist is both complex and
specialised; complex, because behind his characters and
apart from them must stand something stable to which
he relates them; specialised because since he is a single
person with one sensibility the aspects of life in which
he can believe with conviction are strictly limited. So
delicate a balance is easily disturbed. After the middle
period Conrad never again was able to bring his figures
into perfect relation with their background. He never
believed in his later and more highly sophisticated
characters as he had believed in his early seamen.
When he had to indicate their relation to that other
unseen world of novelists, the world of values and

[316]

convictions, he was far less sure what those values were. Then, over and over again, a single phrase, "He steered with care", coming at the end of a storm, carried in it a whole morality. But in this more crowded and complicated world such terse phrases became less and less appropriate. Complex men and women of many interests and relations would not submit to so summary a judgement; or, if they did, much that was important in them escaped the verdict. And yet it was very necessary to Conrad's genius, with its luxuriant and romantic power, to have some law by which its creations could be tried. Essentially—such remained his creed—this world of civilised and self-conscious people is based upon "a few very simple ideas"; but where, in the world of thoughts and personal relations, are we to find them? There are no masts in drawing-rooms; the typhoon does not test the worth of politicians and business men. Seeking and not finding such supports, the world of Conrad's later period has about it an involuntary obscurity, an inconclusiveness, almost a disillusionment which baffles and fatigues. We lay hold in the dusk only of the old nobilities and sonorities: fidelity, compassion, honour, service—beautiful always, but now a little wearily reiterated, as if times had changed. Perhaps it was Marlow who was at fault. His habit of mind was a trifle sedentary. He had sat upon deck too long; splendid in soliloquy, he was less apt in the give and take of conversation; and those "moments of vision" flashing and fading, do not serve as well as steady lamplight to illumine the ripple of life and its long, gradual years. Above all, perhaps, he did not take into account how, if Conrad was to create, it was essential first that he should believe.

Therefore, though we shall make expeditions into the later books and bring back wonderful trophies, large tracts of them will remain by most of us untrodden. It is the earlier books—*Youth*, *Lord Jim*, *Typhoon*, *The Nigger of the "Narcissus"*—that we shall read in their entirety. For when the question is asked, what of Conrad will survive and where in the ranks of novelists we are to place him, these books, with their air of telling us something very old and perfectly true, which had lain hidden but is now revealed, will come to mind and make such questions and comparisons seem a little futile. Complete and still, very chaste and very beautiful, they rise in the memory as, on these hot summer nights, in their slow and stately way first one star comes out and then another.

How It Strikes a Contemporary

In the first place a contemporary can scarcely fail
to be struck by the fact that two critics at the same
table at the same moment will pronounce completely
different opinions about the same book. Here, on the
right, it is declared a masterpiece of English prose;
on the left, simultaneously, a mere mass of waste-
paper which, if the fire could survive it, should be
thrown upon the flames. Yet both critics are in
agreement about Milton and about Keats. They display an exquisite sensibility and have undoubtedly a
genuine enthusiasm. It is only when they discuss the
work of contemporary writers that they inevitably
come to blows. The book in question, which is at once
a lasting contribution to English literature and a mere
farrago of pretentious mediocrity, was published about
two months ago. That is the explanation; that is why
they differ.

The explanation is a strange one. It is equally
disconcerting to the reader who wishes to take his
bearings in the chaos of contemporary literature and to
the writer who has a natural desire to know whether his
own work, produced with infinite pains and in almost
utter darkness, is likely to burn for ever among the
fixed luminaries of English letters or, on the contrary,

to put out the fire. But if we identify ourselves with the reader and explore his dilemma first, our bewilder‧ ment is short-lived enough. The same thing has hap‧ pened so often before. We have heard the doctors dis‧ agreeing about the new and agreeing about the old twice a year on the average, in spring and autumn, ever since Robert Elsmere, or was it Stephen Phillips, some‧ how pervaded the atmosphere, and there was the same disagreement among grown-up people about them. It would be much more marvellous, and indeed much more upsetting, if, for a wonder, both gentlemen agreed, pronounced Blank's book an undoubted mas‧ terpiece, and thus faced us with the necessity of de‧ ciding whether we should back their judgement to the extent of ten and sixpence. Both are critics of reputa‧ tion; the opinions tumbled out so spontaneously here will be starched and stiffened into columns of sober prose which will uphold the dignity of letters in Eng‧ land and America.

It must be some innate cynicism, then, some un‧ generous distrust of contemporary genius, which de‧ termines us automatically as the talk goes on that, were they to agree—which they show no signs of doing —half a guinea is altogether too large a sum to squan‧ der upon contemporary enthusiasms, and the case will be met quite adequately by a card to the library. Still the question remains, and let us put it boldly to the critics themselves. Is there no guidance nowadays for a reader who yields to none in reverence for the dead, but is tormented by the suspicion that reverence for the dead is vitally connected with understanding of the living? After a rapid survey both critics are agreed that there is unfortunately no such person. For what is their own judgement worth where new books are concerned? Certainly not ten and sixpence. And from the stores of their experience they proceed to bring forth terrible examples of past blunders; crimes of criticism which, if they had been committed against the dead and not against the living, would have lost them their jobs and imperilled their reputations. The only advice they can offer is to respect one's own instincts, to follow them fearlessly and, rather than submit them to the control of any critic or reviewer alive, to check them by reading and reading again the masterpieces of the past.

Thanking them humbly, we cannot help reflecting that it was not always so. Once upon a time, we must believe, there was a rule, a discipline, which controlled the great republic of readers in a way which is now unknown. That is not to say that the great critic—the Dryden, the Johnson, the Coleridge, the Arnold—was an impeccable judge of contemporary work, whose verdicts stamped the book indelibly and saved the reader the trouble of reckoning the value for himself. The mistakes of these great men about their own contemporaries are too notorious to be worth recording. But the mere fact of their existence had a centralising influence. That alone, it is not fantastic to suppose, would have controlled the disagreements of the dinner-table and given to random chatter about some book just out an authority now entirely to seek. The diverse schools would have debated as hotly as ever, but at the back of every reader's mind would have been the consciousness that there was at least one man who kept the main principles of literature closely in view; who, if you had taken to him some eccentricity of the moment, would have brought it into touch with permanence and tethered it by his own authority in the contrary blasts of praise and blame.[1] But when it comes to the making of a critic, nature must be generous and society ripe. The scattered dinner-tables of the modern world, the chase and eddy of the various currents which compose the society of our time, could only be dominated by a giant of fabulous dimensions. And where is even the very tall man whom we have the right to expect? Reviewers we have but no critic; a million competent and incorruptible policemen but no judge. Men of taste and learning and ability are for ever lecturing the young and celebrating the dead. But the too frequent result of their able and industrious pens is a desiccation of the living tissues of literature into a network of little bones. Nowhere shall we find the downright vigour of a Dryden, or Keats with his

---

[1] How violent these are two quotations will show. "It [*Told by an Idiot*] should be read as the *Tempest* should be read, and as *Gulliver's Travels* should be read, for if Miss Macaulay's poetic gift happens to be less sublime than those of the author of the *Tempest,* and if her irony happens to be less tremendous than that of the author of *Gulliver's Travels,* her justice and wisdom are no less noble than theirs." —*The Daily News.*
The next day we read: "For the rest one can only say that if Mr. Eliot had been pleased to write in demotic English *The Waste Land* might not have been, as it just is to all but anthropologists, and literati, so much waste-paper."—*The Manchester Guardian.*

fine and natural bearing, his profound insight and sanity, or Flaubert and the tremendous power of his fanaticism, or Coleridge, above all, brewing in his head the whole of poetry and letting issue now and then one of those profound general statements which are caught up by the mind when hot with the friction of reading as if they were of the soul of the book itself.

And to all this, too, the critics generously agree. A great critic, they say, is the rarest of beings. But should one miraculously appear, how should we maintain him, on what should we feed him? Great critics, if they are not themselves great poets, are bred from the profusion of the age. There is some great man to be vindicated, some school to be founded or destroyed. But our age is meagre to the verge of destitution. There is no name which dominates the rest. There is no master in whose workshop the young are proud to serve apprenticeship. Mr. Hardy has long since withdrawn from the arena, and there is something exotic about the genius of Mr. Conrad which makes him not so much an influence as an idol, honoured and admired, but aloof and apart. As for the rest, though they are many and vigorous and in the full flood of creative activity, there is none whose influence can seriously affect his contemporaries, or penetrate beyond our day to that not very distant future which it pleases us to call immortality. If we make a century our test, and ask how much of the work produced in these days in England will be in existence then, we shall have to answer not merely that we cannot agree upon the same book, but that we are more than doubtful whether such a book there is. It is an age of fragments. A few stanzas, a few pages, a chapter here and there, the beginning of this novel, the end of that, are equal to the best of any age or author. But can we go to posterity with a sheaf of loose pages, or ask the readers of those days, with the whole of literature before them, to sift our enormous rubbish heaps for our tiny pearls? Such are the questions which the critics might lawfully put to their companions at table, the novelists and poets.

At first the weight of pessimism seems sufficient to bear down all opposition. Yes, it is a lean age, we repeat, with much to justify its poverty; but, frankly, if we pit one century against another the comparison seems overwhelmingly against us. *Waverley*, *The Excursion*, *Kubla Khan*, *Don Juan*, *Hazlitt's Essays*, *Pride and Prejudice*, *Hyperion*, and *Prometheus Unbound* were all published between 1800 and 1821. Our century has not lacked industry; but if we ask for masterpieces it appears on the face of it that the pessimists are right. It seems as if an age of genius must be succeeded by an age of endeavour; riot and extravagance by cleanliness and hard work. All honour, of course, to those who have sacrificed their immortality to set the house in order. But if we ask for masterpieces, where are we to look? A little poetry, we may feel sure, will survive; a few poems by Mr. Yeats, by Mr. Davies, by Mr. De la Mare. Mr. Lawrence, of course, has moments of greatness, but hours of something very different. Mr. Beerbohm, in his way, is perfect, but it is not a big way. Passages in *Far Away and Long Ago* will undoubtedly go to posterity entire. *Ulysses* was a memorable catastrophe —immense in daring, terrific in disaster. And so, picking and choosing, we select now this, now that, hold it up for display, hear it defended or derided, and finally have to meet the objection that even so we are only agreeing with the critics that it is an age incapable of sustained effort, littered with fragments, and not seriously to be compared with the age that went before.

But it is just when opinions universally prevail and we have added lip service to their authority that we become sometimes most keenly conscious that we do not believe a word that we are saying. It is a barren and exhausted age, we repeat; we must look back with envy to the past. Meanwhile it is one of the first fine days of spring. Life is not altogether lacking in colour. The telephone, which interrupts the most serious conversations and cuts short the most weighty observations, has a romance of its own. And the random talk of people who have no chance of immortality and thus can speak their minds out has a setting, often, of lights, streets, houses, human beings, beautiful or grotesque, which will weave itself into the moment for ever. But this is life; the talk is about literature. We must try to disentangle the two, and justify the rash revolt of optimism against the superior plausibility, the finer distinction, of pessimism.

Our optimism, then, is largely instinctive. It springs from the fine day and the wine and the talk; it springs from the fact that when life throws up such treasures daily, daily suggests more than the most voluble can express, much though we admire the dead, we prefer life as it is. There is something about the present which we would not exchange, though we were offered a choice of all past ages to live in. And modern literature, with all its imperfections, has the same hold on us and the same fascination. It is like a relation whom we snub and scarify daily, but, after all, cannot do without. It has the same endearing quality of being that which we are, that which we have made, that in which we live, instead of being something, however august, alien to ourselves and beheld from the outside. Nor has any generation more need than ours to cherish its contemporaries. We are sharply cut off from our predecessors. A shift in the scale—the war, the sudden slip of masses held in position for ages—has shaken the fabric from top to bottom, alienated us from the past and made us perhaps too vividly conscious of the present. Every day we find ourselves doing, saying, or thinking things that would have been impossible to our fathers. And we feel the differences which have not been noted far more keenly than the resemblances which have been very perfectly expressed. New books lure us to read them partly in the hope that they will reflect this re-arrangement of our attitude—these scenes, thoughts, and apparently fortuitous groupings of incongruous things which impinge upon us with so keen a sense of novelty—and, as literature does, give it back into our keeping, whole and comprehended. Here indeed there is every reason for optimism. No age can have been more rich than ours in writers determined to give expression to the differences which separate them from the past and not to the resemblances which connect them with it. It would be invidious to mention names, but the most casual reader dipping into poetry, into fiction, into biography can hardly fail to be impressed by the courage, the sincerity, in a word, by the widespread originality of our time. But our exhilaration is strangely curtailed. Book after book leaves us with the same sense of promise unachieved, of intellectual poverty, of brilliance which has been snatched from life but not transmuted into literature. Much of what is best in contemporary work has the appearance of being noted under pressure, taken down in a bleak shorthand which preserves with astonishing brilliance the movements and expressions of the figures as they pass across the screen. But the flash is soon over, and there remains with us a profound dissatisfaction. The irritation is as acute as the pleasure was intense.

After all, then, we are back at the beginning, vacillating from extreme to extreme, at one moment enthusiastic, at the next pessimistic, unable to come to any conclusion about our contemporaries. We have asked the critics to help us, but they have deprecated the task. Now, then, is the time to accept their advice and correct these extremes by consulting the master-

pieces of the past. We feel ourselves indeed driven
to them, impelled not by calm judgement but by some
imperious need to anchor our instability upon their
security. But, honestly, the shock of the comparison
between past and present is at first disconcerting. Undoubtedly there is a dullness in great books. There
is an unabashed tranquillity in page after page of
Wordsworth and Scott and Miss Austen which is
sedative to the verge of somnolence. Opportunities
occur and they neglect them. Shades and subtleties
accumulate and they ignore them. They seem deliberately to refuse to gratify those senses which are stimulated so briskly by the moderns; the senses of sight,
of sound, of touch—above all, the sense of the human
being, his depth and the variety of his perceptions, his
complexity, his confusion, his self, in short. There
is little of all this in the works of Wordsworth and
Scott and Jane Austen. From what, then, arises that
sense of security which gradually, delightfully, and
completely overcomes us? It is the power of their
belief—their conviction, that imposes itself upon us.
In Wordsworth, the philosophic poet, this is obvious
enough. But it is equally true of the careless Scott,
who scribbled masterpieces to build castles before
breakfast, and of the modest maiden lady who wrote
furtively and quietly simply to give pleasure. In
both there is the same natural conviction that life is of
a certain quality. They have their judgement of
conduct. They know the relations of human beings
towards each other and towards the universe. Neither

of them probably has a word to say about the matter outright, but everything depends on it. Only believe, we find ourselves saying, and all the rest will come of itself. Only believe, to take a very simple instance which the recent publication of *The Watsons* brings to mind, that a nice girl will instinctively try to soothe the feelings of a boy who has been snubbed at a dance, and then, if you believe it implicitly and unquestioningly, you will not only make people a hundred years later feel the same thing, but you will make them feel it as literature. For certainty of that kind is the condition which makes it possible to write. To believe that your impressions hold good for others is to be released from the cramp and confinement of personality. It is to be free, as Scott was free, to explore with a vigour which still holds us spell-bound the whole world of adventure and romance. It is also the first step in that mysterious process in which Jane Austen was so great an adept. The little grain of experience once selected, believed in, and set outside herself, could be put precisely in its place, and she was then free to make of it, by a process which never yields its secrets to the analyst, into that complete statement which is literature.

So then our contemporaries afflict us because they have ceased to believe. The most sincere of them will only tell us what it is that happens to himself. They cannot make a world, because they are not free of other human beings. They cannot tell stories because they do not believe the stories are true. They cannot generalise. They depend on their senses and emotions, whose testimony is trustworthy, rather than on their intellects whose message is obscure. And they have perforce to deny themselves the use of some of the most powerful and some of the most exquisite of the weapons of their craft. With the whole wealth of the English language at the back of them, they timidly pass about from hand to hand and book to book only the meanest copper coins. Set down at a fresh angle of the eternal prospect they can only whip out their notebooks and record with agonised intensity the flying gleams, which light on what? and the transitory splendours, which may, perhaps, compose nothing whatever. But here the critics interpose, and with some show of justice.

If this description holds good, they say, and is not, as it may well be, entirely dependent upon our position at the table and certain purely personal relationships to mustard pots and flower vases, then the risks of judging contemporary work are greater than ever before. There is every excuse for them if they are wide of the mark; and no doubt it would be better to retreat, as Matthew Arnold advised, from the burning ground of the present to the safe tranquillity of the past. "We enter on burning ground," wrote Matthew Arnold, "as we approach the poetry of times so near to us, poetry like that of Byron, Shelley, and Wordsworth, of which the estimates are so often not only personal, but personal with passion," and this, they remind us, was written in the year 1880. Beware, they say, of putting under the microscope one inch of a ribbon which runs many miles; things sort themselves out if you wait; moderation and a study of the classics are to be recommended. Moreover, life is short; the Byron centenary is at hand; and the burning question of the moment is, did he, or did he not, marry his sister? To sum up, then—if indeed any conclusion is possible when everybody is talking at once and it is time to be going—it seems that it would be wise for the writers of the present to renounce for themselves the hope of creating masterpieces. Their poems, plays, biographies, novels are not books but notebooks, and Time, like a good schoolmaster, will take them in his hands, point to their blots and erasions, and tear them across; but he will not throw them into the waste-paper basket. He will keep them because other students will find them very useful. It is from notebooks of the present that the masterpieces of the future are made. Literature, as the critics were saying just now, has lasted long, has undergone many changes, and it is only a short sight and a parochial mind that will exaggerate the importance of these squalls, however they may agitate the little boats now tossing out at sea. The storm and the drenching are on the surface; and continuity and calm are in the depths.

As for the critics whose task it is to pass judgement upon the books of the moment, whose work, let us admit, is difficult, dangerous, and often distasteful, let us ask them to be generous of encouragement, but sparing of those wreaths and coronets which are so apt to get awry, and fade, and make the wearers, in six months time, look a little ridiculous. Let them take a wider, a less personal view of modern literature, and look indeed upon the writers as if they were engaged upon some vast building, which being built by common effort, the separate workmen may well remain anonymous. Let them slam the door upon the cosy company where sugar is cheap and butter plentiful, give over, for a time at least, the discussion of that fascinating topic—whether Byron married his sister— and, withdrawing, perhaps, a handsbreadth from the table where we sit chattering, say something interesting about literature. Let us buttonhole them as they leave, and recall to their memory that gaunt aristocrat, Lady Hester Stanhope, who kept a milk-white horse in her stable in readiness for the Messiah and was for ever scanning the mountain tops, impatiently but with confidence, for signs of his approach, and ask them to follow her example; scan the horizon; see the past in relation to the future; and so prepare the way for masterpieces to come.

THE SECOND
COMMON READER

MOST of the following papers have appeared in the *Times Literary Supplement*, *Life and Letters*, *The Nation*, *Vogue*, *The New York Herald*, *The Yale Review*, and *Figaro*. For permission to reprint two of them I have to thank the Oxford University Press and Mr. Jonathan Cape. Some are now published for the first time.

The Strange Elizabethans

THERE are few greater delights than to go back three or four hundred years and become in fancy at least an Elizabethan. That such fancies are only fancies, that this "becoming an Elizabethan", this reading sixteenth-century writing as currently and certainly as we read our own is an illusion, is no doubt true. Very likely the Elizabethans would find our pronunciation of their language unintelligible; our fancy picture of what it pleases us to call Elizabethan life would rouse their ribald merriment. Still, the instinct that drives us to them is so strong and the freshness and vigour that blow through their pages are so sweet that we willingly run the risk of being laughed at, of being ridiculous.

And if we ask why we go further astray in this particular region of English literature than in any other, the answer is no doubt that Elizabethan prose, for all its beauty and bounty, was a very imperfect medium. It was almost incapable of fulfilling one of the offices of prose which is to make people talk, simply and naturally, about ordinary things. In an age of utilitarian prose like our own, we know exactly how people spend the hours between breakfast and bed, how they behave when they are neither one thing nor the other, neither angry nor loving, neither happy nor miserable. Poetry ignores these slighter shades; the social student can pick up hardly any facts about daily

life from Shakespeare's plays; and if prose refuses to enlighten us, then one avenue of approach to the men and
women of another age is blocked. Elizabethan prose, still
scarcely separated off from the body of its poetry, could
speak magnificently, of course, about the great themes—
how life is short, and death certain; how spring is lovely,
and winter horrid—perhaps, indeed, the lavish and tower-
ing periods that it raises above these simple platitudes are
due to the fact that it has not cheapened itself upon trifles.
But the price it pays for this soaring splendour is to be
found in its awkwardness when it comes to earth—when
Lady Sidney, for example, finding herself cold at nights,
has to solicit the Lord Chamberlain for a better bedroom
at Court. Then any housemaid of her own age could put
her case more simply and with greater force. Thus, if we
go to the Elizabethan prose-writers to solidify the splendid
world of Elizabethan poetry as we should go now to our
biographers, novelists, and journalists to solidify the world
of Pope, of Tennyson, of Conrad, we are perpetually baffled
and driven from our quest. What, we ask, was the life of
an ordinary man or woman in the time of Shakespeare?
Even the familiar letters of the time give us little help. Sir
Henry Wotton is pompous and ornate and keeps us stiffly at
arm's-length. Their histories resound with drums and trumpets. Their broadsheets reverberate with meditations upon
death and reflections upon the immortality of the soul. Our
best chance of finding them off their guard and so becoming at ease with them is to seek one of those unambitious
men who haunt the outskirts of famous gatherings, listening, observing, sometimes taking a note in a book. But they
are difficult to find. Gabriel Harvey perhaps, the friend of

Spenser and of Sidney, might have fulfilled that function. Unfortunately the values of the time persuaded him that to write about rhetoric, to write about Thomas Smith, to write about Queen Elizabeth in Latin, was better worth doing than to record the table talk of Spenser and Sir Philip Sidney. But he possessed to some extent the modern instinct for preserving trifles, for keeping copies of letters, and for making notes of ideas that struck him in the margins of books. If we rummage among these fragments we shall, at any rate, leave the highroad and perhaps hear some roar of laughter from a tavern door, where poets are drinking; or meet humble people going about their milking and their love-making without a thought that this is the great Elizabethan age, or that Shakespeare is at this moment strolling down the Strand and might tell one, if one plucked him by the sleeve, to whom he wrote the sonnets, and what he meant by Hamlet.

The first person whom we meet is indeed a milkmaid—Gabriel Harvey's sister Mercy. In the winter of 1574 she was milking in the fields near Saffron Walden accompanied by an old woman, when a man approached her and offered her cakes and malmsey wine. When they had eaten and drunk in a wood and the old woman had wandered off to pick up sticks, the man proceeded to explain his business. He came from Lord Surrey, a youth of about Mercy's own age—seventeen or eighteen that is—and a married man. He had been bowling one day and had seen the milkmaid; her hat had blown off and "she had somewhat changed her colour". In short, Lord Surrey had fallen passionately in love with her; and sent her by the same man gloves, a silk girdle, and an enamel posy ring which he had torn

5

from his own hat though his Aunt, Lady W——, had given it him for a very different purpose. Mercy at first stood her ground. She was a poor milkmaid, and he was a noble gentleman. But at last she agreed to meet him at her house in the village. Thus, one very misty, foggy night just before Christmas, Lord Surrey and his servant came to Saffron Walden. They peered in at the malthouse, but saw only her mother and sisters; they peeped in at the parlour, but only her brothers were there. Mercy herself was not to be seen; and "well mired and wearied for their labour", there was nothing for it but to ride back home again. Finally, after further parleys, Mercy agreed to meet Lord Surrey in a neighbour's house alone at midnight. She found him in the little parlour "in his doublet and hose, his points untrust, and his shirt lying round about him". He tried to force her on to the bed; but she cried out, and the good wife, as had been agreed between them, rapped on the door and said she was sent for. Thwarted, enraged, Lord Surrey cursed and swore, "God confound me, God confound me", and by way of lure emptied his pockets of all the money in them —thirteen shillings in shillings and testers it came to—and made her finger it. Still, however, Mercy made off, untouched, on condition that she would come again on Christmas Eve. But when Christmas Eve dawned she was up betimes and had put seven miles between her and Saffron Walden by six in the morning, though it snowed and rained so that the floods were out, and P., the servant, coming later to the place of assignation, had to pick his way through the water in pattens. So Christmas passed. And a week later, in the very nick of time to save her honour, the whole story very strangely was discovered and brought to an end. On

6

New Year's Eve her brother Gabriel, the young fellow of Pembroke Hall, was riding back to Cambridge when he came up with a simple countryman whom he had met at his father's house. They rode on together, and after some country gossip, the man said that he had a letter for Gabriel in his pocket. Indeed, it was addressed "To my loving brother Mr. G. H.", but when Gabriel opened it there on the road, he found that the address was a lie. It was not from his sister Mercy, but to his sister Mercy. "Mine Own Sweet Mercy", it began; and it was signed "Thine more than ever his own Phil". Gabriel could hardly control himself— "could scarcely dissemble my sudden fancies and comprimitt my inward passions"—as he read. For it was not merely a love-letter; it was more; it talked about possessing Mercy according to promise. There was also a fair English noble wrapped up in the paper. So Gabriel, doing his best to control himself before the countryman, gave him back the letter and the coin and told him to deliver them both to his sister at Saffron Walden with this message: "To look ere she leap. She may pick out the English of it herself." He rode on to Cambridge; he wrote a long letter to the young lord, informing him with ambiguous courtesy that the game was up. The sister of Gabriel Harvey was not to be the mistress of a married nobleman. Rather she was to be a maid, "diligent, and trusty and tractable", in the house of Lady Smith at Audley End. Thus Mercy's romance breaks off; the clouds descend again; and we no longer see the milkmaid, the old woman, the treacherous serving man who came with malmsey and cakes and rings and ribbons to tempt a poor girl's honour while she milked her cows.

This is probably no uncommon story; there must have

been many milkmaids whose hats blew off as they milked their cows, and many lords whose hearts leapt at the sight so that they plucked the jewels from their hats and sent their servants to make treaty for them. But it is rare for the girl's own letters to be preserved or to read her own account of the story as she was made to deliver it at her brother's inquisition. Yet when we try to use her words to light up the Elizabethan field, the Elizabethan house and living-room, we are met by the usual perplexities. It is easy enough, in spite of the rain and the fog and the floods, to make a fancy piece out of the milkmaid and the meadows and the old woman wandering off to pick up sticks. Elizabethan songwriters have taught us too well the habit of that particular trick. But if we resist the impulse to make museum pieces out of our reading, Mercy herself gives us little help. She was a milkmaid, scribbling love-letters by the light of a farthing dip in an attic. Nevertheless, the sway of the Elizabethan convention was so strong, the accent of their speech was so masterful, that she bears herself with a grace and expresses herself with a resonance that would have done credit to a woman of birth and literary training. When Lord Surrey pressed her to yield she replied:

The thing you wot of, Milord, were a great trespass towards God, a great offence to the world, a great grief to my friends, a great shame to myself, and, as I think, a great dishonour to your lordship. I have heard my father say, Virginity is ye fairest flower in a maid's garden, and chastity ye richest dowry a poor wench can have. . . . Chastity, they say, is like unto time, which, being once lost, can no more be recovered.

Words chime and ring in her ears, as if she positively enjoyed the act of writing. When she wishes him to know that she is only a poor country girl and no fine lady like his wife, she exclaims, "Good Lord, that you should seek after so bare and country stuff abroad, that have so costly and courtly wares at home!" She even breaks into a jog-trot of jingling rhyme, far less sonorous than her prose, but proof that to write was an art, not merely a means of conveying facts. And if she wants to be direct and forcible, the proverbs she has heard in her father's house come to her pen, the biblical imagery runs in her ears: "And then were I, poor wench, cast up for hawk's meat, to mine utter undoing, and my friends' exceeding grief". In short, Mercy the milkmaid writes a natural and noble style, which is incapable of vulgarity, and equally incapable of intimacy. Nothing, one feels, would have been easier for Mercy than to read her lover a fine discourse upon the vanity of grandeur, the loveliness of chastity, the vicissitudes of fortune. But of emotion as between one particular Mercy and one particular Phillip, there is no trace. And when it comes to dealing exactly in a few words with some mean object—when, for example, the wife of Sir Henry Sidney, the daughter of the Duke of Northumberland, has to state her claim to a better room to sleep in, she writes for all the world like an illiterate servant girl who can neither form her letters nor spell her words nor make one sentence follow smoothly after another. She haggles, she niggles, she wears our patience down with her repetitions and her prolixities. Hence it comes about that we know very little about Mercy Harvey, the milkmaid, who wrote so well, or Mary Sidney, daughter to the Duke of Northumberland, who wrote so badly. The background of Elizabethan life eludes us.

Q

But let us follow Gabriel Harvey to Cambridge, in case we can there pick up something humble and colloquial that will make these strange Elizabethans more familiar to us. Gabriel, having discharged his duty as a brother, seems to have given himself up to the life of an intellectual young man with his way to make in the world. He worked so hard and he played so little that he made himself unpopular with his fellows. For it was obviously difficult to combine an intense interest in the future of English poetry and the capacity of the English language with card-playing, bear-baiting, and such diversions. Nor could he apparently accept everything that Aristotle said as gospel truth. But with congenial spirits he argued, it is clear, hour by hour, night after night, about poetry, and metre, and the raising of the despised English speech and the meagre English literature to a station among the great tongues and literatures of the world. We are sometimes made to think, as we listen, of such arguments as might now be going forward in the new Universities of America. The young English poets speak with a bold yet uneasy arrogance—"England, since it was England, never bred more honourable minds, more adventurous hearts, more valorous hands, or more excellent wits, than of late". Yet, to be English is accounted a kind of crime—"nothing is reputed so contemptible and so basely and vilely accounted of as whatsoever is taken for English". And if, in their hopes for the future and their sensitiveness to the opinion of older civilisations, the Elizabethans show much the same susceptibility that sometimes puzzles us among the younger countries today, the sense that broods over them of what is about to happen, of an undiscovered land on which they are about to set foot, is much like the excitement that science stirs in the minds of imaginative English writers of our own time. Yet however stimulating it is to think that we hear the stir and strife of tongues in Cambridge rooms about the year 1570, it has to be admitted that to read Harvey's pages methodically is almost beyond the limits of human patience. The words seem to run red-hot, molten, hither and thither, until we cry out in anguish for the boon of some meaning to set its stamp on them. He takes the same idea and repeats it over and over again:

In the sovereign workmanship of Nature herself, what garden of flowers without weeds? what orchard of trees without worms? what field of corn without cockle? what pond of fishes without frogs? what sky of light without darkness? what mirror of knowledge without ignorance? what man of earth without frailty? what commodity of the world without discommodity?

It is interminable. As we go round and round like a horse in a mill, we perceive that we are thus clogged with sound because we are reading what we should be hearing. The amplifications and the repetitions, the emphasis like that of a fist pounding the edge of a pulpit, are for the benefit of the slow and sensual ear which loves to dally over sense and luxuriate in sound—the ear which brings in, along with the spoken word, the look of the speaker and his gestures, which gives a dramatic value to what he says and adds to the crest of an extravagance some modulation which makes the word wing its way to the precise spot aimed at in the hearer's heart. Hence, when we lay Harvey's diatribes against Nash or his letters to Spenser upon poetry under the light of the eye alone, we can hardly make headway and lose our sense of any definite direction. We grasp any simple fact that floats to the surface as a drowning man grasps a plank—that the carrier was called Mrs. Kerke, that Perne kept a cub for his pleasure in his rooms at Peterhouse; that "Your last letter . . . was delivered me at mine hostesses by the fireside, being fast hedged in round about on every side with a company of honest, good fellows, and at that time reasonable, honest quaffers"; that Greene died begging Mistress Isam "for a penny pot of Malmsey", had borrowed her husband's shirt when his own was awashing, and was buried yesterday in the new churchyard near Bedlam at a cost of six shillings and fourpence. Light seems to dawn upon the darkness. But no; just as we think to lay hands on Shakespeare's coat-tails, to hear the very words rapped out as Spenser spoke them, up rise the fumes of Harvey's eloquence and we are floated off again into disputation and eloquence, windy, wordy, voluminous, and obsolete. How, we ask, as we slither over the pages, can we ever hope to come to grips with these Elizabethans? And then, turning, skipping and glancing, something fitfully and doubtfully emerges from the violent pages, the voluminous arguments—the figure of a man, the outlines of a face, somebody who is not "an Elizabethan" but an interesting, complex, and individual human being.

We know him, to begin with, from his dealings with his sister. We see him riding to Cambridge, a fellow of his college, when she was milking with poor old women in the fields. We observe with amusement his sense of the conduct that befits the sister of Gabriel Harvey, the Cambridge scholar. Education had put a great gulf between him and his family. He rode to Cambridge from a house in a village street where his father made ropes and his mother worked in the malthouse. Yet though his lowly

birth and the consciousness that he had his way to make
in the world made him severe with his sister, fawning to
the great, uneasy and self-centred and ostentatious, it never
made him ashamed of his family. The father who could
send three sons to Cambridge and was so little ashamed
of his craft that he had himself carved making ropes at his
work and the carving let in above his fireplace, was no
ordinary man. The brothers who followed Gabriel to Cambridge and were his best allies there, were brothers to be
proud of. He could be proud of Mercy even, whose beauty
could make a great nobleman pluck the jewel from his hat.
He was undoubtedly proud of himself. It was the pride of
a self-made man who must read when other people are
playing cards, who owns no undue allegiance to authority
and will contradict Aristotle himself, that made him unpopular at Cambridge and almost cost him his degree. But
it was an unfortunate chance that led him thus early in
life to defend his rights and insist upon his merits. Moreover, since it was true—since he was abler, quicker, and
more learned than other people, handsome in person too,
as even his enemies could not deny ("a smudge piece of a
handsome fellow it hath been in his days" Nash admitted)
he had reason to think that he deserved success and was
denied it only by the jealousies and conspiracies of his col-
leagues. For a time, by dint of much caballing and much
dwelling upon his own deserts, he triumphed over his
enemies in the matter of the degree. He delivered lectures.
He was asked to dispute before the court when Queen
Elizabeth came to Audley End. He even drew her favourable attention. "He lookt something like an Italian", she
said when he was brought to her notice. But the seeds of

13

his downfall were visible even in his moment of triumph.
He had no self-respect, no self-control. He made himself
ridiculous and his friends uneasy. When we read how he
dressed himself up and "came ruffling it out huffty tuffty
in his suit of velvet" how uneasy he was, at one moment
cringing, at another "making no bones to take the wall
of Sir Phillip Sidney", now flirting with the ladies, now
"putting bawdy riddles to them", how when the Queen
praised him he was beside himself with joy and talked the
English of Saffron Walden with an Italian accent, we can
imagine how his enemies jeered and his friends blushed.
And so, for all his merits, his decline began. He was not
taken into Lord Leicester's service; he was not made Public
Orator; he was not given the Mastership of Trinity Hall.
But there was one society in which he succeeded. In the
small, smoky rooms where Spenser and other young men
discussed poetry and language and the future of English
literature, Harvey was not laughed at. Harvey, on the
contrary, was taken very seriously. To friends like these he
seemed as capable of greatness as any of them. He too might
be one of those destined to make English literature illus-
trious. His passion for poetry was disinterested. His learning was profound. When he held forth upon quantity and
metre, upon what the Greeks had written and the Italians,
and what the English might write, no doubt he created for
Spenser that atmosphere of hope and ardent curiosity spiced
with sound learning that serves to spur the imagination of a
young writer and to make each fresh poem as it is written
seem the common property of a little band of adventurers
set upon the same quest. It was thus that Spenser saw him:

Harvey, the happy above happiest men,
I read: that, sitting like a looker-on
Of this world's stage, doest note, with critic pen,
The sharp dislikes of each condition.

Poets need such "lookers-on"; some one who discriminates from a watch-tower above the battle; who warns; who foresees. It must have been pleasant for Spenser to listen as Harvey talked; and then to cease to listen, to let the vehement, truculent voice run on, while he slipped from theory to practise and made up a few lines of his own poetry in his head. But the looker-on may sit too long and hold forth too curiously and domineeringly for his own health. He may make his theories fit too tight to accommodate the formlessness of life. Thus when Harvey ceased to theorise and tried to practise there issued nothing but a thin dribble of arid and unappetising verse or a copious flow of unctuous and servile eulogy. He failed to be a poet as he failed to be a statesman, as he failed to be a professor, as he failed to be a Master, as he failed, it might seem, in everything that he undertook, save that he had won the friendship of Spenser and Sir Phillip Sidney.

But happily Harvey left behind him a commonplace book; he had the habit of making notes in the margins of books as he read. Looking from one to the other, from his public self to his private, we see his face lit from both sides, and the expression changes as it changes so seldom upon the face of the Elizabethans. We detect another Harvey lurking behind the superficial Harvey, shading him with doubt and effort and despondency. For, luckily the commonplace book was small; the margins even of an Elizabethan folio narrow; Harvey was forced to be brief, and because he wrote only for his own eye at the command of some sharp memory or experience he seems to write as if he were talking to himself. That is true, he seems to say; or that reminds me, or again: If only I had done this— We thus become aware of a conflict between the Harvey who blundered among men and the Harvey who sat wisely at home among his books. The one who acts and suffers brings his case to the one who reads and thinks for advice and consolation.

Indeed, he had need of both. From the first his life was full of conflict and difficulty. Harvey the rope-maker's son might put a brave face on it, but still in the society of gentlemen the lowness of his birth galled him. Think, then, the sedentary Harvey counselled him, of all those unknown people who have nevertheless triumphed. Think of "Alexander, an Unexpert Youth"; think of David, "a forward stripling, but vanquished a huge Giant"; think of Judith and of Pope Joan and their exploits; think above all of that "gallant virago . . . Joan of Arc, a most worthy, valiant young wench . . . what may not an industrious and politic man do . . . when a lusty adventurous wench might thus prevail?" And then it seems as if the smart young men at Cambridge twitted the rope-maker's son for his lack of skill in the gentlemanly arts. "Leave writing", Gabriel counselled him "which consumeth unreasonable much time. . . . You have already plagued yourself this way". Make yourself master of the arts of eloquence and persuasion. Go into the world. Learn swordsmanship, riding, and shooting. All three may be learnt in a week. And then the ambitious but uneasy youth began to find the other sex attractive and asked advice of his wise and sedentary brother in the conduct of his love affairs. Manners, the other Harvey was of opinion, are of the utmost importance in dealing with women; one must be discreet, self-controlled. A gentleman, this counsellor continued, is known by his "Good entertainment of Ladies and gentlewomen. No salutation, without much respect and ceremony"—a reflection inspired no doubt by the memory of some snub received at Audley End. Health and the care of the body are of the utmost importance. "We scholars make an Ass of our body and wit". One must "leap out of bed lustily, every morning in ye whole year". One must be sparing in one's diet, and active, and take regular exercise, like brother H., "who never failed to breathe his hound once a day at least". There must be no "buzzing or musing". A learned man must also be a man of the world. Make it your "daily charge" "to exercise, to laugh; to proceed boldly". And if your tormentors brawl and rail and scoff and mock at you, the best answer is "a witty and pleasant Ironie". In any case, do not complain, "It is gross folly, and a vile Sign of a wayward and forward disposition, to be eftsoons complaining of this, or that, to small purpose". And if as time goes on without preferment, one cannot pay one's bills, one is thrust into prison, one has to bear the taunts and insults of landladies, still remember "Glad poverty is no poverty"; and if, as time passes and the struggle increases, it seems as if "Life is warfare", if sometimes the beaten man has to own, "But for hope ye Hart would brust" still his sage counsellor in the study will not let him throw up the sponge. "He beareth his misery best, that hideth it most" he told himself.

So runs the dialogue that we invent between the two Harveys—Harvey the active and Harvey the passive,

Harvey the foolish and Harvey the wise. And it seems on the surface that the two halves, for all their counselling together, made but a sorry business of the whole. For the young man who had ridden off to Cambridge full of conceit and hope and good advice to his sister returned empty-handed to his native village in the end. He dwindled out his last long years in complete obscurity at Saffron Walden. He occupied himself superficially by practising his skill as a doctor among the poor of the neighbourhood. He lived in the utmost poverty off buttered roots and sheep's trotters. But even so he had his consolations, he cherished his dreams. As he pottered about his garden in the old black velvet suit, purloined, Nash says, from a saddle for which he had not paid, his thoughts were all of power and glory; of Stukeley and Drake; of "the winners of gold and the wearers of gold". Memories he had in abundance—"The remembrance of best things will soon pass out of memory; if it be not often renewed and revived", he wrote. But there was some eager stir in him, some lust for action and glory and life and adventure that forbade him to dwell in the past. "The present tense only to be regarded" is one of his notes. Nor did he drug himself with the dust of scholarship. Books he loved as a true reader loves them, not as trophies to be hung up for display, but as living beings that "must be meditated, practised and incorporated into my body and soul". A singularly humane view of learning survived in the breast of the old and disappointed scholar. "The only brave way to learn all things with no study and much pleasure", he remarked. Dreams of the winners of gold and the wearers of gold, dreams of action and power, fantastic though they were in an old beggar who could not pay his reckoning, who pressed simples and lived off buttered roots in a cottage, kept life in him when his flesh had withered and his skin was "riddled and crumpled like a piece of burnt parchment". He had his triumph in the end. He survived both his friends and his enemies—Spenser and Sidney, Nash and Pern. He lived to a very great age for an Elizabethan, to eighty-one or eighty-two; and when we say that Harvey lived we mean that he quarrelled and was tiresome and ridiculous and struggled and failed and had a face like ours —a changing, a variable, a human face.

Donne After Three Centuries

WHEN we think how many millions of words have been written and printed in England in the past three hundred years, and how the vast majority have died out without leaving any trace, it is tempting to wonder what quality the words of Donne possess that we should still hear them distinctly today. Far be it from us to suggest even in this year of celebration and pardonable adulation (1931) that the poems of Donne are popular reading or that the typist, if we look over her shoulder in the Tube, is to be discovered reading Donne as she returns from her office. But he is read; he is audible—to that fact new editions and frequent articles testify, and it is worth perhaps trying to analyse the meaning that his voice has for us as it strikes upon the ear after this long flight across the stormy seas that separate us from the age of Elizabeth.

But the first quality that attracts us is not his meaning, charged with meaning as his poetry is, but something much more unmixed and immediate; it is the explosion with which he bursts into speech. All preface, all parleying have been consumed; he leaps into poetry the shortest way. One phrase consumes all preparation:

> I long to talke with some old lover's ghost,

or

> He is starke mad, whoever sayes,
> That he hath beene in love an houre.

At once we are arrested. Stand still, he commands,

> Stand still, and I will read to thee
> A Lecture, Love, in love's philosophy.

And stand still we must. With the first words a shock passes through us; perceptions, previously numb and torpid, quiver into being; the nerves of sight and hearing are quickened; the "bracelet of bright hair" burns in our eyes. But, more remarkably, we do not merely become aware of beautiful remembered lines; we feel ourselves compelled to a particular attitude of mind. Elements that were dispersed in the usual stream of life become, under the stroke of Donne's passion, one and entire. The world, a moment before, cheerful, humdrum, bursting with character and variety, is consumed. We are in Donne's world now. All other views are sharply cut off.

In this power of suddenly surprising and subjugating the reader, Donne excels most poets. It is his characteristic quality; it is thus that he lays hold upon us, summing up his essence in a word or two. But it is an essence that, as it works in us, separates into strange contraries at odds with one another. Soon we begin to ask ourselves of what this essence is composed, what elements have met together to cut so deep and complex an impression. Some obvious clues lie strewn on the surface of the poems. When we read the *Satyres*, for example, we need no external proof to tell us that these are the work of a boy. He has all the ruthlessness and definiteness of youth, its hatred of the follies of middle age and of convention. Bores, liars, courtiers—detestable humbugs and hypocrites as they are, why not sum them up and sweep them off the face of the earth with a few strokes

of the pen? And so these foolish figures are drubbed with
an ardour that proves how much hope and faith and delight
in life inspire the savagery of youthful scorn. But, as we
read on, we begin to suspect that the boy with the complex
and curious face of the early portrait—bold yet subtle,
sensual yet nerve drawn—possessed qualities that made him
singular among the young. It is not simply that the huddle
and pressure of youth which outthinks its words had urged
him on too fast for grace or clarity. It may be that there
is in this clipping and curtailing, this abrupt heaping of
thought on thought, some deeper dissatisfaction than that of
youth with age, of honesty with corruption. He is in rebellion, not merely against his elders, but against something
antipathetic to him in the temper of his time. His verse has
the deliberate bareness of those who refuse to avail themselves of the current usage. It has the extravagance of those
who do not feel the pressure of opinion, so that sometimes
judgment fails them, and they heap up strangeness for
strangeness' sake. He is one of those nonconformists, like
Browning and Meredith, who cannot resist glorifying their
nonconformity by a dash of wilful and gratuitous eccentricity. But to discover what Donne disliked in his own age,
let us imagine some of the more obvious influences that must
have told upon him when he wrote his early poems—let us
ask what books he read. And by Donne's own testimony we
find that his chosen books were the works of "grave
Divines"; of philosophers; of "jolly Statesmen, which teach
how to tie The sinewes of a cities mistique bodie"; and
chroniclers. Clearly he liked facts and arguments. If there
are also poets among his books, the epithets he applies to
them, "Giddie fantastique", seem to disparage the art, or

at least to show that Donne knew perfectly well what qualities were antipathetic to him in poetry. And yet he was
living in the very spring of English poetry. Some of Spenser
might have been on his shelves; and Sidney's *Arcadia;* and
the *Paradise of Dainty Devices*, and Lyly's *Euphues*. He
had the chance, and apparently took it—"I tell him of new
playes"—of going to the theatre; of seeing the plays of
Marlowe and Shakespeare acted. When he went abroad in
London, he must have met all the writers of that time—
Spenser and Sidney and Shakespeare and Jonson; he must
have heard at this tavern or at that talk of new plays, of
new fashions in verse, heated and learned discussion of the
possibilities of the English language and the future of English poetry. And yet, if we turn to his biography, we find
that he neither consorted with his contemporaries nor read
what they wrote. He was one of those original beings who
cannot draw profit, but are rather disturbed and distracted
by what is being done round them at the moment. If we
turn again to *Satyres*, it is easy to see why this should be so.
Here is a bold and active mind that loves to deal with actual
things, which struggles to express each shock exactly as it
impinges upon his tight-stretched senses. A bore stops him
in the street. He sees him exactly, vividly.

His cloths were strange, though coarse; and black, though bare;
Sleevelesse his jerkin was, and it had beene
Velvet, but t'was now (so much ground was seene)
Become Tufftaffatie;

Then he likes to give the actual words that people say:

He, like to a high stretcht lute string squeakt, O Sir,
'Tis sweet to talke of Kings. At Westminster,

Said I, The man that keepes the Abbey tombes,
And for his price doth with who ever comes,
Of all our Harries, and our Edwards talke,
From King to King and all their kin can walke:
Your eares shall heare nought, but Kings; your eyes meet
Kings only; The way to it, is Kingstreet.

His strength and his weakness are both to be found here. He selects one detail and stares at it until he has reduced it to the few words that express its oddity:

And like a bunch of ragged carrets stand
The short swolne fingers of thy gouty hand,

but he cannot see in the round, as a whole. He cannot stand apart and survey the large outline so that the description is always of some momentary intensity, seldom of the broader aspect of things. Naturally, then, he found it difficult to use the drama with its conflict of other characters; he must always speak from his own centre in soliloquy, in satire, in self-analysis. Spenser, Sidney, and Marlowe provided no helpful models for a man who looked out from this angle of vision. The typical Elizabethan with his love of eloquence, with his longing for brave new words, tended to enlarge and generalise. He loved wide landscapes, heroic virtues, and figures seen sublimely in outline or in heroic conflict. Even the prose-writers have the same habit of aggrandisement. When Dekker sets out to tell us how Queen Elizabeth died in the spring, he cannot describe her death in particular or that spring in particular; he must dilate upon all deaths and all springs:

. . . the Cuckoo (like a single, sole Fiddler, that reels from Tavern to Tavern) plied it all the day long: Lambs frisked up and down in the vallies, kids and Goats leapt to and fro on the

Mountains: Shepherds sat piping, country wenches singing: Lovers made Sonnets for their Lasses, whilst they made Garlands for their Lovers: And as the Country was frolic, so was the City merry . . . no Scritch-Owl frighted the silly Countryman at midnight, nor any Drum the Citizen at noon-day; but all was more calm than a still water, all husht, as if the Spheres had been playing in Consort: In conclusion, heaven lookt like a Pallace, and the great hall of the earth, like a Paradise. But O the short-liv'd Felicity of man! O world, of what slight and thin stuff is thy happiness!

—in short, Queen Elizabeth died, and it is no use asking Dekker what the old woman who swept his room for him said, or what Cheapside looked like that night if one happened to be caught in the thick of the throng. He must enlarge; he must generalise; he must beautify.

Donne's genius was precisely the opposite of this. He diminished; he particularised. Not only did he see each spot and wrinkle which defaced the fair outline; but he noted with the utmost curiosity his own reaction to such contrasts and was eager to lay side by side the two conflicting views and to let them make their own dissonance. It is this desire for nakedness in an age that was florid, this determination to record not the likenesses which go to compose a rounded and seemly whole, but the inconsistencies that break up semblances, the power to make us feel the different emotions of love and hate and laughter at the same time, that separate Donne from his contemporaries. And if the usual traffic of the day—to be buttonholed by a bore, to be snared by a lawyer, to be snubbed by a courtier—made so sharp an impression on Donne, the effect of falling in love was bound to be incomparably greater. Falling in love meant, to Donne, a thousand things; it meant being tormented and disgusted, disillusioned and enraptured; but it also meant speaking the truth. The love poems, the elegies, and the letters thus reveal a figure of a very different calibre from the typical figure of Elizabethan love poetry. That great ideal, built up by a score of eloquent pens, still burns bright in our eyes. Her body was of alabaster, her legs of ivory; her hair was golden wire and her teeth pearls from the Orient. Music was in her voice and stateliness in her walk. She could love and sport and be faithless and yielding and cruel and true; but her emotions were simple, as befitted her person. Donne's poems reveal a lady of a very different cast. She was brown but she was also fair; she was solitary but also sociable; she was rustic yet also fond of city life; she was sceptical yet devout, emotional but reserved—in short she was as various and complex as Donne himself. As for choosing one type of human perfection and restricting himself to love her and her only, how could Donne, or any man who allowed his senses full play and honestly recorded his own moods, so limit his nature and tell such lies to placate the conventional and the decorous? Was not "love's sweetest part, Variety"? "Of music, joy, life and eternity Change is the nursery", he sang. The timid fashion of the age might limit a lover to one woman. For his part he envied and admired the ancients, "who held plurality of loves no crime":

> But since this title honour hath been us'd,
> Our weak credulity hath been abus'd.

We have fallen from our high estate; the golden laws of nature are repealed.

So through the glass of Donne's poetry now darkly clouded, now brilliantly clear, we see pass in procession the many women whom he loved and hated—the common Julia whom he despised; the simpleton, to whom he taught the art of love; she who was married to an invalid husband, "cag'd in a basket chair"; she who could only be loved dangerously by strategy; she who dreamt of him and saw him murdered as he crossed the Alps; she whom he had to dissuade from the risk of loving him; and lastly, the autumnal, the aristocratic lady for whom he felt more of reverence than of love—so they pass, common and rare, simple and sophisticated, young and old, noble and plebeian, and each casts a different spell and brings out a different lover, although the man is the same man, and the women, perhaps, are also phases of womanhood rather than separate and distinct women. In later years the Dean of St. Paul's would willingly have edited some of these poems and suppressed one of these lovers—the poet presumably of "Going to Bed" and "Love's Warr". But the Dean would have been wrong. It is the union of so many different desires that gives Donne's love poetry not only its vitality but also a quality that is seldom found with such strength in the conventional and orthodox lover—its spirituality. If we do not love with the body, can we love with the mind? If we do not love variously, freely, admitting the lure first of this quality and then of that, can we at length choose out the one quality that is essential and adhere to it and so make peace among the warring elements and pass into a state of being which transcends the "Hee and Shee"? Even while he was at his most fickle and gave fullest scope to his youthful lusts, Donne could predict the season of maturity when he would love differently, with pain and difficulty, one and one only. Even while he scorned and railed and abused, he divined another relationship which transcended change and parting and might, even in the bodies' absence, lead to unity and communion:

> Rend us in sunder, thou canst not divide,
> Our bodies so, but that our souls are ty'd,
> And we can love by letters still and gifts,
> And thoughts and dreams;

Again,

> They who one another keepe alive
> N'er parted be.

And again,

> So to one neutrall thing both sexes fit,
> Wee dye and rise the same, and prove
> Mysterious by this love.

Such hints and premonitions of a further and finer state urge him on and condemn him to perpetual unrest and dissatisfaction with the present. He is tantalised by the sense that there is a miracle beyond any of these transient delights and disgusts. Lovers can, if only for a short space, reach a state of unity beyond time, beyond sex, beyond the body. And at last, for one moment, they reach it. In the "Extasie" they lie together on a bank,

> All day, the same our postures were,
> And wee said nothing, all the day. . . .

> This Extasie doth unperplex
> (We said) and tell us what we love,
> Wee see by this, it was not sexe,
> Wee see, we saw not what did move: . . .

> Wee then, who are this new soule, know,
> Of what we are compos'd, and made,
> For, th' Atomies of which we grow,
> Are soules, whom no change can invade.

But O alas, so long, so farre
Our bodies, why doe wee forbeare? . . .

But O alas, he breaks off, and the words remind us that
however much we may wish to keep Donne in one posture
—for it is in these Extasies that lines of pure poetry suddenly flow as if liquefied by a great heat—so to remain in
one posture was against his nature. Perhaps it is against
the nature of things also. Donne snatches the intensity because he is aware of the change that must alter, of the discord that must interrupt.

Circumstances, at any rate, put it beyond his power to
maintain that ecstasy for long. He had married secretly; he
was a father; he was, as we are soon reminded, a very poor
yet a very ambitious man, living in a damp little house at
Mitcham with a family of small children. The children were
frequently ill. They cried, and their cries, cutting through
the thin walls of the jerry-built house, disturbed him at his
work. He sought sanctuary naturally enough elsewhere, and
naturally had to pay rent for that relief. Great ladies—
Lady Bedford, Lady Huntingdon, Mrs. Herbert—with
well-spread tables and fair gardens, must be conciliated;
rich men with the gift of rooms in their possession must be
placated. Thus, after Donne the harsh satirist, and Donne
the imperious lover, comes the servile and obsequious figure
of Donne the devout servant of the great, the extravagant
eulogist of little girls. And our relationship with him suddenly changes. In the satires and the love poems there was
a quality—some psychological intensity and complexity—
that brings him closer than his contemporaries, who often
seem to be caught up in a different world from ours and to
exist immune from our perplexities and swept by passions

which we admire but cannot feel. Easy as it is to exaggerate affinities, still we may claim to be akin to Donne in our readiness to admit contrasts, in our desire for openness, in that psychological intricacy which the novelists have taught us with their slow, subtle, and analytic prose. But now, as we follow Donne in his progress, he leaves us in the lurch. He becomes more remote, inaccessible, and obsolete than any of the Elizabethans. It is as if the spirit of the age, which he had scorned and flouted, suddenly asserted itself and made this rebel its slave. And as we lose sight of the outspoken young man who hated society, and of the passionate lover, seeking some mysterious unity with his love and finding it miraculously, now here, now there, it is natural to abuse the system of patrons and patronage that thus seduced the most incorruptible of men. Yet it may be that we are too hasty. Every writer has an audience in view, and it may well be doubted if the Bedfords and the Drurys and the Herberts were worse influences than the libraries and the newspaper proprietors who fill the office of patron nowadays.

The comparison, it is true, presents great difficulties. The noble ladies who brought so strange an element into Donne's poetry, live only in the reflection, or in the distortion, that we find in the poems themselves. The age of memoirs and letter-writing was still to come. If they wrote themselves, and it is said that both Lady Pembroke and Lady Bedford were poets of merit, they did not dare to put their names to what they wrote, and it has vanished. But a diary here and there survives from which we may see the patroness more closely and less romantically. Lady Ann Clifford, for example, the daughter of a Clifford and a Russell, though active and practical and little educated—she was not allowed "to learn any language because her father would not permit it"—felt, we can gather from the bald statements of her diary, a duty towards literature and to the makers of it as her mother, the patroness of the poet Daniel, had done before her. A great heiress, infected with all the passion of her age for lands and houses, busied with all the cares of wealth and property, she still read good English books as naturally as she ate good beef and mutton. She read *The Faërie Queene* and Sidney's *Arcadia;* she acted in Ben Jonson's Masques at Court; and it is proof of the respect in which reading was held that a girl of fashion should be able to read an old corrupt poet like Chaucer without feeling that she was making herself a target for ridicule as a blue-stocking. The habit was part of a normal and well-bred life. It persisted even when she was mistress of one estate and claimant to even vaster possession of her own. She had Montaigne read aloud to her as she sat stitching at Knole; she sat absorbed in Chaucer while her husband worked. Later, when years of strife and loneliness had saddened her, she returned to her Chaucer with a deep sigh of content: ". . . if I had not excellent Chaucer's book here to comfort me", she wrote, "I were in a pitiable case having as many troubles as I have here, but, when I read in that, I scorn and make light of them all, and a little part of his beauteous spirit infuses itself in me". The woman who said that, though she never attempted to set up a salon or to found a library, felt it incumbent on her to respect the men of low birth and no fortune who could write *The Canterbury Tales* or *The Faërie Queene.* Donne preached before her at Knole. It was she who paid for the first monument to Spenser in

Westminster Abbey, and if, when she raised a tomb to her old tutor, she dwelt largely upon her own virtues and titles, she still acknowledged that even so great a lady as herself owed gratitude to the makers of books. Words from great writers nailed to the walls of the room in which she sat, eternally transacting business, surrounded her as she worked, as they surrounded Montaigne in his tower in Burgundy.

Thus we may infer that Donne's relation to the Countess of Bedford was very different from any that could exist between a poet and a countess at the present time. There was something distant and ceremonious about it. To him she was "as a vertuous Prince farre off". The greatness of her office inspired reverence apart from her personality, just as the rewards within her gift inspired humility. He was her Laureate, and his songs in her praise were rewarded by invitations to stay with her at Twickenham and by those friendly meetings with men in power which were so effective in furthering the career of an ambitious man—and Donne was highly ambitious, not indeed for the fame of a poet, but for the power of a statesman. Thus when we read that Lady Bedford was "God's Masterpiece", that she excelled all women in all ages, we realise that John Donne is not writing to Lucy Bedford; Poetry is saluting Rank. And this distance served to inspire reason rather than passion. Lady Bedford must have been a very clever woman, well versed in the finer shades of theology, to derive an instant or an intoxicating pleasure from the praises of her servant. Indeed, the extreme subtlety and erudition of Donne's poems to his patrons seem to show that one effect of writing for such an audience is to exaggerate the poet's ingenuity. What is not poetry but something tortured and difficult will prove to the patron that the poet is exerting his skill on her behalf. Then again, a learned poem can be handed round among statesmen and men of affairs to prove that the poet is no mere versifier, but capable of office and responsibility. But a change of inspiration that has killed many poets—witness Tennyson and the *Idylls of the King* —only stimulated another side of Donne's many-sided nature and many-faceted brain. As we read the long poems written ostensibly in praise of Lady Bedford, or in celebration of Elizabeth Drury (*An Anatomie of the World* and the *Progresse of the Soul*), we are made to reflect how much remains for a poet to write about when the season of love is over. When May and June are passed, most poets cease to write or sing the songs of their youth out of tune. But Donne survived the perils of middle age by virtue of the acuteness and ardour of his intellect. When "the satyrique fires which urg'd me to have writt in skorne of all" were quenched, when "My muse (for I had one), because I'm cold, Divorced herself", there still remained the power to turn upon the nature of things and dissect that. Even in the passionate days of youth Donne had been a thinking poet. He had dissected and analysed his own love. To turn from that to the anatomy of the world, from the personal to the impersonal, was the natural development of a complex nature. And the new angle to which his mind now pointed under the influence of middle age and traffic with the world, released powers that were held in check when they were directed against some particular courtier or some particular woman. Now his imagination, as if freed from impediment, goes rocketing up in flights of extravagant exaggeration. True, the rocket bursts; it scatters in a shower of minute, separate particles—curious speculations, wire-drawn comparisons, obsolete erudition; but, winged by the double pressure of mind and heart, of reason and imagination, it soars far and fast into a finer air. Working himself up by his own extravagant praise of the dead girl, he shoots on:

> We spur, we reine the starres, and in their race
> They're diversly content t'obey our pace.
> But keepes the earth her round proportion still?
> Doth not a Tenarif, or higher Hill
> Rise so high like a Rocke, that one might thinke
> The floating Moone would shipwracke there, and sinke?
> Seas are so deepe, that Whales being strooke today,
> Perchance tomorrow, scarce at middle way
> Of their wish'd journies end, the bottome, die.
> And men, to sound depths, so much line untie,
> As one might justly thinke, that there would rise
> At end thereof, one of th'Antipodies:

Or again, Elizabeth Drury is dead and her soul has escaped:

> she stayes not in the ayre,
> To looke what Meteors there themselves prepare;
> She carries no desire to know, nor sense,
> Whether th'ayres middle region be intense;
> For th'Element of fire, she doth not know,
> Whether she past by such a place or no;
> She baits not at the Moone, nor cares to trie
> Whether in that new world, men live, and die.
> *Venus* retards her not, to'enquire, how shee
> Can, (being one starre) *Hesper*, and *Vesper* bee;
> Hee that charm'd *Argus* eyes, sweet *Mercury*,
> Workes not on her, who now is growne all eye;

So we penetrate into distant regions, and reach rare and remote speculations a million miles removed from the simple girl whose death fired the explosion. But to break off

34

fragments from poems whose virtue lies in their close-knit sinews and their long-breathed strength is to diminish them. They need to be read currently rather to grasp the energy and power of the whole than to admire those separate lines which Donne suddenly strikes to illumine the stages of our long climb.

Thus finally we reach the last section of the book, the Holy Sonnets and Divine Poems. Again the poetry changes with the change of circumstances and of years. The patron has gone with the need of patronage. Lady Bedford has been replaced by a Prince still more virtuous and still more remote. To Him the prosperous, the important, the famous Dean of St. Paul's now turns. But how different is the divine poetry of this great dignitary from the divine poetry of the Herberts and the Vaughans! The memory of his sins returns to him as he writes. He has been burnt with "lust and envy"; he has followed profane loves; he has been scornful and fickle and passionate and servile and ambitious. He has attained his end; but he is weaker and worse than the horse or the bull. Now too he is lonely. "Since she whom I lov'd" is dead "My good is dead." Now at last his mind is "wholly sett on heavenly things". And yet how could Donne—that "little world made cunningly of elements"—be wholly set on any one thing?

> Oh, to vex me, contraryes meet in one:
> Inconstancy unnaturally hath begott
> A constant habit; that when I would not
> I change in vowes, and in devotione.

It was impossible for the poet who had noted so curiously the flow and change of human life, and its contrasts, who was at once so inquisitive of knowledge and so sceptical—

Doubt wisely; in strange way,
To stand inquiring right, is not to stray;
To sleep, or run wrong, is

—who had owned allegiance to so many great Princes, the
body, the King, the Church of England, to reach that state
of wholeness and certainty which poets of purer life were
able to maintain. His devotions themselves were feverish
and fitful. "My devout fitts come and goe away like a fantastique Ague." They are full of contraries and agonies.
Just as his love poetry at its most sensual will suddenly reveal the desire for a transcendent unity "beyond the Hee
and Shee", and his most reverential letters to great ladies
will suddenly become love poems addressed by an amorous
man to a woman of flesh and blood, so these last divine
poems are poems of climbing and falling, of incongruous
clamours and solemnities, as if the church door opened on
the uproar of the street. That perhaps is why they still
excite interest and disgust, contempt and admiration. For
the Dean still retained the incorrigible curiosity of his
youth. The temptation to speak the truth in defiance of the
world even when he had taken all that the world had to
give, still worked in him. An obstinate interest in the nature
of his own sensations still troubled his age and broke its
repose as it had troubled his youth and made him the most
vigorous of satirists and the most passionate of lovers.
There was no rest, no end, no solution even at the height
of fame and on the edge of the grave for a nature plaited
together of such diverse strands. The famous preparations
that he made, lying in his shroud, being carved for his
tomb, when he felt death approach are poles asunder from
the falling asleep of the tired and content. He must still cut

a figure and still stand erect—a warning perhaps, a portent certainly, but always consciously and conspicuously himself. That, finally, is one of the reasons why we still seek out Donne; why after three hundred years and more we still hear the sound of his voice speaking across the ages so distinctly. It may be true that when from curiosity we come to cut up and "survey each part", we are like the doctors and "know not why"—we cannot see how so many different qualities meet together in one man. But we have only to read him, to submit to the sound of that passionate and penetrating voice, and his figure rises again across the waste of the years more erect, more imperious, more inscrutable than any of his time. Even the elements seem to have respected that identity. When the fire of London destroyed almost every other monument in St. Paul's, it left Donne's figure untouched, as if the flames themselves found that knot too hard to undo, that riddle too difficult to read, and that figure too entirely itself to turn to common clay.

"The Countess of Pembroke's Arcadia"

IF IT is true that there are books written to escape from the present moment, and its meanness and its sordidity, it is certainly true that readers are familiar with a corresponding mood. To draw the blinds and shut the door, to muffle the noises of the street and shade the glare and flicker of its lights—that is our desire. There is then a charm even in the look of the great volumes that have sunk, like the "Countess of Pembroke's Arcadia", as if by their own weight down to the very bottom of the shelf. We like to feel that the present is not all; that other hands have been before us, smoothing the leather until the corners are rounded and blunt, turning the pages until they are yellow and dog-eared. We like to summon before us the ghosts of those old readers who have read their *Arcadia* from this very copy—Richard Porter, reading with the splendours of the Elizabethans in his eyes; Lucy Baxter, reading in the licentious days of the Restoration; Thos. Hake, still reading, though now the eighteenth century has dawned with a distinction that shows itself in the upright elegance of his signature. Each has read differently, with the insight and the blindness of his own generation. Our reading will be equally partial. In 1930 we shall miss a great deal that was obvious to 1655; we shall see some things that the eighteenth century ignored. But let us keep up the long succession of readers; let us in our turn bring the insight and the blindness of our own generation to bear upon the "Countess of Pembroke's Arcadia", and so pass it on to our successors.

If we choose the *Arcadia* because we wish to escape, certainly the first impression of the book is that Sidney wrote it with very much the same intention: ". . . it is done only for you, only to you", he tells his "dear lady and sister, the Countess of Pembroke". He is not looking at what is before him here at Wilton; he is not thinking of his own troubles or of the tempestuous mood of the great Queen in London. He is absenting himself from the present and its strife. He is writing merely to amuse his sister, not for "severer eyes". "Your dear self can best witness the manner, being done in loose sheets of Paper, most of it in your presence, the rest, by sheets sent unto you, as fast as they were done." So, sitting at Wilton under the downs with Lady Pembroke, he gazes far away into a beautiful land which he calls Arcadia. It is a land of fair valleys and fertile pastures, where the houses are "lodges of yellow stone built in the form of a star"; where the inhabitants are either great princes or humble shepherds; where the only business is to love and to adventure; where bears and lions surprise nymphs bathing in fields red with roses; where princesses are immured in the huts of shepherds; where disguise is perpetually necessary; where the shepherd is really a prince and the woman a man; where, in short, anything may be and happen except what actually is and happens here in England in the year 1580. It is easy to see why, as Sidney handed these dream pages to his sister, he smiled, entreating her indulgence. "Read it then at your idle times, and the follies your good judgment

39

will find in it, blame not, but laugh at." Even for the Sidneys and the Pembrokes life was not quite like that. And yet the life that we invent, the stories we tell, as we sink back with half-shut eyes and pour forth our irresponsible dreams, have perhaps some wild beauty; some eager energy; we often reveal in them the distorted and decorated image of what we soberly and secretly desire. Thus the *Arcadia*, by wilfully flouting all contact with the fact, gains another reality. When Sidney hinted that his friends would like the book for its writer's sake, he meant perhaps that they would find there something that he could say in no other form, as the shepherds singing by the river's side will "deliver out, sometimes joys, sometimes lamentations, sometimes challengings one of the other, sometimes, under hidden forms, uttering such matters as otherwise they durst not deal with". There may be under the disguise of the *Arcadia* a real man trying to speak privately about something that is close to his heart. But in the first freshness of the early pages the disguise itself is enough to enchant us. We find ourselves with shepherds in spring on those sands which "lie against the Island of Cithera". Then, behold, something floats on the waters. It is the body of a man, and he grasps to his breast a small square coffer; and he is young and beautiful— "though he were naked, his nakedness was to him an apparel"; and his name is Musidorus; and he has lost his friend. So, warbling melodiously, the shepherds revive the youth, and row out in a bark from the haven in search of Pyrocles; and a stain appears on the sea, with sparks and smoke issuing from it. For the ship upon which the two princes Musidorus and Pyrocles were voyaging has caught fire; it floats blazing on the water with a great store of rich

40

things round it, and many drowned bodies. "In sum, a defeat, where the conquered kept both field and spoil: a shipwrack without storm or ill footing: and a waste of fire in the midst of the water."

There in a little space we have some of the elements that are woven together to compose this vast tapestry. We have beauty of scene; a pictorial stillness; and something floating towards us, not violently but slowly and gently in time to the sweet warbling of the shepherds' voices. Now and again this crystallises into a phrase that lingers and haunts the ear —"and a waste of fire in the midst of the waters"; "having in their faces a certain waiting sorrow". Now the murmur broadens and expands into some more elaborate passage of description: "each pasture stored with sheep, feeding with sober security, while the pretty lambs with bleating oratory crav'd the dam's comfort: here a shepherd's boy piping, as though he should never be old: there a young shepherdess knitting, and withal singing, and it seemed that her voice comforted her hands to work, and her hands kept time to her voice-music"—a passage that reminds us of a famous description in Dorothy Osborne's *Letters*.

Beauty of scene; stateliness of movement; sweetness of sound—these are the graces that seem to reward the mind that seeks enjoyment purely for its own sake. We are drawn on down the winding paths of this impossible landscape because Sidney leads us without any end in view but sheer delight in wandering. The syllabling of the words even causes him the liveliest delight. Mere rhythm we feel as we sweep over the smooth backs of the undulating sentences intoxicates him. Words in themselves delight him. Look, he seems to cry, as he picks up the glittering handfuls, can it be true that there are such numbers of beautiful words lying about for the asking? Why not use them, lavishly and abundantly? And so he luxuriates. Lambs do not suck—"with bleating oratory [they] crav'd the dam's comfort"; girls do not undress—they "take away the eclipsing of their apparel"; a tree is not reflected in a river—"it seemed she looked into it and dressed her green locks by that running river". It is absurd; and yet there is a world of difference between writing like this with zest and wonder at the images that form upon one's pen and the writing of later ages when the dew was off the language—witness the little tremor that stirs and agitates a sentence that a more formal age would have made coldly symmetrical:

> And the boy fierce though beautiful; and beautiful, though dying, not able to keep his falling feet, fell down to the earth, which he bit for anger, repining at his fortune, and as long as he could, resisting death, which might seem unwilling too; so long he was in taking away his young struggling soul.

It is this inequality and elasticity that lend their freshness to Sidney's vast pages. Often as we rush through them, half laughing, half in protest, the desire comes upon us to shut the ear of reason completely and lie back and listen to this unformed babble of sound; this chorus of intoxicated voices singing madly like birds round the house before any one is up.

But it is easy to lay too much stress upon qualities that delight us because they are lost. Sidney doubtless wrote the *Arcadia* partly to wile away the time, partly to exercise his pen and experiment with the new instrument of the English language. But even so he remained young and a man; even in Arcadia the roads had ruts, and coaches were upset and ladies dislocated their shoulders; even the Princes Musidorus and Pyrocles have passions; Pamela and Philoclea, for all their sea-coloured satins and nets strung with pearls, are women and can love. Thus we stumble upon scenes that cannot be reeled off with a flowing pen; there are moments where Sidney stopped and thought, like any other novelist, what a real man or woman in this particular situation would say; where his own emotions come suddenly to the surface and light up the vague pastoral landscape with an incongruous glare. For a moment we get a surprising combination; crude daylight overpowers the silver lights of the tapers; shepherds and princesses suddenly stop their warbling and speak a few rapid words in their eager human voices.

... many times have I, leaning to yonder Palm, admired the blessedness of it, that it could bear love without sense of pain; many times, when my Master's cattle came hither to chew their cud in this fresh place, I might see the young Bull testify his love; but how? with proud looks and joyfulness. O wretched mankind (said I then to myself) in whom wit (which should be the governor of his welfare) become's the traitor to his blessedness: these beasts like children to nature, inherit her blessings quietly; we like bastards are laid abroad, even as foundlings, to be trained up by grief and sorrow. Their minds grudge not at their bodies comfort, nor their senses are letted from enjoying their objects; we have the impediments of honour, and the torments of conscience.

The words ring strangely on the finicking, dandified lips of Musidorus. There is Sidney's own anger in them and his pain. And then the novelist Sidney suddenly opens his eyes. He watches Pamela as she takes the jewel in the figure of a crab-fish to signify "because it looks one way and goes another" that though he pretended to love Mopsa his heart was Pamela's. And she takes it, he notes,

43

with a calm carelessness letting each thing slide (just as we do by their speeches who neither in matter nor person do any way belong unto us) which kind of cold temper, mixt with that lightning of her natural majesty, is of all others most terrible unto me. . . .

Had she despised him, had she hated him, it would have been better.

But this cruel quietness, neither retiring to mislike, nor proceeding to favour; gracious, but gracious still after one manner; all her courtesies having this engraven in them, that what is done, is for virtue's sake, not for the parties. . . . This (I say) heavenliness of hers . . . is so impossible to reach unto that I almost begin to submit myself unto the tyranny of despair, not knowing any way of persuasion. . . .

—surely an acute and subtle observation made by a man who had felt what he describes. For a moment the pale and legendary figures, Gynecia, Philoclea, and Zelmane, become alive; their featureless faces work with passion; Gynecia, realising that she loves her daughter's lover, foams into grandeur, "crying vehemently Zelmane help me, O Zelmane have pity on me"; and the old King, in whom the beautiful strange Amazon has awakened a senile amorosity, shows himself old and foolish, looking "very curiously upon himself, sometimes fetching a little skip, as if he had said his strength had not yet forsaken him".

But that moment of illumination, as it dies down and the princes once more resume their postures and the shepherds apply themselves to their lutes, throws a curious light upon the book as a whole. We realise more clearly the boundaries within which Sidney was working. For a moment he could note and observe and record as keenly and exactly as any modern novelist. And then, after this one glimpse in our direction, he turns aside, as if he heard other voices calling him and must obey their commands. In prose, he bethinks himself, one must not use the common words of daily speech. In a romance one must not make princes and princesses feel like ordinary men and women. Humour is the attribute of peasants. They can behave ridiculously; they can talk naturally; like Dametas they can come "whistling, and counting upon his fingers, how many load of hay seventeen fat oxen eat up on a year"; but the language of great people must always be long-winded and abstract and full of metaphors. Further, they must either be heroes of stainless virtue, or villains untouched by humanity. Of human oddities and littleness they must show no trace. Prose also must be careful to turn away from what is actually before it. Sometimes for a moment in looking at Nature one may fit the word to the sight; note the heron "wagling" as it rises from the marsh, or observe the water-spaniel hunting the duck "with a snuffling grace". But this realism is only to be applied to Nature and animals and peasants. Prose, it seems, is made for slow, noble, and generalised emotions; for the description of wide landscapes; for the conveyance of long, equable discourses uninterrupted for pages together by any other speaker. Verse, on the other hand, had quite a different office. It is curious to observe how, when Sidney wished to sum up, to strike hard, to register a single and definite impression, he turns to verse. Verse in the *Arcadia* performs something of the function of dialogue in the modern novel. It breaks up the monotony and strikes a high light. In those snatches of song that are scattered about the interminable adventures of Pyrocles and Musidorus our interest is once more fanned into flame. Often the realism and vigour of the verse comes with a shock after the drowsy languor of the prose:

> What needed so high spirits such mansions blind?
> Or wrapt in flesh what do they here obtain,
> But glorious name of wretched human kind?
> Balls to the stars, and thralls to fortune's reign;
> Turn'd from themselves, infected with their cage,
> Where death is fear'd, and life is held with pain.
> Like players plac't to fill a filthy stage. . . .

—one wonders what the indolent princes and princesses will make of that vehement speaking? Or of this:

> A shop of shame, a Book where blots be rife,
> This body is . . .
> This man, this talking beast, this walking tree

—thus the poet turns upon his languid company as if he loathed their self-complacent foppery; and yet must indulge them. For though it is clear that the poet Sidney had shrewd eyes—he talks of "hives of wisely painful bees", and knew like any other country-bred Englishman "how shepherds spend their days. At blow-point, hot-cockles or else at keels",—still he must drone on about Plangus and Erona, and Queen Andromana and the intrigues of Amphialus and his mother Cecropia in deference to his audience. Incongruously enough, violent as they were in their lives, with their plots and their poisonings, nothing can be too sweet, too vague, too long-winded for those Elizabethan listeners. Only the fact that Zelmane had received a blow from a lion's paw that morning can shorten the story and suggest to Basilius that it might be better to reserve the complaint of Klaius till another day.

Which she, perceiving the song had already worn out much time, and not knowing when Lamon would end, being even now stepping over to a new matter, though much delighted with what was spoken, willingly agreed unto. And so of all sides they went to recommend themselves to the elder brother of death.

And as the story winds on its way, or rather as the succession of stories fall on each other like soft snowflakes, one obliterating the other, we are much tempted to follow their example. Sleep weighs down our eyes. Half dreaming, half yawning, we prepare to seek the elder brother of death. What, then, has become of that first intoxicating sense of freedom? We who wished to escape have been caught and enmeshed. Yet how easy it seemed in the beginning to tell a story to amuse a sister—how inspiriting to escape from here and now and wander wildly in a world of lutes and roses! But alas, softness has weighed down our steps; brambles have caught at our clothing. We have come to long for some plain statement, and the decoration of the style, at first so enchanting, has dulled and decayed. It is not difficult to find the reason. High spirited, flown with words, Sidney seized his pen too carelessly. He had no notion when he set out where he was going. Telling stories, he thought, was enough—one could follow another interminably. But where there is no end in view there is no sense of direction to draw us on. Nor, since it is part of his scheme to keep his characters simply bad and simply good without distinction, can he gain variety from the complexity of character. To supply change and movement he must have recourse to mystification. These changes of dress, these disguises of princes as peasants, of men as women, serve instead of psychological subtlety to relieve the stagnancy of people collected together with nothing to talk about. But when the charm of that childish device falls flat, there is no breath left to fill his sails. Who is talking, and to whom, and about what we no longer feel sure. So slack indeed becomes Sidney's grasp upon these ambling phantoms that in the middle he has forgotten what his relation to them is—is it "I" the author who is speaking or is it "I" the character? No reader can be kept in bondage, whatever the grace and the charm, when the ties between him and the writer are so irresponsibly doffed and assumed. So by degrees the book floats away into the thin air of limbo. It becomes one of those half-forgotten and deserted places where the grasses grow over fallen statues and the rain drips and the marble steps are green with moss and vast weeds flourish in the flower-beds. And yet it is a beautiful garden to wander in now and then; one stumbles over lovely broken faces, and here and there a flower blooms and the nightingale sings in the lilac-tree.

Thus when we come to the last page that Sidney wrote before he gave up the hopeless attempt to finish the *Arcadia*, we pause for a moment before we return the folio to its place on the bottom shelf. In the *Arcadia*, as in some luminous globe, all the seeds of English fiction lie latent. We can trace infinite possibilities: it may take any one of many different directions. Will it fix its gaze upon Greece and prince and princesses, and seek as it might so nobly, the statuesque, the impersonal? Will it keep to simple lines and great masses and the vast landscapes of the epic? Or will it look closely and carefully at what is actually before it? Will it take for its heroes Dametas and Mopsa, ordinary people of low birth and rough natural speech, and deal with the normal course of daily human life? Or will it brush through those barriers and penetrate within to the anguish and complexity of some unhappy woman loving where she may not love; to the senile absurdity of some old man tortured by an incongruous passion? Will it make its dwelling in their psychology and the adventures of the soul? All these possibilities are present in the *Arcadia*—romance and realism, poetry and psychology. But as if Sidney knew that he had broached a task too large for his youth to execute, had bequeathed a legacy for other ages to inherit, he put down his pen, mid-way, and left unfinished in all its beauty and absurdity this attempt to wile away the long days at Wilton, telling a story to his sister.

"Robinson Crusoe"

THERE are many ways of approaching this classical volume; but which shall we choose? Shall we begin by saying that, since Sidney died at Zutphen leaving the *Arcadia* unfinished, great changes had come over English life, and the novel had chosen, or had been forced to choose, its direction? A middle class had come into existence, able to read and anxious to read not only about the loves of princes and princesses, but about themselves and the details of their humdrum lives. Stretched upon a thousand pens, prose had accommodated itself to the demand; it had fitted itself to express the facts of life rather than the poetry. That is certainly one way of approaching *Robinson Crusoe*—through the development of the novel; but another immediately suggests itself—through the life of the author. Here too, in the heavenly pastures of biography, we may spend many more hours than are needed to read the book itself from cover to cover. The date of Defoe's birth, to begin with, is doubtful—was it 1660 or 1661? Then again, did he spell his name in one word or in two? And who were his ancestors? He is said to have been a hosier; but what, after all, was a hosier in the seventeenth century? He became a pamphleteer, and enjoyed the confidence of William the Third; one of his pamphlets caused him to be stood in the pillory and imprisoned at Newgate; he was employed by Harley and later by Godolphin; he was the first of the hireling journalists; he wrote innumerable pamphlets and articles; also *Moll Flanders* and *Robinson Crusoe;* he had a wife and six children; was spare in figure, with a hooked nose, a sharp chin, grey eyes and a large mole near his mouth. Nobody who has any slight acquaintance with English literature needs to be told how many hours can be spent and how many lives have been spent in tracing the development of the novel and in examining the chins of the novelists. Only now and then, as we turn from theory to biography and from biography to theory, a doubt insinuates itself—if we knew the very moment of Defoe's birth and whom he loved and why, if we had by heart the history of the origin, rise, growth, decline, and fall of the English novel from its conception (say) in Egypt to its decease in the wilds (perhaps) of Paraquay, should we suck an ounce of additional pleasure from *Robinson Crusoe* or read it one whit more intelligently?

For the book itself remains. However we may wind and wriggle, loiter and dally in our approach to books, a lonely battle waits us at the end. There is a piece of business to be transacted between writer and reader before any further dealings are possible, and to be reminded in the middle of this private interview that Defoe sold stockings, had brown hair, and was stood in the pillory is a distraction and a worry. Our first task, and it is often formidable enough, is to master his perspective. Until we know how the novelist orders his world, the ornaments of that world, which the critics press upon us, the adventures of the writer, to which biographers draw attention, are superfluous possessions of which we can make no use. All alone we must climb upon the novelist's shoulders and gaze through his eyes until we, too, understand in what order he ranges the large common objects upon which novelists are fated to gaze: man and men; behind them Nature; and above them that power which for convenience and brevity we may call God. And at once confusion, misjudgment, and difficulty begin. Simple as they appear to us, these objects can be made monstrous and indeed unrecognisable by the manner in which the novelist relates them to each other. It would seem to be true that people who live cheek by jowl and breathe the same air vary enormously in their sense of proportion; to one the human being is vast, the tree minute; to the other, trees are huge and human beings insignificant little objects in the background. So, in spite of the text-books, writers may live at the same time and yet see nothing the same size. Here is Scott, for example, with his mountains looming huge and his men therefore drawn to scale; Jane Austen picking out the roses on her tea-cups to match the wit of her dialogues; while Peacock bends over heaven and earth one fantastic distorting mirror in which a tea-cup may be Vesuvius or Vesuvius a tea-cup. Nevertheless Scott, Jane Austen, and Peacock lived through the same years; they saw the same world; they are covered in the text-books by the same stretch of literary history. It is in their perspective that they are different. If, then, it were granted us to grasp this firmly, for ourselves, the battle would end in victory; and we could turn, secure in our intimacy, to enjoy the various delights with which the critics and biographers so generously supply us.

But here many difficulties arise. For we have our own vision of the world; we have made it from our own experience and prejudices, and it is therefore bound up with our

own vanities and loves. It is impossible not to feel injured
and insulted if tricks are played and our private harmony is
upset. Thus when *Jude the Obscure* appears or a new volume
of Proust, the newspapers are flooded with protests. Major
Gibbs of Cheltenham would put a bullet through his head
tomorrow if life were as Hardy paints it; Miss Wiggs of
Hampstead must protest that though Proust's art is wonderful, the real world, she thanks God, has nothing in common
with the distortions of a perverted Frenchman. Both the
gentleman and the lady are trying to control the novelist's
perspective so that it shall resemble and reinforce their own.
But the great writer—the Hardy or the Proust—goes on his
way regardless of the rights of private property; by the sweat
of his brow he brings order from chaos; he plants his tree
there, and his man here; he makes the figure of his deity remote or present as he wills. In masterpieces—books, that is,
where the vision is clear and order has been achieved—he
inflicts his own perspective upon us so severely that as often
as not we suffer agonies—our vanity is injured because our
own order is upset; we are afraid because the old supports
are being wrenched from us; and we are bored—for what
pleasure or amusement can be plucked from a brand new
idea? Yet from anger, fear, and boredom a rare and lasting
delight is sometimes born.

Robinson Crusoe, it may be, is a case in point. It is a
masterpiece, and it is a masterpiece largely because Defoe
has throughout kept consistently to his own sense of perspective. For this reason he thwarts us and flouts us at every
turn. Let us look at the theme largely and loosely, comparing it with our preconceptions. It is, we know, the story of
a man who is thrown, after many perils and adventures,

alone upon a desert island. The mere suggestion—peril and solitude and a desert island—is enough to rouse in us the expectation of some far land on the limits of the world; of the sun rising and the sun setting; of man, isolated from his kind, brooding alone upon the nature of society and the strange ways of men. Before we open the book we have perhaps vaguely sketched out the kind of pleasure we expect it to give us. We read; and we are rudely contradicted on every page. There are no sunsets and no sunrises; there is no solitude and no soul. There is, on the contrary, staring us full in the face nothing but a large earthenware pot. We are told, that is to say, that it was the 1st of September 1651; that the hero's name is Robinson Crusoe; and that his father has the gout. Obviously, then, we must alter our attitude. Reality, fact, substance is going to dominate all that follows. We must hastily alter our proportions throughout; Nature must furl her splendid purples; she is only the giver of drought and water; man must be reduced to a struggling, life-preserving animal; and God shrivel into a magistrate whose seat, substantial and somewhat hard, is only a little way above the horizon. Each sortie of ours in pursuit of information upon these cardinal points of perspective—God, man, Nature—is snubbed back with ruthless common-sense. Robinson Crusoe thinks of God: "sometimes I would expostulate with myself, why providence should thus completely ruin its creatures. . . . But something always return'd swift upon me to check these thoughts." God does not exist. He thinks of Nature, the fields "adorn'd with flowers and grass, and full of very fine woods", but the important thing about a wood is that it harbours an abundance of parrots who may be tamed and taught to speak. Nature

54

does not exist. He considers the dead, whom he has killed himself. It is of the utmost importance that they should be buried at once, for "they lay open to the sun and would presently be offensive". Death does not exist. Nothing exists except an earthenware pot. Finally, that is to say, we are forced to drop our own preconceptions and to accept what Defoe himself wishes to give us.

Let us then go back to the beginning and repeat again, "I was born in the year 1632 in the city of York of a good family". Nothing could be plainer, more matter of fact, than that beginning. We are drawn on soberly to consider all the blessings of orderly, industrious middle-class life. There is no greater good fortune we are assured than to be born of the British middle class. The great are to be pitied and so are the poor; both are exposed to distempers and un-easiness; the middle station between the mean and the great is the best; and its virtues—temperance, moderation, quiet-ness, and health—are the most desirable. It was a sorry thing, then, when by some evil fate a middle class youth was bitten with the foolish love of adventure. So he proses on, drawing, little by little, his own portrait, so that we never forget it—imprinting upon us indelibly, for he never forgets it either, his shrewdness, his caution, his love of order and comfort and respectability; until by whatever means, we find ourselves at sea, in a storm; and, peering out, everything is seen precisely as it appears to Robinson Crusoe. The waves, the seamen, the sky, the ship—all are seen through those shrewd, middle-class, unimaginative eyes. There is no escaping him. Everything appears as it would appear to that naturally cautious, apprehensive, conven-tional, and solidly matter-of-fact intelligence. He is in-

capable of enthusiasm. He has a natural slight distaste for
the sublimities of Nature. He suspects even Providence of
exaggeration. He is so busy and has such an eye to the main
chance that he notices only a tenth part of what is going on
round him. Everything is capable of a rational explanation,
he is sure, if only he had time to attend to it. We are much
more alarmed by the "vast great creatures" that swim out
in the night and surround his boat than he is. He at once
takes his gun and fires at them, and off they swim—whether
they are lions or not he really cannot say. Thus before we
know it we are opening our mouths wider and wider. We
are swallowing monsters that we should have jibbed at if
they had been offered us by an imaginative and flamboyant
traveller. But anything that this sturdy middle-class man
notices can be taken for a fact. He is for ever counting his
barrels, and making sensible provisions for his water supply;
nor do we ever find him tripping even in a matter of detail.
Has he forgotten, we wonder, that he has a great lump of
beeswax on board? Not at all. But as he had already made
candles out of it, it is not nearly as great on page thirty-
eight as it was on page twenty-three. When for a wonder he
leaves some inconsistency hanging loose—why if the wild
cats are so very tame are the goats so very shy?—we are not
seriously perturbed, for we are sure that there was a reason,
and a very good one, had he time to give it us. But the pressure of life when one is fending entirely for oneself alone on
a desert island is really no laughing matter. It is no crying
one either. A man must have an eye to everything; it is no
time for raptures about Nature when the lightning may explode one's gunpowder—it is imperative to seek a safer
lodging for it. And so by means of telling the truth undevi-

atingly as it appears to him—by being a great artist and forgoing this and daring that in order to give effect to his prime quality, a sense of reality—he comes in the end to make common actions dignified and common objects beautiful. To dig, to bake, to plant, to build—how serious these simple occupations are; hatchets, scissors, logs, axes—how beautiful these simple objects become. Unimpeded by comment, the story marches on with magnificent downright simplicity. Yet how could comment have made it more impressive? It is true that he takes the opposite way from the psychologist's—he describes the effect of emotion on the body, not on the mind. But when he says how, in a moment of anguish, he clinched his hands so that any soft thing would have been crushed; how "my teeth in my head would strike together, and set against one another so strong, that for the time I could not part them again", the effect is as deep as pages of analysis could have made it. His own instinct in the matter is right. "Let the naturalists", he says, "explain these things, and the reason and manner of them; all I can say to them is, to describe the fact. . . ." If you are Defoe, certainly to describe the fact is enough; for the fact is the right fact. By means of this genius for fact Defoe achieves effects that are beyond any but the great masters of descriptive prose. He has only to say a word or two about "the grey of the morning" to paint vividly a windy dawn. A sense of desolation and of the deaths of many men is conveyed by remarking in the most prosaic way in the world, "I never saw them afterwards, or any sign of them except three of their hats, one cap, and two shoes that were not fellows". When at last he exclaims, "Then to see how like a king I din'd too all alone, attended by my servants"—his parrot and his dog and his two cats, we cannot help but feel that all humanity is on a desert island alone—though Defoe at once informs us, for he has a way of snubbing off our enthusiasms, that the cats were not the same cats that had come in the ship. Both of those were dead; these cats were new cats, and as a matter of fact cats became very troublesome before long from their fecundity, whereas dogs, oddly enough, did not breed at all.

Thus Defoe, by reiterating that nothing but a plain earthenware pot stands in the foreground, persuades us to see remote islands and the solitudes of the human soul. By believing fixedly in the solidity of the pot and its earthiness, he has subdued every other element to his design; he has roped the whole universe into harmony. And is there any reason, we ask as we shut the book, why the perspective that a plain earthenware pot exacts should not satisfy us as completely, once we grasp it, as man himself in all his sublimity standing against a background of broken mountains and tumbling oceans with stars flaming in the sky?

Dorothy Osborne's "Letters"

IT MUST sometimes strike the casual reader of English literature that there is a bare season in it, sometimes like early spring in our country-side. The trees stand out; the hills are unmuffled in green; there is nothing to obscure the mass of the earth or the lines of the branches. But we miss the tremor and murmur of June, when the smallest wood seems full of movement, and one has only to stand still to hear the whispering and the pattering of nimble, inquisitive animals going about their affairs in the undergrowth. So in English literature we have to wait till the sixteenth century is over and the seventeenth well on its way before the bare landscape becomes full of stir and quiver and we can fill in the spaces between the great books with the voices of people talking.

Doubtless great changes in psychology were needed and great changes in material comfort—arm-chairs and carpets and good roads—before it was possible for human beings to watch each other curiously or to communicate their thoughts easily. And it may be that our early literature owes something of its magnificence to the fact that writing was an uncommon art, practised, rather for fame than for money, by those whose gifts compelled them. Perhaps the dissipation of our genius in biography, and journalism, and letter- and memoir-writing has weakened its strength in any one direction. However, this may be, there is a bareness about an age that has neither letter-writers nor biographers. Lives and characters appear in stark outline. Donne, says Sir Edmund Gosse, is inscrutable; and that is largely because, though we know what Donne thought of Lady Bedford, we have not the slightest inkling what Lady Bedford thought of Donne. She had no friend to whom she described the effect of that strange visitor; nor, had she had a confidante, could she have explained for what reasons Donne seemed to her strange.

And the conditions that made it impossible for Boswell or Horace Walpole to be born in the sixteenth century were obviously likely to fall with far heavier force upon the other sex. Besides the material difficulty—Donne's small house at Mitcham with its thin walls and crying children typifies the discomfort in which the Elizabethans lived—the woman was impeded also by her belief that writing was an act unbefitting her sex. A great lady here and there whose rank secured her the toleration and it may be the adulation of a servile circle, might write and print her writings. But the act was offensive to a woman of lower rank. "Sure the poore woman is a little distracted, she could never bee soe ridiculous else as to venture writeing book's and in verse too", Dorothy Osborne exclaimed when the Duchess of Newcastle published one of her books. For her own part, she added, "If I could not sleep this fortnight I should not come to that". And the comment is the more illuminating in that it was made by a woman of great literary gift. Had she been born in 1827, Dorothy Osborne would have written novels; had she been born in 1527, she would never have written at all. But she was born in 1627, and at that date though writing books was ridiculous for a woman there was nothing unseemly in writing a letter. And so by degrees the silence is

broken; we begin to hear rustlings in the undergrowth; for
the first time in English literature we hear men and women
talking together over the fire.

But the art of letter-writing in its infancy was not the art
that has since filled so many delightful volumes. Men and
women were ceremoniously Sir and Madam; the language
was still too rich and stiff to turn and twist quickly and
freely upon half a sheet of notepaper. The art of letter-
writing is often the art of essay-writing in disguise. But
such as it was, it was an art that a woman could practise
without unsexing herself. It was an art that could be carried
on at odd moments, by a father's sick-bed, among a thousand
interruptions, without exciting comment, anonymously as it
were, and often with the pretence that it served some useful
purpose. Yet into these innumerable letters, lost now for
the most part, went powers of observation and of wit that
were later to take rather a different shape in *Evelina* and in
Pride and Prejudice. They were only letters, yet some pride
went to their making. Dorothy, without admitting it, took
pains with her own writing and had views as to the nature
of it: ". . . great Schollers are not the best writer's (of
Letters I mean, of books perhaps they are) . . . all letters
mee thinks should be free and easy as one's discourse". She
was in agreement with an old uncle of hers who threw his
standish at his secretary's head for saying "put pen to paper"
instead of simply "wrote". Yet there were limits, she reflected, to free-and-easiness: ". . . many pritty things
shuffled together" do better spoken than in a letter. And so
we come by a form of literature, if Dorothy Osborne will
let us call it so, which is distinct from any other, and much

to be regretted now that it has gone from us, as it seems, for ever.

For Dorothy Osborne, as she filled her great sheets by her father's bed or by the chimney-corner, gave a record of life, gravely yet playfully, formally yet with intimacy, to a public of one, but to a fastidious public, as the novelist can never give it, or the historian either. Since it is her business to keep her lover informed of what passes in her home, she must sketch the solemn Sir Justinian Isham—Sir Solomon Justinian, she calls him—the pompous widower with four daughters and a great gloomy house in Northamptonshire who wished to marry her. "Lord what would I give that I had a Lattin letter of his for you", she exclaimed, in which he describes her to an Oxford friend and specially commended her that she was "capable of being company and conversation for him"; she must sketch her valetudinarian Cousin Molle waking one morning in fear of the dropsy and hurrying to the doctor at Cambridge; she must draw her own picture wandering in the garden at night and smelling the "Jessomin", "and yet I was not pleased" because Temple was not with her. Any gossip that comes her way is sent on to amuse her lover. Lady Sunderland, for instance, has condescended to marry plain Mr. Smith, who treats her like a princess, which Sir Justinian thinks a bad precedent for wives. But Lady Sunderland tells every one she married him out of pity, and that, Dorothy comments, "was the pitty-full'st sayeing that ever I heard". Soon we have picked up enough about all her friends to snatch eagerly at any further addition to the picture which is forming in our mind's eye.

Indeed, our glimpse of the society of Bedfordshire in the

seventeenth century is the more intriguing for its intermit-
tency. In they come and out they go—Sir Justinian and
Lady Diana, Mr. Smith and his countess—and we never
know when or whether we shall hear of them again. But
with all this haphazardry, the *Letters*, like the letters of all
born letter-writers, provide their own continuity. They make
us feel that we have our seat in the depths of Dorothy's
mind, at the heart of the pageant which unfolds itself page
by page as we read. For she possesses indisputably the gift
which counts for more in letter-writing than wit or brilliance
or traffic with great people. By being herself without effort
or emphasis, she envelops all these odds and ends in the flow
of her own personality. It was a character that was both
attractive and a little obscure. Phrase by phrase we come
closer into touch with it. Of the womanly virtues that befitted her age she shows little trace. She says nothing of sewing or baking. She was a little indolent by temperament.
She browsed casually on vast French romances. She roams
the commons, loitering to hear the milkmaids sing; she walks
in the garden by the side of a small river, "where I sitt
downe and wish you were with mee". She was apt to fall
silent in company and dream over the fire till some talk of
flying, perhaps, roused her, and she made her brother laugh
by asking what they were saying about flying, for the
thought had struck her, if she could fly she could be with
Temple. Gravity, melancholy were in her blood. She looked,
her mother used to say, as if all her friends were dead. She
is oppressed by a sense of fortune and its tyranny and the
vanity of things and the uselessness of effort. Her mother
and sister were grave women too, the sister famed for her
letters, but fonder of books than of company, the mother

"counted as wise a woman as most in England", but sardonic. "I have lived to see that 'tis almost impossible to think People worse than they are and soe will you"—Dorothy could remember her mother saying that. To assuage her spleen, Dorothy herself had to visit the wells at Epsom and to drink water that steel had stood in.

With such a temperament her humour naturally took the form of irony rather than of wit. She loved to mock her lover and to pour a fine raillery over the pomps and ceremonies of existence. Pride of birth she laughed at. Pompous old men were fine subjects for her satire. A dull sermon moved her to laughter. She saw through parties; she saw through ceremonies; she saw through worldliness and display. But with all this clearsightedness there was something that she did not see through. She dreaded with a shrinking that was scarcely sane the ridicule of the world. The meddling of aunts and the tyranny of brothers exasperated her. "I would live in a hollow Tree", she said, "to avoyde them." A husband kissing his wife in public seemed to her as "ill a sight as one would wish to see". Though she cared no more whether people praised her beauty or her wit than whether "they think my name Eliz: or Dor:", a word of gossip about her own behaviour would set her in a quiver. Thus when it came to proving before the eyes of the world that she loved a poor man and was prepared to marry him, she could not do it. "I confess that I have an humor that will not suffer mee to Expose myself to People's Scorne", she wrote. She could be "sattisfyed within as narrow a compasse as that of any person liveing of my rank", but ridicule was intolerable to her. She shrank from any extravagance that could draw the censure of the world upon her. It was a weakness for which Temple had sometimes to reprove her.

For Temple's character emerges more and more clearly as the letters go on—it is a proof of Dorothy's gift as a correspondent. A good letter-writer so takes the colour of the reader at the other end, that from reading the one we can imagine the other. As she argues, as she reasons, we hear Temple almost as clearly as we hear Dorothy herself. He was in many ways the opposite of her. He drew out her melancholy by rebutting it; he made her defend her dislike of marriage by opposing it. Of the two Temple was by far the more robust and positive. Yet there was perhaps something—a little hardness, a little conceit—that justified her brother's dislike of him. He called Temple the "proudest imperious insulting ill-natured man that ever was". But, in the eyes of Dorothy, Temple had qualities that none of her other suitors possessed. He was not a mere country gentleman, nor a pompous Justice of the Peace, nor a town gallant, making love to every woman he met, nor a travelled Monsieur; for had he been any one of these things, Dorothy, with her quick sense of the ridiculous, would have had none of him. To her he had some charm, some sympathy, that the others lacked; she could write to him whatever came into her head; she was at her best with him; she loved him; she respected him. Yet suddenly she declared that marry him she would not. She turned violently against marriage indeed, and cited failure after failure. If people knew each other before marriage, she thought, there would be an end of it. Passion was the most brutish and tyrannical of all our senses. Passion had made Lady Anne Blount the "talk of all the footmen and Boy's in the street". Passion had been the undoing of the lovely Lady Izabella—what use was her beauty now married to "that beast with all his estate"? Torn asunder by her brother's anger, by Temple's jealousy, and by her own dread of ridicule, she wished for nothing but to be left to find "an early and a quiet grave". That Temple overcame her scruples and overrode her brother's opposition is much to the credit of his character. Yet it is an act that we can hardly help deploring. Married to Temple, she wrote to him no longer. The letters almost immediately cease. The whole world that Dorothy had brought into existence is extinguished. It is then that we realise how round and populous and stirring that world has become. Under the warmth of her affection for Temple the stiffness had gone out of her pen. Writing half asleep by her father's side, snatching the back of an old letter to write upon, she had come to write easily though always with the dignity proper to that age, of the Lady Dianas, and the Ishams, of the aunts and the uncles—how they come, how they go; what they say; whether she finds them dull, laughable, charming, or much as usual. More than that, she has suggested, writing her mind out to Temple, the deeper relationships, the more private moods, that gave her life its conflict and its consolation —her brother's tyranny; her own moodiness and melancholy; the sweetness of walking in the garden at night; of sitting lost in thought by the river; of longing for a letter and finding one. All this is around us; we are deep in this world, seizing its hints and suggestions when, in the moment, the scene is blotted out. She married, and her husband was a rising diplomat. She had to follow his fortunes in Brussels, at The Hague, wherever they called him. Seven children were born and seven children died "almost all in their cradle". Innumerable duties and responsibilities fell to the lot of the girl who had made fun of pomp and ceremony, who loved privacy and had wished to live secluded out of the world and "grow old together in our little cottage". Now she was mistress of her husband's house at The Hague with its splendid buffet of plate. She was his confidante in the many troubles of his difficult career. She stayed behind in London to negotiate if possible the payment of his arrears of salary. When her yacht was fired on, she behaved, the King said, with greater courage than the captain himself. She was everything that the wife of an ambassador should be: she was everything, too, that the wife of a man retired from the public service should be. And troubles came upon them —a daughter died; a son, inheriting perhaps his mother's melancholy, filled his boots with stones and leapt into the Thames. So the years passed; very full, very active, very troubled. But Dorothy maintained her silence.

At last, however, a strange young man came to Moor Park as secretary to her husband. He was difficult, ill-mannered, and quick to take offence. But it is through Swift's eyes that we see Dorothy once more in the last years of her life. "Mild Dorothea, peaceful, wise, and great", Swift called her; but the light falls upon a ghost. We do not know that silent lady. We cannot connect her after all these years with the girl who poured her heart out to her lover. "Peaceful, wise, and great"—she was none of those things when we last met her, and much though we honour the admirable ambassadress who made her husband's career her own, there are moments when we would exchange all the benefits of the Triple Alliance and all the glories of the Treaty of Nimue-gen for the letters that Dorothy did not write.

Swift's "Journal to Stella"

IN ANY highly civilised society disguise plays so large a part, politeness is so essential, that to throw off the ceremonies and conventions and talk a "little language" for one or two to understand, is as much a necessity as a breath of air in a hot room. The reserved, the powerful, the admired have the most need of such a refuge. Swift himself found it so. The proudest of men coming home from the company of great men who praised him, of lovely women who flattered him, from intrigue and politics, put all that aside, settled himself comfortably in bed, pursed his severe lips into baby language and prattled to his "two monkies", his "dear Sirrahs", his "naughty rogues" on the other side of the Irish Channel.

Well, let me see you now again. My wax candle's almost out, but however I'll begin. Well then don't be so tedious, Mr. Presto; what can you say to MD's letter? Make haste, have done with your preambles—why, I say, I am glad you are so often abroad.

So long as Swift wrote to Stella in that strain, carelessly, illegibly, for "methinks when I write plain, I do not know how, but we are not alone, all the world can see us. A bad scrawl is so snug . . .", Stella had no need to be jealous. It was true that she was wearing away the flower of her youth in Ireland with Rebecca Dingley, who wore hinged spectacles, consumed large quantities of Brazil tobacco, and stumbled over her petticoats as she walked. Further, the

conditions in which the two ladies lived, for ever in Swift's
company when he was at home, occupying his house when
he was absent, gave rise to gossip; so that though Stella
never saw him except in Mrs. Dingley's presence, she was
one of those ambiguous women who live chiefly in the society of the other sex. But surely it was well worth while.
The packets kept coming from England, each sheet written
to the rim in Swift's crabbed little hand, which she imitated
to perfection, full of nonsense words, and capital letters,
and hints which no one but Stella could understand, and
secrets which Stella was to keep, and little commissions
which Stella was to execute. Tobacco came for Dingley,
and chocolate and silk aprons for Stella. Whatever people
might say, surely it was well worth while.

Of this Presto, who was so different from that formidable
character "t'other I", the world knew nothing. The world
knew only that Swift was over in England again, soliciting
the new Tory government on behalf of the Irish Church for
those First Fruits which he had begged the Whigs in vain to
restore. The business was soon accomplished; nothing indeed could exceed the cordiality and affection with which
Harley and St. John greeted him; and now the world saw
what even in those days of small societies and individual
pre-eminence must have been a sight to startle and amaze—
the "mad parson", who had marched up and down the
coffee-houses in silence and unknown a few years ago, admitted to the inmost councils of State, the penniless boy
who was not allowed to sit down at table with Sir William
Temple dining with the highest Ministers of the Crown,
making dukes do his bidding and so run after for his good
offices that his servant's chief duty was to know how to keep

people out. Addison himself forced his way up only by pretending that he was a gentleman come to pay a bill. For the time being Swift was omnipotent. Nobody could buy his services; everybody feared his pen. He went to Court, and "am so proud I make all the lords come up to me". The Queen wished to hear him preach; Harley and St. John added their entreaties; but he refused. When Mr. Secretary one night dared show his temper, Swift called upon him and warned him

never to appear cold to me, for I would not be treated like a schoolboy. . . . He took all right; said I had reason . . . would have had me dine with him at Mrs. Masham's brother, to make up matters; but I would not. I don't know, but I would not.

He scribbled all this down to Stella without exultation or vanity. That he should command and dictate, prove himself the peer of great men and make rank abase itself before him, called for no comment on his part or on hers. Had she not known him years ago at Moor Park and seen him lose his temper with Sir William Temple, and guessed his greatness and heard from his own lips what he planned and hoped? Did she not know better than any one how strangely good and bad were blent in him and all his foibles and eccentricities of temper? He scandalised the lords with whom he dined by his stinginess, picked the coals off his fire, saved halfpence on coaches; and yet by the help of these very economies he practised, she knew, the most considerate and secret of charities—he gave poor Patty Rolt "a pistole to help her a little forward against she goes to board in the country"; he took twenty guineas to young Harrison, the sick poet, in his garret. She alone knew how he could be coarse in his speech and yet delicate in his behaviour; how he could be cynical superficially and yet cherish a depth of feeling which she had never met with in any other human being. They knew each other in and out; the good and the bad, the deep and the trivial; so that without effort or concealment he could use those precious moments late at night or the first thing on waking to pour out upon her the whole story of his day, with its charities and meannesses, its affections and ambitions and despairs, as though he were thinking aloud.

With such proof of his affection, admitted to intimacy with this Presto whom no one else in the world knew, Stella had no cause to be jealous. It was perhaps the opposite that happened. As she read the crowded pages, she could see him and hear him and imagine so exactly the impression that he must be making on all these fine people that she fell more deeply in love with him than ever. Not only was he courted and flattered by the great; everybody seemed to call upon him when they were in trouble. There was "young Harrison"; he worried to find him ill and penniless; carried him off to Knightsbridge; took him a hundred pounds only to find that he was dead an hour before. "Think what grief this is to me! . . . I could not dine with Lord Treasurer, nor anywhere else; but got a bit of meat toward evening." She could imagine the strange scene, that November morning, when the Duke of Hamilton was killed in Hyde Park, and Swift went at once to the Duchess and sat with her for two hours and heard her rage and storm and rail; and took her affairs, too, on his shoulders as if it were his natural office, and none could dispute his place in the house of mourning. "She has moved my very soul", he said. When young Lady Ashburnham died he burst out, "I hate life when I think it exposed to such accidents; and to see so many thousand wretches burdening the earth, while such as her die, makes me think God did never intend life for a blessing". And then, with that instinct to rend and tear his own emotions which made him angry in the midst of his pity, he would round upon the mourners, even the mother and sister of the dead woman, and part them as they cried together and complain how "people will pretend to grieve more than they really do, and that takes off from their true grief".

All this was poured forth freely to Stella; the gloom and the anger, the kindness and the coarseness and the genial love of little ordinary human things. To her he showed himself fatherly and brotherly; he laughed at her spelling; he scolded her about her health; he directed her business affairs. He gossiped and chatted with her. They had a fund of memories in common. They had spent many happy hours together. "Do not you remember I used to come into your chamber and turn Stella out of her chair, and rake up the fire in a cold morning and cry *uth, uth, uth!*" She was often in his mind; he wondered if she was out walking when he was; when Prior abused one of his puns he remembered Stella's puns and how vile they were; he compared his life in London with hers in Ireland and wondered when they would be together again. And if this was the influence of Stella upon Swift in town among all the wits, the influence of Swift upon Stella marooned in an Irish village alone with Dingley was far greater. He had taught her all the little learning she had when she was a child and he a young man years ago at Moor Park. His influence was everywhere —upon her mind, upon her affections, upon the books she read and the hand she wrote, upon the friends she made and the suitors she rejected. Indeed, he was half responsible for her being.

But the woman he had chosen was no insipid slave. She had a character of her own. She was capable of thinking for herself. She was aloof, a severe critic for all her grace and sympathy, a little formidable perhaps with her love of plain speaking and her fiery temper and her fearlessness in saying what she thought. But with all her gifts she was little known. Her slender means and feeble health and dubious social standing made her way of life very modest. The society which gathered round her came for the simple pleasure of talking to a woman who listened and understood and said very little herself, but in the most agreeable of voices and generally "the best thing that was said in the company". For the rest she was not learned. Her health had prevented her from serious study, and though she had run over a great variety of subjects and had a fine severe taste in letters, what she did read did not stick in her mind. She had been extravagant as a girl, and flung her money about until her good sense took control of her and now she lived with the utmost frugality. "Five nothings on five plates of delf" made her supper. Attractive, if not beautiful, with her fine dark eyes and her raven black hair she dressed very plainly, and thus contrived to lay by enough to help the poor and to bestow upon her friends (it was an extravagance that she could not resist) "the most agreeable presents in the world". Swift never knew her equal in that art, "although it be an affair of as delicate a nature as most in the course of life". She had in addition that sincerity which Swift called "honour", and in spite of the weakness of her

73

body "the personal courage of a hero". Once when a robber
came to her window, she had shot him through the body
with her own hand. Such, then, was the influence which
worked on Swift as he wrote; such the presence that mingled with the thought of his fruit trees and the willows
and the trout stream at Laracor when he saw the trees bud-
ding in St. James's Park and heard the politicians wrangle
at Westminster. Unknown to all of them, he had his retreat;
and if the Ministers again played him false, and once more,
after making his friend's fortunes, he went empty-handed
away, then after all he could retire to Ireland and to Stella
and have "no shuddering at all" at the thought.

But Stella was the last woman in the world to press her
claims. None knew better than she that Swift loved power
and the company of men: that though he had his moods of
tenderness and his fierce spasms of disgust at society, still
for the most part he infinitely preferred the dust and bustle
of London to all the trout streams and cherry trees in the
world. Above all, he hated interference. If any one laid a
finger upon his liberty or hinted the least threat to his independence, were they men or women, queens or kitchen-
maids, he turned upon them with a ferocity which made a
savage of him on the spot. Harley once dared to offer him a
banknote; Miss Waring dared hint that the obstacles to
their marriage were now removed. Both were chastised, the
woman brutally. But Stella knew better than to invite such
treatment. Stella had learnt patience; Stella had learnt discretion. Even in a matter like this of staying in London or
coming back to Ireland she allowed him every latitude. She
asked nothing for herself and therefore got more than she
asked. Swift was half annoyed:

. . . your generosity makes me mad; I know you repine inwardly at Presto's absence; you think he has broken his word, of coming in three months, and that this is always his trick: and now Stella says, she does not see possibly how I can come away in haste, and that MD is satisfied, etc. An't you a rogue to overpower me thus?

But it was thus that she kept him. Again and again he burst into language of intense affection:

Farewell dear Sirrahs, dearest lives: there is peace and quiet with MD, and nowhere else. . . . Farewell again, dearest rogues: I am never happy, but when I write or think of MD. . . . You are as welcome as my blood to every farthing I have in the world: and all that grieves me is, I am not richer, for MD's sake.

One thing alone dashed the pleasure that such words gave her. It was always in the plural that he spoke of her; it was always "dearest Sirrahs, dearest lives"; MD stood for Stella and Mrs. Dingley together. Swift and Stella were never alone. Grant that this was for form's sake merely, grant that the presence of Mrs. Dingley, busy with her keys and her lap-dog and never listening to a word that was said to her, was a form too. But why should such forms be necessary? Why impose a strain that wasted her health and half spoilt her pleasure and kept "perfect friends" who were happy only in each other's company apart? Why indeed? There was a reason; a secret that Stella knew; a secret that Stella did not impart. Divided they had to be. Since, then, no bond bound them, since she was afraid to lay the least claim upon her friend, all the more jealously must she have searched into his words and analysed his conduct to ascertain the temper of his mood and acquaint herself instantly with the least change in it. So long as he told her frankly of his "favourites" and showed himself the bluff tyrant who required every woman to make advances to him, who lectured fine ladies and let them tease him, all was well. There was nothing in that to rouse her suspicions. Lady Berkeley might steal his hat; the Duchess of Hamilton might lay bare her agony; and Stella, who was kind to her sex, laughed with the one and grieved with the other.

But were there traces in the *Journal* of a different sort of influence—something far more dangerous because more equal and more intimate? Suppose that there were some woman of Swift's own station, a girl, like the girl that Stella herself had been when Swift first knew her, dissatisfied with the ordinary way of life, eager, as Stella put it, to know right from wrong, gifted, witty, and untaught—she indeed, if she existed, might be a rival to be feared. But was there such a rival? If so, it was plain that there would be no mention of her in the *Journal*. Instead, there would be hesitations, excuses, an occasional uneasiness and embarrassment when, in the midst of writing freely and fully, Swift was brought to a stop by something that he could not say. Indeed, he had only been a month or two in England when some such silence roused Stella's suspicions. Who was it, she asked, that boarded near him, that he dined with now and then? "I know no such person," Swift replied; "I do not dine with boarders. What the pox! You know whom I have dined with every day since I left you, better than I do. What do you mean, Sirrah?" But he knew what she meant: she meant Mrs. Vanhomrigh, the widow who lived near him; she meant her daughter Esther. "The Vans" kept coming again and again after that in the *Journal*. Swift was too proud to conceal the fact that he saw them, but he sought nine times out of ten to excuse it. When he was in Suffolk

76

Street the Vanhomrighs were in St. James's Street and thus saved him a walk. When he was in Chelsea they were in London, and it was convenient to keep his best gown and periwig there. Sometimes the heat kept him there and sometimes the rain; now they were playing cards, and young Lady Ashburnham reminded him so much of Stella that he stayed on to help her. Sometimes he stayed out of listlessness; again he stayed because he was very busy and they were simple people who did not stand on ceremony. At the same time Stella had only to hint that these Vanhomrighs were people of no consequence for him to retort, "Why, they keep as good female company as I do male. . . . I saw two lady Bettys there this afternoon." In short, to tell the whole truth, to write whatever came into his head in the old free way, was no longer easy.

Indeed, the whole situation was full of difficulty. No man detested falsehood more than Swift or loved truth more whole-heartedly. Yet here he was compelled to hedge, to hide, and to prevaricate. Again, it had become essential to him to have some "sluttery" or private chamber where he could relax and unbend and be Presto and not "t'other I". Stella satisfied this need as no one else could. But then Stella was in Ireland; Vanessa was on the spot. She was younger and fresher; she too had her charms. She too could be taught and improved and scolded into maturity as Stella had been. Obviously Swift's influence upon her was all to the good. And so with Stella in Ireland and Vanessa in London, why should it not be possible to enjoy what each could give him, confer benefits on both and do no serious harm to either? It seemed possible; at any rate he allowed himself to make the experiment. Stella, after all, had con-

trived for many years to make shift with her portion; Stella
had never complained of her lot.

But Vanessa was not Stella. She was younger, more vehement, less disciplined, less wise. She had no Mrs. Dingley
to restrain her. She had no memories of the past to solace
her. She had no journals coming day by day to comfort
her. She loved Swift and she knew no reason why she should
not say so. Had he not himself taught her "to act what was
right, and not to mind what the world said"? Thus when
some obstacle impeded her, when some mysterious secret
came between them she had the unwisdom to question
him. "Pray what can be wrong in seeing and advising an
unhappy young woman? I can't imagine." "You have
taught me to distinguish," she burst out, "and then you
leave me miserable." Finally in her anguish and her bewilderment she had the temerity to force herself upon Stella.
She wrote and demanded to be told the truth—what was
Stella's connection with Swift? But it was Swift himself
who enlightened her. And when the full force of those bright
blue eyes blazed upon her, when he flung her letter on the
table and glared at her and said nothing and rode off, her
life was ended. It was no figure of speech when she said that
"his killing, killing words" were worse than the rack to her;
when she cried out that there was "something in your look
so awful that it strikes me dumb". Within a few weeks of
that interview she was dead; she had vanished, to become
one of those uneasy ghosts who haunted the troubled background of Stella's life, peopling its solitude with fears.

Stella was left to enjoy her intimacy alone. She lived on
to practise those sad arts by which she kept her friend at
her side until, worn out with the strain and the concealment,

with Mrs. Dingley and her lap-dogs, with the perpetual fears and frustrations, she too died. As they buried her, Swift sat in a back room away from the lights in the church-yard and wrote an account of the character of "the truest, most virtuous, and valuable friend, that I, or perhaps any other person, was ever blessed with". Years passed; insanity overcame him; he exploded in violent outbursts of mad rage. Then by degrees he fell silent. Once they caught him murmuring. "I am what I am", they heard him say.

The "Sentimental Journey"

TRISTRAM SHANDY, though it is Sterne's first novel, was written at a time when many have written their twentieth, that is, when he was forty-five years old. But it bears every sign of maturity. No young writer could have dared to take such liberties with grammar and syntax and sense and propriety and the long-standing tradition of how a novel should be written. It needed a strong dose of the assurance of middle age and its indifference to censure to run such risks of shocking the lettered by the unconventionality of one's style, and the respectable by the irregularity of one's morals. But the risk was run and the success was prodigious. All the great, all the fastidious were enchanted. Sterne became the idol of the town. Only in the roar of laughter and applause which greeted the book, the voice of the simple-minded public at large was to be heard protesting that it was a scandal coming from a clergyman and that the Archbishop of York ought to administer, to say the least of it, a scolding. The Archbishop, it seems, did nothing. But Sterne, however little he let it show on the surface, laid the criticism to heart. That heart too had been afflicted since the publication of *Tristram Shandy*. Eliza Draper, the object of his passion, had sailed to join her husband in Bombay. In his next book Sterne was determined to give effect to the change that had come over him, and to prove, not only the brilliance of his wit, but the depths of his sen-

sibility. In his own words, "my design in it was to teach us
to love the world and our fellow creatures better than we
do". It was with such motives animating him that he sat
down to write that narrative of a little tour in France which
he called *A Sentimental Journey*.

But if it were possible for Sterne to correct his manners,
it was impossible for him to correct his style. That had
become as much a part of himself as his large nose or his
brilliant eyes. With the first words—They order, said I,
this matter better in France—we are in the world of *Tristram Shandy*. It is a world in which anything may happen.
We hardly know what jest, what jibe, what flash of poetry
is not going to glance suddenly through the gap which this
astonishingly agile pen has cut in the thick-set hedge of
English prose. Is Sterne himself responsible? Does he know
what he is going to say next for all his resolve to be on his
best behaviour this time? The jerky, disconnected sentences
are as rapid and it would seem as little under control as the
phrases that fall from the lips of a brilliant talker. The very
punctuation is that of speech, not writing, and brings the
sound and associations of the speaking voice in with it. The
order of the ideas, their suddenness and irrelevancy, is more
true to life than to literature. There is a privacy in this intercourse which allows things to slip out unreproved that
would have been in doubtful taste had they been spoken
in public. Under the influence of this extraordinary style
the book becomes semi-transparent. The usual ceremonies
and conventions which keep reader and writer at arm's
length disappear. We are as close to life as we can be.

That Sterne achieved this illusion only by the use of extreme art and extraordinary pains is obvious without going

to his manuscript to prove it. For though the writer is always haunted by the belief that somehow it must be possible to brush aside the ceremonies and conventions of writing and to speak to the reader as directly as by word of mouth, any one who has tried the experiment has either been struck dumb by the difficulty, or waylaid into disorder and diffusity unutterable. Sterne somehow brought off the astonishing combination. No writing seems to flow more exactly into the very folds and creases of the individual mind, to express its changing moods, to answer its lightest whim and impulse, and yet the result is perfectly precise and composed. The utmost fluidity exists with the utmost permanence. It is as if the tide raced over the beach hither and thither and left every ripple and eddy cut on the sand in marble.

Nobody, of course, stood more in need of the liberty to be himself than Sterne. For while there are writers whose gift is impersonal, so that a Tolstoy, for example, can create a character and leave us alone with it, Sterne must always be there in person to help us in our intercourse. Little or nothing of *A Sentimental Journey* would be left if all that we call Sterne himself were extracted from it. He has no valuable information to give, no reasoned philosophy to impart. He left London, he tells us, "with so much precipitation that it never enter'd my mind that we were at war with France". He has nothing to say of pictures or churches or the misery or well-being of the country-side. He was travelling in France indeed, but the road was often through his own mind, and his chief adventures were not with brigands and precipices but with the emotions of his own heart.

This change in the angle of vision was in itself a daring

innovation. Hitherto, the traveller had observed certain laws of proportion and perspective. The Cathedral had always been a vast building in any book of travels and the man a little figure, properly diminutive, by its side. But Sterne was quite capable of omitting the Cathedral altogether. A girl with a green satin purse might be much more important than Notre-Dame. For there is, he seems to hint, no universal scale of values. A girl may be more interesting than a cathedral; a dead donkey more instructive than a living philosopher. It is all a question of one's point of view. Sterne's eyes were so adjusted that small things often bulked larger in them than big. The talk of a barber about the buckle of his wig told him more about the character of the French than the grandiloquence of her statesmen.

I think I can see the precise and distinguishing marks of national characters more in these nonsensical *minutiae*, than in the most important matters of state; where great men of all nations talk and stalk so much alike, that I would not give nine-pence to chuse amongst them.

So too if one wishes to seize the essence of things as a sentimental traveller should, one should seek for it, not at broad noonday in large and open streets, but in an unobserved corner up a dark entry. One should cultivate a kind of shorthand which renders the several turns of looks and limbs into plain words. It was an art that Sterne had long trained himself to practise.

For my own part, by long habitude, I do it so mechanically that when I walk the streets of London, I go translating all the way; and have more than once stood behind in the circle, where not three words had been said, and have brought off twenty different dialogues with me, which I could have fairly wrote down and swore to.

It is thus that Sterne transfers our interest from the outer to the inner. It is no use going to the guide-book; we must consult our own minds; only they can tell us what is the comparative importance of a cathedral, of a donkey, and of a girl with a green satin purse. In this preference for the windings of his own mind to the guide-book and its hammered high road, Sterne is singularly of our own age. In this interest in silence rather than in speech Sterne is the forerunner of the moderns. And for these reasons he is on far more intimate terms with us today than his great contemporaries the Richardsons and the Fieldings.

Yet there is a difference. For all his interest in psychology Sterne was far more nimble and less profound than the masters of this somewhat sedentary school have since become. He is after all telling a story, pursuing a journey, however arbitrary and zigzag his methods. For all our divagations, we do make the distance between Calais and Modane within the space of a very few pages. Interested as he was in the way in which he saw things, the things themselves also interested him acutely. His choice is capricious and individual, but no realist could be more brilliantly successful in rendering the impression of the moment. *A Sentimental Journey* is a succession of portraits—the Monk, the lady, the Chevalier selling *pâtés*, the girl in the bookshop, La Fleur in his new breeches;—it is a succession of scenes. And though the flight of this erratic mind is as zigzag as a dragon-fly's, one cannot deny that this dragon-fly has some method in its flight, and chooses the flowers not at random but for some exquisite harmony or for some brilliant discord. We laugh, cry, sneer, sympathise by turns. We change from one emotion to its opposite in the twinkling of an eye. This light attachment to the accepted reality, this neglect of the orderly sequence of narrative, allows Sterne almost the licence of a poet. He can express ideas which ordinary novelists would have to ignore in language which, even if the ordinary novelist could command it, would look intolerably outlandish upon his page.

I walked up gravely to the window in my dusty black coat, and looking through the glass saw all the world in yellow, blue, and green, running at the ring of pleasure.—The old with broken lances, and in helmets which had lost their vizards—the young in armour bright which shone like gold, beplumed with each gay feather of the east—all—all tilting at it like fascinated knights in tournaments of yore for fame and love.

There are many passages of such pure poetry in Sterne. One can cut them out and read them apart from the text, and yet—for Sterne was a master of the art of contrast — they lie harmoniously side by side on the printed page. His freshness, his buoyancy, his perpetual power to surprise and startle are the result of these contrasts. He leads us to the very brink of some deep precipice of the soul; we snatch one short glance into its depths; next moment, we are whisked round to look at the green pastures glowing on the other side.

If Sterne distresses us, it is for another reason. And here the blame rests partly at least upon the public—the public which had been shocked, which had cried out after the publication of *Tristram Shandy* that the writer was a cynic who deserved to be unfrocked. Sterne, unfortunately, thought it necessary to reply.

The world has imagined [he told Lord Shelburne] because I wrote *Tristram Shandy*, that I was myself more Shandean than I really ever was. . . . If it (*A Sentimental Journey*) is not thought a chaste book, mercy on them that read it, for they must have warm imaginations, indeed!

Thus in *A Sentimental Journey* we are never allowed to forget that Sterne is above all things sensitive, sympathetic, humane; that above all things he prizes the decencies, the simplicities of the human heart. And directly a writer sets out to prove himself this or that our suspicions are aroused. For the little extra stress he lays on the quality he desires us to see in him, coarsens it and over-paints it, so that instead of humour, we get farce, and instead of sentiment, sentimentality. Here, instead of being convinced of the tenderness of Sterne's heart—which in *Tristram Shandy* was never in question—we begin to doubt it. For we feel that Sterne is thinking not of the thing itself but of its effect upon our opinion of him. The beggars gather round him and he gives the *pauvre honteux* more than he had meant to. But his mind is not solely and simply on the beggars; his mind is partly on us, to see that we appreciate his goodness. Thus his conclusion, "and I thought he thank'd me more than them all", placed, for more emphasis, at the end of the chapter, sickens us with its sweetness like the drop of pure sugar at the bottom of a cup. Indeed, the chief fault of *A Sentimental Journey* comes from Sterne's concern for our good opinion of his heart. It has a monotony about it, for all its brilliance, as if the author had reined in the natural variety and vivacity of his tastes, lest they should give offence. The mood is subdued to one that is too uniformly kind, tender, and compassionate to be quite natural. One misses the variety, the vigour, the ribaldry of *Tristram Shandy*. His concern for his sensibility has blunted his natural sharpness, and we are called upon to gaze rather too long at modesty, simplicity, and virtue standing rather too still to be looked at.

But it is significant of the change of taste that has come over us that it is Sterne's sentimentality that offends us and not his immorality. In the eyes of the nineteenth century all that Sterne wrote was clouded by his conduct as husband and lover. Thackeray lashed him with his righteous indignation, and exclaimed that "There is not a page of Sterne's writing but has something that were better away, a latent corruption—a hint as of an impure presence". To us at the present time, the arrogance of the Victorian novelist seems at least as culpable as the infidelities of the eighteenth-century parson. Where the Victorians deplored his lies and his levities, the courage which turned all the rubs of life to laughter and the brilliance of the expression are far more apparent now.

Indeed *A Sentimental Journey*, for all its levity and wit, is based upon something fundamentally philosophic. It is true that it is a philosophy that was much out of fashion in the Victorian age—the philosophy of pleasure; the philosophy which holds that it is as necessary to behave well in small things as in big, which makes the enjoyment, even of other people, seem more desirable than their suffering. The shameless man had the hardihood to confess to "having been in love with one princess or another almost all my life", and to add, "and I hope I shall go on so till I die, being firmly persuaded that if ever I do a mean action, it must be in some interval betwixt one passion and another". The wretch had the audacity to cry through the mouth of one of his characters, "Mais vive la joie . . . Vive l'amour! et vive la bagatelle!" Clergyman though he was, he had the irreverence to reflect, when he watched the French peas-

ants dancing, that he could distinguish an elevation of
spirit, different from that which is the cause or the effect of
simple jollity.—"In a word, I thought I beheld *Religion*
mixing in the dance."

It was a daring thing for a clergyman to perceive a relationship between religion and pleasure. Yet it may, perhaps, excuse him that in his own case the religion of happiness had a great deal of difficulty to overcome. If you are
no longer young, if you are deeply in debt, if your wife is
disagreeable, if, as you racket about France in a post-chaise,
you are dying of consumption all the time, then the pursuit
of happiness is not so easy after all. Still, pursue it one
must. One must pirouette about the world, peeping and
peering, enjoying a flirtation here, bestowing a few coppers
there, and sitting in whatever little patch of sunshine one
can find. One must crack a joke, even if the joke is not altogether a decent one. Even in daily life one must not forget
to cry "Hail ye, small, sweet courtesies of life, for smooth
do ye make the road of it!" One must—but enough of
must; it is not a word that Sterne was fond of using. It
is only when one lays the book aside and recalls its symmetry, its fun, its whole-hearted joy in all the different
aspects of life, and the brilliant ease and beauty with which
they are conveyed to us, that one credits the writer with a
backbone of conviction to support him. Was not Thackeray's coward—the man who trifled so immorally with so
many women and wrote love-letters on gilt-edged paper
when he should have been lying on a sick-bed or writing
sermons—was he not a stoic in his own way and a moralist,
and a teacher? Most great writers are, after all. And that
Sterne was a very great writer we cannot doubt.

Lord Chesterfield's Letters to His Son

WHEN Lord Mahon edited the letters of Lord Chesterfield he thought it necessary to warn the intending reader that they are "by no means fitted for early or indiscriminate perusal". Only "those people whose understandings are fixed and whose principles are matured" can, so his Lordship said, read them with impunity. But that was in 1845. And 1845 looks a little distant now. It seems to us now the age of enormous houses without any bathrooms. Men smoke in the kitchen after the cook has gone to bed. Albums lie upon drawing-room tables. The curtains are very thick and the women are very pure. But the eighteenth century also has undergone a change. To us in 1930 it looks less strange, less remote than those early Victorian years. Its civilisation seems more rational and more complete than the civilisation of Lord Mahon and his contemporaries. Then at any rate a small group of highly educated people lived up to their ideals. If the world was smaller it was also more compact; it knew its own mind; it had its own standards. Its poetry is affected by the same security. When we read the *Rape of the Lock* we seem to find ourselves in an age so settled and so circumscribed that masterpieces were possible. Then, we say to ourselves, a poet could address himself whole-heartedly to his task and keep his mind upon it, so that the little boxes on a lady's dressing-table are fixed among the solid possessions of our imaginations.

A game at cards or a summer's boating party upon the Thames has power to suggest the same beauty and the same sense of things vanishing that we receive from poems aimed directly at our deepest emotions. And just as the poet could spend all his powers upon a pair of scissors and a lock of hair, so too, secure in his world and its values, the aristocrat could lay down precise laws for the education of his son. In that world also there was a certainty, a security that we are now without. What with one thing and another times have changed. We can now read Lord Chesterfield's letters without blushing, or, if we do blush, we blush in the twentieth century at passages that caused Lord Mahon no discomfort whatever.

When the letters begin, Philip Stanhope, Lord Chesterfield's natural son by a Dutch governess, was a little boy of seven. And if we are to make any complaint against the father's moral teaching, it is that the standard is too high for such tender years. "Let us return to oratory, or the art of speaking well; which should never be entirely out of our thoughts", he writes to the boy of seven. "A man can make no figure without it in Parliament, or the Church, or in the law", he continues, as if the little boy were already considering his career. It seems, indeed, that the father's fault, if fault it be, is one common to distinguished men who have not themselves succeeded as they should have done and are determined to give their children—and Philip was an only child—the chances that they have lacked. Indeed, as the letters go on one may suppose that Lord Chesterfield wrote as much to amuse himself by turning over the stores of his experience, his reading, his knowledge of the world, as to instruct his son. The letters show an eagerness, an animation which prove that to write to Philip was not a task, but a delight. Tired, perhaps, with the duties of office and disillusioned with its disappointments, he takes up his pen and, in the relief of free communication at last, forgets that his correspondent is, after all, only a schoolboy who cannot understand half the things that his father says to him. But, even so, there is nothing to repel us in Lord Chesterfield's preliminary sketch of the unknown world. He is all on the side of moderation, toleration, ratiocination. Never abuse whole bodies of people, he counsels; frequent all churches, laugh at none; inform yourself about all things. Devote your mornings to study, your evenings to good society. Dress as the best people dress, behave as they behave, never be eccentric, egotistical, or absent-minded. Observe the laws of proportion, and live every moment to the full.

So, step by step, he builds up the figure of the perfect man—the man that Philip may become, he is persuaded, if he will only—and here Lord Chesterfield lets fall the words which are to colour his teaching through and through—cultivate the Graces. These ladies are, at first, kept discreetly in the background. It is well that the boy should be indulged in fine sentiments about women and poets to begin with. Lord Chesterfield adjures him to respect them both. "For my own part, I used to think myself in company as much above me when I was with Mr. Addison and Mr. Pope, as if I had been with all the Princes in Europe", he writes. But as time goes on the Virtues are more and more taken for granted. They can be left to take care of themselves. But the Graces assume tremendous proportions. The Graces dominate the life of man in this world. Their service cannot for an instant be neglected. And the service is certainly exacting. For consider what it implies, this art of pleasing. To begin with, one must know how to come into a room and then how to go out again. As human arms and legs are notoriously perverse, this by itself is a matter needing considerable dexterity. Then one must be dressed so that one's clothes seem perfectly fashionable without being new or striking; one's teeth must be perfect; one's wig beyond reproach; one's finger-nails cut in the segment of a circle; one must be able to carve, able to dance, and, what is almost as great an art, able to sit gracefully in a chair. These things are the alphabet of the art of pleasing. We now come to speech. It is necessary to speak at least three languages to perfection. But before we open our lips we must take a further precaution—we must be on our guard never to laugh. Lord Chesterfield himself never laughed. He always smiled. When at length the young man is pronounced capable of speech he must avoid all proverbs and vulgar expressions; he must enunciate clearly and use perfect grammar; he must not argue; he must not tell stories; he must not talk about himself. Then, at last, the young man may begin to practise the finest of the arts of pleasing—the art of flattery. For every man and every woman has some prevailing vanity. Watch, wait, pry, seek out their weakness "and you will then know what to bait your hook with to catch them". For that is the secret of success in the world.

It is at this point, such is the idiosyncrasy of our age, that we begin to feel uneasy. Lord Chesterfield's views upon success are far more questionable than his views upon love. For what is to be the prize of this endless effort and self-

abnegation? What do we gain when we have learnt to come
into rooms and to go out again; to pry into people's secrets;
to hold our tongues and to flatter, to forsake the society of
low-born people which corrupts and the society of clever
people which perverts? What is the prize which is to reward us? It is simply that we shall rise in the world. Press
for a further definition, and it amounts perhaps to this:
one will be popular with the best people. But if we are so
exacting as to demand who the best people are we become
involved in a labyrinth from which there is no returning.
Nothing exists in itself. What is good society? It is the
society that the best people believe to be good. What is
wit? It is what the best people think to be witty. All value
depends upon somebody else's opinion. For it is the essence
of this philosophy that things have no independent existence, but live only in the eyes of other people. It is a looking-glass world, this, to which we climb so slowly; and its
prizes are all reflections. That may account for our baffled
feeling as we shuffle, and shuffle vainly, among these urbane
pages for something hard to lay our hands upon. Hardness
is the last thing we shall find. But, granted the deficiency,
how much that is ignored by sterner moralists is here seized
upon, and who shall deny, at least while Lord Chesterfield's
enchantment is upon him, that these imponderable qualities
have their value and these shining Graces have their radi-
ance? Consider for a moment what the Graces have done
for their devoted servant, the Earl.

Here is a disillusioned politician, who is prematurely
aged, who has lost his office, who is losing his teeth, who,
worst fate of all, is growing deafer day by day. Yet he
never allows a groan to escape him. He is never dull; he

is never boring; he is never slovenly. His mind is as well groomed as his body. Never for a second does he "welter in an easy-chair". Private though these letters are, and apparently spontaneous, they play with such ease in and about the single subject which absorbs them that it never becomes tedious or, what is still more remarkable, never becomes ridiculous. It may be that the art of pleasing has some connection with the art of writing. To be polite, considerate, controlled, to sink one's egotism, to conceal rather than to obtrude one's personality may profit the writer even as they profit the man of fashion.

Certainly there is much to be said in favour of the training, however we define it, which helped Lord Chesterfield to write his Characters. The little papers have the precision and formality of some old-fashioned minuet. Yet the symmetry is so natural to the artist that he can break it where he likes; it never becomes pinched and formal, as it would in the hands of an imitator. He can be sly; he can be witty; he can be sententious, but never for an instant does he lose his sense of time, and when the tune is over he calls a halt. "Some succeeded, and others burst" he says of George the First's mistresses: the King liked them fat. Again, "He was fixed in the house of lords, that hospital of incurables." He smiles: he does not laugh. Here the eighteenth century, of course, came to his help. Lord Chesterfield, though he was polite to everything, even to the stars and Bishop Berkeley's philosophy, firmly refused, as became a son of his age, to dally with infinity or to suppose that things are not quite as solid as they seem. The world was good enough and the world was big enough as it was. This prosaic temper, while it keeps him within the bounds of impeccable common

sense, limits his outlook. No single phrase of his reverber-
ates or penetrates as so many of La Bruyère's do. But he
would have been the first to deprecate any comparison with
that great writer; besides, to write as La Bruyère wrote, one
must perhaps believe in something, and then how difficult
to observe the Graces! One might perhaps laugh; one might
perhaps cry. Both are equally deplorable.

But while we amuse ourselves with this brilliant nobleman and his views on life we are aware, and the letters owe
much of their fascination to this consciousness, of a dumb
yet substantial figure on the farther side of the page. Philip
Stanhope is always there. It is true that he says nothing,
but we feel his presence in Dresden, in Berlin, in Paris,
opening the letters and poring over them and looking dole-
fully at the thick packets which have been accumulating
year after year since he was a child of seven. He had grown
into a rather serious, rather stout, rather short young man.
He had a taste for foreign politics. A little serious reading
was rather to his liking. And by every post the letters came
—urbane, polished, brilliant, imploring and commanding
him to learn to dance, to learn to carve, to consider the
management of his legs, and to seduce a lady of fashion.
He did his best. He worked very hard in the school of the
Graces, but their service was too exacting. He sat down
half-way up the steep stairs which lead to the glittering
hall with all the mirrors. He could not do it. He failed in
the House of Commons; he subsided into some small post
in Ratisbon; he died untimely. He left it to his widow to
break the news which he had lacked the heart or the courage
to tell his father—that he had been married all these years
to a lady of low birth, who had borne him children.

The Earl took the blow like a gentleman. His letter to his daughter-in-law is a model of urbanity. He began the education of his grandsons. But he seems to have become a little indifferent to what happened to himself after that. He did not care greatly if he lived or died. But still to the very end he cared for the Graces. His last words were a tribute of respect to those goddesses. Some one came into the room when he was dying; he roused himself: "Give Dayrolles a chair," he said, and said no more.

Two Parsons

I. JAMES WOODFORDE

ONE could wish that the psycho-analysts would go into the question of diary-keeping. For often it is the one mysterious fact in a life otherwise as clear as the sky and as candid as the dawn. Parson Woodforde is a case in point—his diary is the only mystery about him. For forty-three years he sat down almost daily to record what he did on Monday and what he had for dinner on Tuesday; but for whom he wrote or why he wrote it is impossible to say. He does not unburden his soul in his diary; yet it is no mere record of engagements and expenses. As for literary fame, there is no sign that he ever thought of it, and finally, though the man himself is peaceable above all things, there are little indiscretions and criticisms which would have got him into trouble and hurt the feelings of his friends had they read them. What purpose, then, did the sixty-eight little books fulfil? Perhaps it was the desire for intimacy. When James Woodforde opened one of his neat manuscript books he entered into conversation with a second James Woodforde, who was not quite the same as the reverend gentleman who visited the poor and preached in the church. These two friends said much that all the world might hear; but they had a few secrets which they shared with each other only. It was a great comfort, for example, that Christmas when

Nancy, Betsy, and Mr. Walker seemed to be in conspiracy against him, to exclaim in the diary, "The treatment I meet with for my Civility this Christmas is to me abominable". The second James Woodforde sympathised and agreed. Again, when a stranger abused his hospitality it was a relief to inform the other self who lived in the little book that he had put him to sleep in the attic story, "and I treated him as one that would be too free if treated kindly". It is easy to understand why, in the quiet life of a country parish, these two bachelor friends became in time inseparable. An essential part of him would have died had he been forbidden to keep his diary. When indeed he thought himself in the grip of death he still wrote on and on. And as we read—if reading is the word for it—we seem to be listening to some one who is murmuring over the events of the day to himself in the quiet space which precedes sleep. It is not writing, and, to speak of the truth, it is not reading. It is slipping through half a dozen pages and strolling to the window and looking out. It is going on thinking about the Woodfordes while we watch the people in the street below. It is taking a walk and making up the life and character of James Woodforde as we go. It is not reading any more than it is writing—what to call it we scarcely know.

James Woodforde, then, was one of those smooth-cheeked, steady-eyed men, demure to look at, whom we can never imagine except in the prime of life. He was of an equable temper, with only such acerbities and touchinesses as are generally to be found in those who have had a love affair in their youth and remained, as they fancy, unwed because of it. The Parson's love affair, however, was nothing very tremendous. Once when he was a young man in Somerset he liked to walk over to Shepton and to visit a certain "sweet tempered" Betsy White who lived there. He had a great mind "to make a bold stroke" and ask her to marry him. He went so far, indeed, as to propose marriage "when opportunity served", and Betsy was willing. But he delayed; time passed; four years passed indeed, and Betsy went to Devonshire, met a Mr. Webster, who had five hundred pounds a year, and married him. When James Woodforde met them in the turnpike road he could say little, "being shy", but to his diary he remarked—and this no doubt was his private version of the affair ever after—"she has proved herself to me a mere jilt".

But he was a young man then, and as time went on we cannot help suspecting that he was glad to consider the question of marriage shelved once and for all so that he might settle down with his niece Nancy at Weston Longueville, and give himself simply and solely, every day and all day, to the great business of living. Again, what else to call it we do not know.

For James Woodforde was nothing in particular. Life had it all her own way with him. He had no special gift; he had no oddity or infirmity. It is idle to pretend that he was a zealous priest. God in Heaven was much the same to him as King George upon the throne—a kindly Monarch, that is to say, whose festivals one kept by preaching a sermon on Sunday much as one kept the Royal birthday by firing a blunderbuss and drinking a toast at dinner. Should anything untoward happen, like the death of a boy who was dragged and killed by a horse, he would instantly, but rather perfunctorily exclaim, "I hope to God the Poor Boy is happy", and add, "We all came home singing"; just as when Justice

Creed's peacock spread its tail—"and most noble it is"—
he would exclaim, "How wonderful are Thy Works O God
in every Being". But there was no fanaticism, no enthusiasm, no lyric impulse about James Woodforde. In all these
pages, indeed, each so neatly divided into compartments,
and each of those again filled, as the days themselves were
filled, quietly and fully in a hand steady as the pacing of a
well-tempered nag, one can only call to mind a single poetic
phrase about the transit of Venus. "It appeared as a black
patch upon a fair Lady's face", he says. The words themselves are mild enough, but they hang over the undulating
expanse of the Parson's prose with the resplendence of the
star itself. So in the Fen country a barn or a tree appears
twice its natural size against the surrounding flats. But
what led him to this palpable excess that summer's night
we cannot tell. It cannot have been that he was drunk. He
spoke out too roundly against such failings in his brother
Jack to be guilty himself. Temperamentally he was among
the eaters of meat and not among the drinkers of wine.
When we think of the Woodfordes, uncle and niece, we
think of them as often as not waiting with some impatience
for their dinner. Gravely they watch the joint as it is set
upon the table; swiftly they get their knives to work upon
the succulent leg or loin; without much comment, unless a
word is passed about the gravy or the stuffing, they go on
eating. So they munch, day after day, year in year out, until
between them they must have devoured herds of sheep and
oxen, flocks of poultry, an odd dozen or so of swans and
cygnets, bushels of apples and plums, while the pastries and
the jellies crumble and squash beneath their spoons in mountains, in pyramids, in pagodas. Never was there a book so

stuffed with food as this one is. To read the bill of fare
respectfully and punctually set forth gives one a sense of
repletion. Trout and chicken, mutton and peas, pork and
apple sauce—so the joints succeed each other at dinner, and
there is supper with more joints still to come, all, no doubt,
home grown, and of the juciest and sweetest; all cooked,
often by the mistress herself, in the plainest English way,
save when the dinner was at Weston Hall and Mrs. Custance surprised them with a London dainty—a pyramid of
jelly, that is to say, with a "landscape appearing through
it". After dinner sometimes, Mrs. Custance, for whom
James Woodforde had a chivalrous devotion, would play
the "Sticcardo Pastorale", and make "very soft music indeed"; or would get out her work-box and show them how
neatly contrived it was, unless indeed she were giving birth
to another child upstairs. These infants the Parson would
baptize and very frequently he would bury them. They died
almost as frequently as they were born. The Parson had a
deep respect for the Custances. They were all that country
gentry should be—a little given to the habit of keeping
mistresses, perhaps, but that peccadillo could be forgiven
them in view of their generosity to the poor, the kindness
they showed to Nancy, and their condescension in asking
the Parson to dinner when they had great people staying
with them. Yet great people were not much to James's liking. Deeply though he respected the nobility, "one must
confess", he said, "that being with our equals is much more
agreeable".

Not only did Parson Woodforde know what was agreeable; that rare gift was by the bounty of Nature supple-
mented by another equally rare—he could have what he

wanted. The age was propitious. Monday, Tuesday,
Wednesday—they follow each other and each little compartment seems filled with content. The days were not
crowded, but they were enviably varied. Fellow of New
College though he was, he did things with his own hands,
not merely with his own head. He lived in every room of
the house—in the study he wrote sermons, in the dining-
room he ate copiously; he cooked in the kitchen, he played
cards in the parlour. And then he took his coat and stick
and went coursing his greyhounds in the fields. Year in,
year out, the provisioning of the house and its defence
against the cold of winter and the drought of summer fell
upon him. Like a general he surveyed the seasons and took
steps to make his own little camp safe with coal and wood
and beef and beer against the enemy. His day thus had to
accommodate a jumble of incongruous occupations. There
is religion to be served, and the pig to be killed; the sick to
be visited and dinner to be eaten; the dead to be buried
and beer to be brewed; Convocation to be attended and the
cow to be bolused. Life and death, mortality and immortality, jostle in his pages and make a good mixed marriage
of it: ". . . found the old gentleman almost at his last
gasp. Totally senseless with rattlings in his Throat. Dinner
today boiled beef and Rabbit rosted". All is as it should be;
life is like that.

Surely, surely, then, here is one of the breathing-spaces
in human affairs—here in Norfolk at the end of the
eighteenth century at the Parsonage. For once man is content with his lot; harmony is achieved; his house fits him; a
tree is a tree; a chair is a chair; each knows its office and
fulfils it. Looking through the eyes of Parson Woodforde,

the different lives of men seem orderly and settled. Far
away guns roar; a King falls; but the sound is not loud
enough to scare the rooks here in Norfolk. The proportions
of things are different. The Continent is so distant that it
looks a mere blur; America scarcely exists; Australia is unknown. But a magnifying glass is laid upon the fields of
Norfolk. Every blade of grass is visible there. We see every
lane and every field; the ruts on the roads and the peasants'
faces. Each house stands in its own breadth of meadow isolated and independent. No wires link village to village. No
voices thread the air. The body also is more present and
more real. It suffers more acutely. No anaesthetic deadens
physical pain. The surgeon's knife hovers real and sharp
above the limb. Cold strikes unmitigated upon the house.
The milk freezes in the pans; the water is thick with ice in
the basins. One can scarcely walk from one room to another
in the parsonage in winter. Poor men and women are frozen
to death upon the roads. Often no letters come and there are
no visitors and no newspapers. The Parsonage stands alone
in the midst of the frost-bound fields. At last, Heaven be
praised, life circulates again; a man comes to the door with
a Madagascar monkey; another brings a box containing a
child with two distinct perfect heads; there is a rumour that
a balloon is going to rise at Norwich. Every little incident
stands out sharp and clear. The drive to Norwich even is
something of an adventure. One must trundle every step of
the way behind a horse. But look how distinct the trees
stand in the hedges; how slowly the cattle move their heads
as the carriage trots by; how gradually the spires of Norwich raise themselves above the hill. And then how clear-
cut and familiar are the faces of the few people who are our

friends—the Custances, Mr. du Quesne. Friendship has time to solidify, to become a lasting, a valuable possession.

True, Nancy of the younger generation is visited now and then by a flighty notion that she is missing something, that she wants something. One day she complained to her uncle that life was very dull: she complained "of the dismal situation of my house, nothing to be seen, and little or no visiting or being visited, &c.", and made him very uneasy. We could read Nancy a little lecture upon the folly of wanting that "et cetera". Look what your "et cetera" has brought to pass, we might say; half the countries of Europe are bankrupt; there is a red line of villas on every green hillside; your Norfolk roads are black as tar; there is no end to "visiting or being visited". But Nancy has an answer to make us, to the effect that our past is her present. You, she says, think it a great privilege to be born in the eighteenth century, because one called cowslips pagles and rode in a curricle instead of driving in a car. But you are utterly wrong, you fanatical lovers of memoirs, she goes on. I can assure you, my life was often intolerably dull. I did not laugh at the things that make you laugh. It did not amuse me when my uncle dreamt of a hat or saw bubbles in the beer, and said that meant a death in the family; I thought so too. Betsy Davy mourned young Walker with all her heart in spite of dressing in sprigged paduasoy. There is a great deal of humbug talked of the eighteenth century. Your delight in old times and old diaries is half impure. You make up something that never had any existence. Our sober reality is only a dream to you—so Nancy grieves and complains, living through the eighteenth century day by day, hour by hour.

Still, if it is a dream, let us indulge it a moment longer. Let us believe that some things last, and some places and some people are not touched by change. On a fine May morning, with the rooks rising and the hares scampering and the plover calling among the long grass, there is much to encourage the illusion. It is we who change and perish. Parson Woodforde lives on. It is the kings and queens who lie in prison. It is the great towns that are ravaged with anarchy and confusion. But the river Wensum still flows; Mrs. Custance is brought to bed of yet another baby; there is the first swallow of the year. The spring comes, and summer with its hay and strawberries; then autumn, when the walnuts are exceptionally fine though the pears are poor; so we lapse into winter, which is indeed boisterous, but the house, thank God, withstands the storm; and then again there is the first swallow, and Parson Woodforde takes his greyhounds out a-coursing.

II. THE REV. JOHN SKINNER

A WHOLE world separates Woodforde, who was born in 1740 and died in 1803, from Skinner, who was born in 1772 and died in 1839.

For the few years that separated the two parsons are those momentous years that separate the eighteenth century from the nineteenth. Camerton, it is true, lying in the heart of Somersetshire, was a village of the greatest antiquity; nevertheless, before five pages of the diary are turned we read of coal-works, and how there was a great shouting at the coal-works because a fresh vein of coal had been dis-

covered, and the proprietors had given money to the workmen to celebrate an event which promised such prosperity
to the village. Then, though the country gentlemen seemed
set as firmly in their seats as ever, it happened that the
manor house at Camerton, with all the rights and duties per-
taining to it, was in the hands of the Jarretts, whose fortune
was derived from the Jamaica trade. This novelty, this in-
cursion of an element quite unknown to Woodforde in his
day, had its disturbing influence no doubt upon the character of Skinner himself. Irritable, nervous, apprehensive, he
seems to embody, even before the age itself had come into
existence, all the strife and unrest of our distracted times.
He stands, dressed in the prosaic and unbecoming stocks and
pantaloons of the early nineteenth century, at the parting
of the ways. Behind him lay order and discipline and all
the virtues of the heroic past, but directly he left his study
he was faced with drunkenness and immorality; with indis-
cipline and irreligion; with Methodism and Roman Cathol-
icism; with the Reform Bill and the Catholic Emancipation
Act, with a mob clamouring for freedom, with the over-
throw of all that was decent and established and right.
Tormented and querulous, at the same time conscientious
and able, he stands at the parting of the ways, unwilling to
yield an inch, unable to concede a point, harsh, peremptory,
apprehensive, and without hope.

Private sorrow had increased the natural acerbity of his
temper. His wife had died young, leaving him with four
small children, and of these the best-loved, Laura, a child
who shared his tastes and would have sweetened his life,
for she already kept a diary and had arranged a cabinet of
shells with the utmost neatness, died too. But these losses,

though they served nominally to make him love God the better, in practice led him to hate men more. By the time the diary opens in 1822 he was fixed in his opinion that the mass of men are unjust and malicious, and that the people of Camerton are more corrupt even than the mass of men. But by that date he was also fixed in his profession. Fate had taken him from the lawyer's office, where he would have been in his element, dealing out justice, filling up forms, keeping strictly to the letter of the law, and had planted him at Camerton among church-wardens and farmers, the Gullicks and the Padfields, the old woman who had dropsy, the idiot boy, and the dwarf. Nevertheless, however sordid his tasks and disgusting his parishioners, he had his duty to them; and with them he would remain. Whatever insults he suffered, he would live up to his principles, uphold the right, protect the poor, and punish the wrongdoer. By the time the diary opens, this strenuous and unhappy career is in full swing.

Perhaps the village of Camerton in the year 1822, with its coal-miners and the disturbance they brought, was no fair sample of English village life. Certainly it is difficult, as one follows the Rector on his daily rounds, to indulge in pleasant dreams about the quaintness and amenity of old English rural life. Here, for instance, he was called to see Mrs. Gooch—a woman of weak mind, who had been locked up alone in her cottage and fallen into the fire and was in agony. "Why do you not help me, I say? Why do you not help me?" she cried. And the Rector, as he heard her screams, knew that she had come to this through no fault of her own. Her efforts to keep a home together had led to drink, and so she had lost her reason, and what with

the squabbles between the Poor Law officials and the family
as to who should support her, what with her husband's
extravagance and drunkenness, she had been left alone, had
fallen into the fire, and so died. Who was to blame? Mr.
Purnell, the miserly magistrate, who was all for cutting
down the allowance paid to the poor, or Hicks the Overseer,
who was notoriously harsh, or the ale-houses, or the Methodists, or what? At any rate the Rector had done his duty.
However he might be hated for it, he always stood up for
the rights of the down-trodden; he always told people of
their faults, and convicted them of evil. Then there was
Mrs. Somer, who kept a house of ill fame and was bringing
up her daughters to the same profession. Then there was
Farmer Lippeatt, who, turned out of the Red Post at midnight, dead drunk, missed his way, fell into a quarry, and
died of a broken breastbone. Wherever one turned there was
suffering, wherever one looked one found cruelty behind
that suffering. Mr. and Mrs. Hicks, for example, the Over-
seers, let an infirm pauper lie for ten days in the Poor House
without care, "so that maggots had bred in his flesh and
eaten great holes in his body". His only attendant was an
old woman, who was so failing that she was unable to lift
him. Happily the pauper died. Happily poor Garratt, the
miner, died too. For to add to the evils of drink and poverty
and the cholera there was constant peril from the mine itself. Accidents were common and the means of treating
them elementary. A fall of coal had broken Garratt's back,
but he lingered on, though exposed to the crude methods of
country surgeons, from January to November, when at last
death released him. Both the stern Rector and the flippant
Lady of the Manor, to do them justice, were ready with

their half-crowns, with their soups and their medicines, and visited sick-beds without fail. But even allowing for the natural asperity of Mr. Skinner's temper, it would need a very rosy pen and a very kindly eye to make a smiling picture of life in the village of Camerton a century ago. Half-crowns and soup went a very little way to remedy matters; sermons and denunciations made them perhaps even worse.

The Rector found refuge from Camerton neither in dissipation like some of his neighbours, nor in sport like others. Occasionally he drove over to dine with a brother cleric, but he noted acrimoniously that the entertainment was "better suited to Grosvenor Square than a clergyman's home —French dishes and French wines in profusion", and records with a note of exclamation that it was eleven o'clock before he drove home. When his children were young he sometimes walked with them in the fields, or amused himself by making them a boat, or rubbed up his Latin in an epitaph for the tomb of some pet dog or tame pigeon. And sometimes he leant back peacefully and listened to Mrs. Fenwick as she sang the songs of Moore to her husband's accompaniment on the flute. But even such harmless pleasures were poisoned with suspicion. A farmer stared insolently as he passed; some one threw a stone from a window; Mrs. Jarrett clearly concealed some evil purpose behind her cordiality. No, the only refuge from Camerton lay in Camalodunum. The more he thought of it the more certain he became that he had the singular good fortune to live on the identical spot where lived the father of Caractacus, where Ostorius established his colony, where Arthur had fought the traitor Modred, where Alfred very nearly came in his misfortunes. Camerton was undoubtedly the Camalo-

dunum of Tacitus. Shut up in his study alone with his docu-
ments, copying, comparing, proving indefatigably, he was
safe, at rest, even happy. He was also, he became convinced,
on the track of an important etymological discovery, by
which it could be proved that there was a secret significance
"in every letter that entered into the composition of Celtic
names". No archbishop was as content in his palace as Skinner the antiquary was content in his cell. To these pursuits
he owed, too, those rare and delightful visits to Stourhead,
the seat of Sir Richard Hoare, when at last he mixed with
men of his own calibre, and met the gentlemen who were
engaged in examining the antiquities of Wiltshire. However hard it froze, however high the snow lay heaped on the
roads, Skinner rode over to Stourhead; and sat in the
library, with a violent cold, but in perfect content, making
extracts from Seneca, and extracts from Diodorum Siculus,
and extracts from Ptolemy's *Geography*, or scornfully dis-
posed of some rash and ill-informed fellow-antiquary who
had the temerity to assert that Camalodunum was really
situated at Colchester. On he went with his extracts, with
his theories, with his proofs, in spite of the malicious present
of a rusty nail wrapped in paper from his parishioners, in
spite of the laughing warning of his host: "Oh, Skinner, you
will bring everything at last to Camalodunum; be content
with what you have already discovered, if you fancy too
much you will weaken the authority of real facts". Skinner
replied with a sixth letter thirty-four pages long; for Sir
Richard did not know how necessary Camalodunum had become to an embittered man who had daily to encounter
Hicks the Overseer and Purnell the magistrate, the brothels,
the ale-houses, the Methodists, the dropsies and bad legs of

Camerton. Even the floods were mitigated if one could reflect that thus Camalodunum must have looked in the time of the Britons.

So he filled three iron chests with ninety-eight volumes of manuscript. But by degrees the manuscripts ceased to be entirely concerned with Camalodunum; they began to be largely concerned with John Skinner. It was true that it was important to establish the truth about Camalodunum, but it was also important to establish the truth about John Skinner. In fifty years after his death, when the diaries were published, people would know not only that John Skinner was a great antiquary, but that he was a much wronged, much suffering man. His diary became his confidante, as it was to become his champion. For example, was he not the most affectionate of fathers, he asked the diary? He had spent endless time and trouble on his sons; he had sent them to Winchester and Cambridge, and yet now when the farmers were so insolent about paying him his tithes, and gave him a broken-backed lamb for his share, or fobbed him off with less than his due of cocks, his son Joseph refused to help him. His son said that the people of Camerton laughed at him; that he treated his children like servants; that he suspected evil where none was meant. And then he opened a letter by chance and found a bill for a broken gig; and then his sons lounged about smoking cigars when they might have helped him to mount his drawings. In short, he could not stand their presence in his house. He dismissed them in a fury to Bath. When they had gone he could not help admitting that perhaps he had been at fault. It was his querulous temper again—but then he had so much to make him querulous. Mrs. Jarrett's peacock screamed under his window all night. They jangled the church bells on purpose to annoy him. Still, he would try; he would let them come back. So Joseph and Owen came back. And then the old irritation overcame him again. He "could not help saying" something about being idle, or drinking too much cider, upon which there was a terrible scene and Joseph broke one of the parlour chairs. Owen took Joseph's part. So did Anna. None of his children cared for him. Owen went further. Owen said "I was a madman and ought to have a commission of lunacy to investigate my conduct". And, further, Owen cut him to the quick by pouring scorn on his verses, on his diaries and archaeological theories. He said: "No one would read the nonsense I had written. When I mentioned having gained a prize at Trinity College . . . his reply was that none but the most stupid fellows ever thought of writing for the college prize". Again there was a terrible scene; again they were dismissed to Bath, followed by their father's curses. And then Joseph fell ill with the family consumption. At once his father was all tenderness and remorse. He sent for doctors, he offered to take him for a sea trip to Ireland, he took him indeed to Weston and went sailing with him on the sea. Once more the family came together. And once more the querulous, exacting father could not help, for all his concern, exasperating the children whom, in his own crabbed way, he yet genuinely loved. The question of religion cropped up. Owen said his father was no better than a Deist or a Socinian. And Joseph, lying ill upstairs, said he was too tired for argument; he did not want his father to bring drawings to show him; he did not want his father to read prayers to him, "he would rather have some other person to converse with than me".

So in the crisis of their lives, when a father should have been closest to them, even his children turned away from him. There was nothing left to live for. Yet what had he done to make every one hate him? Why did the farmers call him mad? Why did Joseph say that no one would read what he wrote? Why did the villagers tie tin cans to the tail of his dog? Why did the peacocks shriek and the bells ring? Why was there no mercy shown to him and no respect and no love? With agonising repetition the diary asks these questions; but there was no answer. At last, one morning in December 1839, the Rector took his gun, walked into the beech wood near his home, and shot himself dead.

Dr. Burney's Evening Party

THE party was given either in 1777 or in 1778; on which day or month of the year is not known, but the night was cold. Fanny Burney, from whom we get much of our information, was accordingly either twenty-five or twenty-six, as we choose. But in order to enjoy the party to the full it is necessary to go back some years and to scrape acquaintance with the guests.

Fanny, from the earliest days, had always been fond of writing. There was a cabin at the end of her stepmother's garden at King's Lynn, where she used to sit and write of an afternoon till the oaths of the seamen sailing up and down the river drove her in. But it was only in the afternoon and in remote places that her half-suppressed, uneasy passion for writing had its way. Writing was held to be slightly ridiculous in a girl; rather unseemly in a woman. Besides, one never knew, if a girl kept a diary, whether she might not say something indiscreet—so Miss Dolly Young warned her; and Miss Dolly Young, though exceedingly plain, was esteemed a woman of the highest character in King's Lynn. Fanny's stepmother also disapproved of writing. Yet so keen was the joy—"I cannot express the pleasure I have in writing down my thoughts at the very moment, and my opinion of people when I first see them"—that scribble she must. Loose sheets of paper fell from her pocket and were picked up and read by her father to her agony and

114

shame; once she was forced to make a bonfire of all her papers in the back garden. At last some kind of compromise seems to have been arrived at. The morning was sacred to serious tasks like sewing; it was only in the afternoon that she allowed herself to scribble—letters, diaries, stories, verses in the look-out place which overhung the river, till the oaths of the sailors drove her in.

There was something strange in that, perhaps, for the eighteenth century was the age of oaths. Fanny's early diary is larded with them. "God help me", "Split me", "Stap my vitals", together with damneds and devilishes dropped daily and hourly from the lips of her adored father and her venerated Daddy Crisp. Perhaps Fanny's attitude to language was altogether a little abnormal. She was immensely susceptible to the power of words, but not nervously or acutely as Jane Austen was. She adored fluency and the sound of language pouring warmly and copiously over the printed page. Directly she read *Rasselas*, enlarged and swollen sentences formed on the tip of her childish pen in the manner of Dr. Johnson. Quite early in life she would go out of her way to avoid the plain name of Tomkins. Thus, whatever she heard from her cabin at the end of the garden was sure to affect her more than most girls, and it is also clear that while her ears were sensitive to sound, her soul was sensitive to meaning. There was something a little prudish in her nature. Just as she avoided the name of Tomkins, so she avoided the roughnesses, the asperities, the plainnesses of daily life. The chief fault that mars the extreme vivacity and vividness of the early diary is that the profusion of words tends to soften the edges of the sentences, and the sweetness of the sentiment to smooth out the outlines of the thought. Thus, when she heard the sailors swearing, though Maria Allen, her half-sister, would, one believes, have liked to stay and toss a kiss over the water—her future history allows us to take the liberty of thinking so—Fanny went indoors.

Fanny went indoors, but not to solitary meditation. The house, whether it was in Lynn or in London—and by far the greater part of the year was spent in Poland Street—hummed with activity. There was the sound of the harpsichord; the sound of singing; there was the sound—for such concentration seems to pervade a whole house with its murmur—of Dr. Burney writing furiously, surrounded by notebooks, in his study; and there were great bursts of chatter and laughter when, returning from their various occupations, the Burney children met together. Nobody enjoyed family life more than Fanny did. For there her shyness only served to fasten the nickname of Old Lady upon her; there she had a familiar audience for her humour; there she need not bother about her clothes; there—perhaps the fact that their mother had died when they were all young was partly the cause of it—was that intimacy which expresses itself in jokes and legends and a private language ("The wig is wet", they would say, winking at each other); there were endless confabulations, and confidences between sisters and brothers and brothers and sisters. Nor could there be any doubt that the Burneys—Susan and James and Charles and Fanny and Hetty and Charlotte—were a gifted race. Charles was a scholar; James was a humorist; Fanny was a writer; Susan was musical—each had some special gift or characteristic to add to the common stock. And besides their natural gifts they were happy in the fact that their father

was a very popular man; a man, too, so admirably situated
by his talents, which were social, and his birth, which was
gentle, that they could mix without difficulty either with
lords or with bookbinders, and had, in fact, as free a run
of life as could be wished.

As for Dr. Burney himself, there are some points about
which, at this distance of time, one may feel dubious. It is
difficult to be sure what, had one met him now, one would
have felt for him. One thing is certain—one would have
met him everywhere. Hostesses would be competing to catch
him. Notes would wait for him. Telephone bells would interrupt him. For he was the most sought-after, the most occupied of men. He was always dashing in and dashing out.
Sometimes he dined off a box of sandwiches in his carriage.
Sometimes he went out at seven in the morning, and was not
back from his round of music lessons till eleven at night.
The "habitual softness of his manners", his great social
charm, endeared him to everybody. His haphazard untidy
ways—everything, notes, money, manuscripts, was tossed
into a drawer, and he was robbed of all his savings once,
but his friends were delighted to make it up for him; his odd
adventures—did he not fall asleep after a bad crossing at
Dover, and so return to France and so have to cross the
Channel again?—gave him a claim upon people's kindness
and sympathy. It is, perhaps, his diffuseness that makes him
a trifle nebulous. He seems to be for ever writing and then
re-writing, and requiring his daughters to write for him, endless books and articles, while over him, unchecked, unfiled,
unread perhaps, pour down notes, letters, invitations to
dinner which he cannot destroy and means some day to
annotate and collect, until he seems to melt away at last in

a cloud of words. When he died at the age of eighty-eight, there was nothing to be done by the most devoted of daughters but to burn the whole accumulation entire. Even Fanny's love of language was suffocated. But if we fumble a little as to our feeling for Dr. Burney, Fanny certainly did not. She adored her father. She never minded how many times she had to lay aside her own writing in order to copy out his. And he returned her affection. Though his ambition for her success at Court was foolish, perhaps, and almost cost her her life, she had only to cry when a distasteful suitor was pressed on her, "Oh, Sir, I wish for nothing! Only let me live with you!" for the emotional doctor to reply, "My Life! Thou shalt live with me for ever if thou wilt. Thou canst not think I meant to get rid of thee?" And not only were his eyes full of tears, but, what was more remarkable, he never mentioned Mr. Barlow again. Indeed, the Burneys were a happy family; a mixed composite, oddly assorted family; for there were the Allens, too, and little half-brothers and half-sisters were being born and growing up.

So time passed, and the passage of the years made it impossible for the family to continue in Poland Street any longer. First they moved to Queen Square, and then, in 1774, to the house where Newton had lived, in St. Martin's Street, Leicester Fields; where his Observatory still stood, and his room with the painted panels was still to be seen. Here in a mean street, but in the centre of the town, the Burneys set up their establishment. Here Fanny went on scribbling, stealing to the Observatory as she had stolen to the cabin at Lynn, for she exclaimed, "I cannot any longer resist what I find to be irresistible, the pleasure of popping

down my thoughts from time to time upon paper". Here
came so many famous people either to be closeted with the
doctor, or, like Garrick, to sit with him while his fine head
of natural hair was brushed, or to join the lively family
dinner, or, more formally to gather together in a musical
party, where all the Burney children played and their father
"dashed away" on the harpsichord, and perhaps some foreign musician of distinction performed a solo—so many
people came for one reason or another to the house in St.
Martin's Street that it is only the eccentrics, the grotesques,
that catch the eye. One remembers, for instance, the Ajujari,
the astonishing soprano, because she had been "mauled as an
infant by a pig, in consequence of which she is reported to
have a silver side". One remembers Bruce, the traveller, because he had a

most extraordinary complaint. When he attempted to speak, his whole
stomach suddenly seemed to heave like an organ bellows. He did not
wish to make any secret about it, but spoke of it as having originated
in Abyssinia. However, one evening, when he appeared rather agi-
tated, it lasted much longer than usual, and was so violent that it
alarmed the company.

One seems to remember, for she paints herself while she
paints the others, Fanny herself slipping eagerly and lightly
in and out of all this company, with her rather prominent
gnat-like eyes, and her shy, awkward manners. But the gnat-
like eyes, the awkward manners, concealed the quickest
observation, the most retentive memory. As soon as the
company had gone, she stole to the Observatory and wrote
down every word, every scene, in letters twelve pages long,
for her beloved Daddy Crisp at Chessington. That old hermit—he had retired to a house in a field in dudgeon with

society—though professing to be better pleased with a bottle of wine in his cellar and a horse in his stable, and a game of backgammon at night, than with all the fine company in the world, was always agog for news. He scolded his Fannikin if she did not tell him all about her fine goings-on. And he scolded her again if she did not write at full tilt exactly as the words came into her head.

Mr. Crisp wanted to know in particular "about Mr. Greville and his notions". For, indeed, Mr. Greville was a perpetual source of curiosity. It is a thousand pities that time with her poppy dust has covered Mr. Greville so that only his most prominent features, his birth, his person, and his nose emerge. Fulke Greville was the descendant—he must, one fancies, have emphasised the fact from the way in which it is repeated—of the friend of Sir Philip Sidney. A coronet, indeed, "hung almost suspended over his head". In person he was tall and well proportioned. "His face, features, and complexion were striking for masculine beauty." "His air and carriage were noble with conscious dignity"; his bearing was "lofty, yet graceful". But all these gifts and qualities, to which one must add that he rode and fenced and danced and played tennis to admiration, were marred by prodigious faults. He was supercilious in the extreme; he was selfish; he was fickle. He was a man of violent temper. His introduction to Dr. Burney in the first place was due to his doubt whether a musician could be fit company for a gentleman. When he found that young Burney not only played the harpsichord to perfection, but curved his finger and rounded his hand as he played; that he answered plain "Yes, Sir", or "No, Sir", being more interested in the music than in his patron; that it was only indeed when Greville himself thrummed pertinaciously from memory that he could stand it no longer, and broke into vivacious conversation—it was only when he found that young Burney was both gifted and well bred that, being himself a very clever man, he no longer stood upon his dignity. Burney became his friend and his equal. Burney, indeed, almost became his victim. For if there was one thing that the descendant of the friend of Sir Philip Sidney detested it was what he called "fogrum". By that expressive word he seems to have meant the middle-class virtues of discretion and respectability, as opposed to the aristocratic virtues of what he called *"ton"*. Life must be lived dashingly, daringly, with perpetual display, even if the display was extremely expensive, and, as seemed possible to those who trailed dismally round his grounds praising the improvements, as boring to the man who made it as to the unfortunate guests whose admiration he insisted upon extorting. But Greville could not endure fogrum in himself or in his friends. He threw the obscure young musician into the fast life of White's and Newmarket, and watched with amusement to see if he sank or swam. Burney, most adroit of men, swam as if born to the water, and the descendant of the friend of Sir Philip Sidney was pleased. From being his protégé, Burney became his confidant. Indeed, the splendid gentleman, for all his high carriage, was in need of one. For Greville, could one wipe away the poppy dust that covers him, was one of those tortured and unhappy souls who find themselves torn asunder by opposite desires. On the one hand he was consumed with the wish to be in the first flight of fashion and to do "the thing", however costly or dreary "the thing" might be. On the other, he was secretly persuaded that "the proper bent of his mind and understanding was for metaphysics". Burney, perhaps, was a link between the world of *ton* and the world of fogrum. He was a man of breeding who could dice and bet with the bloods; he was also a musician who could talk of intellectual things and ask clever people to his house.

Thus Greville treated the Burneys as his equals, and came to their house, though his visits were often interrupted by the violent quarrels which he managed to pick even with the amiable Dr. Burney himself. Indeed, as time went on there was nobody with whom Greville did not quarrel. He had lost heavily at the gambling-tables. His prestige in society was sunk. His habits were driving his family from him. Even his wife, by nature gentle and conciliatory, though excessive thinness made her seem fitted to sit for a portrait "of a penetrating, puissant and sarcastic fairy queen", was wearied by his infidelities. Inspired by them she had suddenly produced that famous Ode to Indifference, "which had passed into every collection of fugitive pieces in the English language" and (it is Madam D'Arblay who speaks) "twined around her brow a garland of wide-spreading and unfading fragrance". Her fame, it may be, was another thorn in her husband's side; for he, too, was an author. He himself had produced a volume of Maxims and Characters; and having "waited for fame with dignity rather than anxiety, because with expectation unclogged with doubt", was beginning perhaps to become a little impatient when fame delayed. Meanwhile he was fond of the society of clever people, and it was largely at his desire that the famous party in St. Martin's Street met together that very cold night.

II

IN THOSE days, when London was so small, it was easier than now for people to stand on an eminence which they scarcely struggled to keep, but enjoyed by unanimous consent. Everybody knew and remembered when they saw her that Mrs. Greville had written an Ode to Indifference; everybody knew that Mr. Bruce had travelled in Abyssinia; so, too, everybody knew that there was a house at Streatham presided over by a lady called Mrs. Thrale. Without troubling to write an Ode, without hazarding her life among savages, without possessing either high rank or vast wealth, Mrs. Thrale was a celebrity. By the exercise of powers difficult to define—for to feel them one must have sat at table and noticed a thousand audacities and deftnesses and skilful combinations which die with the moment—Mrs. Thrale had the reputation of a great hostess. Her fame spread far beyond her house. People who had never seen her discussed her. People wanted to know what she was like; whether she was really so witty and so well read; whether it was a pose; whether she had a heart; whether she loved her husband the brewer, who seemed a dull dog; why she had married him; whether Dr. Johnson was in love with her—what, in short, was the truth of her story, the secret of her power. For power she had—that was indisputable.

Even then perhaps, it would have been difficult to say in what it consisted. For she possessed the one quality which can never be named; she enjoyed the one gift which never ceases to excite discussion. Somehow or other she was a personality. The young Burneys, for instance, had never seen Mrs. Thrale or been to Streatham, but the stir which she set going round her had reached them in St. Martin's Street. When their father came back from giving his first music lesson to Miss Thrale at Streatham they flocked about him to hear his account of her mother. Was she as brilliant as people made out? Was she kind? Was she cruel? Had he liked her? Dr. Burney was in high good temper—in itself a proof of his hostess's power—and he replied, not, we may be sure, as Fanny rendered it, that she was a "star of the first constellation of female wits: surpassing, rather than equalising the reputation which her extraordinary endowments, and the splendid fortune which made them conspicuous, had blazoned abroad"—that was written when Fanny's style was old and tarnished, and its leaves were fluttering and falling profusely to the ground; the doctor, we may suppose, answered briskly that he had enjoyed himself hugely; that the lady was a very clever lady; that she had interrupted the lesson all the time; that she had a very sharp tongue—there was no doubt of that; but he would go to the stake for it that she was a good-hearted woman at bottom. Then they must have pressed to know what she looked like. She looked younger than her age—which was about forty. She was rather plump, very small, fair with very blue eyes, and had a scar or cut on her lip. She painted her cheeks, which was unnecessary, because her complexion was rosy by nature. The whole impression she made was one of bustle and gaiety and good temper. She was, he said, a woman "full of sport", whom nobody could have taken for a creature that the doctor could not bear, a learned lady. Less obviously, she was very observant, as her anecdotes were to prove; capable of passion, though that was not yet visible at Streatham; and, while curiously careless and good-tempered about her dues as a wit or a blue-stocking, had an amusing pride in being descended from a long line of Welsh gentry (whereas the Thrales were obscure), and drew satisfaction now and then from the reflection that in her veins ran the blood, as the College of Heralds acknowledged, of Adam of Salzburg.

Many women might have possessed these qualities without being remembered for them. Mrs. Thrale possessed besides one that has given her immortality: the power of being the friend of Dr. Johnson. Without that addition, her life might have fizzled and flamed to extinction, leaving nothing behind it. But the combination of Dr. Johnson and Mrs. Thrale created something as solid, as lasting, as remarkable in its way as a work of art. And this was an achievement that called for much rarer powers on the part of Mrs. Thrale than the qualities of a good hostess. When the Thrales first met Johnson he was in a state of profound gloom, crying out such lost and terrible words that Mr. Thrale put his hand before his mouth to silence him. Physically, too, he was afflicted with asthma and dropsy; his manners were rough; his habits were gross; his clothes were dirty; his wig was singed; his linen was soiled; and he was the rudest of men. Yet Mrs. Thrale carried this monster off with her to Brighton and then domesticated him in her house at Streatham, where he was given a room to himself, and where he spent habitually some days in the middle of every week. This might have been, it is true, but the enthusiasm of a curiosity hunter, ready to put up with a host of disagreeables for the sake of having at her house the original Dr. Johnson, whom anybody in England would gladly pay to see. But it is clear that her connoisseurship was of a finer type. She understood—her anecdotes prove it —that Dr. Johnson was somehow a rare, an important, an impressive human being whose friendship might be a burden but was certainly an honour. And it was not by any means so easy to know this then as it is now. What one knew then was that Dr. Johnson was coming to dinner. And when Dr. Johnson came to dinner one had to ask one's self who was coming too? For if it was a Cambridge man there might be an outburst. If it was a Whig there would certainly be a scene. If it was a Scotsman anything might happen. Such were his whims and prejudices. Next one would have to bethink one, what food had been ordered for dinner? For the food never went uncriticised; and even when one had provided him with young peas from the garden, one must not praise them. Were not the young peas charming, Mrs. Thrale asked once? and he turned upon her, after gobbling down masses of pork and veal pie with lumps of sugar in it, and snapped "Perhaps they would be so—to a pig". Then what would the talk be about—that was another cause for anxiety. If it got upon painting or music he was apt to dismiss it with scorn, for both arts were indifferent to him. Then if a traveller told a tale he was sure to pooh-pooh it, because he believed nothing that he had not seen himself. Then if any one were to express sympathy in his presence it might well draw down upon one a rebuke for insincerity:

When, one day, I lamented the loss of a cousin killed in America: "Prithee, my dear," said he, "have done with canting: how would the world be the worse for it, I may ask, if all your relations were at once spitted like larks, and roasted for Presto's supper?"

In short, the meal would be strewn with difficulties; the whole affair might run upon the rocks at any moment.

Had Mrs. Thrale been a shallow curiosity hunter she would have shown him for a season or so and then let him drop. But Mrs. Thrale realised even at the moment that one must submit to be snubbed and bullied and irritated and offended by Dr. Johnson because—well, what was the force that sent an impudent and arrogant young man like Boswell slinking back to his chair like a beaten boy when Johnson bade him? Why did she herself sit up till four in the morning pouring out tea for him? There was a force in him that awed even a competent woman of the world, that subdued even a thick-skinned, conceited boy. He had a right to scold Mrs. Thrale for inhumanity, when she knew that he spent only seventy pounds a year on himself and with the rest of his income supported a houseful of decrepit and ungrateful lodgers. If he gobbled at table and tore the peaches from the wall, he went back punctually to London to see that his wretched inmates had their three good meals over the week-end. Moreover, he was a warehouse of knowledge. If the dancing-master talked about dancing, Johnson could out-talk him. He could keep one amused by the hour with his tales of the underworld, of the topers and scallywags who haunted his lodgings and claimed his bounty. He said things casually that one never forgot. But what was perhaps more engaging than all this learning and virtue, was his love of pleasure, his detestation of the mere bookworm, his passion for life and society. And then, as a woman would, Mrs. Thrale loved him for his courage—that he had separated two fierce dogs that were tearing each other to pieces in Mr. Beauclerc's sitting-room; that he had thrown

a man, chair and all, into the pit of a theatre; that, blind
and twitching as he was, he rode to hounds on Brightelm-
stone Downs, and followed the hunt as if he had been a gay
dog instead of a huge and melancholy old man. Moreover,
there was a natural affinity between them. She drew him
out: she made him say what without her he would never
have said; indeed, he had confessed to her some painful
secret of his youth which she never revealed to anybody.
Above all, they shared the same passion. Of talk they could
neither of them ever have enough.

Thus Mrs. Thrale could always be counted on to produce
Dr. Johnson; and it was, of course, Dr. Johnson whom
Mr. Greville most particularly wished to meet. As it happened, Dr. Burney had renewed his acquaintance with Dr.
Johnson after many years, when he went to Streatham to
give his first music lesson, and Dr. Johnson had been there,
"wearing his mildest aspect". For he remembered Dr. Burney with kindness. He remembered a letter that Dr. Burney
had written to him in praise of the dictionary; he remembered, too, that Dr. Burney having called upon him, years
ago, and found him out, had dared to cut some bristles from
the hearth broom to send to an admirer. When he met Dr.
Burney again at Streatham, he had instantly taken a liking
to him; soon he was brought by Mrs. Thrale to see Dr. Burney's books; it was quite easy, therefore, for Dr. Burney to
arrange that on a certain night in the early spring of 1777
or 1778, Mr. Greville's great wish to meet Dr. Johnson and
Mrs. Thrale should be gratified. A day was fixed and the
engagement was made.

Whatever the day was it must have been marked in the
host's calendar with a note of interrogation. Anything

might happen. Any extreme of splendour or disaster might spring from the meeting of so many marked and distinguished characters. Dr. Johnson was formidable. Mr. Greville was domineering. Mrs. Greville was a celebrity in one way; Mrs. Thrale was a celebrity in another. Then it was an occasion. Everybody felt it to be so. Wits would be on the strain; expectation on tiptoe. Dr. Burney foresaw these difficulties and took steps to avert them, but there was, one vaguely feels, something a little obtuse about Dr. Burney. The eager, kind, busy man, with his head full of music and his desk stuffed with notes, lacked discrimination. The precise outline of people's characters was covered with a rambling pink haze. To his innocent mind music was the universal specific. Everybody must share his own enthusiasm for music. If there was going to be any difficulty, music could solve it. He therefore asked Signor Piozzi to be of the party.

The night arrived and the fire was lit. The chairs were placed and the company arrived. As Dr. Burney had foreseen, the awkwardness was great. Things indeed seemed to go wrong from the start. Dr. Johnson had come in his worsted wig, very clean and prepared evidently for enjoyment. But after one look at him, Mr. Greville seemed to decide that there was something formidable about the old man; it would be better not to compete; it would be better to play the fine gentleman, and leave it to literature to make the first advances. Murmuring, apparently, something about having the toothache, Mr. Greville "assumed his most supercilious air of distant superiority and planted himself, immovable as a noble statue, upon the hearth". He said nothing. Then Mrs. Greville, though longing to distinguish herself, judged it proper for Dr. Johnson to begin, so that she said nothing. Mrs. Thrale, who might have been expected to break up the solemnity, felt, it seemed, that the party was not her party and, waiting for the principals to engage, resolved to say nothing either. Mrs. Crewe, the Grevilles' daughter, lovely and vivacious as she was, had come to be entertained and instructed and therefore very naturally she, too, said nothing. Nobody said anything. Complete silence reigned. Here was the very moment for which Dr. Burney in his wisdom had prepared. He nodded to Signor Piozzi; and Signor Piozzi stepped to the instrument and began to sing. Accompanying himself on the pianoforte, he sang an *aria parlante*. He sang beautifully, he sang his best. But far from breaking the awkwardness and loosing the tongues, the music increased the constraint. Nobody spoke. Everybody waited for Dr. Johnson to begin. There, indeed, they showed their fatal ignorance, for if there was one thing that Dr. Johnson never did, it was to begin. Somebody had always to start a topic before he consented to pursue it or to demolish it. Now he waited in silence to be challenged. But he waited in vain. Nobody spoke. Nobody dared speak. The roulades of Signor Piozzi continued uninterrupted. As he saw his chance of a pleasant evening's talk drowned in the rattle of a piano, Dr. Johnson sank into silent abstraction and sat with his back to the piano gazing at the fire. The *aria parlante* continued uninterrupted. At last the strain became unendurable. At last Mrs. Thrale could stand it no longer. It was the attitude of Mr. Greville, apparently, that roused her resentment. There he stood on the hearth in front of the fire "staring around him at the whole company in curious silence sardonically".

What right had he, even if he were the descendant of the friend of Sir Philip Sidney, to despise the company and absorb the fire? Her own pride of ancestry suddenly asserted itself. Did not the blood of Adam of Salzburg run in her veins? Was it not as blue as that of the Grevilles and far more sparkling? Giving rein to the spirit of recklessness which sometimes bubbled in her, she rose, and stole on tiptoe to the pianoforte. Signor Piozzi was still singing and accompanying himself dramatically as he sang. She began a ludicrous mimicry of his gestures: she shrugged her shoulders, she cast up her eyes, she reclined her head on one side just as he did. At this singular display the company began to titter—indeed, it was a scene that was to be described "from coterie to coterie throughout London, with comments and sarcasms of endless variety". People who saw Mrs. Thrale at her mockery that night never forgot that this was the beginning of that criminal affair, the first scene of that "most extraordinary drama" which lost Mrs. Thrale the respect of friends and children, which drove her in ignominy from England, and scarcely allowed her to show herself in London again—this was the beginning of her most reprehensible, her most unnatural passion for one who was not only a musician but a foreigner. But all this still lay on the laps of the gods. Nobody yet knew of what iniquity the vivacious lady was capable. She was still the respected wife of a wealthy brewer. Happily, Dr. Johnson was staring at the fire, and knew nothing of the scene at the piano. But Dr. Burney put a stop to the laughter instantly. He was shocked that a guest, even if a foreigner and a musician, should be ridiculed behind his back, and stealing to Mrs. Thrale he whispered kindly but with authority in her ear that if she had no taste for music herself she should consider the feelings of those who had. Mrs. Thrale took the rebuke with admirable sweetness, nodded her acquiescence and returned to her chair. But she had done her part. After that nothing more could be expected from her. Let them now do what they chose—she washed her hands of it, and seated herself "like a pretty little Miss", as she said afterwards, to endure what yet remained to be endured "of one of the most humdrum evenings that she had ever passed".

If no one had dared to tackle Dr. Johnson in the beginning it was scarcely likely that they would dare now. He had apparently decided that the evening was a failure so far as talk was concerned. If he had not come dressed in his best clothes he might have had a book in his pocket which he could have pulled out and read. As it was, nothing but the resources of his own mind were left him; but these were huge; and these he explored as he sat with his back to the piano looking the very image of gravity, dignity, and composure.

At last the *aria parlante* came to an end. Signor Piozzi indeed, finding nobody to talk to, fell asleep in his solitude. Even Dr. Burney by this time must have been aware that music is not an infallible specific; but there was nothing for it now. Since people would not talk, the music must continue. He called upon his daughters to sing a duet. And then, when that was over, there was nothing for it but that they must sing another. Signor Piozzi still slept, or still feigned sleep. Dr. Johnson explored still further the magnificent resources of his own mind. Mr. Greville still stood superciliously upon the hearth-rug. And the night was cold.

But it was a grave mistake to suppose that because Dr.

Johnson was apparently lost in thought, and certainly almost blind, he was not aware of anything, particularly of anything reprehensible, that was taking place in the room. His "starts of vision" were always astonishing and almost always painful. So it was on the present occasion. He suddenly woke up. He suddenly roused himself. He suddenly uttered the words for which the company had been waiting all the evening.

"If it were not for depriving the ladies of the fire", he said, looking fixedly at Mr. Greville, "I should like to stand upon the hearth myself!" The effect of the outburst was prodigious. The Burney children said afterwards that it was as good as a comedy. The descendant of the friend of Sir Philip Sidney quailed before the Doctor's glance. All the blood of all the Brookes rallied itself to overcome the insult. The son of a bookseller should be taught his place. Greville did his best to smile—a faint, scoffing smile. He did his best to stand where he had stood the whole evening. He stood smiling, he stood trying to smile, for two or perhaps for three minutes more. But when he looked round the room and saw all eyes cast down, all faces twitching with amusement, all sympathies plainly on the side of the bookseller's son, he could stand there no longer. Fulke Greville slunk away, sloping even his proud shoulders, to a chair. But as he went, he rang the bell "with force". He demanded his carriage.

"The party then broke up; and no one from amongst it ever asked, or wished for its repetition."

Jack Mytton

ARE you curious to know what sort of person your neighbour is in a deck-chair on Brighton pier? Watch, then, which column of *The Times*—she has brought it, rolled like a French roll, and it lies on the top of her bag—she reads first. Politics, presumably, or an article upon a temple in Jerusalem? Not a bit of it—she reads the sporting news. Yet one could have sworn, to look at her—boots, stockings, and all —that she was a public servant of some sort; with an Act of Parliament, a blue-book or two, and a frugal lunch of biscuits and bananas in her bag. If for a moment she basks on Brighton pier while Madame Rosalba, poised high on a platform above the sea, dives for coins or soup-plates it is only to refresh herself before renewing her attack upon the iniquities of our social system. Yet she begins by reading the sporting news.

Perhaps there is nothing so strange in it after all. The great English sports are pursued almost as fiercely by sedentary men who cannot sit a donkey, and by quiet women who cannot drown a mouse, as by the booted and spurred. They hunt in imagination. They follow the fortunes of the Berkeley, the Cattistock, the Quorn, and the Belvoir upon phantom hunters. They roll upon their lips the odd-sounding, beautifully crabbed English place-names—Humblebee, Doddles Hill, Caroline Bog, Winniats Brake. They imagine as they read (hanging to a strap in the Underground or propping the paper against a suburban teapot) now a "slow, twisting hunt", now a "brilliant gallop". The rolling meadows are in their eyes; they hear the thunder and the whimper of horses and hounds; the shapely slopes of Leicestershire unfold before them, and in imagination they ride home again, when evening falls, soothed and satisfied, and watch the lights coming out in farmhouse windows. Indeed the English sporting writers, Beckford, St. John, Surtees, Nimrod, make no mean reading. In their slapdash, gentlemanly way they have ridden their pens as boldly as they have ridden their horses. They have had their effect upon the language. This riding and tumbling, this being blown upon and rained upon and splashed from head to heels with mud, have worked themselves into the very texture of English prose and given it that leap and dash, that stripping of images from flying hedge and tossing tree which distinguish it not indeed above the French but so emphatically from it. How much English poetry depends upon English hunting this is not the place to enquire. That Shakespeare was a bold if erratic horseman scarcely needs proving. Therefore that an Englishwoman should choose to read the sporting news rather than the political gossip need cause us no surprise; nor need we condemn her if, when she has folded up her paper, she takes from her bag not a blue-book but a red book and proceeds, while Madame Rosalba dives and the band blares and the green waters of the English channel sparkle and sway between the chinks of the pier, to read the Life of Jack Mytton.

Jack Mytton was by no means an estimable character. Of an old Shropshire family (the name was Mutton once; so Brontë was Prunty), he had inherited a fine property and

a large income. The little boy who was born in the year
1796 should have carried on the tradition of politics and
sport which his ancestors had pursued respectably for five
centuries before him. But families have their seasons, like
the year. After months of damp and drizzle, growth and
prosperity, there come the wild equinoctial gales, a roaring
in the trees all day, fruit destroyed and blossom wasted.
Lightning strikes the house and its rooftree goes up in fire.
Indeed, Nature and society between them had imposed upon
the Mytton of 1796 a burden which might have crushed a
finer spirit—a body hewn from the solid rock, a fortune of
almost indestructible immensity. Nature and society dared
him, almost, to defy them. He accepted the challenge. He
went shooting in the thinnest silk stockings, he let the rain
pelt on his bare skin, he swam rivers, charged gates,
crouched naked on the snow, but still his body remained
obdurate and upright. He had his breeches made without
pockets; wads of bank-notes were picked up in the woods,
but still his fortune survived. He begot children and tossed
them in the air and pelted them with oranges; he married
wives whom he tormented and imprisoned until one died
and the other snatched her chance and ran away. While he
shaved, a glass of port stood by his side, and as the day
wore on he worked through five or six bottles of wine and
sopped them up with pound upon pound of filberts. There
was an extremity about his behaviour which raises it from
the particular to the general. The shaggy body of primeval
man, with all his appetites and aptitudes, seemed to have
risen from his grave under the barrows, where the great
stones were piled on top of him, where once he sacrificed
rams and did homage to the rising sun, to carouse with tip-

pling fox-hunters of the time of George the Fourth. His
limbs themselves seemed carved from more primitive materials than modern men's. He had neither beauty of countenance nor grace of manner, yet he bore himself, for all his
violence of body and mind, with an air of natural breeding
which one can imagine in a savage stepping on his native
turf. When he talked, says Nimrod, which he did sparely,
he said, in a very few words, things which made everybody
laugh; but, unequally gifted as he was, acute in some senses,
dull in others, he had a deafness which made him unwieldy
in general society.

What, then, could a primeval man do, who was born in
England in the reign of George the Fourth? He could take
bets and make them. Was it a watery winter's night? He
would drive his gig across country under the moon. Was it
freezing? He would make his stable-boys hunt rats upon
skates. Did some moderately cautious guest admit that he
had never been upset in a gig? Mytton at once ran the wheel
up the bank and flung them both into the road. Put any
obstacle in his way and he leapt it, swam it, smashed it,
somehow surmounted it, at the cost of a broken bone or a
broken carriage. To yield to danger or to own to pain were
both unthinkable. And so the Shropshire peasantry were
amazed (as we see them in Alken's and Rawlins's pictures)
by the apparition of a gentleman setting his tandem at a
gate, riding a bear round his drawing-room, beating a bull-
dog with naked fists, lying between the hoofs of a nervous
horse, riding with broken ribs unmurmuring when every jar
was agony. They were amazed; they were scandalised; his
eccentricities and infidelities and generosities were the talk
of every inn and farmhouse for miles; yet somehow no

bailiff in the four counties would arrest him. They looked up at him as one looks at something removed from ordinary duties and joys—a monument, a menace—with contempt and pity and some awe.

But Jack Mytton himself—what was he feeling meanwhile? The thrill of perfect satisfaction, the delight of joys snatched unhesitatingly without compunction? The barbarian surely should have been satisfied. But the by no means introspective mind of Nimrod was puzzled. "Did the late Mr. Mytton really enjoy life amidst all this profusion of expenditure?" No; Nimrod was of opinion that he did not. He had everything that the human heart could desire, but he lacked "the art of enjoyment". He was bored. He was unhappy. "There was that about him which resembled the restlessness of the hyena." He hurried from thing to thing, determined to taste and enjoy, but somehow blunted and bruised his pleasures as he touched them. Two hours before his own exquisite dinner he devoured fat bacon and strong ale at a farmhouse, and then blamed his cook. Still, without an appetite, he would eat; still he would drink, only instead of port it must be brandy to lash his flagging palate into sensation. A "sort of destroying spirit egged him on". He was magnificent, wasteful, extravagant in every detail. ". . . it was his largeness of heart that ruined Mr. Mytton", said Nimrod, "added to the lofty pride which disdained the littleness of prudence."

By the time he was thirty, at any rate, Jack Mytton had done two things that to most men would have been impossible: he had almost ruined his health; he had almost spent his money. He had to leave the ancestral home of the Myttons. But it was no primeval man, glowing with health, bristling with energy, but a "round-shouldered, tottering old-young man bloated by drink" who joined the company of shady adventurers whose necessities obliged them to live at Calais. Even in that society his burden was upon him; still he must shine; still he must excel. No one should call him Johnny Mytton with impunity. Four horses must draw Mr. Mytton the three hundred yards to his rooms or he preferred to walk. And then the hiccough attacked him. Seizing his bedroom candle, he set alight to his shirt and staggered, burning and blazing, to show his friends how Jack Mytton cured the hiccough. What more could human beings ask of him? To what further frenzies would the gods dare their victim? Now that he had burnt himself alive, it seemed as if he had discharged his obligation to society and could lay the primeval man to rest. He might perhaps allow that other spirit, the civilised gentleman who was so incongruously coupled with the barbarian, to come to the surface. He had once learnt Greek. Now as he lay burnt and bloated in bed he quoted Sophocles—"the beautiful passage . . . wherein Oedipus recommends his children to the care of Creon". He remembered the Greek anthology. When they moved him to the seaside he began to pick up shells, and could hardly sit out dinner in his eagerness to be at the work of brushing them "with a nail brush dipped in vinegar". "He to whom the whole world had appeared insufficient to afford pleasure . . . was now completely happy." But alas, shells and Sophocles, peace and happiness, were whelmed in the general dissolution which could not be delayed. The King's Bench prison seized him, and there, corrupt in body, ruined in fortune, worn out in mind, he died at the age of thirty-eight. And his wife cried that she could not help loving him with all his faults", and four horses drew him to the grave, and three thousand poor people sobbed for the loss of one who had somehow acted out for the benefit of the crowd an odious, monstrous part, laid on him by the gods, for the edification of mankind and their pleasure too, but for his own unutterable misery.

For the truth is we like these exhibitions of human nature. We like to see exalted above us some fox-hunter, like Jack Mytton, burning himself alive to cure the hiccough, some diver like Madame Rosalba, who, mounting higher and higher, wraps herself about in sacking, and then, with a look of indifference and satiety as if she had renounced and suffered and dedicated herself to some insane act of defiance for no pleasure of her own, dives into the Channel and brings up a twopenny-halfpenny soup-plate between her teeth. The lady on the pier feels gratified. It is because of this, she says, that I love my kind.

De Quincey's Autobiography

IT MUST often strike the reader that very little criticism worthy of being called so has been written in English of prose—our great critics have given the best of their minds to poetry. And the reason perhaps why prose so seldom calls out the higher faculties of the critic, but invites him to argue a case or to discuss the personality of the writer— to take a theme from the book and make his criticism an air played in variation on it—is to be sought in the prose-writer's attitude to his own work. Even if he writes as an artist, without a practical end in view, still he treats prose as a humble beast of burden which must accommodate all sorts of odds and ends; as an impure substance in which dust and twigs and flies find lodgment. But more often than not the prose-writer has a practical aim in view, a theory to argue, or a cause to plead, and with it adopts the moralist's view that the remote, the difficult, and the complex are to be abjured. His duty is to the present and the living. He is proud to call himself a journalist. He must use the simplest words and express himself as clearly as possible in order to reach the greatest number in the plainest way. Therefore he cannot complain of the critics if his writing, like the irritation in the oyster, serves only to breed other art; nor be surprised if his pages, once they have delivered their message, are thrown on the rubbish heap like other objects that have served their turn.

But sometimes we meet even in prose with writing that seems inspired by other aims. It does not wish to argue or to convert or even to tell a story. We can draw all our pleasure from the words themselves; we have not to enhance it by reading between the lines or by making a voyage of discovery into the psychology of the writer. De Quincey, of course, is one of these rare beings. When we bring his work to mind we recall it by some passage of stillness and completeness, like the following:

"*Life is Finished!*" was the secret misgiving of my heart; for the heart of infancy is as apprehensive as that of maturest wisdom in relation to any capital wound inflicted on the happiness. "*Life is Finished! Finished it is!*" was the hidden meaning that, half-unconsciously to myself, lurked within my sighs; and, as bells heard from a distance on a summer evening seem charged at times with an articulate form of words, some monitory message, that rolls round unceasingly, even so for me some noiseless and subterraneous voice seemed to chant continually a secret word, made audible only to my own heart—that "now is the blossoming of life withered for ever".

Such passages occur naturally, for they consist of visions and dreams, not of actions or of dramatic scenes, in his autobiographic sketches. And yet we are not made to think of him, De Quincey, as we read. If we try to analyse our sensations we shall find that we are worked upon as if by music—the senses are stirred rather than the brain. The rise and fall of the sentence immediately soothes us to a mood and removes us to a distance in which the near fades and detail is extinguished. Our minds, thus widened and lulled to a width of apprehension, stand open to receive one by one in slow and stately procession the ideas which De Quincey wishes us to receive; the golden fullness of life; the pomps of the heaven above; the glory of the flowers below, as he stands "between an open window and a dead body on a summer's day". The theme is supported and amplified and varied. The idea of hurry and trepidation, of reaching towards something that for ever flies, intensifies the impression of stillness and eternity. Bells heard on summer evenings, palm-trees waving, sad winds that blow for ever keep us by successive waves of emotion in the same mood. The emotion is never stated; it is suggested and brought slowly by repeated images before us until it stays, in all its complexity, complete.

The effect is one that is very rarely attempted in prose and is rarely appropriate to it because of this very quality of finality. It does not lead anywhere. We do not add to our sense of high summer and death and immortality any consciousness of who is hearing, seeing, and feeling. De Quincey wished to shut out from us everything save the picture "of a solitary infant, and its solitary combat with grief—a mighty darkness, and a sorrow without a voice", to make us fathom and explore the depths of that single emotion. It is a state which is general and not particular. Therefore De Quincey was at odds with the aims of the prose-writer and his morality. His reader was to be put in possession of a meaning of that complex kind which is largely a sensation. He had to become fully aware not merely of the fact that a child was standing by a bed, but of stillness, sunlight, flowers, the passage of time and the presence of death. None of this could be conveyed by simple words in their logical order; clarity and simplicity would merely travesty and deform such a meaning. De Quincey, of course, was fully aware of the gulf that lay between him as a writer who wished to convey such ideas and his contemporaries. He turned from the neat precise speech of his time to Milton and Jeremy Taylor and Sir Thomas Browne; from them he learnt the roll of the long sentence that sweeps its coils in and out, that piles its summit higher and higher. Then followed a discipline exacted, most drastically, by the fineness of his own ear—the weighing of cadences, the consideration of pauses; the effect of repetitions and consonances and assonances—all this was part of the duty of a writer who wishes to put a complex meaning fully and completely before his reader.

When, therefore, we come to consider critically one of the passages that has made so deep an impression we find that it has been produced much as a poet like Tennyson would produce it. There is the same care in the use of sound; the same variety of measure; the length of the sentence is varied and its weight shifted. But all these measures are diluted to a lower degree of strength and their force is spread over a much greater space, so that the transition from the lowest compass to the highest is by a gradation of shallow steps and we reach the utmost heights without violence. Hence the difficulty of stressing the particular quality of any single line as in a poem and the futility of taking one passage apart from the context, since its effect is compound of suggestions that have been received sometimes several pages earlier. Moreover, De Quincey, unlike some of his masters, was not at his best in sudden majesty of phrase; his power lay in suggesting large and generalised visions; landscapes in which nothing is seen in detail; faces without features; the stillness of midnight or summer; the tumult and trepidation of flying multitudes; anguish that for ever falls and rises and casts its arms upwards in despair.

But De Quincey was not merely the master of separate passages of beautiful prose; if that had been so his achievement would have been far less than it is. He was also a writer of narrative, an autobiographer, and one, if we consider that he wrote in the year 1833, with very peculiar views of the art of autobiography. In the first place he was convinced of the enormous value of candour.

If he were really able to pierce the haze which so often envelops, even to himself, his own secret springs of action and reserve, there cannot be a life moving at all under intellectual impulses that would not, through that single force of absolute frankness, fall within the reach of a deep, solemn, and sometimes even of a thrilling interest.

He understood by autobiography the history not only of the external life but of the deeper and more hidden emotions. And he realised the difficulty of making such a confession: ". . . vast numbers of people, though liberated from all reasonable motives of self-restraint, *cannot* be confidential—have it not in their power to lay aside reserve". Aerial chains, invisible spells, bind and freeze the free spirit of communication. "It is because a man cannot see and measure these mystical forces which palsy him that he cannot deal with them effectually." With such perceptions and intentions it is strange that De Quincey failed to be among the great autobiographers of our literature. Certainly he was not tongue-tied or spellbound. Perhaps one of the reasons that led him to fail in his task of self-delineation was not the lack of expressive power, but the superfluity. He was profusely and indiscriminately loquacious. Discursiveness— the disease that attacked so many of the nineteenth-century English writers—had him in her coils. But while it is easy to see why the works of Ruskin or Carlyle are huge and formless—every kind of heterogeneous object had to be found room for somehow, somewhere—De Quincey had not their excuse. The burden of the prophet was not laid upon him. He was, moreover, the most careful of artists. Nobody tunes the sound and modulates the cadence of a sentence more carefully and more exquisitely. But strangely enough, the sensibility which was on the alert to warn him instantly if a sound clashed or a rhythm flagged failed him completely when it came to the architecture of the whole. Then he could tolerate a disproportion and profusion that make his book as dropsical and shapeless as each sentence is symmetrical and smooth. He is indeed, to use the expressive word coined by his brother to describe De Quincey's tendency as a small boy "to plead some distinction or verbal demur", the prince of Pettifogulisers. Not only did he find "in everybody's words an unintentional opening left for double interpretations"; he could not tell the simplest story without qualifying and illustrating and introducing additional information until the point that was to be cleared up has long since become extinct in the dim mists of the distance.

Together with this fatal verbosity and weakness of architectural power, De Quincey suffered too as an autobiographer from a tendency to meditative abstraction. "It was my disease", he said, "to meditate too much and to observe too little." A curious formality diffuses his vision to a general vagueness, lapsing into a colourless monotony. He shed over everything the lustre and the amenity of his own dreaming, pondering absent-mindedness. He approached even the two disgusting idiots with their red eyes with the elaboration of a great gentleman who has by mistake wandered into a slum. So too he slipped mellifluously across all the fissures of the social scale—talking on equal terms with the young aristocrats at Eton or with the working-class family as they chose a joint of meat for their Sunday dinner. De Quincey indeed prided himself upon the ease with which he passed from one sphere to another: ". . . from my very earliest youth", he observed, "it has been my pride to converse familiarly, *more Socratico*, with all human beings, man, woman, and child, that chance might fling in my way". But as we read his descriptions of these men, women, and children we are led to think that he talked to them so easily because to him they differed so little. The same manner served equally for them all. His relations even with those with whom he was most intimate, whether it was Lord Altamont, his schoolboy friend, or Ann the prostitute, were equally ceremonial and gracious. His portraits have the flowing contours, the statuesque poses, the undifferentiated features of Scott's heroes and heroines. Nor is his own face exempted from the general ambiguity. When it came to telling the truth about himself he shrank from the task with all the horror of a well-bred English gentleman. The candour which fascinates us in the confessions of Rousseau—the determination to reveal the ridiculous, the mean, the sordid in himself—was abhorrent to him. "Nothing indeed is more revolting to English feelings", he wrote, "than the spectacle of a human being obtruding on our notice his moral ulcers and scars."

Clearly, therefore, De Quincey as an autobiographer labours under great defects. He is diffuse and redundant; he is aloof and dreamy and in bondage to the old pruderies and conventions. At the same time he was capable of being transfixed by the mysterious solemnity of certain emotions; of realising how one moment may transcend in value fifty years. He was able to devote to their analysis a skill which the professed analysts of the human heart—the Scotts, the Jane Austens, the Byrons—did not then possess. We find him writing passages which, in their self-consciousness, are scarcely to be matched in the fiction of the nineteenth century:

> And, recollecting it, I am struck with the truth, that far more of our deepest thoughts and feelings pass to us through perplexed combinations of *concrete* objects, pass to us as *involutes* (if I may coin that word) in compound experiences incapable of being disentangled, than ever reach us *directly* and in their own abstract shapes. . . . Man is doubtless *one* by some subtle *nexus*, some system of links, that we cannot perceive, extending from the new-born infant to the superannuated dotard: but, as regards many affections and passions incident to his nature at different stages, he is *not* one, but an intermitting creature, ending and beginning anew; the unity of man, in this respect, is co-extensive only with the particular stage to which the passion belongs. Some passions, as that of sexual love, are celestial by one-half of their origin, animal and earthly by the other half. These will not survive their own appropriate stage. But love, which is *altogether* holy, like that between two children, is privileged to revisit by glimpses the silence and the darkness of declining years. . . .

When we read such passages of analysis, when such states of mind seem in retrospect to be an important element in life and so to deserve scrutiny and record, the art of autobiography as the eighteenth century knew it is changing its character. The art of biography also is being transformed. Nobody after that could maintain that the whole truth of life can be told without "piercing the haze"; without revealing "his own secret springs of action and reserve". Yet external events also have their importance. To tell the whole story of a life the autobiographer must devise some means by which the two levels of existence can be recorded —the rapid passage of events and actions; the slow opening up of single and solemn moments of concentrated emotion. It is the fascination of De Quincey's pages that the two levels are beautifully, if unequally, combined. For page after page we are in company with a cultivated gentleman who describes with charm and eloquence what he has seen and known—the stage coaches, the Irish rebellion, the appearance and conversation of George the Third. Then suddenly the smooth narrative parts asunder, arch opens beyond arch, the vision of something for ever flying, for ever escaping, is revealed, and time stands still.

Four Figures

I. COWPER AND LADY AUSTEN

IT HAPPENED, of course, many years ago, but there must have been something remarkable about the meeting, since people still like to bring it before their eyes. An elderly gentleman was looking out of his window in a village street in the summer of 1781 when he saw two ladies go into a draper's shop opposite. The look of one of them interested him very much, and he seems to have said so, for soon a meeting was arranged.

A quiet and solitary life that must have been, in which a gentleman stood in the morning looking out of the window, in which the sight of an attractive face was an event. Yet perhaps it was an event partly because it revived some half-forgotten but still pungent memories. For Cowper had not always looked at the world from the windows of a house in a village street. Time was when the sight of ladies of fashion had been familiar enough. In his younger days he had been very foolish. He had flirted and giggled; he had gone smartly dressed to Vauxhall and Marylebone Gardens. He had taken his work at the Law Courts with a levity that alarmed his friends—for he had nothing whatever to live upon. He had fallen in love with his cousin Theodora Cowper. Indeed, he had been a thoughtless, wild young man. But suddenly in the heyday of his youth, in the midst of his gaiety, something terrible had happened. There lurked beneath that levity and perhaps inspired it a morbidity that sprang from some defect of person, a dread which made action, which made marriage, which made any public exhibition of himself insupportable. If goaded to it, and he was now committed to a public career in the House of Lords, he must fly, even into the jaws of death. Rather than take up his appointment he would drown himself. But a man sat on the quay when he came to the water's edge; some invisible hand mysteriously forced the laudanum from his lips when he tried to drink it; the knife which he pressed to his heart broke; and the garter with which he tried to hang himself from the bed-post let him fall. Cowper was condemned to live.

When, therefore, that July morning he looked out of the window at the ladies shopping, he had come through gulfs of despair, but he had reached at last not only the haven of a quiet country town, but a settled state of mind, a settled way of life. He was domesticated with Mrs. Unwin, a widow six years his elder. By letting him talk, and listening to his terrors and understanding them, she had brought him very wisely, like a mother, to something like peace of mind. They had lived side by side for many years in methodical monotony. They began the day by reading the Scriptures together; they then went to church; they parted to read or walk; they met after dinner to converse on religious topics or to sing hymns together; then again they walked if it were fine, or read and talked if it were wet, and at last the day ended with more hymns and more prayers. Such for many years had been the routine of Cowper's life with Mary Unwin. When his fingers found their way to a

pen they traced the lines of a hymn, or if they wrote a letter
it was to urge some misguided mortal, his brother John,
for instance, at Cambridge, to seek salvation before it was
too late. Yet this urgency was akin perhaps to the old levity;
it, too, was an attempt to ward off some terror, to propitiate
some deep unrest that lurked at the bottom of his soul. Suddenly the peace was broken. One night in February 1773
the enemy rose; it smote once and for ever. An awful voice
called out to Cowper in a dream. It proclaimed that he was
damned, that he was outcast, and he fell prostrate before it.
After that he could not pray. When the others said grace
at table, he took up his knife and fork as a sign that he
had no right to join their prayers. Nobody, not even Mrs.
Unwin, understood the terrific import of the dream. Nobody
realised why he was unique; why he was singled out from
all mankind and stood alone in his damnation. But that
loneliness had a strange effect—since he was no longer
capable of help or direction he was free. The Rev. John
Newton could no longer guide his pen or inspire his muse.
Since doom had been pronounced and damnation was inevitable, he might sport with hares, cultivate cucumbers,
listen to village gossip, weave nets, make tables; all that
could be hoped was to while away the dreadful years without the ability to enlighten others or to be helped himself.
Never had Cowper written more enchantingly, more gaily,
to his friends than now that he knew himself condemned.
It was only at moments, when he wrote to Newton or to
Unwin, that the terror raised its horrid head above the
surface and that he cried aloud: "My days are spent in
vanity. . . . Nature revives again; but a soul once slain
lives no more." For the most part, as he idled his time away

in pleasant pastimes, as he looked with amusement at what passed in the street below, one might think him the happiest of men. There was Geary Ball going to the "Royal Oak" to drink his dram—that happened as regularly as Cowper brushed his teeth; but behold—two ladies were going into the draper's shop opposite. That was an event.

One of the ladies he knew already—she was Mrs. Jones, the wife of a neighbouring clergyman. But the other was a stranger. She was arch and sprightly, with dark hair and round dark eyes. Though a widow—she had been the wife of a Sir Robert Austen—she was far from old and not at all solemn. When she talked, for she and Cowper were soon drinking tea together, "she laughs and makes laugh, and keeps up a conversation without seeming to labour at it". She was a lively, well-bred woman who had lived much in France, and, having seen much of the world, "accounts it a great simpleton as it is". Such were Cowper's first impressions of Ann Austen. Ann's first impressions of the queer couple who lived in the large house in the village street were even more enthusiastic. But that was natural—Ann was an enthusiast by nature. Moreover, though she had seen a great deal of the world and had a town house in Queen Anne Street, she had no friends or relations in that world much to her liking. Clifton Reynes, where her sister lived, was a rude, rough English village where the inhabitants broke into the house if a lady were left unprotected. Lady Austen was dissatisfied; she wanted society, but she also wanted to be settled and to be serious. Neither Clifton Reynes nor Queen Anne Street gave her altogether what she wanted. And then in the most opportune way—quite by chance—she met a refined, well-bred couple who were ready

to appreciate what she had to give and ready to invite her
to share the quiet pleasures of the countryside which were
so dear to them. She could heighten those pleasures de-
liciously. She made the days seem full of movement and
laughter. She organised picnics—they went to the Spinnie
and ate their dinner in the root-house and drank their tea
on the top of a wheelbarrow. And when autumn came and
the evenings drew in, Ann Austen enlivened them too; she
it was who stirred William to write a poem about a sofa
and told him, just as he was sinking into one of his fits of
melancholy, the story of John Gilpin, so that he leapt out
of bed, shaking with laughter. But beneath her sprightliness
they were glad to find that she was seriously inclined. She
longed for peace and quietude, "for with all that gaiety",
Cowper wrote, "she is a great thinker".

And with all that melancholy, to paraphrase his words,
Cowper was a man of the world. As he said himself, he was
not by nature a recluse. He was no lean and solitary hermit.
His limbs were sturdy; his cheeks were ruddy; he was
growing plump. In his younger days he, too, had known the
world, and provided, of course, that you have seen through
it, there is something to be said for having known it. Cowper,
at any rate, was a little proud of his gentle birth. Even at
Olney he kept certain standards of gentility. He must have
an elegant box for his snuff and silver buckles for his shoes;
if he wanted a hat it must be "not a round slouch, which I
abhor, but a smart, well-cocked, fashionable affair". His
letters preserve this serenity, this good sense, this sidelong,
arch humour embalmed in page after page of beautiful clear
prose. As the post went only three times a week he had
plenty of time to smooth out every little crease in daily life

to perfection. He had time to tell how a farmer was thrown from his cart and one of the pet hares had escaped; Mr. Grenville had called; they had been caught in a shower and Mrs. Throckmorton had asked them to come into the house —some little thing of the kind happened every week very aptly for his purpose. Or if nothing happened and it was true that the days went by at Olney "shod with felt", then he was able to let his mind play with rumours that reached him from the outer world. There was talk of flying. He would write a few pages on the subject of flying and its impiety; he would express his opinion of the wickedness, for Englishwomen at any rate, of painting the cheeks. He would discourse upon Homer and Virgil and perhaps attempt a few translations himself. And when the days were dark and even he could no longer trudge through the mud, he would open one of his favourite travellers and dream that he was voyaging with Cook or with Anson, for he travelled widely in imagination, though in body he moved no further than from Buckingham to Sussex and from Sussex back to Buckingham again.

His letters preserve what must have made the charm of his company. It is easy to see that his wit, his stories, his sedate, considerate ways, must have made his morning visits —and he had got into the habit of visiting Lady Austen at eleven every morning—delightful. But there was more in his society than that—there was some charm, some peculiar fascination, that made it indispensable. His cousin Theodora had loved him—she still loved him anonymously; Mrs. Unwin loved him; and now Ann Austen was beginning to feel something stronger than friendship rise within her. That strain of intense and perhaps inhuman passion which rested with tremulous ecstasy like that of a hawk moth over a flower, upon some tree, some hill-side—did that not tensify the quiet of the country morning, and give to intercourse with him some keener interest than belonged to the society of other men? "The very stones in the garden walls are my intimate acquaintance", he wrote. "Everything I see in the fields is to me an object, and I can look at the same rivulet, or at a handsome tree, every day of my life with new pleasure." It is this intensity of vision that gives his poetry, with all its moralising and didacticism, its unforgettable qualities. It is this that makes passages in *The Task* like clear windows let into the prosaic fabrics of the rest. It was this that gave the edge and zest to his talk. Some finer vision suddenly seized and possessed him. It must have given to the long winter evenings, to the early morning visits, an indescribable combination of pathos and charm. Only, as Theodora could have warned Ann Austen, his passion was not for men and women; it was an abstract ardour; he was a man singularly without thought of sex.

Already early in their friendship Ann Austen had been warned. She adored her friends, and she expressed her adoration with the enthusiasm that was natural to her. At once Cowper wrote to her kindly but firmly admonishing her of the folly of her ways. "When we embellish a creature with colours taken from our fancy," he wrote, "we make it an idol . . . and shall derive nothing from it but a painful conviction of our error." Ann read the letter, flew into a rage, and left the country in a huff. But the breach was soon healed; she worked him ruffles; he acknowledged them with a present of his book. Soon she had embraced Mary Unwin and was back again on more intimate terms than ever. In another month indeed, with such rapidity did her plans take effect, she had sold the lease of her town house, taken part of the vicarage next door to Cowper, and declared that she had now no home but Olney and no friends but Cowper and Mary Unwin. The door between the gardens was opened; the two families dined together on alternate nights; William called Ann sister; and Ann called William brother. What arrangement could have been more idyllic? "Lady Austen and we pass our days alternately at each other's chateau. In the morning I walk with one or other of the ladies, and in the afternoon wind thread", wrote Cowper, playfully comparing himself to Hercules and Samson. And then the evening came, the winter evening which he loved best, and he dreamt in the firelight and watched the shadows dance uncouthly and the sooty films play upon the bars until the lamp was brought, and in that level light he had out his netting, or wound silk, and then, perhaps, Ann sang to the harpsichord and Mary and William played battledore and shuttlecock together. Secure, innocent, peaceful, where then was that "thistly sorrow" that grows inevitably, so Cowper said, beside human happiness? Where would discord come, if come it must? The danger lay perhaps with the women. It might be that Mary would notice one evening that Ann wore a lock of William's hair set in diamonds. She might find a poem to Ann in which he expressed more than a brotherly affection. She would grow jealous. For Mary Unwin was no country simpleton, she was a well-read woman with "the manners of a Duchess"; she had nursed and consoled William for years before Ann came to flutter the "still life" which they both loved best. Thus the two ladies would compete; discord would enter at that point. Cowper would be forced to choose between them.

But we are forgetting another presence at that innocent evening's entertainment. Ann might sing; Mary might play; the fire might burn brightly and the frost and the wind outside make the fireside calm all the sweeter. But there was a shadow among them. In that tranquil room a gulf opened. Cowper trod on the verge of an abyss. Whispers mingled with the singing, voices hissed in his ear words of doom and damnation. He was haled by a terrible voice to perdition. And then Ann Austen expected him to make love to her! Then Ann Austen wanted him to marry her! The thought was odious; it was indecent; it was intolerable. He wrote her another letter, a letter to which there could be no reply. In her bitterness Ann burnt it. She left Olney and no word ever passed between them again. The friendship was over.

And Cowper did not mind very much. Everybody was extremely kind to him. The Throckmortons gave him the key of their garden. An anonymous friend—he never guessed her name—gave him fifty pounds a year. A cedar desk with silver handles was sent him by another friend who wished also to remain unknown. The kind people at Olney supplied him with almost too many tame hares. But if you are damned, if you are solitary, if you are cut off from God and man, what does human kindness avail? "It is all vanity. . . . Nature revives again; but a soul once slain lives no more." He sank from gloom to gloom, and died in misery.

As for Lady Austen, she married a Frenchman. She was happy—so people said.

II. BEAU BRUMMELL

WHEN Cowper, in the seclusion of Olney, was roused to anger by the thought of the Duchess of Devonshire and predicted a time when "instead of a girdle there will be a rent, and instead of beauty, baldness", he was acknowledging the power of the lady whom he thought so despicable. Why, otherwise, should she haunt the damp solitudes of Olney? Why should the rustle of her silken skirts disturb those gloomy meditations? Undoubtedly the Duchess was a good haunter. Long after those words were written, when she was dead and buried beneath a tinsel coronet, her ghost mounted the stairs of a very different dwelling-place. An old man was sitting in his arm-chair at Caen. The door opened, and the servant announced, "The Duchess of Devonshire". Beau Brummell at once rose, went to the door and made a bow that would have graced the Court of St. James's. Only, unfortunately, there was nobody there. The cold air blew up the staircase of an Inn. The Duchess was long dead, and Beau Brummell, in his old age and imbecility, was dreaming that he was back in London again giving a party. Cowper's curse had come true for both of them. The Duchess lay in her shroud, and Brummell, whose clothes had been the envy of kings, had now only one pair of much-mended trousers, which he hid as best he could under a tattered cloak. As for his hair, that had been shaved by order of the doctor.

But though Cowper's sour predictions had thus come to pass, both the Duchess and the dandy might claim that they had had their day. They had been great figures in their time.

Of the two, perhaps Brummell might boast the more miraculous career. He had no advantage of birth, and but little of fortune. His grandfather had let rooms in St. James's Street. He had only a moderate capital of thirty thousand pounds to begin with, and his beauty, of figure rather than of face, was marred by a broken nose. Yet without a single noble, important, or valuable action to his credit he cuts a figure; he stands for a symbol; his ghost walks among us still. The reason for this eminence is now a little difficult to determine. Skill of hand and nicety of judgment were his, of course, otherwise he would not have brought the art of tying neck-cloths to perfection. The story is, perhaps, too well known—how he drew his head far back and sunk his chin slowly down so that the cloth wrinkled in perfect symmetry, or if one wrinkle were too deep or too shallow, the cloth was thrown into a basket and the attempt renewed, while the Prince of Wales sat, hour after hour, watching. Yet skill of hand and nicety of judgment were not enough. Brummell owed his ascendency to some curious combination of wit, of taste, of insolence, of independence—for he was never a toady—which it were too heavy handed to call a philosophy of life, but served the purpose. At any rate, ever since he was the most popular boy at Eton coolly jesting when they were for throwing a bargee into the river, "My good fellows, don't send him into the river; the man is evidently in a high state of perspiration, and it almost amounts to a certainty that he will catch cold", he floated buoyantly and gaily and without apparent effort to the top of whatever society he found himself among. Even when he was a captain in the Tenth Hussars and so scandalously inattentive to duty that he only knew his troop by "the very large blue nose" of one of the men, he was liked and tolerated. When he resigned his commission, for the regiment was to be sent to Manchester—and "I really could not go—think, your Royal Highness, Manchester!"—he had only to set up house in Chesterfield Street to become the head of the most jealous and exclusive society of his time. For example, he was at Almack's one night talking to Lord ——. The Duchess of —— was there, escorting her young daughter, Lady Louisa. The Duchess caught sight of Mr. Brummell, and at once warned her daughter that if that gentleman near the door came and spoke to them she was to be careful to impress him favourably, "for", and she sank her voice to a whisper, "he is the celebrated Mr. Brummell". Lady Louisa might well have wondered why a Mr. Brummell was celebrated, and why a Duke's daughter need take care to impress a Mr. Brummell. And then directly he began to move towards them the reason of her mother's warning became apparent. The grace of his carriage was so astonishing; his bows were so exquisite. Everybody looked over-dressed or badly dressed—some, indeed, looked positively dirty beside him. His clothes seemed to melt into each other with the perfection of their cut and the quiet harmony of their colour. Without a single point of emphasis everything was distinguished—from his bow to the way he opened his snuff-box, with his left hand invariably. He was the person-ification of freshness and cleanliness and order. One could well believe that he had his chair brought into his dressing-room and was deposited at Almack's without letting a puff of wind disturb his curls or a spot of mud stain his shoes. When he actually spoke to her, Lady Louisa would be at first enchanted—no one was more agreeable, more amusing, had a manner that was more flattering and enticing—and then she would be puzzled. It was quite possible that before the evening was out he would ask her to marry him, and yet his manner of doing it was such that the most ingenuous débutante could not believe that he meant it seriously. His odd grey eyes seemed to contradict his lips; they had a look in them which made the sincerity of his compliments very doubtful. And then he said very cutting things about other people. They were not exactly witty; they were certainly not profound; but they were so skilful, so adroit—they had a twist in them which made them slip into the mind and stay there when more important phrases were forgotten. He had downed the Regent himself with his dexterous "Who's your fat friend?" and his method was the same with humbler people who snubbed him or bored him. "Why, what could I do, my good fellow, but cut the connection? I discovered that Lady Mary actually ate cabbage!"—so he explained to a friend his failure to marry a lady. And, again, when some dull citizen pestered him about his tour to the North, "Which of the lakes do I admire?" he asked his valet. "Windermere, sir." "Ah, yes—Windermere, so it is—Windermere." That was his style, flickering, sneering, hovering on the verge of insolence, skimming the edge of nonsense, but always keeping within some curious mean, so that one knew the false Brummell story from the true by its exaggeration. Brummell could never have said, "Wales, ring the bell", any more than he could have worn a brightly coloured waistcoat or a glaring necktie. That "certain exquisite propriety" which Lord Byron remarked in his dress, stamped his whole being, and made him appear cool, refined, and debonair among the gentlemen who talked

162

only of sport, which Brummell detested, and smelt of the stable, which Brummell never visited. Lady Louisa might well be on tenter-hooks to impress Mr. Brummell favourably. Mr. Brummell's good opinion was of the utmost importance in the world of Lady Louisa.

And unless that world fell into ruins his rule seemed assured. Handsome, heartless, and cynical, the Beau seemed invulnerable. His taste was impeccable, his health admirable; and his figure as fine as ever. His rule had lasted many years and survived many vicissitudes. The French Revolution had passed over his head without disordering a single hair. Empires had risen and fallen while he experimented with the crease of a neck-cloth and criticised the cut of a coat. Now the battle of Waterloo had been fought and peace had come. The battle left him untouched; it was the peace that undid him. For some time past he had been winning and losing at the gaming-tables. Harriette Wilson had heard that he was ruined, and then, not without disappointment, that he was safe again. Now, with the armies disbanded, there was let loose upon London a horde of rough, ill-mannered men who had been fighting all those years and were determined to enjoy themselves. They flooded the gaming-houses. They played very high. Brummell was forced into competition. He lost and won and vowed never to play again, and then he did play again. At last his remaining ten thousand pounds was gone. He borrowed until he could borrow no more. And finally, to crown the loss of so many thousands, he lost the six-penny-bit with a hole in it which had always brought him good luck. He gave it by mistake to a hackney coachman: that rascal Rothschild got hold of it, he said, and that was the end of his luck. Such was his own account of the affair—other people put a less innocent interpretation on the matter. At any rate there came a day, 16th May 1816, to be precise— it was a day upon which everything was precise—when he dined alone off a cold fowl and a bottle of claret at Watier's, attended the opera, and then took coach for Dover. He drove rapidly all through the night and reached Calais the day after. He never set foot in England again.

And now a curious process of disintegration set in. The peculiar and highly artificial society of London had acted as a preservative; it had kept him in being; it had concentrated him into one single gem. Now that the pressure was removed, the odds and ends, so trifling separately, so brilliant in combination, which had made up the being of the Beau, fell asunder and revealed what lay beneath. At first his lustre seemed undiminished. His old friends crossed the water to see him and made a point of standing him a dinner and leaving a little present behind them at his bankers. He held his usual levee at his lodgings; he spent the usual hours washing and dressing; he rubbed his teeth with a red root, tweezed out hairs with a silver tweezer, tied his cravat to admiration, and issued at four precisely as perfectly equipped as if the Rue Royale had been St. James's Street and the Prince himself had hung upon his arm. But the Rue Royale was not St. James's Street; the old French Countess who spat on the floor was not the Duchess of Devonshire; the good bourgeois who pressed him to dine off goose at four was not Lord Alvanley; and though he soon won for himself the title of Roi de Calais, and was known to workmen as "George, ring the bell", the praise was gross, the society coarse, and the amusements of Calais

very slender. The Beau had to fall back upon the resources
of his own mind. These might have been considerable. According to Lady Hester Stanhope, he might have been, had
he chosen, a very clever man; and when she told him so, the
Beau admitted that he had wasted his talents because a
dandy's way of life was the only one "which could place
him in a prominent light, and enable him to separate himself from the ordinary herd of men, whom he held in considerable contempt". That way of life allowed of verse-
making—his verses, called "The Butterfly's Funeral", were
much admired; and of singing, and of some dexterity with
the pencil. But now, when the summer days were so long
and so empty, he found that such accomplishments hardly
served to while away the time. He tried to occupy himself
with writing his memoirs; he bought a screen and spent
hours pasting it with pictures of great men and beautiful
ladies whose virtues and frailties were symbolised by
hyenas, by wasps, by profusions of cupids, fitted together
with extraordinary skill; he collected Buhl furniture; he
wrote letters in a curiously elegant and elaborate style to
ladies. But these occupations palled. The resources of his
mind had been whittled away in the course of years; now
they failed him. And then the crumbling process went a little
farther, and another organ was laid bare—the heart. He
who had played at love all these years and kept so adroitly
beyond the range of passion, now made violent advances to
girls who were young enough to be his daughters. He wrote
such passionate letters to Mademoiselle Ellen of Caen that
she did not know whether to laugh or to be angry. She was
angry, and the Beau, who had tyrannised over the daughters
of Dukes, prostrated himself before her in despair. But it

was too late—the heart after all these years was not a very engaging object even to a simple country girl, and he seems at last to have lavished his affections upon animals. He mourned his terrier Vick for three weeks; he had a friendship with a mouse; he became the champion of all the neglected cats and starving dogs in Caen. Indeed, he said to a lady that if a man and a dog were drowning in the same pond he would prefer to save the dog—if, that is, there were nobody looking. But he was still persuaded that everybody was looking; and his immense regard for appearances gave him a certain stoical endurance. Thus, when paralysis struck him at dinner he left the table without a sign; sunk deep in debt as he was, he still picked his way over the cobbles on the points of his toes to preserve his shoes, and when the terrible day came and he was thrown into prison he won the admiration of murderers and thieves by appearing among them as cool and courteous as if about to pay a morning call. But if he were to continue to act his part, it was essential that he should be supported—he must have a sufficiency of boot polish, gallons of eau-de-Cologne, and three changes of linen every day. His expenditure upon these items was enormous. Generous as his old friends were, and persistently as he supplicated them, there came a time when they could be squeezed no longer. It was decreed that he was to content himself with one change of linen daily, and his allowance was to admit of necessaries only. But how could a Brummell exist upon necessaries only? The demand was absurd. Soon afterwards he showed his sense of the gravity of the situation by mounting a black silk neck-cloth. Black silk neck-cloths had always been his aversion. It was a signal of despair, a sign that the end was in sight. After that everything that had supported him and kept him in being dissolved. His self-respect vanished. He would dine with any one who would pay the bill. His memory weakened and he told the same story over and over again till even the burghers of Caen were bored. Then his manners degenerated. His extreme cleanliness lapsed into carelessness, and then into positive filth. People objected to his presence in the dining-room of the hotel. Then his mind went—he thought that the Duchess of Devonshire was coming up the stairs when it was only the wind. At last but one passion remained intact among the crumbled debris of so many— an immense greed. To buy Rheims biscuits he sacrificed the greatest treasure that remained to him—he sold his snuffbox. And then nothing was left but a heap of disagreeables, a mass of corruption, a senile and disgusting old man fit only for the charity of nuns and the protection of an asylum. There the clergyman begged him to pray. " 'I do try', he said, but he added something which made me doubt whether he understood me." Certainly, he would try; for the clergyman wished it and he had always been polite. He had been polite to thieves and to duchesses and to God Himself. But it was no use trying any longer. He could believe in nothing now except a hot fire, sweet biscuits and another cup of coffee if he asked for it. And so there was nothing for it but that the Beau who had been compact of grace and sweetness should be shuffled into the grave like any other illdressed, ill-bred, unneeded old man. Still, one must remember that Byron, in his moments of dandyism, "always pronounced the name of Brummell with a mingled emotion of respect and jealousy".

[NOTE.—Mr. Berry of St. James's Street has courteously

drawn my attention to the fact that Beau Brummell certainly visited England in 1822. He came to the famous wine-shop on 26th July 1822 and was weighed as usual. His weight was then 10 stones 13 pounds. On the previous occasion, 6th July 1815, his weight was 12 stones 10 pounds. Mr. Berry adds that there is no record of his coming after 1822.]

III. MARY WOLLSTONECRAFT

GREAT wars are strangely intermittent in their effects. The French Revolution took some people and tore them asunder; others it passed over without disturbing a hair of their heads. Jane Austen, it is said, never mentioned it; Charles Lamb ignored it; Beau Brummell never gave the matter a thought. But to Wordsworth and to Godwin it was the dawn; unmistakably they saw

> France standing on the top of golden hours,
> And human nature seeming born again.

Thus it would be easy for a picturesque historian to lay side by side the most glaring contrasts—here in Chesterfield Street was Beau Brummell letting his chin fall carefully upon his cravat and discussing in a tone studiously free from vulgar emphasis the proper cut of the lapel of a coat; and here in Somers Town was a party of ill-dressed, excited young men, one with a head too big for his body and a nose too long for his face, holding forth day by day over the tea-cups upon human perfectibility, ideal unity, and the rights of man. There was also a woman present with very bright eyes and a very eager tongue, and the young men, who had middle-class names, like Barlow and Holcroft and Godwin, called her simply "Wollstonecraft", as if it did not matter whether she were married or unmarried, as if she were a young man like themselves.

Such glaring discords among intelligent people—for Charles Lamb and Godwin, Jane Austen and Mary Wollstonecraft were all highly intelligent—suggest how much influence circumstances have upon opinions. If Godwin had been brought up in the precincts of the Temple and had drunk deep of antiquity and old letters at Christ's Hospital, he might never have cared a straw for the future of man and his rights in general. If Jane Austen had lain as a child on the landing to prevent her father from thrashing her mother, her soul might have burnt with such a passion against tyranny that all her novels might have been consumed in one cry for justice.

Such had been Mary Wollstonecraft's first experience of the joys of married life. And then her sister Everina had been married miserably and had bitten her wedding ring to pieces in the coach. Her brother had been a burden on her; her father's farm had failed, and in order to start that disreputable man with the red face and the violent temper and the dirty hair in life again she had gone into bondage among the aristocracy as a governess—in short, she had never known what happiness was, and, in its default, had fabricated a creed fitted to meet the sordid misery of real human life. The staple of her doctrine was that nothing mattered save independence. "Every obligation we receive from our fellow-creatures is a new shackle, takes from our native freedom, and debases the mind." Independence was the first necessity for a woman; not grace or charm, but energy and courage and the power to put her will into effect were her necessary qualities. It was her highest boast to be able to say, "I never yet resolved to do anything of consequence that I did not adhere readily to it". Certainly Mary could say this with truth. When she was a little more than thirty she could look back upon a series of actions which she had carried out in the teeth of opposition. She had taken a house by prodigious efforts for her friend Fanny, only to find that Fanny's mind was changed and she did not want a house after all. She had started a school. She had persuaded Fanny into marrying Mr. Skeys. She had thrown up her school and gone to Lisbon alone to nurse Fanny when she died. On the voyage back she had forced the captain of the ship to rescue a wrecked French vessel by threatening to expose him if he refused. And when, overcome by a passion for Fuseli, she declared her wish to live with him and was refused flatly by his wife, she had put her principle of decisive action instantly into effect, and had gone to Paris determined to make her living by her pen.

The Revolution thus was not merely an event that had happened outside her; it was an active agent in her own blood. She had been in revolt all her life—against tyranny, against law, against convention. The reformer's love of humanity, which has so much of hatred in it as well as love, fermented within her. The outbreak of revolution in France expressed some of her deepest theories and convictions, and she dashed off in the heat of that extraordinary moment those two eloquent and daring books—the *Reply to Burke* and the *Vindication of the Rights of Woman*, which are so true that they seem now to contain nothing new in them—

their originality has become our commonplace. But when she was in Paris lodging by herself in a great house, and saw with her own eyes the King whom she despised driving past surrounded by National Guards and holding himself with greater dignity than she expected, then, "I can scarcely tell you why", the tears came to her eyes. "I am going to bed," the letter ended, "and, for the first time in my life, I cannot put out the candle." Things were not so simple after all. She could not understand even her own feelings. She saw the most cherished of her convictions put into practice—and her eyes filled with tears. She had won fame and independence and the right to live her own life—and she wanted something different. "I do not want to be loved like a goddess," she wrote, "but I wish to be necessary to you." For Imlay, the fascinating American to whom her letter was addressed, had been very good to her. Indeed, she had fallen passionately in love with him. But it was one of her theories that love should be free—"that mutual affection was marriage and that the marriage tie should not bind after the death of love, if love should die". And yet at the same time that she wanted freedom she wanted certainty. "I like the word affection," she wrote, "because it signifies something habitual."

The conflict of all these contradictions shows itself in her face, at once so resolute and so dreamy, so sensual and so intelligent, and beautiful into the bargain with its great coils of hair and the large bright eyes that Southey thought the most expressive he had ever seen. The life of such a woman was bound to be tempestuous. Every day she made theories by which life should be lived; and every day she came smack against the rock of other people's prejudices.

Every day too—for she was no pedant, no cold-blooded theorist—something was born in her that thrust aside her theories and forced her to model them afresh. She acted upon her theory that she had no legal claim upon Imlay; she refused to marry him; but when he left her alone week after week with the child she had borne him her agony was unendurable.

Thus distracted, thus puzzling even to herself, the plausible and treacherous Imlay cannot be altogether blamed for failing to follow the rapidity of her changes and the alternate reason and unreason of her moods. Even friends whose liking was impartial were disturbed by her discrepancies. Mary had a passionate, an exuberant, love of Nature, and yet one night when the colours in the sky were so exquisite that Madeleine Schweizer could not help saying to her, "Come, Mary—come, nature lover—and enjoy this wonderful spectacle—this constant transition from colour to colour", Mary never took her eyes off the Baron de Wolzogen. "I must confess," wrote Madame Schweizer, "that this erotic absorption made such a disagreeable impression on me, that all my pleasure vanished." But if the sentimental Swiss was disconcerted by Mary's sensuality, Imlay, the shrewd man of business, was exasperated by her intelligence. Whenever he saw her he yielded to her charm, but then her quickness, her penetration, her uncompromising idealism harassed him. She saw through his excuses; she met all his reasons; she was even capable of managing his business. There was no peace with her—he must be off again. And then her letters followed him, torturing him with their sincerity and their insight. They were so outspoken; they pleaded so passionately to be told the truth; they showed such a contempt for soap and alum and wealth and comfort; they repeated, as he suspected, so truthfully that he had only to say the word, "and you shall never hear of me more", that he could not endure it. Tickling minnows he had hooked a dolphin, and the creature rushed him through the waters till he was dizzy and only wanted to escape. After all, though he had played at theory-making too, he was a business man, he depended upon soap and alum; "the secondary pleasures of life", he had to admit, "are very necessary to my comfort". And among them was one that for ever evaded Mary's jealous scrutiny. Was it business, was it politics, was it a woman that perpetually took him away from her? He shillied and shallied; he was very charming when they met; then he disappeared again. Exasperated at last, and half insane with suspicion, she forced the truth from the cook. A little actress in a strolling company was his mistress, she learnt. True to her own creed of decisive action, Mary at once soaked her skirts so that she might sink unfailingly, and threw herself from Putney Bridge. But she was rescued; after unspeakable agony she recovered, and then her "unconquerable greatness of mind", her girlish creed of independence, asserted itself again, and she determined to make another bid for happiness and to earn her living without taking a penny from Imlay for herself or their child.

It was in this crisis that she again saw Godwin, the little man with the big head, whom she had met when the French Revolution was making the young men in Somers Town think that a new world was being born. She met him—but that is a euphemism, for in fact Mary Wollstonecraft actually visited him in his own house. Was it the effect of

the French Revolution? Was it the blood she had seen spilt
on the pavement and the cries of the furious crowd that had
rung in her ears that made it seem a matter of no importance
whether she put on her cloak and went to visit Godwin in
Somers Town, or waited in Judd Street West for Godwin
to come to her? And what strange upheaval of human life
was it that inspired that curious man, who was so queer a
mixture of meanness and magnanimity, of coldness and deep
feeling—for the memoir of his wife could not have been
written without unusual depth of heart—to hold the view
that she did right—that he respected Mary for trampling
upon the idiotic convention by which women's lives were
tied down? He held the most extraordinary views on many
subjects, and upon the relations of the sexes in particular.
He thought that reason should influence even the love between men and women. He thought that there was something spiritual in their relationship. He had written that
"marriage is a law, and the worst of all laws . . . marriage
is an affair of property, and the worst of all properties". He
held the belief that if two people of the opposite sex like
each other, they should live together without any ceremony,
or, for living together is apt to blunt love, twenty doors off,
say, in the same street. And he went further; he said that if
another man liked your wife "this will create no difficulty.
We may all enjoy her conversation, and we shall all be wise
enough to consider the sensual intercourse a very trivial
object." True, when he wrote those words he had never
been in love; now for the first time he was to experience
that sensation. It came very quietly and naturally, growing
"with equal advances in the mind of each" from those talks
in Somers Town, from those discussions upon everything

under the sun which they held so improperly alone in his rooms. "It was friendship melting into love . . .", he wrote. "When, in the course of things, the disclosure came, there was nothing in a manner for either party to disclose to the other." Certainly they were in agreement upon the most essential points; they were both of opinion, for instance, that marriage was unnecessary. They would continue to live apart. Only when Nature again intervened, and Mary found herself with child, was it worth while to lose valued friends, she asked, for the sake of a theory? She thought not, and they were married. And then that other theory— that it is best for husband and wife to live apart—was not that also incompatible with other feelings that were coming to birth in her? "A husband is a convenient part of the furniture of the house", she wrote. Indeed, she discovered that she was passionately domestic. Why not, then, revise that theory too, and share the same roof? Godwin should have a room some doors off to work in; and they should dine out separately if they liked—their work, their friends, should be separate. Thus they settled it, and the plan worked admirably. The arrangement combined "the novelty and lively sensation of a visit with the more delicious and heart-felt pleasures of domestic life". Mary admitted that she was happy; Godwin confessed that, after all one's philosophy, it was "extremely gratifying" to find that "there is some one who takes an interest in one's happiness". All sorts of powers and emotions were liberated in Mary by her new satisfaction. Trifles gave her an exquisite pleasure —the sight of Godwin and Imlay's child playing together; the thought of their own child who was to be born; a day's jaunt into the country. One day, meeting Imlay in the New

Road, she greeted him without bitterness. But, as Godwin wrote, "Ours is not an idle happiness, a paradise of selfish and transitory pleasures". No, it too was an experiment, as Mary's life had been an experiment from the start, an attempt to make human conventions conform more closely to human needs. And their marriage was only a beginning; all sorts of things were to follow after. Mary was going to have a child. She was going to write a book to be called *The Wrongs of Women*. She was going to reform education. She was going to come down to dinner the day after her child was born. She was going to employ a midwife and not a doctor at her confinement—but that experiment was her last. She died in child-birth. She whose sense of her own existence was so intense, who had cried out even in her misery, "I cannot bear to think of being no more—of losing myself—nay, it appears to me impossible that I should cease to exist", died at the age of thirty-six. But she has her revenge. Many millions have died and been forgotten in the hundred and thirty years that have passed since she was buried; and yet as we read her letters and listen to her arguments and consider her experiments, above all that most fruitful experiment, her relation with Godwin, and realise the high-handed and hot-blooded manner in which she cut her way to the quick of life, one form of immortality is hers undoubtedly: she is alive and active, she argues and experiments, we hear her voice and trace her influence even now among the living.

IV. DOROTHY WORDSWORTH

TWO highly incongruous travellers, Mary Wollstonecraft and Dorothy Wordsworth, followed close upon each other's footsteps. Mary was in Altona on the Elbe in 1795 with her baby; three years later Dorothy came there with her brother and Coleridge. Both kept a record of their travels; both saw the same places, but the eyes with which they saw them were very different. Whatever Mary saw served to start her mind upon some theory, upon the effect of government, upon the state of the people, upon the mystery of her own soul. The beat of the oars on the waves made her ask, "Life, what are you? Where goes this breath? This *I* so much alive? In what element will it mix, giving and receiving fresh energy?" And sometimes she forgot to look at the sunset and looked instead at the Baron Wolzogen. Dorothy, on the other hand, noted what was before her accurately, literally, and with prosaic precision. "The walk very pleasing between Hamburgh and Altona. A large piece of ground planted with trees, and intersected by gravel walks. . . . The ground on the opposite side of the Elbe appears marshy." Dorothy never railed against "the cloven hoof of despotism". Dorothy never asked "men's questions" about exports and imports; Dorothy never confused her own soul with the sky. This "*I* so much alive" was ruthlessly subordinated to the trees and the grass. For if she let "I" and its rights and its wrongs and its passions and its suffering get between her and the object, she would be calling the moon "the Queen of the Night"; she would be talking of dawn's "orient beams"; she would be soaring

into reveries and rhapsodies and forgetting to find the exact
phrase for the ripple of moonlight upon the lake. It was
like "herrings in the water"—she could not have said that
if she had been thinking about herself. So while Mary
dashed her head against wall after wall, and cried out,
"Surely something resides in this heart that is not perishable
—and life is more than a dream", Dorothy went on methodically at Alfoxden noting the approach of spring. "The sloe
in blossom, the hawthorn green, the larches in the park
changed from black to green, in two or three days." And
next day, 14th April 1798, "the evening very stormy, so
we staid indoors. Mary Wollstonecraft's life, &c., came."
And the day after they walked in the squire's grounds and
noticed that "Nature was very successfully striving to make
beautiful what art had deformed—ruins, hermitages, &c.,
&c.". There is no reference to Mary Wollstonecraft; it
seems as if her life and all its storms had been swept away
in one of those compendious et ceteras, and yet the next
sentence reads like an unconscious comment. "Happily we
cannot shape the huge hills, or carve out the valleys according to our fancy." No, we cannot reform, we must not
rebel; we can only accept and try to understand the message
of Nature. And so the notes go on.

Spring passed; summer came; summer turned to autumn;
it was winter, and then again the sloes were in blossom
and the hawthorns green and spring had come. But it was
spring in the North now, and Dorothy was living alone
with her brother in a small cottage at Grasmere in the
midst of the hills. Now after the hardships and separations
of youth they were together under their own roof; now
they could address themselves undisturbed to the absorb-

ing occupation of living in the heart of Nature and trying, day by day, to read her meaning. They had money enough at last to let them live together without the need of earning a penny. No family duties or professional tasks distracted them. Dorothy could ramble all day on the hills and sit up talking to Coleridge all night without being scolded by her aunt for unwomanly behaviour. The hours were theirs from sunrise to sunset, and could be altered to suit the season. If it was fine, there was no need to come in; if it was wet, there was no need to get up. One could go to bed at any hour. One could let the dinner cool if the cuckoo were shouting on the hill and William had not found the exact epithet he wanted. Sunday was a day like any other. Custom, convention, everything was subordinated to the absorbing, exacting, exhausting task of living in the heart of Nature and writing poetry. For exhausting it was. William would make his head ache in the effort to find the right word. He would go on hammering at a poem until Dorothy was afraid to suggest an alteration. A chance phrase of hers would run in his head and make it impossible for him to get back into the proper mood. He would come down to breakfast and sit "with his shirt neck unbuttoned, and his waistcoat open", writing a poem on a Butterfly which some story of hers had suggested, and he would eat nothing, and then he would begin altering the poem and again would be exhausted.

It is strange how vividly all this is brought before us considering that the diary is made up of brief notes such as any quiet woman might make of her garden's changes and her brother's moods and the progress of the seasons. It was warm and mild, she notes, after a day of rain. She met a cow in a field. "The cow looked at me, and I looked at the cow, and whenever I stirred the cow gave over eating." She met an old man who walked with two sticks—for days on end she met nothing more out of the way than a cow eating and an old man walking. And her motives for writing are common enough—"because I will not quarrel with myself, and because I shall give William pleasure by it when he comes home again". It is only gradually that the difference between this rough notebook and others discloses itself; only by degrees that the brief notes unfurl in the mind and open a whole landscape before us, that the plain statement proves to be aimed so directly at the object that if we look exactly along the line that it points we shall see precisely what she saw. "The moonlight lay upon the hills like snow." "The air was become still, the lake of a bright slate colour, the hills darkening. The bays shot into the low fading shores. Sheep resting. All things quiet." "There was no one waterfall above another—it was the sound of waters in the air—the voice of the air." Even in such brief notes one feels the suggestive power which is the gift of the poet rather than of the naturalist, the power which, taking only the simplest facts, so orders them that the whole scene comes before us, heightened and composed, the lake in its quiet, the hills in their splendour. Yet she was no descriptive writer in the usual sense. Her first concern was to be truthful—grace and symmetry must be made subordinate to truth. But then truth is sought because to falsify the look of the stir of the breeze on the lake is to tamper with the spirit which inspires appearances. It is that spirit which goads her and urges her and keeps her faculties for ever on the stretch. A sight or a sound would not let her be till she had traced her perception along its course and fixed it in words, though they might be bald, or in an image, though it might be angular. Nature was a stern taskmistress. The exact prosaic detail must be rendered as well as the vast and visionary outline. Even when the distant hills trembled before her in the glory of a dream she must note with literal accuracy "the glittering silver line on the ridge of the backs of the sheep", or remark how "the crows at a little distance from us became white as silver as they flew in the sunshine, and when they went still further, they looked like shapes of water passing over the green fields". Always trained and in use, her powers of observation became in time so expert and so acute that a day's walk stored her mind's eye with a vast assembly of curious objects to be sorted at leisure. How strange the sheep looked mixed with the soldiers at Dumbarton Castle! For some reason the sheep looked their real size, but the soldiers looked like puppets. And then the movements of the sheep were so natural and fearless, and the motion of the dwarf soldiers was so restless and apparently without meaning. It was extremely queer. Or lying in bed she would look up at the ceiling and think how the varnished beams were "as glossy as black rocks on a sunny day cased in ice". Yes, they

crossed each other in almost as intricate and fantastic a manner as I have seen the underboughs of a large beech-tree withered by the depth of the shade above. . . . It was like what I should suppose an underground cave or temple to be, with a dripping or moist roof, and the moonlight entering in upon it by some means or other, and yet the colours were more like melted gems. I lay looking up till the light of the fire faded away. . . . I did not sleep much.

Indeed, she scarcely seemed to shut her eyes. They looked and they looked, urged on not only by an indefatigable curiosity but also by reverence, as if some secret of the utmost importance lay hidden beneath the surface. Her pen sometimes stammers with the intensity of the emotion that she controlled as De Quincey said that her tongue stammered with the conflict between her ardour and her shyness when she spoke. But controlled she was. Emotional and impulsive by nature, her eyes "wild and starting", tormented by feelings which almost mastered her, still she must control, still she must repress, or she would fail in her task— she would cease to see. But if one subdued oneself, and resigned one's private agitations, then, as if in reward, Nature would bestow an exquisite satisfaction. "Rydale was very beautiful, with spear-shaped streaks of polished steel. . . . It calls home the heart to quietness. I had been very melancholy", she wrote. For did not Coleridge come walking over the hills and tap at the cottage door late at night—did she not carry a letter from Coleridge hidden safe in her bosom?

Thus giving to Nature, thus receiving from Nature, it seemed, as the arduous and ascetic days went by, that Nature and Dorothy had grown together in perfect sympathy —a sympathy not cold or vegetable or inhuman because at the core of it burnt that other love for "my beloved", her brother, who was indeed its heart and inspiration. William and Nature and Dorothy herself, were they not one being? Did they not compose a trinity, self-contained and self-sufficient and independent whether indoors or out? They sit indoors. It was

about ten o'clock and a quiet night. The fire flickers and the watch ticks. I hear nothing but the breathing of my Beloved as he now and then pushes his book forward, and turns over a leaf.

And now it is an April day, and they take the old cloak
and lie in John's grove out of doors together.

William heard me breathing, and rustling now and then, but we
both lay still and unseen by one another. He thought that it would
be sweet thus to lie in the grave, to hear the peaceful sounds of the
earth, and just to know that our dear friends were near. The lake
was still; there was a boat out.

It was a strange love, profound, almost dumb, as if brother
and sister had grown together and shared not the speech
but the mood, so that they hardly knew which felt, which
spoke, which saw the daffodils or the sleeping city; only
Dorothy stored the mood in prose, and later William came
and bathed in it and made it into poetry. But one could
not act without the other. They must feel, they must think,
they must be together. So now, when they had lain out on
the hill-side they would rise and go home and make tea,
and Dorothy would write to Coleridge, and they would
sow the scarlet beans together, and William would work
at his "Leech Gatherer", and Dorothy would copy the lines
for him. Rapt but controlled, free yet strictly ordered, the
homely narrative moves naturally from ecstasy on the hills
to baking bread and ironing linen and fetching William
his supper in the cottage.

The cottage, though its garden ran up into the fells, was
on the highroad. Through her parlour window Dorothy
looked out and saw whoever might be passing—a tall beggar
woman perhaps with her baby on her back; an old soldier;
a coroneted landau with touring ladies peering inquisitively
inside. The rich and the great she would let pass—they
interested her no more than cathedrals or picture galleries or
great cities; but she could never see a beggar at the door

without asking him in and questioning him closely. Where
had he been? What had he seen? How many children had
he? She searched into the lives of the poor as if they held
in them the same secret as the hills. A tramp eating cold
bacon over the kitchen fire might have been a starry night,
so closely she watched him; so clearly she noted how his
old coat was patched "with three bell-shaped patches of
darker blue behind, where the buttons had been", how his
beard of a fortnight's growth was like "grey *plush*". And
then as they rambled on with their tales of seafaring and
the pressgang and the Marquis of Granby, she never failed
to capture the one phrase that sounds on in the mind after
the story is forgotten, "What, you are stepping westward?"
"To be sure there is great promise for virgins in Heaven."
"She could trip lightly by the graves of those who died
when they were young." The poor had their poetry as the
hills had theirs. But it was out of doors, on the road or on
the moor, not in the cottage parlour, that her imagination
had freest play. Her happiest moments were passed tramp-
ing beside a jibbing horse on a wet Scottish road without
certainty of bed or supper. All she knew was that there was
some sight ahead, some grove of trees to be noted, some
waterfall to be inquired into. On they tramped hour after
hour in silence for the most part, though Coleridge, who
was of the party, would suddenly begin to debate aloud the
true meaning of the words majestic, sublime, and grand.
They had to trudge on foot because the horse had thrown
the cart over a bank and the harness was only mended with
string and pocket-handkerchiefs. They were hungry, too,
because Wordsworth had dropped the chicken and the bread
into the lake, and they had nothing else for dinner. They

were uncertain of the way, and did not know where they would find lodging: all they knew was that there was a waterfall ahead. At last Coleridge could stand it no longer. He had rheumatism in the joints; the Irish jaunting car provided no shelter from the weather; his companions were silent and absorbed. He left them. But William and Dorothy tramped on. They looked like tramps themselves. Dorothy's cheeks were brown as a gipsy's, her clothes were shabby, her gait was rapid and ungainly. But still she was indefatigable; her eye never failed her; she noticed everything. At last they reached the waterfall. And then all Dorothy's powers fell upon it. She searched out its character, she noted its resemblances, she defined its differences, with all the ardour of a discoverer, with all the exactness of a naturalist, with all the rapture of a lover. She possessed it at last—she had laid it up in her mind for ever. It had become one of those "inner visions" which she could call to mind at any time in their distinctness and in their particularity. It would come back to her long years afterwards when she was old and her mind had failed her; it would come back stilled and heightened and mixed with all the happiest memories of her past—with the thought of Racedown and Alfoxden and Coleridge reading "Christabel", and her beloved, her brother William. It would bring with it what no human being could give, what no human relation could offer—consolation and quiet. If, then, the passionate cry of Mary Wollstonecraft had reached her ears—"Surely something resides in this heart that is not perishable—and life is more than a dream"—she would have had no doubt whatever as to her answer. She would have said quite simply, "We looked about us, and felt that we were happy".

William Hazlitt

HAD one met Hazlitt no doubt one would have liked him on his own principle that "We can scarcely hate any one we know". But Hazlitt has been dead now a hundred years, and it is perhaps a question how far we can know him well enough to overcome those feelings of dislike, both personal and intellectual, which his writings still so sharply arouse. For Hazlitt—it is one of his prime merits—was not one of those non-committal writers who shuffle off in a mist and die of their own insignificance. His essays are emphatically himself. He has no reticence and he has no shame. He tells us exactly what he thinks, and he tells us—the confidence is less seductive—exactly what he feels. As of all men he had the most intense consciousness of his own existence, since never a day passed without inflicting on him some pang of hate or of jealousy, some thrill of anger or of pleasure, we cannot read him for long without coming in contact with a very singular character—ill-conditioned yet high-minded; mean yet noble; intensely egotistical yet inspired by the most genuine passion for the rights and liberties of mankind.

Soon, so thin is the veil of the essay as Hazlitt wore it, his very look comes before us. We see him as Coleridge saw him, "browhanging, shoe-contemplative, strange". He comes shuffling into the room, he looks nobody straight in the face, he shakes hands with the fin of a fish; occasionally he darts a malignant glance from his corner. "His manners are 99 in a 100 singularly repulsive", Coleridge said. Yet now and again his face lit up with intellectual beauty, and his manner became radiant with sympathy and understanding. Soon, too, as we read on, we become familiar with the whole gamut of his grudges and his grievances. He lived, one gathers, mostly at inns. No woman's form graced his board. He had quarrelled with all his old friends, save perhaps with Lamb. Yet his only fault had been that he had stuck to his principles and "not become a government tool". He was the object of malignant persecution—Blackwood's reviewers called him "pimply Hazlitt", though his cheek was pale as alabaster. These lies, however, got into print, and then he was afraid to visit his friends because the footman had read the newspaper and the housemaid tittered behind his back. He had—no one could deny it—one of the finest minds, and he wrote indisputably the best prose style of his time. But what did that avail with women? Fine ladies have no respect for scholars, nor chambermaids either —so the growl and plaint of his grievances keeps breaking through, disturbing us, irritating us; and yet there is something so independent, subtle, fine, and enthusiastic about him—when he can forget himself he is so rapt in ardent speculation about other things—that dislike crumbles and turns to something much warmer and more complex. Hazlitt was right:

It is the mask only that we dread and hate; the man may have something human about him! The notions in short which we entertain of people at a distance, or from partial representation, or from guess-work, are simple, uncompounded ideas, which answer to nothing in reality; those which we derive from experience are mixed modes, the only true and, in general, the most favourable ones.

Certainly no one could read Hazlitt and maintain a simple and uncompounded idea of him. From the first he was a twy-minded man—one of those divided natures which are inclined almost equally to two quite opposite careers. It is significant that his first impulse was not to essay-writing but to painting and philosophy. There was something in the remote and silent art of the painter that offered a refuge to his tormented spirit. He noted enviously how happy the old age of painters was—"their minds keep alive to the last"; he turned longingly to the calling that takes one out of doors, among fields and woods, that deals with bright pigments, and has solid brush and canvas for its tools and not merely black ink and white paper. Yet at the same time he was bitten by an abstract curiosity that would not let him rest in the contemplation of concrete beauty. When he was a boy of fourteen he heard his father, the good Unitarian minister, dispute with an old lady of the congregation as they were coming out of Meeting as to the limits of religious toleration, and, he said, "it was this circumstance that decided the fate of my future life". It set him off "forming in my head . . . the following system of political rights and general jurisprudence". He wished "to be satisfied of the reason of things". The two ideals were ever after to clash. To be a thinker and to express in the plainest and most accurate of terms "the reason of things", and to be a painter gloating over blues and crimsons, breathing fresh air and living sensually in the emotions—these were two different, perhaps incompatible ideals, yet like all Hazlitt's emotions both were tough and each strove for mastery. He yielded now to one, now to the other. He spent months in Paris copying pictures at the Louvre. He came home and toiled laboriously at the portrait of an old woman in a bonnet day after day, seeking by industry and pains to discover the secret of Rembrandt's genius; but he lacked some quality—perhaps it was invention—and in the end cut the canvas to ribbons in a rage or turned it against the wall in despair. At the same time he was writing the *Essay on the Principles of Human Action* which he preferred to all his other works. For there he wrote plainly and truthfully, without glitter or garishness, without any wish to please or to make money, but solely to gratify the urgency of his own desire for truth. Naturally, "the book dropped still-born from the press". Then, too, his political hopes, his belief that the age of freedom had come and that the tyranny of kingship was over, proved vain. His friends deserted to the Government, and he was left to uphold the doctrines of liberty, fraternity, and revolution in that perpetual minority which requires so much self-approval to support it.

Thus he was a man of divided tastes and of thwarted ambition; a man whose happiness, even in early life, lay behind. His mind had set early and bore for ever the stamp of first impressions. In his happiest moods he looked not forwards but backwards—to the garden where he had played as a child, to the blue hills of Shropshire and to all those landscapes which he had seen when hope was still his, and peace brooded upon him and he looked up from his painting or his book and saw the fields and woods as if they were the outward expression of his own inner quietude. It is to the books that he read then that he returns—to Rousseau and to Burke and to the *Letters of Junius*. The impression that they made upon his youthful imagination was never effaced and scarcely overlaid; for after youth was over he ceased to read for pleasure, and youth and the pure and intense pleasures of youth were soon left behind.

Naturally, given his susceptibility to the charms of the other sex, he married; and naturally, given his consciousness of his own "misshapen form made to be mocked", he married unhappily. Miss Sarah Stoddart pleased him when he met her at the Lambs by the commonsense with which she found the kettle and boiled it when Mary absent-mindedly delayed. But of domestic talents she had none. Her little income was insufficient to meet the burden of married life, and Hazlitt soon found that instead of spending eight years in writing eight pages he must turn journalist and write articles upon politics and plays and pictures and books of the right length, at the right moment. Soon the mantelpiece of the old house at York Street where Milton had lived was scribbled over with ideas for essays. As the habit proves, the house was not a tidy house, nor did geniality and comfort excuse the lack of order. The Hazlitts were to be found eating breakfast at two in the afternoon, without a fire in the grate or a curtain to the window. A valiant walker and a clear-sighted woman, Mrs. Hazlitt had no delusions about her husband. He was not faithful to her, and she faced the fact with admirable commonsense. But "he said that I had always despised him and his abilities", she noted in her diary, and that was carrying commonsense too far. The prosaic marriage came lamely to an end. Free at last from the encumbrance of home and husband, Sarah Hazlitt pulled on her boots and set off on a walking tour through Scotland, while Hazlitt, incapable of attachment or comfort, wandered from inn to inn, suffered tortures of humiliation and disillusionment, but, as he drank cup after cup of very strong tea and made love to the innkeeper's daughter, he wrote those essays that are of course among the very best that we have.

That they are not quite the best—that they do not haunt the mind and remain entire in the memory as the essays of Montaigne or Lamb haunt the mind—is also true. He seldom reaches the perfection of these great writers or their unity. Perhaps it is the nature of these short pieces that they need unity and a mind at harmony with itself. A little jar there makes the whole composition tremble. The essays of Montaigne, Lamb, even Addison, have the reticence which springs from composure, for with all their familiarity they never tell us what they wish to keep hidden. But with Hazlitt it is different. There is always something divided and discordant even in his finest essays, as if two minds were at work who never succeed save for a few moments in making a match of it. In the first place there is the mind of the inquiring boy who wishes to be satisfied of the reason of things—the mind of the thinker. It is the thinker for the most part who is allowed the choice of the subject. He chooses some abstract idea, like Envy, or Egotism, or Reason and Imagination. He treats it with energy and independence. He explores its ramifications and scales its narrow paths as if it were a mountain road and the ascent both difficult and inspiring. Compared with this athletic progress, Lamb's seems the flight of a butterfly cruising capriciously among the flowers and perching for a second incongruously here upon a barn, there upon a wheelbarrow. But every sentence in Hazlitt carries us forward. He has his end in view and, unless some accident intervenes, he strides towards it in that "pure conversational prose style" which, as he points out, is so much more difficult to practise than fine writing.

There can be no question that Hazlitt the thinker is an admirable companion. He is strong and fearless; he knows his mind and he speaks his mind forcibly yet brilliantly too, for the readers of newspapers are a dull-eyed race who must be dazzled in order to make them see. But besides Hazlitt the thinker there is Hazlitt the artist. There is the sensuous and emotional man, with his feeling for colour and touch, with his passion for prize-fighting and Sarah Walker, with his sensibility to all those emotions which disturb the reason and make it often seem futile enough to spend one's time slicing things up finer and finer with the intellect when the body of the world is so firm and so warm and demands so imperatively to be pressed to the heart. To know the reason of things is a poor substitute for being able to feel them. And Hazlitt felt with the intensity of a poet. The most abstract of his essays will suddenly glow red-hot or white-hot if something reminds him of his past. He will drop his fine analytic pen and paint a phrase or two with a full brush brilliantly and beautifully if some landscape stirs his imagination or some book brings back the hour when he first read it. The famous passages about reading *Love for Love* and drinking coffee from a silver pot, and reading *La Nouvelle Héloïse* and eating a cold chicken are known to all, and yet how oddly they often break into the context, how violently we are switched from reason to rhapsody—how embarrassingly our austere thinker falls upon our shoulders and demands our sympathy! It is this disparity and the sense of two forces in conflict that trouble the serenity and cause the inconclusiveness of some of Hazlitt's finest essays. They set out to give us a proof and they end by giving us a picture. We are about to plant our feet upon the solid rock of Q.E.D., and behold the rock turns to quagmire and we are knee-deep in mud and water and flowers. "Faces pale as the primrose with hyacinthine locks" are in our eyes; the woods of Tuderly breathe their mystic voices in our ears. Then suddenly we are recalled, and the thinker, austere, muscular, and sardonic, leads us on to analyse, to dissect, and to condemn.

Thus if we compare Hazlitt with the other great masters in his line it is easy to see where his limitations lie. His range is narrow and his sympathies few if intense. He does not open the doors wide upon all experience like Montaigne, rejecting nothing, tolerating everything, and watching the play of the soul with irony and detachment. On the contrary, his mind shut hard with egotistic tenacity upon his first impressions and froze them to unalterable convictions. Nor was it for him to make play, like Lamb, with the figures of his friends, creating them afresh in fantastic flights of imagination and reverie. His characters are seen with the same quick sidelong glance full of shrewdness and suspicion which he darted upon people in the flesh. He does not use the essayist's licence to circle and meander. He is tethered by his egotism and by his convictions to one time and one place and one being. We never forget that this is England in the early days of the nineteenth century; indeed, we feel ourselves in the Southampton Buildings or in the inn parlour that looks over the downs and on to the high road at Winterslow. He has an extraordinary power of making us contemporary with himself. But as we read on through the many volumes which he filled with so much energy and yet with so little love of his task, the comparison with the other essayists drops from us. These are not essays, it seems, independent and self-sufficient, but fragments broken off from some larger book—some searching enquiry into the reason for human actions or into the nature of human institutions. It is only accident that has cut them short, and only deference to the public taste that has decked them out with gaudy images and bright colours. The phrase which occurs in one form or another so frequently and indicates the structure which if he were free he would follow —"I will here try to go more at large into the subject and then give such instances and illustrations of it as occur to me"—could by no possibility occur in the *Essays of Elia* or *Sir Roger de Coverley*. He loves to grope among the curious depths of human psychology and to track down the reason of things. He excels in hunting out the obscure causes that lie behind some common saying or sensation, and the drawers of his mind are well stocked with illustrations and arguments. We can believe him when he says that for twenty years he had thought hard and suffered acutely. He is speaking of what he knows from experience when he exclaims, "How many ideas and trains of sentiment, long and deep and intense, often pass through the mind in only one day's thinking or reading!" Convictions are his life-blood; ideas have formed in him like stalactites, drop by drop, year by year. He has sharpened them in a thousand solitary walks; he has tested them in argument after argument, sitting in his corner, sardonically observant, over a late supper at the Southampton Inn. But he has not changed them. His mind is his own and it is made up.

Thus however threadbare the abstraction—*Hot and Cold*, or *Envy*, or *The Conduct of Life*, or *The Picturesque and the Ideal*—he has something solid to write about. He never lets his brain slacken or trusts to his great gift of picturesque phrasing to float him over a stretch of shallow thought. Even when it is plain from the savagery and contempt with which he attacks his task that he is out of the mood and only keeps his mind to the grindstone by strong tea and sheer force of will we still find him mordant and searching and acute. There is a stir and trouble, a vivacity and conflict in his essays as if the very contrariety of his gifts kept him on the stretch. He is always hating, loving, thinking, and suffering. He could never come to terms with authority or doff his own idiosyncrasy in deference to opinion. Thus chafed and goaded the level of his essays is extraordinarily high. Often dry, garish in their bright imagery, monotonous in the undeviating energy of their rhythm—for Hazlitt believed too implicitly in his own saying, "mediocrity, insipidity, want of character, is the great fault", to be an easy writer to read for long at a stretch—there is scarcely an essay without its stress of thought, its thrust of insight, its moment of penetration. His pages are full of fine sayings and unexpected turns and independence and originality. "All that is worth remembering of life is the poetry of it." "If the truth were known, the most disagreeable people are the most amiable." "You will hear more good things on the outside of a stage-coach from London to Oxford, than if you were to pass a twelve-month with the undergraduates or heads of colleges of that famous University." We are constantly plucked at by sayings that we would like to put by to examine later.

But besides the volumes of Hazlitt's essays there are the volumes of Hazlitt's criticism. In one way or another, either as lecturer or reviewer, Hazlitt strode through the greater part of English literature and delivered his opinion of the majority of famous books. His criticism has the rapidity and the daring, if it has also the looseness and the roughness, which arise from the circumstances in which it was written. He must cover a great deal of ground, make his points clear to an audience not of readers but of listeners, and has time only to point to the tallest towers and the brightest pinnacles in the landscape. But even in his most perfunctory criticism of books we feel that faculty for seizing on the important and indicating the main outline which learned critics often lose and timid critics never acquire. He is one of those rare critics who have thought so much that they can dispense with reading. It matters very little that Hazlitt had read only one poem by Donne; that he found Shakespeare's sonnets unintelligible; that he never read a book through after he was thirty; that he came indeed to dislike reading altogether. What he had read he had read with fervour. And since in his view it was the duty of a critic to "reflect the colours, the light and shade, the soul and body of a work", appetite, gusto, enjoyment were far more important than analytic subtlety or prolonged and extensive study. To communicate his own fervour was his aim. Thus he first cuts out with vigorous and direct strokes the figure of one author and contrasts it with another, and next builds up with the freest use of imagery and colour the brilliant ghost that the book has left glimmering in his mind. The poem is re-created in glowing phrases—"A rich distilled perfume emanates from it like the breath of genius; a golden cloud envelops it; a honeyed paste of poetic diction encrusts it, like the candied coat of the auricula". But since the analyst in Hazlitt is never far from the surface, this painter's imagery is kept in check by a nervous sense of the hard and lasting in literature, of what a book means and where it should be placed, which models his enthusiasm and gives it angle and outline. He singles out the peculiar quality of his author and stamps it vigorously. There is the "deep, internal, sustained sentiment" of Chaucer; "Crabbe is the only poet who has attempted and succeeded in the *still life* of tragedy". There is nothing flabby, weak, or merely ornamental in his criticism of Scott —sense and enthusiasm run hand in hand. And if such criticism is the reverse of final, if it is initiatory and inspiring rather than conclusive and complete, there is something to be said for the critic who starts the reader on a journey and fires him with a phrase to shoot off on adventures of his own. If one needs an incentive to read Burke, what is better than "Burke's style was forked and playful like the lightning, crested like the serpent"? Or again, should one be trembling on the brink of a dusty folio, the following passage is enough to plunge one in midstream:

It is delightful to repose on the wisdom of the ancients; to have some great name at hand, besides one's own initials always staring one in the face; to travel out of one's self into the Chaldee, Hebrew, and Egyptian characters; to have the palm-trees waving mystically in the margin of the page, and the camels moving slowly on in the distance of three thousand years. In that dry desert of learning, we gather strength and patience, and a strange and insatiable thirst of knowledge. The ruined monuments of antiquity are also there, and the fragments of buried cities (under which the adder lurks) and cool springs, and green sunny spots, and the whirlwind and the lion's roar, and the shadow of angelic wings.

Needless to say that is not criticism. It is sitting in an arm-chair and gazing into the fire, and building up image after image of what one has seen in a book. It is loving and taking the liberties of a lover. It is being Hazlitt.

But it is likely that Hazlitt will survive not in his lectures, nor in his travels, nor in his *Life of Napoleon*, nor in his *Conversations of Northcote*, full as they are of energy and integrity, of broken and fitful splendour and shadowed with the shape of some vast unwritten book that looms on the horizon. He will live in a volume of essays in which is distilled all those powers that are dissipated and distracted elsewhere, where the parts of his complex and tortured spirit come together in a truce of amity and concord. Perhaps a fine day was needed, or a game of fives or a long walk in the country, to bring about this consummation. The body has a large share in everything that Hazlitt writes. Then a mood of intense and spontaneous reverie came over him; he soared into what Patmore called "a calm so pure and serene that one did not like to interrupt it". His brain worked smoothly and swiftly and without consciousness of its own operations; the pages dropped without an erasure from his pen. Then his mind ranged in a rhapsody of well-being over books and love, over the past and its beauty, the present and its comfort, and the future that would bring a partridge hot from the oven or a dish of sausages sizzling in the pan.

I look out of my window and see that a shower has just fallen: the fields look green after it, and a rosy cloud hangs over the brow of the hill; a lily expands its petals in the moisture, dressed in its lovely green and white; a shepherd-boy has just brought some pieces of turf with daisies and grass for his young mistress to make a bed for her skylark, not doomed to dip his wings in the dappled dawn— my cloudy thoughts draw off, the storm of angry politics has blown over—Mr. Blackwood, I am yours—Mr. Croker, my service to you— Mr. T. Moore, I am alive and well.

There is then no division, no discord, no bitterness. The different faculties work in harmony and unity. Sentence follows sentence with the healthy ring and chime of a blacksmith's hammer on the anvil; the words glow and the sparks fly; gently they fade and the essay is over. And as his writing had such passages of inspired description, so, too, his life had its seasons of intense enjoyment. When he lay dying a hundred years ago in a lodging in Soho his voice rang out with the old pugnacity and conviction: "Well, I have had a happy life". One has only to read him to believe it.

Geraldine and Jane

GERALDINE JEWSBURY would certainly not have expected anybody at this time of day to bother themselves about her novels. If she had caught one pulling them down from the shelf in some library she would have expostulated. "They're such nonsense, my dear", she would have said. And then one likes to fancy that she would have burst out in that irresponsible, unconventional way of hers against libraries and literature and love and life and all the rest of it with a "Damn it all!" or a "Confound it!" for Geraldine was fond of swearing.

The odd thing about Geraldine Jewsbury, indeed, was the way in which she combined oaths and endearments, sense and effervescence, daring and gush: ". . . defenceless and tender on the one hand, and strong enough to cleave the very rocks on the other"—that is how Mrs. Ireland, her biographer, puts it; or again: "Intellectually she was a man, but the heart within her was as womanly as ever daughter of Eve could boast". Even to look at there was, it would seem, something incongruous, queer, provocative about her. She was very small and yet boyish; very ugly yet attractive. She dressed very well, wore her reddish hair in a net, and ear-rings made in the form of miniature parrots swung in her ears as she talked. There, in the only portrait we have of her, she sits reading, with her face half-turned away, defenceless and tender at the moment rather than cleaving the very rocks.

But what had happened to her before she sat at the photographer's table reading her book it is impossible to say. Until she was twenty-nine we know nothing of her except that she was born in the year 1812, was the daughter of a merchant, and lived in Manchester, or near it. In the first part of the nineteenth century a woman of twenty-nine was no longer young; she had lived her life or she had missed it. And though Geraldine, with her unconventional ways, was an exception, still it cannot be doubted that something very tremendous had happened in those dim years before we know her. Something had happened in Manchester. An obscure male figure looms in the background—a faithless but fascinating creature who had taught her that life is treacherous, life is hard, life is the very devil for a woman. A dark pool of experience had formed in the back of her mind into which she would dip for the consolation or for the instruction of others. "Oh! it is too frightful to talk about. For two years I lived only in short respites from this blackness of darkness", she exclaimed from time to time. There had been seasons "like dreary, calm November days when there is but one cloud, but that one covers the whole heaven". She had struggled, "but struggling is no use". She had read Cudworth through. She had written an essay upon materialism before giving way. For, though the prey to so many emotions, she was also oddly detached and speculative. She liked to puzzle her head with questions about "matter and spirit and the nature of life" even while her heart was bleeding. Upstairs there was a box full of extracts, abstracts, and conclusions.

Yet what conclusion could a woman come to? Did anything avail a woman when love had deserted her, when her lover had played her false? No. It was useless to struggle; one had better let the wave engulf one, the cloud close over one's head. So she meditated, lying often on a sofa with a piece of knitting in her hands and a green shade over her eyes. For she suffered from a variety of ailments—sore eyes, colds, nameless exhaustion; and Greenheys, the suburb outside Manchester, where she kept house for her brother, was very damp. "Dirty, half-melted snow and fog, a swampy meadow, set off by a creeping cold damp"—that was the view from her window. Often she could hardly drag herself across the room. And then there were incessant interruptions: somebody had come unexpectedly for dinner; she had to jump up and run into the kitchen and cook a fowl with her own hands. That done, she would put on her green shade and peer at her book again, for she was a great reader. She read metaphysics, she read travels, she read old books and new books—and especially the wonderful books of Mr. Carlyle.

Early in the year 1841 she came to London and secured an introduction to the great man, whose works she so much admired. She met Mrs. Carlyle. They must have become intimate with great rapidity. In a few weeks Mrs. Carlyle was "dearest Jane". They must have discussed everything. They must have talked about life and the past and the present, and certain "individuals" who were sentimentally interested or were not sentimentally interested in Geraldine. Mrs. Carlyle, so metropolitan, so brilliant, so deeply versed in life and scornful of its humbugs, must have captivated the young woman from Manchester completely, for directly

Geraldine returned to Manchester she began writing long
letters to Jane which echo and continue the intimate conversations of Cheyne Row. "A man who has had *le plus
grand succès* among women, and who was the most passionate and poetically refined lover in his manners and conversation you would wish to find, once said to me . . ."
So she would begin. Or she would reflect:

It may be that we women are made as we are in order that they
may in some sort fertilise the world. We shall go on loving, they
[the men] will go on struggling and toiling, and we are all alike
mercifully allowed to die—after a while. I don't know whether you
will agree to this, and I cannot see to argue, for my eyes are very
bad and painful.

Probably Jane agreed to very little of all this. For Jane
was eleven years the elder. Jane was not given to abstract
reflections upon the nature of life. Jane was the most caustic, the most concrete, the most clear-sighted of women.
But it is perhaps worth noting that when she first fell in
with Geraldine she was beginning to feel those premonitions of jealousy, that uneasy sense that old relationships
had shifted and that new ones were forming themselves,
which had come to pass with the establishment of her husband's fame. No doubt, in the course of those long talks in
Cheyne Row, Geraldine had received certain confidences,
heard certain complaints, and drawn certain conclusions.
For besides being a mass of emotion and sensibility, Geraldine was a clever, witty woman who thought for herself
and hated what she called "respectability" as much as Mrs.
Carlyle hated what she called "humbug". In addition, Geraldine had from the first the strangest feelings about Mrs.
Carlyle. She felt "vague undefined yearnings to be yours in

some way". "You will let me be yours and think of me as such, will you not?" she urged again and again. "I think of you as Catholics think of their saints", she said: ". . . you will laugh, but I feel towards you much more like a lover than a female friend!" No doubt Mrs. Carlyle did laugh, but also she could scarcely fail to be touched by the little creature's adoration.

Thus when Carlyle himself early in 1843 suggested unexpectedly that they should ask Geraldine to stay with them, Mrs. Carlyle, after debating the question with her usual candour, agreed. She reflected that a little of Geraldine would be "very enlivening", but, on the other hand, much of Geraldine would be very exhausting. Geraldine dropped hot tears on to one's hands; she watched one; she fussed one; she was always in a state of emotion. Then "with all her good and great qualities" Geraldine had in her "a born spirit of intrigue" which might make mischief between husband and wife, though not in the usual way, for, Mrs. Carlyle reflected, her husband "had the habit" of preferring her to other women, "and habits are much stronger in him than passions". On the other hand, she herself was getting lazy intellectually; Geraldine loved talk and clever talk; with all her aspirations and enthusiasms it would be a kindness to let the young woman marooned in Manchester come to Chelsea; and so she came.

She came on the 1st or 2nd of February, and she stayed till the Saturday, the 11th of March. Such were visits in the year 1843. And the house was very small, and the servant was inefficient. Geraldine was always there. All the morning she scribbled letters. All the afternoon she lay fast asleep on the sofa in the drawing-room. She dressed herself

in a low-necked dress to receive visitors on Sunday. She
talked too much. As for her reputed intellect, "she is sharp
as a meat axe, but as narrow". She flattered. She wheedled.
She was insincere. She flirted. She swore. Nothing would
make her go. The charges against her rose in a crescendo
of irritation. Mrs. Carlyle almost had to turn her out of the
house. At last they parted; and Geraldine, as she got into
the cab, was in floods of tears, but Mrs. Carlyle's eyes were
dry. Indeed, she was immensely relieved to see the last of
her visitor. Yet when Geraldine had driven off and she
found herself alone she was not altogether easy in her mind.
She knew that her behaviour to a guest whom she herself
had invited had been far from perfect. She had been "cold,
cross, ironical, disobliging". Above all, she was angry with
herself for having taken Geraldine for a *confidante*.
"Heaven grant that the consequences may be only *boring*
—not *fatal*", she wrote. But it is clear that she was very
much out of temper; and with herself as much as with
Geraldine.

Geraldine, returned to Manchester, was well aware that
something was wrong. Estrangement and silence fell between them. People repeated malicious stories which she
half believed. But Geraldine was the least vindictive of
women—"very noble in her quarrels", as Mrs. Carlyle herself admitted—and, if foolish and sentimental, neither conceited nor proud. Above all, her love for Jane was sincere.
Soon she was writing to Mrs. Carlyle again "with an assi-
duity and disinterestedness that verge on the superhuman",
as Jane commented with a little exasperation. She was
worrying about Jane's health and saying that she did not
want witty letters, but only dull letters telling the truth

about Jane's state. For—it may have been one of those things that made her so trying as a visitor—Geraldine had not stayed for four weeks in Cheyne Row without coming to conclusions which it is not likely that she kept entirely to herself. "You have no one who has any sort of consideration for you", she wrote. "You have had patience and endurance till I am sick of the virtues, and what have they done for you? Half-killed you." "Carlyle", she burst out, "is much too grand for everyday life. A sphinx does not fit in comfortably to our parlour life arrangements." But she could do nothing. "The more one loves, the more helpless one feels", she moralised. She could only watch from Manchester the bright kaleidoscope of her friend's existence and compare it with her own prosaic life, all made up of little odds and ends; but somehow, obscure though her own life was, she no longer envied Jane the brilliance of her lot.

So they might have gone on corresponding in a desultory way at a distance—and "I am tired to death of writing letters into space", Geraldine exclaimed; "one only writes after a long separation, to oneself, instead of one's friend" —had it not been for the Mudies. The Mudies and Mudie-ism, as Geraldine called it, played a vast, if almost unrecorded, part in the obscure lives of Victorian gentlewomen. In this case the Mudies were two girls, Elizabeth and Juliet: "flary, staring, and conceited, stolid-looking girls", Carlyle called them, the daughters of a Dundee schoolmaster, a respectable man who had written books on natural history and died, leaving a foolish widow and little or no provision for his family. Somehow the Mudies arrived in Cheyne Row inconveniently, if one may hazard a guess, just as dinner was on the table. But the Victorian lady never minded that—she put herself to any inconvenience to help the Mudies. The question at once presented itself to Mrs. Carlyle, what could be done for them? Who knew of a place? who had influence with a rich man? Geraldine flashed into her mind. Geraldine was always wishing she could be of use. Geraldine might fairly be asked if there were situations to be had for the Mudies in Manchester. Geraldine acted with a promptitude that was much to her credit. She "placed" Juliet at once. Soon she had heard of another place for Elizabeth. Mrs. Carlyle, who was in the Isle of Wight, at once procured stays, gown, and petticoat for Elizabeth, came up to London, took Elizabeth all the way across London to Euston Square at half past seven in the evening, put her in charge of a benevolent-looking, fat old man, saw that a letter to Geraldine was pinned to her stays, and returned home, exhausted, triumphant, yet, as happens often with the devotees of Mudieism, a prey to secret misgivings. Would the Mudies be happy? Would they thank her for what she had done? A few days later the inevitable bugs appeared in Cheyne Row, and were ascribed, with or without reason, to Elizabeth's shawl. What was far worse, Elizabeth herself appeared four months later, having proved herself "wholly inapplicable to any practical purpose", having "sewed a *black* apron with *white* thread", and, on being mildly scolded, having "thrown herself on the kitchen floor and kicked and screamed". "Of course, her immediate dismissal is the result." Elizabeth vanished—to sew more black aprons with white thread, to kick and scream and be dismissed—who knows what happened eventually to poor Elizabeth Mudie? She disappears from the world altogether, swallowed up in the dark shades of her sisterhood. Juliet, however, remained. Geraldine made Juliet her charge. She superintended and advised. The first place was unsatisfactory. Geraldine engaged herself to find another. She went off and sat in the hall of a "very stiff old lady" who wanted a maid. The very stiff old lady said she would want Juliet to clearstarch collars, to iron cuffs, and to wash and iron petticoats. Juliet's heart failed her. All this clear-starching and ironing, she exclaimed, were beyond her. Off went Geraldine again, late in the evening, and saw the old lady's daughter. It was arranged that the petticoats should be "put out" and only the collars and frills left for Juliet to iron. Off went Geraldine and arranged with her own milliner to give her lessons in quilling and trimming. And Mrs. Carlyle wrote kindly to Juliet and sent her a packet. So it went on with more places and more bothers, and more old ladies, and more interviews till Juliet wrote a novel, which a gentleman praised very highly, and Juliet told Miss Jewsbury that she was annoyed by another gentleman who followed her home from church; but still she was a very nice girl, and everybody spoke well of her until the year 1849, when suddenly, without any reason given, silence descends upon the last of the Mudies. It covers, one cannot doubt, another failure. The novel, the stiff old lady, the gentleman, the caps, the petticoats, the clear-starching—what was the cause of her downfall? Nothing is known. "The wretched stalking blockheads", wrote Carlyle, "stalked fatefully, in spite of all that could be done and said, steadily downwards towards perdition and sank altogether out of view." For all her endeavours Mrs. Carlyle had to admit that Mudieism was always a failure.

But Mudieism had unexpected results. Mudieism brought Jane and Geraldine together again. Jane could not deny that "the fluff of feathers" whom she had served up, as her way was, in so many a scornful phrase for Carlyle's amusement, had "taken up the matter with an enthusiasm even surpassing my own". She had grit in her as well as fluff. Thus when Geraldine sent her the manuscript of her first novel, *Zoe*, Mrs. Carlyle bestirred herself to find a publisher ("for", she wrote, "what is to become of her when she is old without ties, without purposes?") and with surprising success. Chapman & Hall at once agreed to publish the book, which, their reader reported, "had taken hold of him with a grasp of iron". The book had been long on the way. Mrs. Carlyle herself had been consulted at various stages of its career. She had read the first sketch "with a feeling little short of terror! So much power of genius rushing so recklessly into unknown space." But she had also been deeply impressed.

Geraldine in particular shows herself here a far more profound and daring speculator than ever I had fancied her. I do not believe there is a woman alive at the present day, not even Georges Sand herself, that could have written some of the best passages in this book . . . but they must not publish it—decency forbids!

There was, Mrs. Carlyle complained, an indecency or "want of reserve in the spiritual department", which no respectable public would stand. Presumably Geraldine consented to make alterations, though she confessed that she "had no vocation for propriety as such"; the book was rewritten, and it appeared at last in February 1845. The usual buzz and conflict of opinion at once arose. Some were enthusiastic, others were shocked. The "old and young

roués of the Reform Club almost go off into hysterics over
—its *indecency*". The publisher was a little alarmed; but
the scandal helped the sale, and Geraldine became a lioness.

And now, of course, as one turns the pages of the three
little yellowish volumes, one wonders what reason there
was for approval or disapproval, what spasm of indignation
or admiration scored that pencil mark, what mysterious
emotion pressed violets, now black as ink, between the
pages of the love scenes. Chapter after chapter glides ami-
ably, fluently past. In a kind of haze we catch glimpses of
an illegitimate girl called Zoe; of an enigmatic Roman
Catholic priest called Everhard; of a castle in the country;
of ladies lying on sky-blue sofas; of gentlemen reading
aloud; of girls embroidering hearts in silk. There is a con-
flagration. There is an embrace in a wood. There is incessant conversation. There is a moment of terrific emotion
when the priest exclaims, "Would that I had never been
born!" and proceeds to sweep a letter from the Pope asking
him to edit a translation of the principal works of the
Fathers of the first four centuries and a parcel containing
a gold chain from the University of Göttingen into a
drawer because Zoe has shaken his faith. But what indecency there was pungent enough to shock the roués of the
Reform Club, what genius there was brilliant enough to
impress the shrewd intellect of Mrs. Carlyle, it is impossible to guess. Colours that were fresh as roses eighty years
ago have faded to a feeble pink; nothing remains of all
those scents and savours but a faint perfume of faded violets, of stale hair-oil, we know not which. What miracles,
we exclaim, are within the power of a few years to accom-
plish! But even as we exclaim, we see, far away, a trace

perhaps of what they meant. The passion, in so far as it issues from the lips of living people, is completely spent. The Zoes, the Clothildes, the Everhards moulder on their perches; but, nevertheless, there is somebody in the room with them; an irresponsible spirit, a daring and agile woman, if one considers that she is cumbered with crinoline and stays; an absurd sentimental creature, languishing, expatiating, but for all that still strangely alive. We catch a sentence now and then rapped out boldly, a thought subtly conceived. "How much better to do right without religion!" "Oh! if they really believed all they preach, how would any priest or preacher be able to sleep in his bed!" "Weakness is the only state for which there is no hope." "To love rightly is the highest morality of which mankind is capable." Then how she hated the "compacted, plausible theories of men"! And what is life? For what end was it given us? Such questions, such convictions, still hurtle past the heads of the stuffed figures mouldering on their perches. They are dead, but Geraldine Jewsbury herself still survives, independent, courageous, absurd, writing page after page without stopping to correct, and coming out with her views upon love, morality, religion, and the relations of the sexes, whoever may be within hearing, with a cigar between her lips.

Some time before the publication of *Zoe*, Mrs. Carlyle had forgotten, or overcome, her irritation with Geraldine, partly because she had worked so zealously in the cause of the Mudies, partly also because by Geraldine's painstaking she was "almost over-persuaded back into my old illusion that she has some sort of strange, passionate . . . incomprehensible *attraction* towards me". Not only was she

211

drawn back into correspondence—after all her vows to the contrary she again stayed under the same roof with Geraldine, at Seaforth House near Liverpool, in July 1844. Not many days had passed before Mrs. Carlyle's "illusion" about the strength of Geraldine's affection for her proved to be no illusion but a monstrous fact. One morning there was some slight tiff between them: Geraldine sulked all day; at night Geraldine came to Mrs. Carlyle's bedroom and made a scene which was "a revelation to me, not only of Geraldine, but of human nature! Such mad, lover-like jealousy on the part of one woman towards another it had never entered into my heart to conceive." Mrs. Carlyle was angry and outraged and contemptuous. She saved up a full account of the scene to entertain her husband with. A few days later she turned upon Geraldine in public and sent the whole company into fits of laughter by saying: "I wondered she should expect me to behave decently to her after she had for a whole evening been making love before my very face to *another man!*" The trouncing must have been severe, the humiliation painful. But Geraldine was incorrigible. A year later she was again sulking and raging and declaring that she had a right to rage because "she loves me better than all the rest of the world"; and Mrs. Carlyle was getting up and saying, "Geraldine, until you can behave like a gentlewoman . . ." and leaving the room. And again there were tears and apologies and promises to reform.

Yet though Mrs. Carlyle scolded and jeered, though they were estranged, and though for a time they ceased to write to each other, still they always came together again. Geraldine, it is abundantly clear, felt that Jane was in every way wiser, better, stronger than she was. She depended on Jane. She needed Jane to keep her out of scrapes; for Jane never got into scrapes herself. But though Jane was so much wiser and cleverer than Geraldine, there were times when the foolish and irresponsible one of the two became the counsellor. Why, she asked, waste your time in mending old clothes? Why not work at something that will really employ your energies? Write, she advised her. For Jane, who was so profound, so far-seeing, could, Geraldine was convinced, write something that would help women in "their very complicated duties and difficulties". She owed a duty to her sex. But, the bold woman proceeded, "do not go to Mr. Carlyle for sympathy, do not let him dash you with cold water. You must respect your own work, and your own motives"—a piece of advice that Jane, who was afraid to accept the dedication of Geraldine's new novel *The Half Sisters*, lest Mr. Carlyle might object, would have done well to follow. The little creature was in some ways the bolder and the more independent of the two.

She had, morever, a quality that Jane with all her brilliancy lacked—an element of poetry, a trace of the speculative imagination. She browsed upon old books and copied out romantic passages about the palm trees and cinnamon of Arabia and sent them to lie, incongruously enough, upon the breakfast table in Cheyne Row. Jane's genius, of course, was the very opposite; it was positive, direct, and practical. Her imagination concentrated itself upon people. Her letters owe their incomparable brilliancy to the hawk-like swoop and descent of her mind upon facts. Nothing escapes her. She sees through clear water down to the rocks at the bottom. But the intangible eluded her; she dismissed the poetry of Keats with a sneer; something of the narrowness and something of the prudery of a Scottish country doctor's daughter clung to her. Though infinitely the less masterly, Geraldine was sometimes the broader minded.

Such sympathies and antipathies bound the two women together with an elasticity that made for permanence. The tie between them could stretch and stretch indefinitely without breaking. Jane knew the extent of Geraldine's folly; Geraldine had felt the full lash of Jane's tongue. They had learnt to tolerate each other. Naturally, they quarrelled again; but their quarrels were different now; they were quarrels that were bound to be made up. And when after her brother's marriage in 1854 Geraldine moved to London, it was to be near Mrs. Carlyle at Mrs. Carlyle's own wish. The woman who in 1843 would never be a friend of hers again was now the most intimate friend she had in the world. She was to lodge two streets off; and perhaps two streets off was the right space to put between them. The emotional friendship was full of misunderstandings at a distance; it was intolerably exacting under the same roof. But when they lived round the corner their relationship broadened and simplified; it became a natural intercourse whose ruffles and whose calms were based upon the depths of intimacy. They went about together. They went to hear *The Messiah;* and, characteristically, Geraldine wept at the beauty of the music and Jane had much ado to prevent herself from shaking Geraldine for crying and from crying herself at the ugliness of the chorus women. They went to Norwood for a jaunt, and Geraldine left a silk handkerchief and an aluminium brooch ("a love token from Mr. Barlow") in the hotel and a new silk parasol in the waiting-room. Also Jane noted with sardonic satisfaction that Geraldine, in an attempt at economy, bought two second-class tickets, while the cost of a return ticket first class was precisely the same.

Meanwhile Geraldine lay on the floor and generalised and speculated and tried to formulate some theory of life from her own tumultuous experience. "How loathsome" (her language was always apt to be strong—she knew that she "sinned against Jane's notions of good taste" very often), how loathsome the position of women was in many ways! How she herself had been crippled and stunted! How her blood boiled in her at the power that men had over women! She would like to kick certain gentlemen— "the lying hypocritical beggars! Well, it's no good swearing—only, I am angry and it eases my mind."

And then her thoughts turned to Jane and herself and to the brilliant gifts—at any rate, Jane had brilliant gifts —which had borne so little visible result. Nevertheless, except when she was ill,

I do not think that either you or I are to be called failures. We are indications of a development of womanhood which as yet is not recognised. It has, so far, no ready-made channels to run in, but still we have looked and tried, and found that the present rules for women will not hold us—that something better and stronger is needed. . . . There are women to come after us, who will approach nearer the fullness of the measure of the stature of a woman's nature. I regard myself as a mere faint indication, a rudiment of the idea, of certain higher qualities and possibilities that lie in women, and all the eccentricities and mistakes and miseries and absurdities I have made are only the consequences of an imperfect formation, an immature growth.

So she theorised, so she speculated; and Mrs. Carlyle listened, and laughed, and contradicted no doubt, but with more of sympathy than of derision: she could have wished that Geraldine were more precise; she could have wished her to moderate her language. Carlyle might come in at any moment; and if there was one creature that Carlyle hated, it was a strong-minded woman of the George Sand species. Yet she could not deny that there was an element of truth in what Geraldine said; she had always thought that Geraldine "was born to spoil a horn or make a spoon". Geraldine was no fool in spite of appearances.

But what Geraldine thought and said; how she spent her mornings; what she did in the long evenings of the London winter—all, in fact, that constituted her life at Markham Square—is but slightly and doubtfully known to us. For, fittingly enough, the bright light of Jane extinguished the paler and more flickering fire of Geraldine. She had no need to write to Jane any more. She was in and out of the house—now writing a letter for Jane because Jane's fingers were swollen, now taking a letter to the post and forgetting, like the scatter-brained romantic creature she was, to post it. A crooning domestic sound like the purring of a kitten or the humming of a tea-kettle seems to rise, as we turn the pages of Mrs. Carlyle's letters, from the intercourse of the two incompatible but deeply attached women. So the years passed. At length, on Saturday, 21st April 1866, Geraldine was to help Jane with a tea-party. Mr. Carlyle was in Scotland, and Mrs. Carlyle hoped to get through some necessary civilities to admirers in his absence. Geraldine was actually dressing for the occasion when Mr. Froude appeared suddenly at her house. He had just had a message from Cheyne Row to say that "something had happened to Mrs. Carlyle". Geraldine flung on her cloak.

They hastened together to St. George's Hospital. There, writes Froude, they saw Mrs. Carlyle beautifully dressed as usual

as if she had sat upon the bed after leaving the brougham, and had fallen back upon it asleep. . . . The brilliant mockery, the sad softness with which the mockery alternated, both were alike gone. The features lay composed in a stern majestic calm. . . . [Geraldine] could not speak.

Nor indeed can we break that silence. It deepened. It became complete. Soon after Jane's death she went to live at Sevenoaks. She lived there alone for twenty-two years. It is said that she lost her vivacity. She wrote no more books. Cancer attacked her and she suffered much. On her deathbed she began tearing up Jane's letters, as Jane had wished, and she had destroyed all but one before she died. Thus, just as her life began in obscurity, so it ended in obscurity. We know her well only for a few years in the middle. But let us not be too sanguine about "knowing her well". Intimacy is a difficult art, as Geraldine herself reminds us.

Oh, my dear [she wrote to Mrs. Carlyle], if you and I are drowned, or die, what would become of us if any superior person were to go and write our "life and errors"? What a precious mess a "truthful person" would go and make of us, and how very different to what we really are or were!

The echo of her mockery, ungrammatical, colloquial, but as usual with the ring of truth in it, reaches us from where she lies in Lady Morgan's vault in the Brompton cemetery.

"Aurora Leigh"

BY ONE of those ironies of fashion that might have amused the Brownings themselves, it seems likely that they are now far better known in the flesh than they have ever been in the spirit. Passionate lovers, in curls and side whiskers, oppressed, defiant, eloping—in this guise thousands of people must know and love the Brownings who have never read a line of their poetry. They have become two of the most conspicuous figures in that bright and animated company of authors who, thanks to our modern habit of writing memoirs and printing letters and sitting to be photographed, live in the flesh, not merely as of old in the word; are known by their hats, not merely by their poems. What damage the art of photography has inflicted upon the art of literature has yet to be reckoned. How far we are going to read a poet when we can read about a poet is a problem to lay before biographers. Meanwhile, nobody can deny the power of the Brownings to excite our sympathy and rouse our interest. "Lady Geraldine's Courtship" is glanced at perhaps by two professors in American universities once a year; but we all know how Miss Barrett lay on her sofa; how she escaped from the dark house in Wimpole Street one September morning; how she met health and happiness, freedom, and Robert Browning in the church round the corner.

But fate has not been kind to Mrs. Browning as a writer.

Nobody reads her, nobody discusses her, nobody troubles to put her in her place. One has only to compare her reputation with Christina Rossetti's to trace her decline. Christina Rossetti mounts irresistibly to the first place among English women poets. Elizabeth, so much more loudly applauded during her lifetime, falls farther and farther behind. The primers dismiss her with contumely. Her importance, they say, "has now become merely historical. Neither education nor association with her husband ever succeeded in teaching her the value of words and a sense of form." In short, the only place in the mansion of literature that is assigned her is downstairs in the servants' quarters, where, in company with Mrs. Hemans, Eliza Cook, Jean Ingelow, Alexander Smith, Edwin Arnold, and Robert Montgomery she bangs the crockery about and eats vast handfuls of peas on the point of her knife.

If, therefore, we take *Aurora Leigh* from the shelf it is not so much in order to read it as to muse with kindly condescension over this token of bygone fashion, as we toy with the fringes of our grandmothers' mantles and muse over the alabaster models of the Taj Mahal which once adorned their drawing-room tables. But to the Victorians, undoubtedly, the book was very dear. Thirteen editions of *Aurora Leigh* had been demanded by the year 1873. And, to judge from the dedication, Mrs. Browning herself was not afraid to say that she set great store by it—"the most mature of my works," she calls it, "and the one into which my highest convictions upon Life and Art have entered". Her letters show that she had had the book in mind for many years. She was brooding over it when she first met Browning, and her intention with regard to it forms almost the first of those confidences about their work which the lovers delighted to share.

... my chief *intention* [she wrote] just now is the writing of a sort of novel-poem ... running into the midst of our conventions, and rushing into drawing-rooms and the like, "where angels fear to tread"; and so, meeting face to face and without mask the Humanity of the age, and speaking the truth of it out plainly. That is my intention.

But for reasons which later became clear, she hoarded her intention throughout the ten astonishing years of escape and happiness; and when at last the book appeared in 1856 she might well feel that she had poured into it the best that she had to give. Perhaps the hoarding and the saturation which resulted have something to do with the surprise that awaits us. At any rate we cannot read the first twenty pages of *Aurora Leigh* without becoming aware that the Ancient Mariner who lingers, for unknown reasons, at the porch of one book and not of another has us by the hand, and makes us listen like a three years child while Mrs. Browning pours out in nine volumes of blank verse the story of Aurora Leigh. Speed and energy, forthrightness and complete self-confidence—these are the qualities that hold us enthralled. Floated off our feet by them, we learn how Aurora was the child of an Italian mother "whose rare blue eyes were shut from seeing her when she was scarcely four years old". Her father was "an austere Englishman, Who, after a dry life-time spent at home In college-learning, law and parish talk, Was flooded with a passion unaware", but died, too, and the child was sent back to England to be brought up by an aunt. The aunt, of the well-known family of the Leighs, stood upon the hall step of her country house dressed in

black to welcome her. Her somewhat narrow forehead was
braided tight with brown hair pricked with grey; she had
a close, mild mouth; eyes of no colour; and cheeks like roses
pressed in books, "Kept more for ruth than pleasure,—if
past bloom, Past fading also". The lady had lived a quiet
life, exercising her Christian gifts upon knitting stockings
and stitching petticoats "because we are of one flesh, after
all, and need one flannel". At her hand Aurora suffered the
education that was thought proper for women. She learnt
a little French, a little algebra; the internal laws of the
Burmese empire; what navigable river joins itself to Lara;
what census of the year five was taken at Klagenfurt; also
how to draw nereids neatly draped, to spin glass, to stuff
birds, and model flowers in wax. For the Aunt liked a
woman to be womanly. Of an evening she did cross-stitch
and, owing to some mistake in her choice of silk, once em-
broidered a shepherdess with pink eyes. Under this torture
of women's education, the passionate Aurora exclaimed,
certain women have died; others pine; a few have, as Aurora had, "relations with the unseen", survive, and walk
demurely, and are civil to their cousins and listen to the
vicar and pour out tea. Aurora herself was blessed with a
little room. It was green papered, had a green carpet and
there were green curtains to the bed, as if to match the
insipid greenery of the English countryside. There she retired; there she read. "I had found the secret of a garret
room Piled high with cases in my father's name, Piled
high, packed large, where, creeping in and out . . . like
some small nimble mouse between the ribs of a mastodon"
she read and read. The mouse indeed (it is the way with
Mrs. Browning's mice) took wings and soared, for "It is

rather when We gloriously forget ourselves and plunge Soul-forward, headlong, into a book's profound, Impassioned for its beauty and salt of truth—'Tis then we get the right good from a book". And so she read and read, until her cousin Romney called to walk with her, or the painter, Vincent Carrington "whom men judge hardly as bee-bonneted Because he holds that paint a body well you paint a soul by implication", tapped on the window.

This hasty abstract of the first volume of *Aurora Leigh* does it of course no sort of justice; but having gulped down the original much as Aurora herself advises, soul-forward, headlong, we find ourselves in a state where some attempt at the ordering of our multitudinous impressions becomes imperative. The first of these impressions and the most pervasive is the sense of the writer's presence. Through the voice of Aurora the character, the circumstances, the idiosyncrasies of Elizabeth Barrett Browning ring in our ears. Mrs. Browning could no more conceal herself than she could control herself, a sign no doubt of imperfection in an artist, but a sign also that life has impinged upon art more than life should. Again and again in the pages we have read, Aurora the fictitious seems to be throwing light upon Elizabeth the actual. The idea of the poem, we must remember, came to her in the early forties when the connexion between a woman's art and a woman's life was unnaturally close, so that it is impossible for the most austere of critics not sometimes to touch the flesh when his eyes should be fixed upon the page. And as everybody knows, the life of Elizabeth Barrett was of a nature to affect the most authentic and individual of gifts. Her mother had died when she was a child; she had read profusely and privately; her favourite brother was drowned; her health broke down; she had been immured by the tyranny of her father in almost conventual seclusion in a bedroom in Wimpole Street. But instead of rehearsing the well-known facts, it is better to read in her own words her own account of the effect they had upon her.

I have lived only inwardly [she wrote] or with *sorrow*, for a strong emotion. Before this seclusion of my illness, I was secluded still, and there are few of the youngest women in the world who have not seen more, heard more, known more, of society, than I, who am scarcely to be called young now. I grew up in the country—I had no social opportunities, had my heart in books and poetry, and my experience in reveries. And so time passed and passed—and afterwards, when my illness came . . . and no prospect (as appeared at one time) of ever passing the threshold of one room again; why then, I turned to thinking with some bitterness . . . that I had stood blind in this temple I was about to leave—that I had seen no Human nature, that my brothers and sisters of the earth were *names* to me, that I had beheld no great mountain or river, nothing in fact. . . . And do you also know what a disadvantage this ignorance is to my art? Why, if I live on and yet do not escape from this seclusion, do you not perceive that I labour under signal disadvantages—that I am, in a manner as a *blind poet?* Certainly, there is compensation to a degree. I have had much of the inner life, and from the habit of self-consciousness and self-analysis, I make great guesses at Human nature in the main. But how willingly I would as a poet exchange some of this lumbering, ponderous, helpless knowledge of books, for some experience of life and man, for some . . .

She breaks off, with three little dots, and we may take advantage of her pause to turn once more to *Aurora Leigh*.

What damage had her life done her as a poet? A great one, we cannot deny. For it is clear, as we turn the pages of *Aurora Leigh* or of the *Letters*—one often echoes the other—that the mind which found its natural expression in this swift and chaotic poem about real men and women was not the mind to profit by solitude. A lyrical, a scholarly, a fastidious mind might have used seclusion and solitude to perfect its powers. Tennyson asked no better than to live with books in the heart of the country. But the mind of Elizabeth Barrett was lively and secular and satirical. She was no scholar. Books were to her not an end in themselves but a substitute for living. She raced through folios because she was forbidden to scamper on the grass. She wrestled with Aeschylus and Plato because it was out of the question that she should argue about politics with live men and women. Her favourite reading as an invalid was Balzac and George Sand and other "immortal improprieties" because "they kept the colour in my life to some degree". Nothing is more striking when at last she broke the prison bars than the fervour with which she flung herself into the life of the moment. She loved to sit in a café and watch people passing; she loved the arguments, the politics, and the strife of the modern world. The past and its ruins, even the past of Italy and Italian ruins, interested her much less than the theories of Mr. Hume the medium, or the politics of Napoleon, Emperor of the French. Italian pictures, Greek poetry roused in her a clumsy and conventional enthusiasm in strange contrast with the original independence of her mind when it applied itself to actual facts.

Such being her natural bent, it is not surprising that even in the depths of her sick-room her mind turned to modern life as a subject for poetry. She waited, wisely, until her escape had given her some measure of knowledge and proportion. But it cannot be doubted that the long years of seclusion had done her irreparable damage as an artist. She had lived shut off, guessing at what was outside, and inevitably magnifying what was within. The loss of Flush, the spaniel, affected her as the loss of a child might have affected another woman. The tap of ivy on the pane became the thrash of trees in a gale. Every sound was enlarged, every incident exaggerated, for the silence of the sick-room was profound and the monotony of Wimpole Street was intense. When at last she was able to "rush into drawing-rooms and the like and meet face to face without mask the Humanity of the age and speak the truth of it out plainly", she was too weak to stand the shock. Ordinary daylight, current gossip, the usual traffic of human beings left her exhausted, ecstatic, and dazzled into a state where she saw so much and felt so much that she did not altogether know what she felt or what she saw.

Aurora Leigh, the novel-poem, is not, therefore, the masterpiece that it might have been. Rather it is a masterpiece in embryo; a work whose genius floats diffused and fluctuating in some pre-natal stage waiting the final stroke of creative power to bring it into being. Stimulating and boring, ungainly and eloquent, monstrous and exquisite all by turns, it overwhelms and bewilders; but, nevertheless, it still commands our interest and inspires our respect. For it becomes clear as we read that, whatever Mrs. Browning's faults, she was one of those rare writers who risk themselves adventurously and disinterestedly in an imaginative life which is independent of their private lives and demands to be considered apart from personalities. Her "intention" survives; the interest of her theory redeems much that is faulty in her practice. Abridged and simplified from Aurora's argument in the fifth book, that theory runs some-

thing like this. The true work of poets, she said, is to present
their own age, not Charlemagne's. More passion takes place
in drawing-rooms than at Roncesvalles with Roland and
his knights. "To flinch from modern varnish, coat or flounce,
Cry out for togas and the picturesque, Is fatal—foolish
too." For living art presents and records real life, and the
only life we can truly know is our own. But what form,
she asks, can a poem on modern life take? The drama is
impossible, for only servile and docile plays have any
chance of success. Moreover, what we (in 1846) have to
say about life is not fit for "boards, actors, prompters, gas-
light, and costume; our stage is now the soul itself". What
then can she do? The problem is difficult, performance is
bound to fall short of endeavour; but she has at least wrung
her life-blood on to every page of her book, and, for the
rest "Let me think of forms less, and the external. Trust
the spirit . . . Keep up the fire and leave the generous
flames to shape themselves." And so the fire blazed and
the flames leapt high.

The desire to deal with modern life in poetry was not
confined to Miss Barrett. Robert Browning said that he
had had the same ambition all his life. Coventry Patmore's
"Angel in the House" and Clough's "Bothie" were both
attempts of the same kind and preceded *Aurora Leigh* by
some years. It was natural enough. The novelists were dealing triumphantly with modern life in prose. *Jane Eyre*,
Vanity Fair, *David Copperfield*, *Richard Feverel* all trod
fast on each other's heels between the years 1847 and 1860.
The poets may well have felt, with Aurora Leigh, that
modern life had an intensity and a meaning of its own.

Why should these spoils fall solely into the laps of the prose writers? Why should the poet be forced back to the remoteness of Charlemagne and Roland, to the toga and the picturesque, when the humours and tragedies of village life, drawing-room life, club life, and street life all cried aloud for celebration? It was true that the old form in which poetry had dealt with life—the drama—was obsolete; but was there none other that could take its place? Mrs. Browning, convinced of the divinity of poetry, pondered, seized as much as she could of actual experience, and then at last threw down her challenge to the Brontës and the Thackerays in nine books of blank verse. It was in blank verse that she sang of Shoreditch and Kensington; of my aunt and the vicar; of Romney Leigh and Vincent Carrington; of Marian Erle and Lord Howe; of fashionable weddings and drab suburban streets, and bonnets and whiskers and four-wheeled cabs, and railway trains. The poets can treat of these things, she exclaimed, as well as of knights and dames, moats and drawbridges and castle courts. But can they? Let us see what happens to a poet when he poaches upon a novelist's preserves and gives us not an epic or a lyric but the story of many lives that move and change and are inspired by the interests and passions that are ours in the middle of the reign of Queen Victoria.

In the first place there is the story; a tale has to be told; the poet must somehow convey to us the necessary information that his hero has been asked out to dinner. This is a statement that a novelist would convey as quietly and prosaically as possible; for example, "While I was kissing her glove, sadly enough, a note was brought saying that her

father sent his regards and asked me to dine with them next
day". That is harmless. But the poet has to write:

> While thus I grieved, and kissed her glove,
>   My man brought in her note to say,
> Papa had bid her send his love,
>   And would I dine with them next day!

Which is absurd. The simple words have been made to strut
and posture and take on an emphasis which makes them
ridiculous. Then again, what will the poet do with dialogue? In modern life, as Mrs. Browning indicated when
she said that our stage is now the soul, the tongue has su-
perseded the sword. It is in talk that the high moments of
life, the shock of character upon character, are defined. But
poetry when it tries to follow the words on people's lips is
terribly impeded. Listen to Romney in a moment of high
emotion talking to his old love Marian about the baby she
has borne to another man:

> May God so father me, as I do him,
> And so forsake me, as I let him feel
> He's orphaned haply. Here I take the child
> To share my cup, to slumber on my knee,
> To play his loudest gambol at my foot,
> To hold my finger in the public ways . . .

and so on. Romney, in short, rants and reels like any of
those Elizabethan heroes whom Mrs. Browning had warned
so imperiously out of her modern living-room. Blank verse
has proved itself the most remorseless enemy of living
speech. Talk tossed up on the surge and swing of the verse
becomes high, rhetorical, impassioned; and as talk, since
action is ruled out, must go on and on, the reader's mind
stiffens and glazes under the monotony of the rhythm. Fol-

lowing the lilt of her rhythm rather than the emotions of her characters, Mrs. Browning is swept on into generalisation and declamation. Forced by the nature of her medium, she ignores the slighter, the subtler, the more hidden shades of emotion by which a novelist builds up touch by touch a character in prose. Change and development, the effect of one character upon another—all this is abandoned. The poem becomes one long soliloquy, and the only character that is known to us and the only story that is told us are the character and story of Aurora Leigh herself.

Thus, if Mrs. Browning meant by a novel-poem a book in which character is closely and subtly revealed, the relations of many hearts laid bare, and a story unfalteringly unfolded, she failed completely. But if she meant rather to give us a sense of life in general, of people who are unmistakably Victorian, wrestling with the problems of their own time, all brightened, intensified, and compacted by the fire of poetry, she succeeded. Aurora Leigh, with her passionate interest in social questions, her conflict as artist and woman, her longing for knowledge and freedom, is the true daughter of her age. Romney, too, is no less certainly a mid-Victorian gentleman of high ideals who has thought deeply about the social question, and has founded, unfortunately, a phalanstery in Shropshire. The aunt, the antimacassars, and the country house from which Aurora escapes are real enough to fetch high prices in the Tottenham Court Road at this moment. The broader aspects of what it felt like to be a Victorian are seized as surely and stamped as vividly upon us as in any novel by Trollope or Mrs. Gaskell.

And indeed if we compare the prose novel and the novel-poem the triumphs are by no means all to the credit of prose. As we rush through page after page of narrative in which a dozen scenes that the novelist would smooth out separately are pressed into one, in which pages of deliberate description are fused into a single line, we cannot help feeling that the poet has outpaced the prose writer. Her page is packed twice as full as his. Characters, too, if they are not shown in conflict but snipped off and summed up with something of the exaggeration of a caricaturist, have a heightened and symbolical significance which prose with its gradual approach cannot rival. The general aspect of things—market, sunset, church—have a brilliance and a continuity, owing to the compressions and elisions of poetry, which mock the prose writer and his slow accumulations of careful detail. For these reasons *Aurora Leigh* remains, with all its imperfections, a book that still lives and breathes and has its being. And when we think how still and cold the plays of Beddoes or of Sir Henry Taylor lie, in spite of all their beauty, and how seldom in our own day we disturb the repose of the classical dramas of Robert Bridges, we may suspect that Elizabeth Barrett was inspired by a flash of true genius when she rushed into the drawing-room and said that here, where we live and work, is the true place for the poet. At any rate, her courage was justified in her own case. Her bad taste, her tortured ingenuity, her floundering, scrambling, and confused impetuosity have space to spend themselves here without inflicting a deadly wound, while her ardour and abundance, her brilliant descriptive powers, her shrewd and caustic humour infect us with her own enthusiasm. We laugh, we protest, we complain—it is absurd, it is impossible, we cannot tolerate this exaggeration a moment longer—but, nevertheless, we read to the end enthralled. What more can an author ask? But the best compliment that we can pay *Aurora Leigh* is that it makes us wonder why it has left no successors. Surely the street, the drawing-room, are promising subjects; modern life is worthy of the muse. But the rapid sketch that Elizabeth Barrett Browning threw off when she leapt from her couch and dashed into the drawing-room remains unfinished. The conservatism or the timidity of poets still leaves the chief spoils of modern life to the novelist. We have no novel-poem of the age of George the Fifth.

The Niece of an Earl

THERE is an aspect of fiction of so delicate a nature that less has been said about it than its importance deserves. One is supposed to pass over class distinctions in silence; one person is supposed to be as well born as another; and yet English fiction is so steeped in the ups and downs of social rank that without them it would be unrecognisable. When Meredith, in *The Case of General Ople and Lady Camper*, remarks, "He sent word that he would wait on Lady Camper immediately, and betook himself forthwith to his toilette. She was the niece of an Earl", all of British blood accept the statement unhesitatingly, and know that Meredith is right. A General in those circumstances would certainly have given his coat an extra brush. For though the General might have been, we are given to understand that he was not, Lady Camper's social equal. He received the shock of her rank upon a naked surface. No earldom, baronetage, or knighthood protected him. He was an English gentleman merely, and a poor one at that. Therefore, to British readers even now it seems unquestionably fitting that he should "betake himself to his toilette" before appearing in the lady's presence.

It is useless to suppose that social distinctions have vanished. Each may pretend that he knows no such restrictions, and that the compartment in which he lives allows him the run of the world. But it is an illusion. The idlest stroller

down summer streets may see for himself the charwoman's
shawl shouldering its way among the silk wraps of the successful; he sees shop-girls pressing their noses against the
plate glass of motor-cars; he sees radiant youth and august
age waiting their summons within to be admitted to the
presence of King George. There is no animosity, perhaps,
but there is no communication. We are enclosed, and separate, and cut off. Directly we see ourselves in the looking-
glass of fiction we know that this is so. The novelist, and
the English novelist in particular, knows and delights, it
seems, to know that Society is a nest of glass boxes one
separate from another, each housing a group with special
habits and qualities of its own. He knows that there are
Earls and that Earls have nieces; he knows that there are
Generals and that Generals brush their coats before they
visit the nieces of Earls. But this is only the A B C of what
he knows. For in a few short pages, Meredith makes us
aware not only that Earls have nieces, but that Generals
have cousins; that the cousins have friends; that the friends
have cooks; that the cooks have husbands, and that the
husbands of the cooks of the friends of the cousins of the
Generals are carpenters. Each of these people lives in a
glass box of his own, and has peculiarities of which the
novelist must take account. What appears superficially to
be the vast equality of the middle classes is, in truth, nothing of the sort. All through the social mass run curious veins
and streakings separating man from man and woman from
woman; mysterious prerogatives and disabilities too ethereal
to be distinguished by anything so crude as a title impede
and disorder the great business of human intercourse. And
when we have threaded our way carefully through all these

grades from the niece of the Earl to the friend of the cousin
of the General, we are still faced with an abyss; a gulf
yawns before us; on the other side are the working classes.
The writer of perfect judgment and taste, like Jane Austen,
does no more than glance across the gulf; she restricts herself to her own special class and finds infinite shades within
it. But for the brisk, inquisitive, combative writer like Meredith, the temptation to explore is irresistible. He runs up
and down the social scale; he chimes one note against another; he insists that the Earl and the cook, the General
and the farmer shall speak up for themselves and play their
part in the extremely complicated comedy of English
civilised life.

It was natural that he should attempt it. A writer touched
by the comic spirit relishes these distinctions keenly; they
give him something to take hold of; something to make
play with. English fiction without the nieces of Earls and
the cousins of Generals would be an arid waste. It would
resemble Russian fiction. It would have to fall back upon
the immensity of the soul and upon the brotherhood of man.
Like Russian fiction, it would lack comedy. But while we
realise the immense debt that we owe the Earl's niece and
the General's cousin, we doubt sometimes whether the pleasure we get from the play of satire on these broken edges is
altogether worth the price we pay. For the price is a high
one. The strain upon a novelist is tremendous. In two short
stories Meredith gallantly attempts to bridge all gulfs, and
to take half a dozen different levels in his stride. Now he
speaks as an Earl's niece; now as a carpenter's wife. It cannot be said that his daring is altogether successful. One has
a feeling (perhaps it is unfounded) that the blood of the

niece of an Earl is not quite so tart and sharp as he would have it. Aristocracy is not, perhaps, so consistently high and brusque and eccentric as, from his angle, he would represent it. Yet his great people are more successful than his humble. His cooks are too ripe and rotund; his farmers too ruddy and earthy. He overdoes the pith and the sap; the fist-shaking and the thigh-slapping. He has got too far from them to write of them with ease.

It seems, therefore, that the novelist, and the English novelist in particular, suffers from a disability which affects no other artist to the same extent. His work is influenced by his birth. He is fated to know intimately, and so to describe with understanding, only those who are of his own social rank. He cannot escape from the box in which he has been bred. A bird's-eye view of fiction shows us no gentlemen in Dickens; no working men in Thackeray. One hesitates to call Jane Eyre a lady. The Elizabeths and the Emmas of Miss Austen could not possibly be taken for anything else. It is vain to look for dukes or for dustmen—we doubt that such extremes are to be found anywhere in fiction. We are, therefore, brought to the melancholy and tantalising conclusion not only that novels are poorer than they might be, but that we are very largely prevented—for after all, the novelists are the great interpreters—from knowing what is happening either in the heights of Society or in its depths. There is practically no evidence available by which we can guess at the feelings of the highest in the land. What does a King feel? What does a Duke think? We cannot say. For the highest in the land have seldom written at all, and have never written about themselves. We shall never know what the Court of Louis XIV looked

like to Louis XIV himself. It seems likely indeed that the
English aristocracy will pass out of existence, or be merged
with the common people, without leaving any true picture
of themselves behind.

But our ignorance of the aristocracy is nothing compared
with our ignorance of the working classes. At all times the
great families of England and France have delighted to
have famous men at their tables, and thus the Thackerays
and the Disraelis and the Prousts have been familiar enough
with the cut and fashion of aristocratic life to write about
it with authority. Unfortunately, however, life is so framed
that literary success invariably means a rise, never a fall,
and seldom, what is far more desirable, a spread in the
social scale. The rising novelist is never pestered to come
to gin and winkles with the plumber and his wife. His
books never bring him into touch with the cat's-meat man,
or start a correspondence with the old lady who sells matches
and bootlaces by the gate of the British Museum. He becomes rich; he becomes respectable; he buys an evening suit
and dines with peers. Therefore, the later works of successful novelists show, if anything, a slight rise in the social
scale. We tend to get more and more portraits of the successful and the distinguished. On the other hand, the old
rat-catchers and ostlers of Shakespeare's day are shuffled
altogether off the scene, or become, what is far more offensive, objects of pity, examples of curiosity. They serve to
show up the rich. They serve to point the evils of the social
system. They are no longer, as they used to be when Chaucer
wrote, simply themselves. For it is impossible, it would
seem, for working men to write in their own language about
their own lives. Such education as the act of writing implies
at once makes them self-conscious, or class-conscious, or

removes them from their own class. That anonymity, in the shadow of which writers write most happily, is the prerogatives of the middle class alone. It is from the middle class that writers spring, because it is in the middle class only that the practice of writing is as natural and habitual as hoeing a field or building a house. Thus it must have been harder for Byron to be a poet than Keats; and it is as impossible to imagine that a Duke could be a great novelist as that *Paradise Lost* could be written by a man behind a counter.

But things change; class distinctions were not always so hard and fast as they have now become. The Elizabethan age was far more elastic in this respect than our own; we, on the other hand, are far less hidebound than the Victorians. Thus it may well be that we are on the edge of a greater change than any the world has yet known. In another century or so, none of these distinctions may hold good. The Duke and the agricultural labourer as we know them now may have died out as completely as the bustard and the wild cat. Only natural differences such as those of brain and character will serve to distinguish us. General Ople (if there are still Generals) will visit the niece (if there are still nieces) of the Earl (if there are still Earls) without brushing his coat (if there are still coats). But what will happen to English fiction when it has come to pass that there are neither Generals, nieces, Earls, nor coats, we cannot imagine. It may change its character so that we no longer know it. It may become extinct. Novels may be written as seldom and as unsuccessfully by our descendants as the poetic drama by ourselves. The art of a truly democratic age will be—what?

George Gissing

"DO YOU know there are men in London who go the round of the streets selling paraffin oil?" wrote George Gissing in the year 1880, and the phrase because it is Gissing's calls up a world of fog and fourwheelers, of slatternly landladies, of struggling men of letters, of gnawing domestic misery, of gloomy back streets, and ignoble yellow chapels; but also, above this misery, we see tree-crowned heights, the columns of the Parthenon, and the hills of Rome. For Gissing is one of those imperfect novelists through whose books one sees the life of the author faintly covered by the lives of fictitious people. With such writers we establish a personal rather than an artistic relationship. We approach them through their lives as much as through their work, and when we take up Gissing's letters, which have character, but little wit and no brilliance to illumine them, we feel that we are filling in a design which we began to trace out when we read *Demos* and *New Grub Street* and *The Nether World.*

Yet here, too, there are gaps in plenty, and many dark places left unlit. Much information has been kept back, many facts necessarily omitted. The Gissings were poor, and their father died when they were children; there were many of them, and they had to scrape together what education they could get. George, his sister said, had a passion for learning. He would rush off to school with a sharp herring bone in his throat for fear of missing his lesson.

He would copy out from a little book called *That's It* the astonishing number of eggs that the tench lays and the sole lays and the carp lays, "because I think it is a fact worthy of attention". She remembers his "overwhelming veneration" for intellect, and how patiently, sitting beside her, the tall boy with the high white forehead and the short-sighted eyes would help her with her Latin, "giving the same explanation time after time without the least sign of impatience".

Partly because he reverenced facts and had no faculty it seems (his language is meagre and unmetaphorical) for impressions, it is doubtful whether his choice of a novelist's career was a happy one. There was the whole world, with its history and its literature, inviting him to haul it into his mind; he was eager; he was intellectual; yet he must sit down in hired rooms and spin novels about "earnest young people striving for improvement in, as it were, the dawn of a new phase of our civilisation".

But the art of fiction is infinitely accommodating, and it was quite ready about the year 1880 to accept into its ranks a writer who wished to be the "mouthpiece of the advanced Radical Party", who was determined to show in his novels the ghastly condition of the poor and the hideous injustice of society. The art of fiction was ready, that is, to agree that such books were novels; but it was doubtful if such novels would be read. Smith Elder's reader summed up the situation tersely enough. Mr. Gissing's novel, he wrote, "is too painful to please the ordinary novel reader, and treats of scenes that can never attract the subscribers to Mr. Mudie's Library". So, dining off lentils and hearing the men cry paraffin for sale in the streets of Islington, Gissing paid for the publication himself. It was then that he formed the habit of getting up at five in the morning in order to tramp half across London in order to coach Mr. M. before breakfast. Often enough Mr. M. sent down word that he was already engaged, and then another page was added to the dismal chronicle of life in modern *Grub Street*—we are faced by another of those problems with which literature is sown so thick. The writer has dined upon lentils; he gets up at five; he walks across London; he finds Mr. M. still in bed, whereupon he stands forth as the champion of life as it is, and proclaims that ugliness is truth, truth ugliness, and that is all we know and all we need to know. But there are signs that the novel resents such treatment. To use a burning consciousness of one's own misery, of the shackles that cut one's own limbs, to quicken one's sense of life in general, as Dickens did, to shape out of the murk which has surrounded one's childhood some resplendent figure such as Micawber or Mrs. Gamp is admirable: but to use personal suffering to rivet the reader's sympathy and curiosity upon your private case is disastrous. Imagination is at its freest when it is most generalised; it loses something of its sweep and power, it becomes petty and personal, when it is limited to the consideration of a particular case calling for sympathy.

At the same time the sympathy which identifies the author with his hero is a passion of great intensity; it makes the pages fly; it lends what has perhaps little merit artistically another and momentarily perhaps a keener edge. Biffen and Reardon had, we say to ourselves, bread and butter and sardines for supper; so had Gissing; Biffen's overcoat had been pawned, and so had Gissing's; Reardon could not write on Sunday; no more could Gissing. We forget whether it was Reardon who loved cats or Gissing who loved barrel organs. Certainly both Reardon and Gissing bought their copies of Gibbon at a second-hand book-stall, and lugged the volumes home one by one through the fog. So we go on capping these resemblances, and each time we succeed, dipping now into the novel, now into the letters, a little glow of satisfaction comes over us, as if novel-reading were a game of skill in which the puzzle set us is to find the face of the writer.

We know Gissing thus as we do not know Hardy or George Eliot. Where the great novelist flows in and out of his characters and bathes them in an element which seems to be common to us all, Gissing remains solitary, self-centred, apart. His is one of those sharp lights beyond whose edges all is vapour and phantom. But mixed with this sharp light is one ray of singular penetration. With all his narrowness of outlook and meagreness of sensibility, Gissing is one of the extremely rare novelists who believes in the power of the mind, who makes his people think. They are thus differently poised from the majority of fictitious men and women. The awful hierarchy of the passions is slightly displaced. Social snobbery does not exist; money is desired almost entirely to buy bread and butter; love itself takes a second place. But the brain works, and that alone is enough to give us a sense of freedom. For to think is to become complex; it is to overflow boundaries, to cease to be a "character", to merge one's private life in the life of politics or art or ideas, to have relationships based partly on them, and not on sexual desire alone. The impersonal side of life is given its due place in the scheme. "Why don't

people write about the really important things of life?"
Gissing makes one of his characters exclaim, and at the unexpected cry the horrid burden of fiction begins to slip from
the shoulders. Is it possible that we are going to talk of
other things besides falling in love, important though that
is, and going to dinner with Duchesses, fascinating though
that is? Here in Gissing is a gleam of recognition that Darwin had lived, that science was developing, that people read
books and look at pictures, that once upon a time there was
such a place as Greece. It is the consciousness of these things
that makes his books such painful reading; it was this that
made it impossible for them to "attract the subscribers to
Mr. Mudie's Library". They owe their peculiar grimness
to the fact that the people who suffer most are capable of
making their suffering part of a reasoned view of life. The
thought endures when the feeling has gone. Their unhappiness represents something more lasting than a personal
reverse; it becomes part of a view of life. Hence when we
have finished one of Gissing's novels we have taken away
not a character, nor an incident, but the comment of a
thoughtful man upon life as life seemed to him.

But because Gissing was always thinking, he was always
changing. In that lies much of his interest for us. As a young
man he had thought that he would write books to show
up the "hideous injustice of our whole system of society".
Later his views changed; either the task was impossible, or
other tastes were tugging him in a different direction. He
came to think, as he believed finally, that "the only thing
known to us of absolute value is artistic perfection . . .
the works of the artist . . . remain sources of health to the
world". So that if one wishes to better the world one must,

paradoxically enough, withdraw and spend more and more time fashioning one's sentences to perfection in solitude. Writing, Gissing thought, is a task of the utmost difficulty; perhaps at the end of his life he might be able "to manage a page that is decently grammatical and fairly harmonious". There are moments when he succeeded splendidly. For example, he is describing a cemetery in the East End of London:

Here on the waste limits of that dread east, to wander among tombs is to go hand-in-hand with the stark and eyeless emblems of mortality; the spirit fails beneath the cold burden of ignoble destiny. Here lie those who were born for toil; who, when toil has worn them to the uttermost, have but to yield their useless breath and pass into oblivion. For them is no day, only the brief twilight of a winter's sky between the former and the latter night. For them no aspiration; for them no hope of memory in the dust; their very children are wearied into forgetfulness. Indistinguishable units in the vast throng that labours but to support life, the name of each, father, mother, child, is but a dumb cry for the warmth and love of which fate so stinted them. The wind wails above their narrow tenements; the sandy soil, soaking in the rain as soon as it has fallen, is a symbol of the great world which absorbs their toil and straightway blots their being.

Again and again such passages of description stand out like stone slabs, shaped and solid, among the untidy litter with which the pages of fiction are strewn.

Gissing, indeed, never ceased to educate himself. While the Baker Street trains hissed their steam under his window, and the lodger downstairs blew his room out, and the landlady was insolent, and the grocer refused to send the sugar so that he had to fetch it himself, and the fog burnt his throat and he caught cold and never spoke to anybody for three weeks, yet must drive his pen through page after page and vacillated miserably from one domestic disaster to another—while all this went on with a dreary monotony, for which he could only blame the weakness of his own character, the columns of the Parthenon, the hills of Rome still rose above the fogs and the fried-fish shops of the Euston Road. He was determined to visit Greece and Rome. He actually set foot in Athens; he saw Rome; he read his Thucydides in Sicily before he died. Life was changing round him; his comment upon life was changing too. Perhaps the old sordidity, the fog and the paraffin, and the drunken landlady was not the only reality; ugliness is not the whole truth; there is an element of beauty in the world. The past, with its literature and its civilisation, solidifies the present. At any rate his books in future were to be about Rome in the time of Totila, not about Islington in the time of Queen Victoria. He was reaching some point in his perpetual thinking where "one has to distinguish between two forms of intelligence"; one cannot venerate the intellect only. But before he could mark down the spot he had reached on the map of thought, he, who had shared so many of his characters' experiences, shared, too, the death he had given to Edwin Reardon. "Patience, patience", he said to the friend who stood by him as he died—an imperfect novelist, but a highly educated man.

The Novels of George Meredith

TWENTY years ago [1] the reputation of George Meredith was at its height. His novels had won their way to celebrity through all sorts of difficulties, and their fame was all the brighter and the more singular for what it had subdued. Then, too, it was generally discovered that the maker of these splendid books was himself a splendid old man. Visitors who went down to Box Hill reported that they were thrilled as they walked up the drive of the little suburban house by the sound of a voice booming and reverberating within. The novelist, seated among the usual knick-knacks of the drawing-room, was like the bust of Euripides to look at. Age had worn and sharpened the fine features, but the nose was still acute, the blue eyes still keen and ironical. Though he had sunk immobile into an arm-chair, his aspect was still vigorous and alert. It was true that he was almost stone-deaf, but this was the least of afflictions to one who was scarcely able to keep pace with the rapidity of his own ideas. Since he could not hear what was said to him, he could give himself whole-heartedly to the delights of soliloquy. It did not much matter, perhaps, whether his audience was cultivated or simple. Compliments that would have flattered a duchess were presented with equal ceremony to a child. To neither could he speak the simple language of daily life. But all the time this highly wrought,

[1] Written in January 1928.

245

artificial conversation, with its crystallised phrases and its high-piled metaphors, moved and tossed on a current of laughter. His laugh curled round his sentences as if he himself enjoyed their humorous exaggeration. The master of language was splashing and diving in his element of words. So the legend grew; and the fame of George Meredith, who sat with the head of a Greek poet on his shoulders in a suburban villa beneath Box Hill, pouring out poetry and sarcasm and wisdom in a voice that could be heard almost on the high road, made his fascinating and brilliant books seem more fascinating and brilliant still.

But that is twenty years ago. His fame as a talker is necessarily dimmed, and his fame as a writer seems also under a cloud. On none of his successors is his influence now marked. When one of them whose own work has given him the right to be heard with respect chances to speak his mind on the subject, it is not flattering.

Meredith [writes Mr. Forster in his *Aspects of Fiction*] is not the great name he was twenty years ago. . . . His philosophy has not worn well. His heavy attacks on sentimentality—they bore the present generation. . . . When he gets serious and noble-minded there is a strident overtone, a bullying that becomes distressing. . . . What with the faking, what with the preaching, which was never agreeable and is now said to be hollow, and what with the home countries posing as the universe, it is no wonder Meredith now lies in the trough.

The criticism is not, of course, intended to be a finished estimate; but in its conversational sincerity it condenses accurately enough what is in the air when Meredith is mentioned. No, the general conclusion would seem to be, Meredith has not worn well. But the value of centenaries lies in the occasion they offer us for solidifying such airy impressions. Talk, mixed with half-rubbed-out memories, forms a mist by degrees through which we scarcely see plain. To open the books again, to try to read them as if for the first time, to try to free them from the rubbish of reputation and accident—that, perhaps, is the most acceptable present we can offer to a writer on his hundredth birthday.

And since the first novel is always apt to be an unguarded one, where the author displays his gifts without knowing how to dispose of them to the best advantage, we may do well to open *Richard Feverel* first. It needs no great sagacity to see that the writer is a novice at his task. The style is extremely uneven. Now he twists himself into iron knots; now he lies flat as a pancake. He seems to be of two minds as to his intention. Ironic comment alternates with long-winded narrative. He vacillates from one attitude to another. Indeed, the whole fabric seems to rock a little insecurely. The baronet wrapped in a cloak; the county family; the ancestral home; the uncles mouthing epigrams in the dining-room; the great ladies flaunting and swimming; the jolly farmers slapping their thighs: all liberally if spasmodically sprinkled with dried aphorisms from a pepper-pot called the Pilgrim's Scrip—what an odd conglomeration it is! But the oddity is not on the surface; it is not merely that whiskers and bonnets have gone out of fashion: it lies deeper, in Meredith's intention, in what he wishes to bring to pass. He has been, it is plain, at great pains to destroy the conventional form of the novel. He makes no attempt to preserve the sober reality of Trollope and Jane Austen; he has destroyed all the usual staircases by which we have learnt to climb. And what is done so deliberately is done with a purpose. This defiance of the ordinary, these

airs and graces, the formality of the dialogue with its Sirs
and Madams are all there to create an atmosphere that is
unlike that of daily life, to prepare the way for a new and
an original sense of the human scene. Peacock, from whom
Meredith learnt so much, is equally arbitrary, but the virtue
of the assumptions he asks us to make is proved by the fact
that we accept Mr. Skionar and the rest with natural delight. Meredith's characters in *Richard Feverel*, on the other
hand, are at odds with their surroundings. We at once exclaim how unreal they are, how artificial, how impossible.
The baronet and the butler, the hero and the heroine, the
good woman and the bad woman are mere types of baronets
and butler, good women and bad. For what reason, then, has
he sacrificed the substantial advantages of realistic common
sense—the staircase and the stucco? Because, it becomes
clear as we read, he possessed a keen sense not of the complexity of character, but of the splendour of a scene. One
after another in this first book he creates a scene to which
we can attach abstract names—Youth, The Birth of Love,
The Power of Nature. We are galloped to them over every
obstacle on the pounding hoofs of rhapsodical prose.

Away with Systems! Away with a corrupt World! Let us breathe
the air of the Enchanted Island! Golden lie the meadows; golden
run the streams; red gold is on the pine stems.

We forget that Richard is Richard and that Lucy is Lucy;
they are youth; the world runs molten gold. The writer is a
rhapsodist, a poet then; but we have not yet exhausted all
the elements in this first novel. We have to reckon with the
author himself. He has a mind stuffed with ideas, hungry
for argument. His boys and girls may spend their time

picking daisies in the meadows, but they breathe, however unconsciously, an air bristling with intellectual question and comment. On a dozen occasions these incongruous elements strain and threaten to break apart. The book is cracked through and through with those fissures which come when the author seems to be of twenty minds at the same time. Yet it succeeds in holding miraculously together, not certainly by the depths and originality of its character drawing but by the vigour of its intellectual power and by its lyrical intensity.

We are left, then, with our curiosity aroused. Let him write another book or two; get into his stride; control his crudities: and we will open *Harry Richmond* and see what has happened now. Of all the things that might have happened this surely is the strangest. All trace of immaturity is gone; but with it every trace of the uneasy adventurous mind has gone too. The story bowls smoothly along the road which Dickens has already trodden of autobiographical narrative. It is a boy speaking, a boy thinking, a boy adventuring. For that reason, no doubt, the author has curbed his redundance and pruned his speech. The style is the most rapid possible. It runs smooth, without a kink in it. Stevenson, one feels, must have learnt much from this supple narrative, with its precise adroit phrases, its exact quick glance at visible things.

Plunged among dark green leaves, smelling wood-smoke, at night; at morning waking up, and the world alight, and you standing high, and marking the hills where you will see the next morning and the next, morning after morning, and one morning the dearest person in the world surprising you just before you wake: I thought this a heavenly pleasure.

It goes gallantly, but a little self-consciously. He hears himself talking. Doubts begin to rise and hover and settle at last (as in *Richard Feverel*) upon the human figures. These boys are no more real boys than the sample apple which is laid on top of the basket is a real apple. They are too simple, too gallant, too adventurous to be of the same unequal breed as David Copperfield, for example. They are sample boys, novelist's specimens; and again we encounter the extreme conventionality of Meredith's mind where we found it, to our surprise, before. With all his boldness (and there is no risk that he will not run with probability) there are a dozen occasions on which a reach-me-down character will satisfy him well enough. But just as we are thinking that the young gentlemen are altogether too pat, and the adventures which befall them altogether too slick, the shallow bath of illusion closes over our heads and we sink with Richmond Roy and the Princess Ottilia into the world of fantasy and romance, where all holds together and we are able to put our imagination at the writer's service without reserve. That such surrender is above all things delightful: that it adds spring-heels to our boots: that it fires the cold scepticism out of us and makes the world glow in lucid transparency before our eyes, needs no showing, as it certainly submits to no analysis. That Meredith can induce such moments proves him possessed of an extraordinary power. Yet it is a capricious power and highly intermittent. For pages all is effort and agony; phrase after phrase is struck and no light comes. Then, just as we are about to drop the book, the rocket roars into the air; the whole scene flashes into light; and the book, years after, is recalled by that sudden splendour.

If, then, this intermittent brilliancy is Meredith's characteristic excellence it is worth while to look into it more closely. And perhaps the first thing that we shall discover is that the scenes which catch the eye and remain in memory are static; they are illuminations, not discoveries; they do not improve our knowledge of the characters. It is significant that Richard and Lucy, Harry and Ottilia, Clara and Vernon, Beauchamp and Renée are presented in carefully appropriate surroundings—on board a yacht, under a flowering cherry tree, upon some river-bank, so that the landscape always makes part of the emotion. The sea or the sky or the wood is brought forward to symbolise what the human beings are feeling or looking.

The sky was bronze, a vast furnace dome. The folds of light and shadow everywhere were satin rich. That afternoon the bee hummed of thunder and refreshed the ear.

That is a description of a state of mind.

These winter mornings are divine. They move on noiselessly. The earth is still as if waiting. A wren warbles, and flits through the lank, drenched branches; hillside opens green; everywhere is mist, everywhere expectancy.

That is a description of a woman's face. But only some states of mind and some expressions of face can be described in imagery—only those which are so highly wrought as to be simple and, for that reason, will not submit to analysis. This is a limitation; for though we may be able to see these people, very brilliantly, in a moment of illumination, they do not change or grow; the light sinks and leaves us in darkness. We have no such intuitive knowledge of Meredith's characters as we have of Stendhal's, Tchehov's, Jane

Austen's. Indeed, our knowledge of such characters is so intimate that we can almost dispense with "great scenes" altogether. Some of the most emotional scenes in fiction are the quietest. We have been wrought upon by nine hundred and ninety-nine little touches; the thousandth, when it comes, is as slight as the others, but the effect is prodigious. But with Meredith there are no touches; there are hammer-strokes only, so that our knowledge of his characters is partial, spasmodic, and intermittent.

Meredith, then, is not among the great psychologists who feel their way, anonymously and patiently, in and out of the fibres of the mind and make one character differ minutely and completely from another. He is among the poets who identify the character with the passion or with the idea; who symbolise and make abstract. And yet—here lay his difficulty perhaps—he was not a poet-novelist wholly and completely as Emily Brontë was a poet-novelist. He did not steep the world in one mood. His mind was too self-conscious, and too sophisticated to remain lyrical for long. He does not sing only; he dissects. Even in his most lyrical scenes a sneer curls its lash round the phrases and laughs at their extravagance. And as we read on, we shall find that the comic spirit, when it is allowed to dominate the scene, licked the world to a very different shape. *The Egoist* at once modifies our theory that Meredith is pre-eminently the master of great scenes. Here there is none of that precipitate hurry that has rushed us over obstacles to the summit of one emotional peak after another. The case is one that needs argument; argument needs logic; Sir Willoughby, "our original male in giant form", is turned slowly round before a steady fire of scrutiny and criticism which allows no twitch on the victim's part to escape it. That the victim is a wax model and not entirely living flesh and blood is perhaps true. At the same time Meredith pays us a supreme compliment to which as novel-readers we are little accustomed. We are civilised people, he seems to say, watching the comedy of human relations together. Human relations are of profound interest. Men and women are not cats and monkeys, but beings of a larger growth and of a greater range. He imagines us capable of disinterested curiosity in the behaviour of our kind. This is so rare a compliment from a novelist to his reader that we are at first bewildered and then delighted. Indeed his comic spirit is a far more penetrating goddess than his lyrical. It is she who cuts a clear path through the brambles of his manner; she who surprises us again and again by the depth of her observations; she who creates the dignity, the seriousness, and the vitality of Meredith's world. Had Meredith, one is tempted to reflect, lived in an age or in a country where comedy was the rule, he might never have contracted those airs of intellectual superiority, that manner of oracular solemnity which it is, as he points out, the use of the comic spirit to correct.

But in many ways the age—if we can judge so amorphous a shape—was hostile to Meredith, or, to speak more accurately, was hostile to his success with the age we now live in—the year 1928. His teaching seems now too strident and too optimistic and too shallow. It obtrudes; and when philosophy is not consumed in a novel, when we can underline this phrase with a pencil, and cut out that exhortation with a pair of scissors and paste the whole into a system, it is safe to say that there is something wrong with the philosophy or with the novel or with both. Above all, his teaching is too insistent. He cannot, even to hear the profoundest secret, suppress his own opinion. And there is nothing that characters in fiction resent more. If, they seem to argue, we have been called into existence merely to express Mr. Meredith's views upon the universe, we would rather not exist at all. Thereupon they die; and a novel that is full of dead characters, even though it is also full of profound wisdom and exalted teaching, is not achieving its aim as a novel. But here we reach another point upon which the present age may be inclined to have more sympathy with Meredith. When he wrote, in the seventies and eighties of the last century, the novel had reached a stage where it could only exist by moving onward. It is a possible contention that after those two perfect novels, *Pride and Prejudice* and *The Small House at Allington*, English fiction had to escape from the dominion of that perfection, as English poetry had to escape from the perfection of Tennyson. George Eliot, Meredith, and Hardy were all imperfect novelists largely because they insisted upon introducing qualities, of thought and of poetry, that are perhaps incompatible with fiction at its most perfect. On the other hand, if fiction had remained what it was to Jane Austen and Trollope, fiction would by this time be dead. Thus Meredith deserves our gratitude and excites our interest as a great innovator. Many of our doubts about him and much of our inability to frame any definite opinion of his work comes from the fact that it is experimental and thus contains elements that do not fuse harmoniously—the qualities are at odds: the one quality which binds and concentrates has been omitted. To read Meredith, then, to our greatest advantage we must make certain allowances and relax certain standards. We must not expect the perfect quietude of a traditional style nor the triumphs of a patient and pedestrian psychology. On the other hand, his claim, "My method has been to prepare my readers for a crucial exhibition of the personae, and then to give the scene in the fullest of their blood and brain under stress of a fierce situation", is frequently justified. Scene after scene rises on the mind's eye with a flare of fiery intensity. If we are irritated by the dancing-master dandyism which made him write "gave his lungs full play" instead of laughed, or "tasted the swift intricacies of the needle" instead of sewed, we must remember that such phrases prepare the way for the "fierce situations". Meredith is creating the atmosphere from which we shall pass naturally into a highly pitched state of emotion. Where the realistic novelist, like Trollope, lapses into flatness and dullness, the lyrical novelist, like Meredith, becomes meretricious and false; and such falsity is, of course, not only much more glaring than flatness, but it is a greater crime against the phlegmatic nature of prose fiction. Perhaps Meredith had been well advised if he had abjured the novel altogether and kept himself wholly to poetry. Yet we have to remind ourselves that the fault may be ours. Our prolonged diet upon Russian fiction, rendered neutral and negative in translation, our absorption in the convolutions of psychological Frenchmen, may have led us to forget that the English language is naturally exuberant, and the English character full of humours and eccentricities. Meredith's flamboyancy has a great ancestry behind it; we cannot avoid all memory of Shakespeare.

When such questions and qualifications crowd upon us as we read, the fact may be taken to prove that we are neither near enough to be under his spell nor far enough to see him in proportion. Thus the attempt to pronounce a finished estimate is even more illusive than usual. But we can testify even now that to read Meredith is to be conscious of a packed and muscular mind; of a voice booming and reverberating with its own unmistakable accent even though the partition between us is too thick for us to hear what he says distinctly. Still, as we read we feel that we are in the presence of a Greek god though he is surrounded by the innumerable ornaments of a suburban drawing-room; who talks brilliantly, even if he is deaf to the lower tones of the human voice; who, if he is rigid and immobile, is yet marvellously alive and on the alert. This brilliant and uneasy figure has his place with the great eccentrics rather than with the great masters. He will be read, one may guess, by fits and starts; he will be forgotten and discovered and again discovered and forgotten like Donne, and Peacock, and Gerard Hopkins. But if English fiction continues to be read, the novels of Meredith must inevitably rise from time to time into view; his work must inevitably be disputed and discussed.

"I Am Christina Rossetti"

ON THE fifth of this December [1] Christina Rossetti will celebrate her centenary, or, more properly speaking, we shall celebrate it for her, and perhaps not a little to her distress, for she was one of the shyest of women, and to be spoken of, as we shall certainly speak of her, would have caused her acute discomfort. Nevertheless, it is inevitable; centenaries are inexorable; talk of her we must. We shall read her life; we shall read her letters; we shall study her portraits, speculate about her diseases—of which she had a great variety; and rattle the drawers of her writing-table, which are for the most part empty. Let us begin with the biography—for what could be more amusing? As everybody knows, the fascination of reading biographies is irresistible. No sooner have we opened the pages of Miss Sandars's careful and competent book (*Life of Christina Rossetti*, by Mary F. Sandars. [Hutchinson]) than the old illusion comes over us. Here is the past and all its inhabitants miraculously sealed as in a magic tank; all we have to do is to look and to listen and to listen and to look and soon the little figures—for they are rather under life size—will begin to move and to speak, and as they move we shall arrange them in all sorts of patterns of which they were ignorant, for they thought when they were alive that they could go where they liked; and as they speak we shall

[1] 1930.

read into their sayings all kinds of meanings which never struck them, for they believed when they were alive that they said straight off whatever came into their heads. But once you are in a biography all is different.

Here, then, is Hallam Street, Portland Place, about the year 1830; and here are the Rossettis, an Italian family consisting of father and mother and four small children. The street was unfashionable and the home rather poverty-stricken; but the poverty did not matter, for, being foreigners, the Rossettis did not care much about the customs and conventions of the usual middle-class British family. They kept themselves to themselves, dressed as they liked, entertained Italian exiles, among them organ-grinders and other distressed compatriots, and made ends meet by teaching and writing and other odd jobs. By degrees Christina detached herself from the family group. It is plain that she was a quiet and observant child, with her own way of life already fixed in her head—she was to write—but all the more did she admire the superior competence of her elders. Soon we begin to surround her with a few friends and to endow her with a few characteristics. She detested parties. She dressed anyhow. She liked her brother's friends and little gatherings of young artists and poets who were to reform the world, rather to her amusement, for although so sedate, she was also whimsical and freakish, and liked making fun of people who took themselves with egotistic solemnity. And though she meant to be a poet she had very little of the vanity and stress of young poets; her verses seem to have formed themselves whole and entire in her head, and she did not worry very much what she said of them because in her own mind she knew that they were good. She had also immense powers of admiration—for her mother, for example, who was so quiet, and so sagacious, so simple and so sincere; and for her elder sister Maria, who had no taste for painting or for poetry, but was, for that very reason, perhaps more vigorous and effective in daily life. For example, Maria always refused to visit the Mummy Room at the British Museum because, she said, the Day of Resurrection might suddenly dawn and it would be very unseemly if the corpses had to put on immortality under the gaze of mere sight-seers—a reflection which had not struck Christina, but seemed to her admirable. Here, of course, we, who are outside the tank, enjoy a hearty laugh, but Christina, who is inside the tank and exposed to all its heats and currents, thought her sister's conduct worthy of the highest respect. Indeed, if we look at her a little more closely we shall see that something dark and hard, like a kernel, had already formed in the centre of Christina Rossetti's being.

It was religion, of course. Even when she was quite a girl her life-long absorption in the relation of the soul with God had taken possession of her. Her sixty-four years might seem outwardly spent in Hallam Street and Endsleigh Gardens and Torrington Square, but in reality she dwelt in some curious region where the spirit strives towards an unseen God—in her case, a dark God, a harsh God—a God who decreed that all the pleasures of the world were hateful to Him. The theatre was hateful, the opera was hateful, nakedness was hateful—when her friend Miss Thompson painted naked figures in her pictures she had to tell Christina that they were fairies, but Christina saw through the imposture—everything in Christina's life radiated from that knot of agony and intensity in the centre. Her belief regulated her life in the smallest particulars. It taught her that chess was wrong, but that whist and cribbage did not matter. But also it interfered in the most tremendous questions of her heart. There was a young painter called James Collinson, and she loved James Collinson and he loved her, but he was a Roman Catholic and so she refused him. Obligingly he became a member of the Church of England, and she accepted him. Vacillating, however, for he was a slippery man, he wobbled back to Rome, and Christina, though it broke her heart and for ever shadowed her life, cancelled the engagement. Years afterwards another, and it seems better founded, prospect of happiness presented itself. Charles Cayley proposed to her. But alas, this abstract and erudite man who shuffled about the world in a state of absent-minded dishabille, and translated the gospel into Iroquois, and asked smart ladies at a party "whether they were interested in the Gulf Stream", and for a present gave Christina a sea mouse preserved in spirits, was, not unnaturally, a free thinker. Him, too, Christina put from her. Though "no woman ever loved a man more deeply", she would not be the wife of a sceptic. She who loved the "obtuse and furry"—the wombats, toads, and mice of the earth—and called Charles Cayley "my blindest buzzard, my special mole", admitted no moles, wombats, buzzards, or Cayleys to her heaven.

So one might go on looking and listening for ever. There is no limit to the strangeness, amusement, and oddity of the past sealed in a tank. But just as we are wondering which cranny of this extraordinary territory to explore next, the principal figure intervenes. It is as if a fish, whose unconscious gyrations we had been watching in and out of reeds, round and round rocks, suddenly dashed at the glass and broke it. A tea-party is the occasion. For some reason Christina went to a party given by Mrs. Virtue Tebbs. What happened there is unknown—perhaps something was said in a casual, frivolous, tea-party way about poetry. At any rate,

suddenly there uprose from a chair and paced forward into the centre of the room a little woman dressed in black, who announced solemnly, "I am Christina Rossetti!" and having so said, returned to her chair.

With those words the glass is broken. Yes [she seems to say], I am a poet. You who pretend to honour my centenary are no better than the idle people at Mrs. Tebb's tea-party. Here you are rambling among unimportant trifles, rattling my writing-table drawers, making fun of the Mummies and Maria and my love affairs when all I care for you to know is here. Behold this green volume. It is a copy of my collected works. It costs four shillings and sixpence. Read that. And so she returns to her chair.

How absolute and unaccommodating these poets are! Poetry, they say, has nothing to do with life. Mummies and wombats, Hallam Street and omnibuses, James Collinson and Charles Cayley, sea mice and Mrs. Virtue Tebbs, Torrington Square and Endsleigh Gardens, even the vagaries of religious belief are irrelevant, extraneous, superfluous, unreal. It is poetry that matters. The only question of any interest is whether that poetry is good or bad. But this question of poetry, one might point out if only to gain time, is one of the greatest difficulty. Very little of value has been said about poetry since the world began. The judgment of contemporaries is almost always wrong. For example, most of the poems which figure in Christina Rossetti's complete works were rejected by editors. Her annual income from her poetry was for many years about ten pounds. On the other hand, the works of Jean Ingelow, as she noted sardonically, went into eight editions. There were, of course, among her contemporaries one or two poets and one or two critics whose judgment must be respectfully consulted. But what very different impressions they seem to gather from the same works—by what different standards they judge! For instance, when Swinburne read her poetry he exclaimed: "I have always thought that nothing more glorious in poetry has ever been written", and went on to say of her New Year Hymn

that it was touched as with the fire and bathed as in the light of sunbeams, tuned as to chords and cadences of refluent sea-music beyond reach of harp and organ, large echoes of the serene and sonorous tides of heaven.

Then Professor Saintsbury comes with his vast learning, and examines *Goblin Market*, and reports that

The metre of the principal poem ["Goblin Market"] may be best described as a dedoggerelised Skeltonic, with the gathered music of the various metrical progress since Spenser, utilised in the place of the wooden rattling of the followers of Chaucer. There may be discerned in it the same inclination towards line irregularity which has broken out, at different times, in the Pindaric of the late seventeenth and earlier eighteenth centuries, and in the rhymelessness of Sayers earlier and of Mr. Arnold later.

And then there is Sir Walter Raleigh:

I think she is the best poet alive. . . . The worst of it is you cannot lecture on really pure poetry any more than you can talk about the ingredients of pure water—it is adulterated, methylated, sanded poetry that makes the best lectures. The only thing that Christina makes me want to do, is cry, not lecture.

It would appear, then, that there are at least three schools of criticism: the refluent sea-music school; the line-irregularity school, and the school that bids one not criticise but cry. This is confusing; if we follow them all we shall only come to grief. Better perhaps read for oneself, expose the mind bare to the poem, and transcribe in all its haste and imperfection whatever may be the result of the impact. In this case it might run something as follows: O Christina Rossetti, I have humbly to confess that though I know many of your poems by heart, I have not read your works from cover to cover. I have not followed your course and traced your development. I doubt indeed that you developed very much. You were an instinctive poet. You saw the world from the same angle always. Years and the traffic of the mind with men and books did not affect you in the least. You carefully ignored any book that could shake your faith or any human being who could trouble your instincts. You were wise perhaps. Your instinct was so sure, so direct, so intense that it produced poems that sing like music in one's ears—like a melody by Mozart or an air by Gluck. Yet for all its symmetry, yours was a complex song. When you struck your harp many strings sounded together. Like all instinctives you had a keen sense of the visual beauty of the world. Your poems are full of gold dust and "sweet geraniums' varied brightness"; your eye noted incessantly how rushes are "velvet-headed", and lizards have a "strange metallic mail"—your eye, indeed, observed with a sensual pre-Raphaelite intensity that must have surprised Christina the Anglo-Catholic. But to her you owed perhaps

the fixity and sadness of your muse. The pressure of a tremendous faith circles and clamps together these little songs.
Perhaps they owe to it their solidity. Certainly they owe to
it their sadness—your God was a harsh God, your heavenly
crown was set with thorns. No sooner have you feasted on
beauty with your eyes than your mind tells you that beauty
is vain and beauty passes. Death, oblivion, and rest lap
round your songs with their dark wave. And then, incongruously, a sound of scurrying and laughter is heard. There
is the patter of animals' feet and the odd guttural notes of
rooks and the snufflings of obtuse furry animals grunting
and nosing. For you were not a pure saint by any means.
You pulled legs; you tweaked noses. You were at war with
all humbug and pretence. Modest as you were, still you were
drastic, sure of your gift, convinced of your vision. A firm
hand pruned your lines; a sharp ear tested their music.
Nothing soft, otiose, irrelevant cumbered your pages. In a
word, you were an artist. And thus was kept open, even
when you wrote idly, tinkling bells for your own diversion,
a pathway for the descent of that fiery visitant who came
now and then and fused your lines into that indissoluble
connection which no hand can put asunder:

> But bring me poppies brimmed with sleepy death
> And ivy choking what it garlandeth
> And primroses that open to the moon.

Indeed so strange is the constitution of things, and so great
the miracle of poetry, that some of the poems you wrote
in your little back room will be found adhering in perfect
symmetry when the Albert Memorial is dust and tinsel.
Our remote posterity will be singing:

When I am dead, my dearest,

or:

My heart is like a singing bird,

when Torrington Square is a reef of coral perhaps and the fishes shoot in and out where your bedroom window used to be; or perhaps the forest will have reclaimed those pavements and the wombat and the ratel will be shuffling on soft, uncertain feet among the green undergrowth that will then tangle the area railings. In view of all this, and to return to your biography, had I been present when Mrs. Virtue Tebbs gave her party, and had a short elderly woman in black risen to her feet and advanced to the middle of the room, I should certainly have committed some indiscretion —have broken a paper-knife or smashed a teacup in the awkward ardour of my admiration when she said, "I am Christina Rossetti".

The Novels of Thomas Hardy[1]

WHEN we say that the death of Thomas Hardy leaves English fiction without a leader, we mean that there is no other writer whose supremacy would be generally accepted, none to whom it seems so fitting and natural to pay homage. Nobody of course claimed it less. The unworldly and simple old man would have been painfully embarrassed by the rhetoric that flourishes on such occasions as this. Yet it is no less than the truth to say that while he lived there was one novelist at all events who made the art of fiction seem an honourable calling; while Hardy lived there was no excuse for thinking meanly of the art he practised. Nor was this solely the result of his peculiar genius. Something of it sprang from his character in its modesty and integrity, from his life, lived simply down in Dorsetshire without self-seeking or self-advertisement. For both reasons, because of his genius and because of the dignity with which his gift was used, it was impossible not to honour him as an artist and to feel respect and affection for the man. But it is of the work that we must speak, of the novels that were written so long ago that they seem as detached from the fiction of the moment as Hardy himself was remote from the stir of the present and its littleness.

We have to go back more than a generation if we are to trace the career of Hardy as a novelist. In the year 1871

[1] Written in January 1928.

he was a man of thirty-one; he had written a novel, *Desperate Remedies*, but he was by no means an assured craftsman. He "was feeling his way to a method", he said himself; as if he were conscious that he possessed all sorts of gifts, yet did not know their nature, or how to use them to advantage. To read that first novel is to share in the perplexity of its author. The imagination of the writer is powerful and sardonic; he is book-learned in a home-made way; he can create characters but he cannot control them; he is obviously hampered by the difficulties of his technique and, what is more singular, he is driven by some sense that human beings are the sport of forces outside themselves, to make use of an extreme and even melodramatic use of coincidence. He is already possessed of the conviction that a novel is not a toy, nor an argument; it is a means of giving truthful if harsh and violent impressions of the lives of men and women. But perhaps the most remarkable quality in the book is the sound that echoes and booms through its pages of a waterfall. It is the first manifestation of the power that was to assume such vast proportions in the later books. He already proves himself a minute and skilled observer of nature; the rain, he knows, falls differently as it falls upon roots or arable; he knows that the wind sounds differently as it passes through the branches of different trees. But he is aware in a larger sense of Nature as a force; he feels in it a spirit that can sympathise or mock or remain the indifferent spectator of human fortunes. Already that sense was his; and the crude story of Miss Aldclyffe and Cytherea is memorable because it is watched by the eyes of the gods, and worked out in the presence of Nature. That he was a poet should have been obvious; that he was a novelist might still have been held uncertain. But the year after, when *Under the Greenwood Tree* appeared, it was clear that much of the effort of "feeling for a method" had been overcome. Something of the stubborn originality of the earlier book was lost. The second is accomplished, charming, idyllic compared with the first. The writer, it seems, may well develop into one of our English landscape painters, whose pictures are all of cottage gardens and old peasant women, who lingers to collect and preserve from oblivion the old-fashioned ways and words which are rapidly falling into disuse. And yet what kindly lover of antiquity, what naturalist with a microscope in his pocket, what scholar solicitous for the changing shapes of language, ever heard the cry of a small bird killed in the next wood by an owl with such intensity? The cry "passed into the silence without mingling with it". Again we hear, very far away, like the sound of a gun out at sea on a calm summer's morning, a strange and ominous echo. But as we read these early books there is a sense of waste. There is a feeling that Hardy's genius was obstinate and perverse; first one gift would have its way with him and then another. They would not consent to run together easily in harness. Such indeed was likely to be the fate of a writer who was at once poet and realist, a faithful son of field and down, yet tormented by the doubts and despondencies bred of book-learning; a lover of old ways and plain countrymen, yet doomed to see the faith and flesh of his forefathers turn to thin and spectral transparencies before his eyes.

To this contradiction Nature had added another element likely to disorder a symmetrical development. Some writers are born conscious of everything; others are unconscious of many things. Some, like Henry James and Flaubert, are able not merely to make the best use of the spoil their gifts bring in, but control their genius in the act of creation; they are aware of all the possibilities of every situation, and are never taken by surprise. The unconscious writers, on the other hand, like Dickens and Scott, seem suddenly and without their own consent to be lifted up and swept onwards. The wave sinks and they cannot say what has happened or why. Among them—it is the source of his strength and of his weakness—we must place Hardy. His own word, "moments of vision", exactly describes those passages of astonishing beauty and force which are to be found in every book that he wrote. With a sudden quickening of power which we cannot foretell, nor he, it seems, control, a single scene breaks off from the rest. We see, as if it existed alone and for all time, the wagon with Fanny's dead body inside travelling along the road under the dripping trees; we see the bloated sheep struggling among the clover; we see Troy flashing his sword round Bathsheba where she stands motionless, cutting the lock off her head and spitting the caterpillar on her breast. Vivid to the eye, but not to the eye alone, for every sense participates, such scenes dawn upon us and their splendour remains. But the power goes as it comes. The moment of vision is succeeded by long stretches of plain daylight, nor can we believe that any craft or skill could have caught the wild power and turned it to a better use. The novels therefore are full of inequalities; they are lumpish and dull and inexpressive; but they are never arid; there is always about them a little blur of unconsciousness, that halo of freshness and margin of the unexpressed which often produce the most profound sense of satisfaction. It is as if Hardy himself were not quite aware of what he did, as if his consciousness held more than he could produce, and he left it for his readers to make out his full meaning and to supplement it from their own experience.

For these reasons Hardy's genius was uncertain in development, uneven in accomplishment, but, when the moment came, magnificent in achievement. The moment came, completely and fully, in *Far from the Madding Crowd*. The subject was right; the method was right; the poet and the countryman, the sensual man, the sombre reflective man, the man of learning, all enlisted to produce a book which, however fashions may chop and change, must hold its place among the great English novels. There is, in the first place, that sense of the physical world which Hardy more than any novelist can bring before us; the sense that the little prospect of man's existence is ringed by a landscape which, while it exists apart, yet confers a deep and solemn beauty upon his drama. The dark downland, marked by the barrows of the dead and the huts of shepherds, rises against the sky, smooth as a wave of the sea, but solid and eternal; rolling away to the infinite distance, but sheltering in its folds quiet villages whose smoke rises in frail columns by day, whose lamps burn in the immense darkness by night. Gabriel Oak tending his sheep up there on the back of the world is the eternal shepherd; the stars are ancient beacons; and for ages he has watched beside his sheep.

But down in the valley the earth is full of warmth and life; the farms are busy, the barns stored, the fields loud with the lowing of cattle and the bleating of sheep. Nature is prolific, splendid, and lustful; not yet malignant and still the Great Mother of labouring men. And now for the first

time Hardy gives full play to his humour, where it is freest
and most rich, upon the lips of country men. Jan Coggan
and Henry Fray and Joseph Poorgrass gather in the malthouse when the day's work is over and give vent to that
half-shrewd, half-poetic humour which has been brewing
in their brains and finding expression over their beer since
the pilgrims tramped the Pilgrims' Way; which Shakespeare and Scott and George Eliot all loved to overhear,
but none loved better or heard with greater understanding
than Hardy. But it is not the part of the peasants in the
Wessex novels to stand out as individuals. They compose
a pool of common wisdom, of common humour, a fund of
perpetual life. They comment upon the actions of the hero
and heroine, but while Troy or Oak or Fanny or Bathsheba
come in and out and pass away, Jan Coggan and Henry
Fray and Joseph Poorgrass remain. They drink by night
and they plough the fields by day. They are eternal. We
meet them over and over again in the novels, and they
always have something typical about them, more of the
character that marks a race than of the features which belong to an individual. The peasants are the great sanctuary
of sanity, the country the last stronghold of happiness.
When they disappear, there is no hope for the race.

With Oak and Troy and Bathsheba and Fanny Robin
we come to the men and women of the novels at their full
stature. In every book three or four figures predominate,
and stand up like lightning conductors to attract the force
of the elements. Oak and Troy and Bathsheba; Eustacia,
Wildeve, and Venn; Henchard, Lucetta, and Farfrae;
Jude, Sue Bridehead, and Phillotson. There is even a certain likeness between the different groups. They live as in-

dividuals and they differ as individuals; but they also live
as types and have a likeness as types. Bathsheba is Bathsheba, but she is woman and sister to Eustacia and Lucetta
and Sue; Gabriel Oak is Gabriel Oak, but he is man and
brother to Henchard, Venn, and Jude. However lovable
and charming Bathsheba may be, still she is weak; however
stubborn and ill-guided Henchard may be, still he is strong.
This is a fundamental part of Hardy's vision; the staple of
many of his books. The woman is the weaker and the flesh-
lier, and she clings to the stronger and obscures his vision.
How freely, nevertheless, in his greater books life is poured
over the unalterable frame-work! When Bathsheba sits in
the wagon among her plants, smiling at her own loveliness
in the little looking-glass, we may know, and it is proof of
Hardy's power that we do know, how severely she will
suffer and cause others to suffer before the end. But the
moment has all the bloom and beauty of life. And so it is,
time and time again. His characters, both men and women,
were creatures to him of an infinite attraction. For the
women he shows a more tender solicitude than for the men,
and in them, perhaps, he takes a keener interest. Vain might
their beauty be and terrible their fate, but while the glow
of life is in them their step is free, their laughter sweet,
and theirs is the power to sink into the breast of Nature
and become part of her silence and solemnity, or to rise and
put on them the movement of the clouds and the wildness
of the flowering woodlands. The men who suffer, not like
the women through dependence upon other human beings,
but through conflict with fate, enlist our sterner sympathies.
For such a man as Gabriel Oak we need have no passing
fears. Honour him we must, though it is not granted us

to love him quite so freely. He is firmly set upon his feet and can give as shrewd a blow, to men at least, as any he is likely to receive. He has a prevision of what is to be expected that springs from character rather than from education. He is stable in his temperament, steadfast in his affections, and capable of open-eyed endurance without flinching. But he, too, is no puppet. He is a homely, humdrum fellow on ordinary occasions. He can walk the street without making people turn to stare at him. In short, nobody can deny Hardy's power—the true novelist's power—to make us believe that his characters are fellow-beings driven by their own passions and idiosyncrasies, while they have—and this is the poet's gift—something symbolical about them which is common to us all.

And it is when we are considering Hardy's power of creating men and women that we become most conscious of the profound differences that distinguish him from his peers. We look back at a number of these characters and ask ourselves what it is that we remember them for. We recall their passions. We remember how deeply they have loved each other and often with what tragic results. We remember the faithful love of Oak for Bathsheba; the tumultuous but fleeting passions of men like Wildeve, Troy, and Fitzpiers; we remember the filial love of Clym for his mother, the jealous paternal passion of Henchard for Elizabeth Jane. But we do not remember how they have loved. We do not remember how they talked and changed and got to know each other, finely, gradually, from step to step and from stage to stage. Their relationship is not composed of those intellectual apprehensions and subtleties of perception which seem so slight yet are so profound. In all the

books love is one of the great facts that mould human life.
But it is a catastrophe; it happens suddenly and overwhelmingly, and there is little to be said about it. The talk between the lovers when it is not passionate is practical or
philosophic, as though the discharge of their daily duties
left them with more desire to question life and its purpose
than to investigate each other's sensibilities. Even if it were
in their power to analyse their emotions, life is too stirring
to give them time. They need all their strength to deal with
the downright blows, the freakish ingenuity, the gradually
increasing malignity of fate. They have none to spend upon
the subtleties and delicacies of the human comedy.

Thus there comes a time when we can say with certainty
that we shall not find in Hardy some of the qualities that
have given us most delight in the works of other novelists.
He has not the perfection of Jane Austen, or the wit of
Meredith, or the range of Thackeray, or Tolstoy's amazing
intellectual power. There is in the work of the great classical writers a finality of effect which places certain of their
scenes, apart from the story, beyond the reach of change.
We do not ask what bearing they have upon the narrative,
nor do we make use of them to interpret problems which
lie on the outskirts of the scene. A laugh, a blush, half a
dozen words of dialogue, and it is enough; the source of
our delight is perennial. But Hardy has none of this concentration and completeness. His light does not fall directly
upon the human heart. It passes over it and out on to the
darkness of the heath and upon the trees swaying in the
storm. When we look back into the room the group by the
fireside is dispersed. Each man or woman is battling with
the storm, alone, revealing himself most when he is least

under the observation of other human beings. We do not know them as we know Pierre or Natasha or Becky Sharp. We do not know them in and out and all round as they are revealed to the casual caller, to the Government official, to the great lady, to the general on the battlefield. We do not know the complication and involvement and turmoil of their thoughts. Geographically, too, they remain fixed to the same stretch of the English country-side. It is seldom, and always with unhappy results, that Hardy leaves the yeoman or farmer to describe the class above theirs in the social scale. In the drawing-room and clubroom and ball-room, where people of leisure and education come together, where comedy is bred and shades of character revealed, he is awkward and ill at ease. But the opposite is equally true. If we do not know his men and women in their relations to each other, we know them in their relations to time, death, and fate. If we do not see them in quick agitation against the lights and crowds of cities, we see them against the earth, the storm, and the seasons. We know their attitude towards some of the most tremendous problems that can confront mankind. They take on a more than mortal size in memory. We see them, not in detail but enlarged and dignified. We see Tess reading the baptismal service in her nightgown "with an impress of dignity that was almost regal". We see Marty South, "like a being who had rejected with indifference the attribute of sex for the loftier quality of abstract humanism", laying the flowers on Winter-bourne's grave. Their speech has a Biblical dignity and poetry. They have a force in them which cannot be defined, a force of love or of hate, a force which in the men is the cause of rebellion against life, and in the women implies an illimitable capacity for suffering, and it is this which dominates the character and makes it unnecessary that we should see the finer features that lie hid. This is the tragic power; and, if we are to place Hardy among his fellows, we must call him the greatest tragic writer among English novelists.

But let us, as we approach the danger-zone of Hardy's philosophy, be on our guard. Nothing is more necessary, in reading an imaginative writer, than to keep at the right distance above his page. Nothing is easier, especially with a writer of marked idiosyncrasy, than to fasten on opinions, convict him of a creed, tether him to a consistent point of view. Nor was Hardy any exception to the rule that the mind which is most capable of receiving impressions is very often the least capable of drawing conclusions. It is for the reader, steeped in the impression, to supply the comment. It is his part to know when to put aside the writer's conscious intention in favour of some deeper intention of which perhaps he may be unconscious. Hardy himself was aware of this. A novel "is an impression, not an argument", he has warned us, and, again

Unadjusted impressions have their value, and the road to a true philosophy of life seems to lie in humbly recording diverse readings of its phenomena as they are forced upon us by chance and change.

Certainly it is true to say of him that, at his greatest, he gives us impressions; at his weakest, arguments. In *The Woodlanders, The Return of the Native, Far from the Madding Crowd*, and, above all, in *The Mayor of Caster-bridge*, we have Hardy's impression of life as it came to him without conscious ordering. Let him once begin to tamper with his direct intuitions and his power is gone. "Did you say the stars were worlds, Tess?" asks little Abraham as they drive to market with their beehives. Tess replies that they are like "the apples on our stubbard-tree, most of them splendid and sound—a few blighted". "Which do we live on—a splendid or a blighted one?" "A blighted one", she replies, or rather the mournful thinker who has assumed her mask speaks for her. The words protrude, cold and raw, like the springs of a machine where we had seen only flesh and blood. We are crudely jolted out of that mood of sympathy which is renewed a moment later when the little cart is run down and we have a concrete instance of the ironical methods which rule our planet.

That is the reason why *Jude the Obscure* is the most painful of all Hardy's books, and the only one against which we can fairly bring the charge of pessimism. In *Jude the Obscure* argument is allowed to dominate impression, with the result that though the misery of the book is over-whelming it is not tragic. As calamity succeeds calamity we feel that the case against society is not being argued fairly or with profound understanding of the facts. Here is nothing of that width and force and knowledge of man-kind which, when Tolstoy criticises society, makes his in-dictment formidable. Here we have revealed to us the petty cruelty of men, not the large injustice of the gods. It is only necessary to compare *Jude the Obscure* with *The Mayor of Casterbridge* to see where Hardy's true power lay. Jude carries on his miserable contest against the deans of colleges and the conventions of sophisticated society. Henchard is pitted, not against another man, but against something outside himself which is opposed to men of his ambition and power. No human being wishes him ill. Even Farfrae and Newson and Elizabeth Jane whom he has wronged all come to pity him, and even to admire his strength of character. He is standing up to fate, and in backing the old Mayor whose ruin has been largely his own fault, Hardy makes us feel that we are backing human nature in an unequal contest. There is no pessimism here. Throughout the book we are aware of the sublimity of the issue, and yet it is presented to us in the most concrete form. From the opening scene in which Henchard sells his wife to the sailor at the fair to his death on Egdon Heath the vigour of the story is superb, its humour rich and racy, its movement large-limbed and free. The skimmity ride, the fight between Farfrae and Henchard in the loft, Mrs. Cuxsom's speech upon the death of Mrs. Henchard, the talk of the ruffians at Peter's Finger with Nature present in the background or mysteriously dominating the foreground, are among the glories of English fiction. Brief and scanty, it may be, is the measure of happiness allowed to each, but so long as the struggle is, as Henchard's was, with the decrees of fate and not with the laws of man, so long as it is in the open air and calls for activity of the body rather than of the brain, there is greatness in the contest, there is pride and pleasure in it, and the death of the broken corn merchant in his cottage on Egdon Heath is comparable to the death of Ajax lord of Salamis. The true tragic emotion is ours.

Before such power as this we are made to feel that the ordinary tests which we apply to fiction are futile enough. Do we insist that a great novelist shall be a master of melodious prose? Hardy was no such thing. He feels his way by dint of sagacity and uncompromising sincerity to the phrase he wants, and it is often of unforgettable pungency. Failing it, he will make do with any homely or clumsy or old-fashioned turn of speech, now of the utmost angularity, now of a bookish elaboration. No style in literature, save Scott's, is so difficult to analyse; it is on the face of it so bad, yet it achieves its aim so unmistakably. As well might one attempt to rationalise the charm of a muddy country road, or of a plain field of roots in winter. And then, like Dorsetshire itself, out of these very elements of stiffness and angularity his prose will put on greatness; will roll with a Latin sonority; will shape itself in a massive and monumental symmetry like that of his own bare downs. Then again, do we require that a novelist shall observe the probabilities, and keep close to reality? To find anything approaching the violence and convolution of Hardy's plots one must go back to the Elizabethan drama. Yet we accept his story completely as we read it; more than that, it becomes obvious that his violence and his melodrama, when they are not due to a curious peasant-like love of the monstrous for its own sake, are part of that wild spirit of poetry which saw with intense irony and grimness that no reading of life can possibly outdo the strangeness of life itself, no symbol of caprice and unreason be too extreme to represent the astonishing circumstances of our existence.

But as we consider the great structure of the Wessex novels it seems irrelevant to fasten on little points—this character, that scene, this phrase of deep and poetic beauty. It is something larger that Hardy has bequeathed to us. The Wessex novels are not one book, but many. They cover an immense stretch; inevitably they are full of imperfections—some are failures, and others exhibit only the wrong side of their maker's genius. But undoubtedly, when we have submitted ourselves fully to them, when we come to take stock of our impression of the whole, the effect is commanding and satisfactory. We have been freed from the cramp and pettiness imposed by life. Our imaginations have been stretched and heightened; our humour has been made to laugh out; we have drunk deep of the beauty of the earth. Also we have been made to enter the shade of a sorrowful and brooding spirit which, even in its saddest mood, bore itself with a grave uprightness and never, even when most moved to anger, lost its deep compassion for the sufferings of men and women. Thus it is no mere transcript of life at a certain time and place that Hardy has given us. It is a vision of the world and of man's lot as they revealed themselves to a powerful imagination, a profound and poetic genius, a gentle and humane soul.

How Should One Read a Book?[1]

IN THE first place, I want to emphasise the note of interrogation at the end of my title. Even if I could answer the question for myself, the answer would apply only to me and not to you. The only advice, indeed, that one person can give another about reading is to take no advice, to follow your own instincts, to use your own reason, to come to your own conclusions. If this is agreed between us, then I feel at liberty to put forward a few ideas and suggestions because you will not allow them to fetter that independence which is the most important quality that a reader can possess. After all, what laws can be laid down about books? The battle of Waterloo was certainly fought on a certain day; but is *Hamlet* a better play than *Lear?* Nobody can say. Each must decide that question for himself. To admit authorities, however heavily furred and gowned, into our libraries and let them tell us how to read, what to read, what value to place upon what we read, is to destroy the spirit of freedom which is the breath of those sanctuaries. Everywhere else we may be bound by laws and conventions —there we have none.

But to enjoy freedom, if the platitude is pardonable, we have of course to control ourselves. We must not squander our powers, helplessly and ignorantly, squirting half the house in order to water a single rose-bush; we must train

[1] A paper read at a School.

them, exactly and powerfully, here on the very spot. This, it may be, is one of the first difficulties that faces us in a library. What is "the very spot"? There may well seem to be nothing but a conglomeration and huddle of confusion. Poems and novels, histories and memoirs, dictionaries and blue-books; books written in all languages by men and women of all tempers, races, and ages jostle each other on the shelf. And outside the donkey brays, the women gossip at the pump, the colts gallop across the fields. Where are we to begin? How are we to bring order into this multitudinous chaos and so get the deepest and widest pleasure from what we read?

It is simple enough to say that since books have classes— fiction, biography, poetry—we should separate them and take from each what it is right that each should give us. Yet few people ask from books what books can give us. Most commonly we come to books with blurred and divided minds, asking of fiction that it shall be true, of poetry that it shall be false, of biography that it shall be flattering, of history that it shall enforce our own prejudices. If we could banish all such preconceptions when we read, that would be an admirable beginning. Do not dictate to your author; try to become him. Be his fellow-worker and accomplice. If you hang back, and reserve and criticise at first, you are preventing yourself from getting the fullest possible value from what you read. But if you open your mind as widely as possible, then signs and hints of almost imperceptible fineness, from the twist and turn of the first sentences, will bring you into the presence of a human being unlike any other. Steep yourself in this, acquaint yourself with this, and soon you will find that your author is giving you, or attempting to give you, something far more definite. The thirty-two chapters of a novel—if we consider how to read a novel first—are an attempt to make something as formed and controlled as a building: but words are more impalpable than bricks; reading is a longer and more complicated process than seeing. Perhaps the quickest way to understand the elements of what a novelist is doing is not to read, but to write; to make your own experiment with the dangers and difficulties of words. Recall, then, some event that has left a distinct impression on you—how at the corner of the street, perhaps, you passed two people talking. A tree shook; an electric light danced; the tone of the talk was comic, but also tragic; a whole vision, an entire conception, seemed contained in that moment.

But when you attempt to reconstruct it in words, you will find that it breaks into a thousand conflicting impressions. Some must be subdued; others emphasised; in the process you will lose, probably, all grasp upon the emotion itself. Then turn from your blurred and littered pages to the opening pages of some great novelist—Defoe, Jane Austen, Hardy. Now you will be better able to appreciate their mastery. It is not merely that we are in the presence of a different person—Defoe, Jane Austen, or Thomas Hardy—but that we are living in a different world. Here, in *Robinson Crusoe*, we are trudging a plain high road; one thing happens after another; the fact and the order of the fact is enough. But if the open air and adventure mean everything to Defoe they mean nothing to Jane Austen. Hers is the drawing-room, and people talking, and by the many mirrors of their talk revealing their characters. And if, when we have accustomed ourselves to the drawing-room and its reflections, we turn to Hardy, we are once more spun round. The moors are round us and the stars are above our heads. The other side of the mind is now exposed—the dark side that comes uppermost in solitude, not the light side that shows in company. Our relations are not towards people, but towards Nature and destiny. Yet different as these worlds are, each is consistent with itself. The maker of each is careful to observe the laws of his own perspective, and however great a strain they may put upon us they will never confuse us, as lesser writers so frequently do, by introducing two different kinds of reality into the same book. Thus to go from one great novelist to another—from Jane Austen to Hardy, from Peacock to Trollope, from Scott to Meredith—is to be wrenched and uprooted; to be thrown this way and then that. To read a novel is a difficult and complex art. You must be capable not only of great fineness of perception, but of great boldness of imagination if you are going to make use of all that the novelist—the great artist—gives you.

But a glance at the heterogeneous company on the shelf will show you that writers are very seldom "great artists"; far more often a book makes no claim to be a work of art at all. These biographies and autobiographies, for example, lives of great men, of men long dead and forgotten, that stand cheek by jowl with the novels and poems, are we to refuse to read them because they are not "art"? Or shall we read them, but read them in a different way, with a different aim? Shall we read them in the first place to satisfy that curiosity which possesses us sometimes when in the evening we linger in front of a house where the lights are lit and the blinds not yet drawn, and each floor of the house shows us a different section of human life in being? Then we are consumed with curiosity about the lives of these people—the servants gossiping, the gentlemen dining, the girl dressing for a party, the old woman at the window with her knitting. Who are they, what are they, what are their names, their occupations, their thoughts, and adventures?

Biographies and memoirs answer such questions, light up innumerable such houses; they show us people going about their daily affairs, toiling, failing, succeeding, eating, hating, loving, until they die. And sometimes as we watch, the house fades and the iron railings vanish and we are out at sea; we are hunting, sailing, fighting; we are among savages and soldiers; we are taking part in great campaigns. Or if we like to stay here in England, in London, still the scene changes; the street narrows; the house becomes small, cramped, diamond-paned, and malodorous. We see a poet, Donne, driven from such a house because the walls were so thin that when the children cried their voices cut through them. We can follow him, through the paths that lie in the pages of books, to Twickenham; to Lady Bedford's Park, a famous meeting-ground for nobles and poets; and then turn our steps to Wilton, the great house under the downs, and hear Sidney read the *Arcadia* to his sister; and ramble among the very marshes and see the very herons that figure in that famous romance; and then again travel north with that other Lady Pembroke, Anne Clifford, to her wild moors, or plunge into the city and control our merriment at the sight of Gabriel Harvey in his black velvet suit arguing about poetry with Spenser. Nothing is more fascinating than to grope and stumble in the alternate

285

darkness and splendour of Elizabethan London. But there is no staying there. The Temples and the Swifts, the Harleys and the St. Johns beckon us on; hour upon hour can be spent disentangling their quarrels and deciphering their characters; and when we tire of them we can stroll on, past a lady in black wearing diamonds, to Samuel Johnson and Goldsmith and Garrick; or cross the channel, if we like, and meet Voltaire and Diderot, Madame du Deffand; and so back to England and Twickenham—how certain places repeat themselves and certain names!—where Lady Bedford had her Park once and Pope lived later, to Walpole's home at Strawberry Hill. But Walpole introduces us to such a swarm of new acquaintances, there are so many houses to visit and bells to ring that we may well hesitate for a moment, on the Miss Berrys' doorstep, for example, when behold, up comes Thackeray; he is the friend of the woman whom Walpole loved; so that merely by going from friend to friend, from garden to garden, from house to house, we have passed from one end of English literature to another and wake to find ourselves here again in the present, if we can so differentiate this moment from all that have gone before. This, then, is one of the ways in which we can read these lives and letters; we can make them light up the many windows of the past; we can watch the famous dead in their familiar habits and fancy sometimes that we are very close and can surprise their secrets, and sometimes we may pull out a play or a poem that they have written and see whether it reads differently in the presence of the author. But this again rouses other questions. How far, we must ask ourselves, is a book influenced by its writer's life

286

—how far is it safe to let the man interpret the writer? How far shall we resist or give way to the sympathies and antipathies that the man himself rouses in us—so sensitive are words, so receptive of the character of the author? These are questions that press upon us when we read lives and letters, and we must answer them for ourselves, for nothing can be more fatal than to be guided by the preferences of others in a matter so personal.

But also we can read such books with another aim, not to throw light on literature, not to become familiar with famous people, but to refresh and exercise our own creative powers. Is there not an open window on the right hand of the bookcase? How delightful to stop reading and look out! How stimulating the scene is, in its unconsciousness, its irrelevance, its perpetual movement—the colts galloping round the field, the woman filling her pail at the well, the donkey throwing back his head and emitting his long, acrid moan. The greater part of any library is nothing but the record of such fleeting moments in the lives of men, women, and donkeys. Every literature, as it grows old, has its rubbish-heap, its record of vanished moments and forgotten lives told in faltering and feeble accents that have perished. But if you give yourself up to the delight of rubbish-reading you will be surprised, indeed you will be overcome, by the relics of human life that have been cast out to moulder. It may be one letter—but what a vision it gives! It may be a few sentences—but what vistas they suggest! Sometimes a whole story will come together with such beautiful humour and pathos and completeness that it seems as if a great novelist had been at work, yet it is only an old actor, Tate Wilkinson, remembering the strange story of Captain Jones; it is only a young subaltern serving under Arthur Wellesley and falling in love with a pretty girl at Lisbon; it is only Maria Allen letting fall her sewing in the empty drawing-room and sighing how she wishes she had taken Dr. Burney's good advice and had never eloped with her Rishy. None of this has any value; it is negligible in the extreme; yet how absorbing it is now and again to go through the rubbish-heaps and find rings and scissors and broken noses buried in the huge past and try to piece them together while the colt gallops round the field, the woman fills her pail at the well, and the donkey brays.

But we tire of rubbish-reading in the long run. We tire of searching for what is needed to complete the half-truth which is all that the Wilkinsons, the Bunburys, and the Maria Allens are able to offer us. They had not the artist's power of mastering and eliminating; they could not tell the whole truth even about their own lives; they have disfigured the story that might have been so shapely. Facts are all that they can offer us, and facts are a very inferior form of fiction. Thus the desire grows upon us to have done with half-statements and approximations; to cease from searching out the minute shades of human character, to enjoy the greater abstractness, the purer truth of fiction. Thus we create the mood, intense and generalised, unaware of detail, but stressed by some regular, recurrent beat, whose natural expression is poetry; and that is the time to read poetry when we are almost able to write it.

> Western wind, when wilt thou blow?
> The small rain down can rain.

> Christ, if my love were in my arms,
> And I in my bed again!

The impact of poetry is so hard and direct that for the moment there is no other sensation except that of the poem itself. What profound depths we visit then—how sudden and complete is our immersion! There is nothing here to catch hold of; nothing to stay us in our flight. The illusion of fiction is gradual; its effects are prepared; but who when they read these four lines stops to ask who wrote them, or conjures up the thought of Donne's house or Sidney's secretary; or enmeshes them in the intricacy of the past and the succession of generations? The poet is always our contemporary. Our being for the moment is centred and constricted, as in any violent shock of personal emotion. Afterwards, it is true, the sensation begins to spread in wider rings through our minds; remoter senses are reached; these begin to sound and to comment and we are aware of echoes and reflections. The intensity of poetry covers an immense range of emotion. We have only to compare the force and directness of

> I shall fall like a tree, and find my grave,
> Only remembering that I grieve,

with the wavering modulation of

> Minutes are numbered by the fall of sands,
> As by an hour glass; the span of time
> Doth waste us to our graves, and we look on it;
> An age of pleasure, revelled out, comes home
> At last, and ends in sorrow; but the life,
> Weary of riot, numbers every sand,
> Wailing in sighs, until the last drop down,
> So to conclude calamity in rest,

or place the meditative calm of

> whether we be young or old,
> Our destiny, our being's heart and home,
> Is with infinitude, and only there;
> With hope it is, hope that can never die,
> Effort, and expectation, and desire,
> And something evermore about to be,

beside the complete and inexhaustible loveliness of

> The moving Moon went up the sky,
> And no where did abide:
> Softly she was going up,
> And a star or two beside—

or the splendid fantasy of

> And the woodland haunter
> Shall not cease to saunter
>   When, far down some glade,
> Of the great world's burning,
> One soft flame upturning
> Seems, to his discerning,
>   Crocus in the shade.

to bethink us of the varied art of the poet; his power to make us at once actors and spectators; his power to run his hand into character as if it were a glove, and be Falstaff or Lear; his power to condense, to widen, to state, once and for ever.

"We have only to compare"—with those words the cat is out of the bag, and the true complexity of reading is admitted. The first process, to receive impressions with the utmost understanding, is only half the process of reading; it must be completed, if we are to get the whole pleasure from a book, by another. We must pass judgment upon these multitudinous impressions; we must make of these fleeting shapes one that is hard and lasting. But not directly. Wait for the dust of reading to settle; for the conflict and the questioning to die down; walk, talk, pull the dead petals from a rose, or fall asleep. Then suddenly without our willing it, for it is thus that Nature undertakes these transitions, the book will return, but differently. It will float to the top of the mind as a whole. And the book as a whole is different from the book received currently in separate phrases. Details now fit themselves into their places. We see the shape from start to finish; it is a barn, a pig-sty, or a cathedral. Now then we can compare book with book as we compare building with building. But this act of comparison means that our attitude has changed; we are no longer the friends of the writer, but his judges; and just as we cannot be too sympathetic as friends, so as judges we cannot be too severe. Are they not criminals, books that have wasted our time and sympathy; are they not the most insidious enemies of society, corrupters, defilers, the writers of false books, faked books, books that fill the air with decay and disease? Let us then be severe in our judgments; let us compare each book with the greatest of its kind. There they hang in the mind the shapes of the books we have read solidified by the judgments we have passed on them—*Robinson Crusoe, Emma, The Return of the Native.* Compare the novels with these—even the latest and least of novels has a right to be judged with the best. And so with poetry—when the intoxication of rhythm has died down and the splendour of words has faded a visionary shape will return to us and this must be compared with *Lear,* with *Phèdre,* with *The Prelude;* or if not with these, with whatever is the best or seems to us to be the best in its own kind. And we may be sure that the newness of new poetry and fiction is its most superficial quality and that we have only to alter slightly, not to recast, the standards by which we have judged the old.

It would be foolish, then, to pretend that the second part of reading, to judge, to compare, is as simple as the first—to open the mind wide to the fast flocking of innumerable impressions. To continue reading without the book before you, to hold one shadow-shape against another, to have read widely enough and with enough understanding to make such comparisons alive and illuminating—that is difficult; it is still more difficult to press further and to say, "Not only is the book of this sort, but it is of this value; here it fails; here it succeeds; this is bad; that is good". To carry out this part of a reader's duty needs such imagination, insight, and learning that it is hard to conceive any one mind sufficiently endowed; impossible for the most self-confident to find more than the seeds of such powers in himself. Would it not be wiser, then, to remit this part of reading and to allow the critics, the gowned and furred authorities of the library, to decide the question of the book's absolute value for us? Yet how impossible! We may stress the value of sympathy; we may try to sink our own identity as we read. But we know that we cannot sympathise wholly or immerse ourselves wholly; there is always a demon in us who whispers, "I hate, I love", and we cannot silence him. Indeed, it is precisely because we hate and we love that our relation with the poets and novelists is so intimate that we find the presence of another person intolerable. And even if the results are abhorrent and our judgments are wrong, still our taste, the nerve of sensation that sends shocks through us, is our chief illuminant; we learn through feeling; we cannot suppress our own idiosyncrasy without impoverishing it. But as time goes on perhaps we can train our taste; perhaps we can make it submit to some control. When it has fed greedily and lavishly upon books of all sorts—poetry, fiction, history, biography—and has stopped reading and looked for long spaces upon the variety, the incongruity of the living world, we shall find that it is changing a little; it is not so greedy, it is more reflective. It will begin to bring us not merely judgments on particular books, but it will tell us that there is a quality common to certain books. Listen, it will say, what shall we call *this?* And it will read us perhaps *Lear* and then perhaps the *Agamemnon* in order to bring out that common quality. Thus, with our taste to guide us, we shall venture beyond the particular book in search of qualities that group books together; we shall give them names and thus frame a rule that brings order into our perceptions. We shall gain a further and a rarer pleasure from that discrimination. But as a rule only lives when it is perpetually broken by contact with the books themselves—nothing is easier and more stultifying than to make rules which exist out of touch with facts, in a vacuum—now at last, in order to steady ourselves in this difficult attempt, it may be well to turn to the very rare writers who are able to enlighten us upon literature as an art. Coleridge and Dryden and Johnson, in their considered criticism, the poets and novelists themselves in their unconsidered sayings, are often surprisingly relevant; they light up and solidify the vague ideas that have been tumbling in the misty depths of our minds. But they are only able to help us if we come to them laden with questions and suggestions won honestly in the course of our own reading. They can do nothing for us if we herd ourselves under their authority and lie down like sheep in the shade of a hedge. We can only understand their ruling when it comes in conflict with our own and vanquishes it.

If this is so, if to read a book as it should be read calls for the rarest qualities of imagination, insight, and judgment, you may perhaps conclude that literature is a very complex art and that it is unlikely that we shall be able, even after a lifetime of reading, to make any valuable contribution to its criticism. We must remain readers; we shall not put on the further glory that belongs to those rare beings who are also critics. But still we have our responsibilities as readers and even our importance. The standards we raise and the judgments we pass steal into the air and become part of the atmosphere which writers breathe as they work. An influence is created which tells upon them even if it never finds its way into print. And that influence, if it were well instructed, vigorous and individual and sincere, might be of great value now when criticism is necessarily in abeyance; when books pass in review like the procession of animals in a shooting gallery, and the critic has only one second in which to load and aim and shoot and may well be pardoned if he mistakes rabbits for tigers, eagles for barndoor fowls, or misses altogether and wastes his shot upon some peaceful cow grazing in a further field. If behind the erratic gunfire of the press the author felt that there was another kind of criticism, the opinion of people reading for the love of reading, slowly and unprofessionally, and judging with great sympathy and yet with great severity, might this not improve the quality of his work? And if by our means books were to become stronger, richer, and more varied, that would be an end worth reaching.

Yet who reads to bring about an end however desirable? Are there not some pursuits that we practise because they are good in themselves, and some pleasures that are final? And is not this among them? I have sometimes dreamt, at least, that when the Day of Judgment dawns and the great conquerors and lawyers and statesmen come to receive their rewards—their crowns, their laurels, their names carved indelibly upon imperishable marble—the Almighty will turn to Peter and will say, not without a certain envy when He sees us coming with our books under our arms, "Look, these need no reward. We have nothing to give them here. They have loved reading."